MW01177998

Michael Vickers
Aristophanes and Alcibiades

Michael Vickers

Aristophanes and Alcibiades

Echoes of Contemporary History in Athenian Comedy

DE GRUYTER

ISBN 978-3-11-043753-9
e-ISBN (PDF) 978-3-11-042791-2
e-ISBN (EPUB) 978-3-11-042795-0

Library of Congress Cataloging-in-Publication Data
A CIP catalog record for this book has been applied for at the Library of Congress.

Bibliographic information published by the Deutsche Nationalbibliothek
The Deutsche Nationalbibliothek lists this publication in the Deutsche Nationalbibliografie;
detailed bibliographic data are available on the Internet at http://dnb.dnb.de.

© 2015 Walter de Gruyter GmbH, Berlin/Boston
Printing and binding: CPI books GmbH, Leck
♾ Printed on acid-free paper
Printed in Germany

www.degruyter.com

In memory of my teachers
A.D. Fitton Brown, R.E. Wycherley
and W.H. Plommer

Contents

Preface

This book is a continuation of my *Pericles on Stage: Political Comedy in Aristophanes' Early Plays* (Austin, Texas, 1997; reprint 2012). The first six of Aristophanes' extant plays were discussed there: *Acharnians* (425 BC), *Knights* (424 BC), *Clouds* (423 BC), *Wasps* (422 BC), *Peace* (421 BC), and *Birds* (414 BC), and a case was made that the principal targets for Aristophanes' humour were the long-dead Pericles, Cleon, and Pericles' foster-son Alcibiades. Caricatures of these individuals served as the hooks upon which were hung old-fashioned values, belligerent politics, and new-fangled excesses. It was argued that Aristophanes wrote in an allegorical manner,[1] and used the public images of prominent citizens in order to divert his audiences with a view to winning the prize at dramatic festivals.

There seemed to be sufficient overlap between Aristophanes' characters and plots and what we know from a range of sources about Pericles and Alcibiades in particular to justify such equations. If this were indeed the case, it would not be surprising to find both historical individuals underlying characters in Aristophanes' five remaining extant plays: in *Lysistrata* (411 BC), *Thesmophoriazusae* (410 BC), *Frogs* (405 BC), *Ecclesiazusae* (391 BC), and *Plutus* (388 BC); indeed, the very fact that this exercise can be done at all should serve to confirm the essential validity of the initial approach. One of the purposes of this book is to draw out these further possibilities; not all of them (for that would be unduly repetitious), but enough to show how Aristophanes went about the task of amusing—and at times edifying—his Athenian audience.

The argument presented here makes certain demands on the reader, who is in the first place required to accept the possibility that all may not be rosy in the garden of classical philology. Those who believe that the story of *Altertumswissenschaft* has been one of continuous progress since it began in the early nineteenth century are in for a shock, but this is not my concern. Those who by contrast are willing to consider the possibility that there may be other ways of looking at our texts—ways that may perhaps be more in keeping with those of the ancients—are in for a diverting read.

What I believe I have discovered is a means of understanding Greek plays not simply in terms of contemporary history, but as personalised in the way that Greek politics were frequently based on the reputations, ambitions and ach-

---

1 Using "allegory" in its primary sense: a "description of a subject under the guise of some other subject of aptly suggestive resemblance" *OCD*[2] *s.v.*; not "impersonated abstractions" as De Quincey 1857, 281; Newiger 1957; 2000; or Hubbard 1998, 374.

ievements of individuals. It was thus for Aristotle: history was personal and dealt in particulars. The example he chose is "what Alcibiades actually did, or what was done to him" (*Po.* 1451*b*.11). Drama, for Aristotle, describes the kind of things that "a person of a certain character would inevitably say or do" given their known proclivities and predilections (*Po.* 1451*b*.8–9). Again, the reference appears to place matters on a personal level.

Alcibiades figures large in this book because his personality dominated Athenian gossip from the early 430s BC, when he was a trend-setting teenager, to well beyond his death in 404. And not simply gossip, though that was paramount (and of direct concern to a theatre that played with men's—and women's—reputations), but Alcibiades constantly played on his wealth and connections, whether acquiescing in the presentation to him of the ἀριστεῖον ("prize for valour") at Potidaea in 431 BC, which should more properly have gone to Socrates; or precociously obtaining a profitable place on the board of commissioners who re-assessed the Athenian tribute in 425 BC; or obtaining a generalship at a very early age for that office in 420 BC. This is by way of meeting a point raised by critics of *Pericles on Stage* that since Alcibiades was not "a crucial figure" or "was not yet prominent in the period 425–21 BC",[2] it is unreasonable to think of him as underlying several characters in Aristophanes' early plays. Alcibiades' further notoriety as a pathic, a thief, a murderer, a traitor, a matrophile, a profaner of the Mysteries, a liar and an adulterer would only have served to embroider the gossip, and have provided writers for the stage with additional material. Thanks to Alcibiades, the Athenian citizenry would have had a constant diet of the juciest imaginable public and private scandal over more than thirty years.

I have argued elsewhere[3] that Sophocles was on to Alcibiades' case from the early 430s BC, when he used Alcibiades' ambivalent sexuality and teenage cross-dressing (of which he boasted), not to mention his disturbed personality, for the characterisation of Antigone, in a play that probably served in the first instance as a vehicle for criticism of Pericles' having left executed prisoners unburied after his Samian triumphs in 439; and that Sophocles had in mind the threat to the Athenian polity presented by Alcibiades' excesses in *Oedipus Tyrannus* of 425 BC when he extrapolated from rumours that he had had an affair with his guardian's mistress Aspasia (elaborated by Aristophanes, and by Euripides in his Hippolytus plays: Appendix 1, below). Contemporary gossip had it that Alcibiades had not only slept with his mother, but with his sister and his daughter,

---

2 Storey 1997; Hubbard 1998, 370.
3 In *Sophocles and Alcibiades.*

and there are many parallels between Oedipus' road rage when the "narrow way" was blocked by Laius' carriage, and the intransigence of the infant Alcibiades before a cart in a "narrow street" in Athens. Oedipus's irrational belligerence is matched by Alcibiades' tendency to fly off the handle, sometimes with fatal results. Other Sophoclean characters that are based in one way or another on Alcibiades include Ajax, Philoctetes, and the Oedipus at Colonus who is initiated into the Mysteries, just as Alcibiades had been shortly before Sophocles composed his last extant play.

It will be argued here that Alcibiades' some-time effeminacy, his dissolute and irreligious life-style, and the constant fears that he was aiming at tyranny underlie most of Aristophanes' extant comedies. I am fully aware that "few Aristophanic specialists are likely to be persuaded" (to quote one reviewer of *Pericles on Stage*), for they have their own way of going about things. For example, they consistently ignore ancient testimony for Alcibiades' paramount role in comedy. The learned Libanius states explicitly: "What play did not include [Alcibiades] among the cast of characters? Eupolis, Aristophanes, did they not show him on the stage? It is to him that comedy owed its success" (Lib. *fr.* 50.2.21), and for Plutarch, Alcibiades was "a powerful speaker, as the comic dramatists bear witness" (Plut. *Alc.* 10.4). Aristophanic specialists, however, ignore this evidence and are at one in scratching their heads over the apparent paucity of references to Alcibiades. "Notable too in our surviving fragments is the almost complete dearth of attacks by comic poets on one of the most controversial figures of the day: the flamboyant aristocrat Alcibiades"[4] is a typical recent statement of this position.

A working hypothesis throughout this book is that the writer known as the Old Oligarch, our only contemporary witness, knew what he was about when he stated that the kind of person who is lampooned in comedy is usually "rich, or aristocratic, or powerful" ([Xen.] *Ath. pol.* 2.18); another is the essential soundness of the tradition that "masks were made to look like the κωμῳδούμενοι, so that before an actor spoke a word, the audience would recognise from the visual likeness who was being attacked" (Platon. 1.64–6). The κωμῳδούμενοι—the truly lampooned—in the plays we have were therefore relatively few in number, and restricted to those who were truly "rich, or aristocratic, or powerful", such as Cleon, Nicias, Pericles, Aspasia, and Alcibiades and his wife Hipparete. Cleon only figures large in *Knights* and *Wasps*, and Nicias appears in supporting roles in *Knights* and *Birds*, but Pericles and Alcibiades underpin the rest of the canon. Yes, Pericles had been dead for some time before Aristophanes began

---

4 Robson 2009, 179.

writing for the stage, as indeed was Alcibiades when the last two extant plays were composed; all Aristophanes was doing was employing the well-document-ed principle of *idolopoeia*, whereby characters might be brought back from the dead in order to make a contemporary point (Aeschylus and Euripides in *Frogs* are an obvious example [although, as we shall see in Chapter 10, matters are not quite so straightforward], and Pericles in Eupolis' *Demi* another). The paucity of di-rect references to the κωμῳδούμενοι may be accounted for by the fact that it was customary, if not actually obligatory by law, to make attacks on them indirect, oblique.

The method that is frequently employed in what follows is what Keith Hop-kins once called the "wigwam argument": "each pole would fall down by itself, but together the poles stand up, by leaning on each other; they point roughly in the same direction and circumscribe 'truth'."[5] I have elswhere observed that "the 'wigwam argument' flies in the face of traditional philological debate, where it is fair game to sniff out any apparently weak evidence, to imply that even to think of using it is a sign of madness, and to declare gleefully that any conclusions based on it must be inherently flawed".[6] Here, I shall nevertheless often be tak-ing note of hitherto unconsidered scraps which, when combined, amount to something substantial, rather in the spirit of William Sebastian Heckscher (1904–1999) who encouraged his followers to disregard what he called "the aca-demic frontier police" and to employ any fact, no matter how small or apparently insignificant, in reconstructing the intellectual framework within which artists and writers of the past may have worked.[7]

Thus, for example, in establishing Dicaeopolis in *Acharnians* as a caricature of Pericles in *Pericles on Stage*, I would maintain that apart from having the actor wear a pointy-headed mask (alluding to the statesman's congenitally mis-shapen skull that contemporaries compared to a vegetable, and which is the object of much crude humour when Dicaeopolis offers to place his head on a chopping-board), Aristophanes delicately creates a verbal portrait by means of allusive ref-erences to the statesman's concern with δικαιοσύνη ("justice"), to his having adorned the Acro*polis*, and to Pindar's epithet δικαιόπολις for Aegina, an island for which Pericles had a bitter hatred. The principal themes of *Acharnians* are food and sex; Pericles' principal public concern was Athens' grain supply, while his private life gave rise to the charge that he was the "King of the Satyrs". The inhabitants of Acharnae had been Pericles' bugbear when they demanded,

---

5 Hopkins 1978, 19.

6 *Sophocles and Alcibiades*, viii.

7 For a biographical sketch of Heckscher, see Sears 1990; for examples of his method in prac-tice, see Heckscher 1958; 1974.

in vain, that he lead the Athenians out to attack the invading Spartans. That Dicaeopolis succeeds in winning the Acharnians over to his side is a parody of Pericles' persuasiveness (Persuasion was said to sit upon his lips). One would have thought that these various elements, not very strong individually perhaps, serve to make a strong Periclean case when taken together; that they constitute a "wigwam". And yet, these very points have been taken by one critic to stand for nothing (e. g. "Pericles was hardly the only Athenian with an interest in food and women"; "Pericles was hardly the only persuasive speaker in Athens"). All one can say is that if Aristophanes did not have Pericles in his sights, then he was being extremely careless and insensitive. Readers may, however, judge for themselves.

Pericles on Stage only discussed Aristophanes' first six extant plays. This volume includes summaries of the case to be made there (in Chapter 3; readers are encouraged to consult *Pericles on Stage* for extended discussions of particular points), as well as more detailed interpretations of the other five. They all go the same way: the principal κωμῳδούμενοι are again for the most part members of Pericles' extended family, and the characterisations can again be established by means of a series of "wigwam arguments". Another working hypothesis is that Aristophanes used a clever device that I have called "polymorphic characterization", whereby different facets of an individual's personality or public image could be played by a different character on the stage. A related phenomenon is portmanteau characterisation, whereby a single dramatic figure might embody features of different well-known historical individuals: Socrates in *Clouds* as an amalgam of the philosphers who were in Pericles' circle, for example, or Pheidippides who combines features of individuals known to have had a filial relationship to Pericles. An immediate gain from the recognition of these devices is that the lack of continuity that is often said to disfigure Aristophanes' plays disappears. The plays are no longer broken-backed or worse, for κωμῳδούμενοι remain on stage in one guise or another throughout.

One critic has suggested that if we had as much information about "Cleon, Hyperbolus, Theorus, Peisander, Nicias, or at least a dozen other politicians" as we do about Pericles and Alcibiades, we might well find an abundance of allusions to them in our extant plays. To some extent we do—at least in the cases of Cleon and Nicias. A working hypothesis in what follows, however, is that the reason why there is a concentration on Pericles and Alcibiades is that the plays we have were deliberately chosen at an early date to show how Aristophanes lampooned Pericles' extended family, rather than Hyperbolus, Theorus or Peisander or anyone else. I tentatively put forward this proposal in *Pericles on Stage*, but the same critic has dismissed it as "manifest nonsense", on the grounds—that no one would dispute—that other plays were known to later scholars. The clue to the elucidation of this issue is perhaps to be found in the Ravenna codex, the only manuscript to contain the text of all eleven plays in the extant Aristophanic canon. There are certain indications to justify a case for a collection of the kind suggested here having been created early in the fourth century BC, and not very long after the performance of *Plutus*.

The tenth century Ravenna codex (R) was only introduced to modern scholarship in 1794, long after the lines of textual criticism of Aristophanes had been laid down, and its status is still controversial. The principal characteristic of R, apart from its "peculiar readings" and line attributions that differ from those of other manuscript traditions, is the plethora of small mistakes: mistakes of spelling, punctuation and accentuation. What has not been noticed hitherto is that many of the mistakes can be best accounted for if they were made by someone who was converting a text written in the old Attic alphabet to the Ionic alphabet. This change became official at Athens in 403/2 BC, but we can envisage Aristophanes (born 460 – 450 BC) as having employed the old alphabet throughout his life (he died in or shortly after 386 BC). Quite when the transliteration of the source of the Ravenna codex took place is uncertain (nor is it germane to the present discussion), but a *terminus post quem* is supplied by the fact that it included Aristophanes' last extant play (and greatest hit) *Plutus* of 388, the text of which is full of "small mistakes". *Plutus* probably comes first of the eleven plays in R because the characters are crystallised, regardless of chronology, and embody the totality of their distinctive features as regularly lampooned by Aristophanes. Recognise these features here, and they fall into place elsewhere.

We shall never know whether the eleven plays were put together soon after *Plutus*, or at the time of Aristophanes' death, or later, but whoever performed the task did so, I believe, knowingly. There is, moreover, a cluster of data that might point to a collection (whose precise contents are of course uncertain) having existed in the 380s. Plato's devotion to Aristophanes is clear from the fact that he wrote his epitaph and kept his works (doubtless a selection) in his bed. He visited Sicily "in his fortieth year", which could be any time between 388 and 385 BC, and he encouraged "Dionysius the tyrant" (who must be Dionysius I) to learn about Athenian government by studying Aristophanes' plays, in particular *Clouds*. Quite when this encouragement took place is uncertain, but the existence of a collection of the kind envisaged here seems possible from the interest taken in Aristophanes in an entirely different quarter. The Great King is said to have asked "which side the comic writer was on". This is the kind of remark that could only have been generated by a political reading, and the question arises as to when a Persian king might have shown such an interest in Athens, an interest that is quite different from that displayed by Persian rulers in Herodotus, where the Athenians are a despised military foe. Possibilities might be: at the time of the Persian support for Athens' anti-Spartan league of the 390s, or at the time of the King's Peace, in 386 BC, an event with which Dionysius I was also involved. Both regal and tyrannical curiosity would have been satisfied by a collection such as that represented by the contents of the Ravenna codex. Note that the claim is not being made here that things necessarily did work out in quite this manner, merely that it is reasonable to suggest that they might have done; it would, however, be "manifest nonsense", indeed "bizarre" (to quote our kind critic again), to insist that they could not.

While the precise date and circumstances of the formation of the collection as we have it are unknown, it will be a working hypothesis in what follows that it was put together with wit and artistry at an early date by someone who was aware of the political references that the plays contained. The order of the plays in R is as follows: *Plutus, Clouds, Frogs, Birds, Knights, Peace, Lysistrata, Acharnians, Wasps, Thesmophoriazusae* and *Ecclesiazusae.* The contents are topped and tailed by the two plays that had been most recently performed. *Plutus* in effect set the scene, and enabled the reader to recall the basic conventions of Aristophanes' characterisation. Then follow the two great classics *Clouds* and *Frogs. Clouds* is in a revised (and never performed) version of the play of 423. In *Pericles on Stage, Clouds* was treated first, not least in order to show why it could have been considered an appropriate text for Dionysius I, tyrant of Syracuse, to learn about Athenian government. Here, I follow the example of the compiler of R, and begin with a discussion of *Plutus* with a view to showing Aristophanes at the top of his game. First, though, it will be necessary to examine Euripides' *Ion*, a play that probably contributed to the plot of *Plutus.* There are several examples of Aristophanes having bounced his conceits off those of Euripides, and some of them will be treated here in their place. Tempting as it is to follow the order of the plays in R, in order to reconstruct the kind of collection that may have existed in the fourth century BC, the rest of Aristophanes' plays will be treated in the order in which they were performed.

This book was written during leave from my employment at the Ashmolean Museum, Oxford, latterly when I was wearing another hat, namely, that of Senior Research Fellow in Classical Studies at Jesus College, Oxford; some of it at the Fondation Hardt in Geneva, where my visits were sponsored by the British Academy and the Fonds national suisse de recherche; some of it as a Visiting Fellow at the Institute for Advanced Studies at the Hebrew University in Jerusalem, some as a Visiting Professor at the University of Colorado at Boulder, and some as a Visiting Scholar at the Getty Villa. It was thanks to a Major Research Grant from Jesus College that I was able to bring the work to completion. Debts of gratitude are owed to the librarians of the Fondation Hardt, Bodleian, Sackler,

Norlin, Getty and Jesus College libraries for their unfailing courtesy. The *Thesaurus Linguae Graecae* proved to be an invaluable tool.

Obligations are owed to colleagues who, alas, are no longer with us: to Ernst Badian, Peter Bicknell, Peter Derow, George Forrest, Don Fowler, E.D. Francis, William Heckscher, Pierre Lévêque, Peter Levi, David Lewis, Roger Moorey, Martin Ostwald, Roy Porter, Ihor Ševčenko, Andrew Sherratt, and Christiane Sourvinou-Inwood.

Many thanks are also due to Frederick Ahl, Laura Biondi, Daphne Nash Briggs, Edmund Bloedow, Ewen Bowie, Roger Brock, Douglas Cairns, William M. Calder III, Mortimer Chambers, Angelos Chaniotis, Michael Chase, Stephen Colvin, G.O. Cowan, David Crystal, Armand D'Angour, Elspeth Dusinberre, Barrie Fleet, Michael Flower, Clive Foss, Karl Galinsky, John Gibert, David Gill, Rismag Gordeziani, David Gribble, Edith Hall, Eric Handley, Jeffrey Henderson, Gabriel Herman, Peter Hunt, Michael Inwood, Paulina Kewes, Kenneth Lapatin, François Lissarague, Cyril Mango, Andreas Markantonatos, Harold B. Mattingly, Robin Mitchell-Boyask, Akiko Moroo, Mark Munn, Oswyn Murray, William Murray, Manana Odisheli, Robin Osborne, Douglass Parker, Gertrud Platz-Horster, Maurice Pope, Nancy Ramage, Walter Redfern, John Richmond, Laurentiu Ristache, Ralph Rosen, Kenneth Rothwell, Ingrid Rowland, Alexander Rubel, Richard Seaford, Nicholas Sekunda, Susan Sherratt, Philip Stadter, Barry Strauss, Ronald S. Stroud, Daniel P. Tompkins, Christopher Tuplin, R.G. Ussher, Robert Wallace, Nigel Wilson, Martin Winkler, and Norman Yoffee, for advice, encouragement and restraint in various measure. Benjamin Lazarus very kindly read through the text at a late stage. Any remaining shortcomings are my own. Several chapters are based on material that has appeared elsewhere in various guises: in *Pericles on Stage, Athenaeum, Classical Quarterly, Classical World, Dialogues d'histoire ancienne, Historia* and *Nomodeiktes*. I am grateful to Texas University Press and to the respective editors for having entertained these contributions in the first instance. Anonymous readers for the press made many valuable comments and suggestions for improvement.

Perhaps my greatest debt, however, has been to the utter wrong-headedness of the late Sir Kenneth Dover, which has acted as a constant goad. Aristophanic studies have suffered immeasurably from his baleful influence. I thus take exception to Sir Kenneth's view that Aristophanes' humour was "rarely sophisticated" and I provide evidence in support of the scholiast's opinion that "the jokes in comedy are witty and urbane". Perhaps even more damaging to a proper understanding of Aristophanes is "Dover's Law": the principle of "one thing at a time", according to which we should "not turn our attention to two different levels of humour operating simultaneously", a position that is beyond the reach of parody. I also expose the essential weakness of Dover's claim that with very few exceptions "the rich anecdotal material" about Alcibiades in Andocides and Plutarch "finds no echo in Aristophanes", for my endeavour has been to spell out some, but by no means all, of the ways in which there is a huge overlap between, on the one hand, the anecdotal tradition relating not simply to Alcibiades, but to his foster-father Pericles and to Pericles' mistress, Aspasia, and, on the other, Aristophanes' remarkable plots—or at least those we still have. Those who see his (Aristophanes', not Sir Kenneth's) unique genius as a sufficient explanation of his achievement might see any work such as this as undermining Aristophanes' claim to fame, but I can only hope that most readers will feel, after reflecting on the evidence presented here, that his (again, Aristophanes', not Sir Kenneth's) reputation is enhanced rather than diminished, and that we can continue to admire him with a greater appreciation of his sophisticated wit. A by-product of this research has been the discovery of contemporary admirers, notably Thucydides and Xenophon, who drew their inspiration from what Plato called the "temple that would never fall ... the soul of Aristophanes".

Michael Vickers   *Tbilisi, Summer 2015*

Abbreviations

Abbreviations used in the text and notes are based on H.G. Liddell, R. Scott and H.S. Jones, *A Greek-English Lexicon*, 9th edition (with supplement) (Oxford: Clarendon Press, 1968) [LSJ] and S. Hornblower, A. Spawforth and E. Eidinow, *The Oxford Classical Dictionary*, 4th edition (Oxford: Clarendon Press, 2012 [*OCD*[4]].

Pericles on Stage	= M. Vickers, *Pericles on Stage: Political Comedy in Aristophanes' Early Plays* (Austin: Texas University Press, 1997; reprint 2012).
Sophocles and Alcibiades	= M. Vickers, *Sophocles and Alcibiades: Athenian Politics in Ancient Greek Literature* (Stocksfield and Ithaca, NY: Acumen Publishing and Cornell University Press, 2008).

Chapter 1

Political Allegory in Aristophanes

The purpose of this book is to suggest that Aristophanes wrote in an allegorical manner, using the public images of a limited number of prominent politicians and members of their families in order to make his points. His use, not to say abuse, of the figure of the demagogue Cleon in *Knights* and *Wasps* is already familiar, but there were other targets of his wit, the κωμῳδούμενοι. There were not many in his eleven extant plays, but they include Alcibiades, Pericles, Aspasia and Alcibiades' wife Hipparete, Pericles' sons Xanthippus and Paralus, the generals Nicias, Demosthenes and Lamachus, and the Persian satrap Tissaphernes.

"Emphasis"

Since "the kind of person who [was] usually lampooned on the stage [was] rich, or aristocratic, or powerful", attacks had to be carried out with considerable discretion. Aristophanes had been prosecuted for lampooning Cleon in the *Babylonians* in 426 BC, but those who crossed Alcibiades faced less formal sanctions that ranged from a beating to murder.

The technique regularly employed by writers of comedy to ridicule influential figures is to be found in the plot-summary of Cratinus' *Dionysalexandros*. Cratinus "satirized Pericles with great plausibility by means of *emphasis*, because he brought the war on the Athenians".[1] "Emphasis" did not carry the meaning of "explicitness" as it has today; rather it meant "innuendo", or even "subliminal suggestion". "We [today] are simply not attuned to writing which proceeds by indirect suggestion rather than by direct statement .... When we 'emphasize' something, we proclaim it to our readers, leaving no doubt that we want its presence known. The ancient writer does the exact opposite"[2] "Emphasis" was defined by Quintilian as "the process of digging out some lurking meaning from something said",[3] and the rhetorician Demetrius, writing in the fourth century BC, stated that "the effect of an argument is more formidable (δεινότερος) because it is ach-

---

1 *POxy* 663, 44–8; *CGFP*, 70; *PCG*, Cratin. *Dionysalexandros* i. See further *Pericles on Stage* Appendix A; "Postumous Parody in Cratinus' *Dionysalexandros*"; subsequent bibliography in Revermann 1997, 197; Storey 2009.
2 Ahl 1984, 179; Ahl 1991, 22–4.
3 Quint. 9.2.64 (trans. Ahl 1984, 176).

ieved by letting the fact make itself manifest (ἐμφαίνοντος) rather than having the speaker make the point for himself".[4] Such "covert allusion", which was widely used in antiquity, was akin to δεινότης ("cleverness, shrewdness") or ὑποδήλωσις ("insinuation"; Pl. *Phdr.* 267a).[5] Frederick Ahl cites a good modern example of "emphasis" in Czesław Miłosz's description of the ways in which poets in post-war Poland went to some lengths to make it dangerous for those who had noticed their covert subversion to bring charges. One story involves a poet complaining that the only flaw in an otherwise perfect city of Moscow was the all-pervasive smell of oranges. To denounce this would simply draw attention to the fact that oranges were notoriously unavailable.[6] In 2003, there was a graffito in the men's room of the Boulderado Hotel that read "Why is our oil in their soil?": at one level it seemed to be an extreme "redneck" statement; at another (and this was presumably the intended meaning) it raised interesting questions about war aims. But such examples are comparatively rare today; in antiquity they would have been the norm.

The device was said to be one of the distinguishing characteristics of Greek comedy, which "differs from abuse, since abuse delivers the insults in an unconcealed manner, whereas comedy needs what is called ἔμφασις" (*Tract. Coisl.* 31–2 Koster).[7] Crates is said to have been the first to give up invective and to begin "to universalise truth and fiction".[8] This has been interpreted as "to advance beyond the ridiculing of real individuals",[9] but better perhaps to understand it as "the first to have introduced allegory", the more subtly to ridicule real individuals, who were still, it should be recalled, "the rich, or the aristocratic, or the powerful". "Emphasis" contributes greatly to the allegorical pictures Aristophanes creates, but finding hidden meanings in Greek drama is not to everyone's taste, indeed might be said to be taboo in the eyes of many scholars. We shall see presently how this came about, and when the break with the pattern that had prevailed in antiquity and the middle ages occurred.

A good example of the technique of expressing in riddles what the writer wanted to say is to be found near the beginning of *Peace*, where two slaves feed the dung beetle on which Trygaeus will fly up to Olympus. One says:

---

4 Demetr. *Eloc.* 288.9 (trans. Ahl 1991, 22–5).

5 Cf. Volkmann 1885, 445 ff; Janko 1984, 202 ff.

6 Ahl 1984, 186.

7 On the possible derivation of the *Tractatus* from Aristotle's lost *Poetics*, see Janko 1984. Cf. Plut. *Per.* 16.1: in describing how comic writers lampooned Pericles, Plutarch calls their technique παρέμφασις.

8 Arist. *Po.* 1449b.9... τῶν δὲ Ἀθήνησιν Κράτης πρῶτος ἦρξεν ἀφέμενος τῆς ἰαμβικῆς ἰδέας καθόλου ποιεῖν λόγους καὶ μύθους.

9 Dover in *OCD*[3], 406.

"Some bright spark in the audience may be saying, 'What is this about? What does the beetle mean?'" The explanation given is that "he is hinting at Cleon, saying that he shamelessly eats dung" (43–48). The word for "hint" is αἰνίττεται, cognate with αἴνιγμα ("enigma" or "riddle"). This is far from being the only instance of such "hinting", which was widespread throughout Greek comedy, as we shall see, and where it is usually put across "emphatically", or "allegorically".

Alcibiades' Violence

But Cleon was not the only powerful Athenian politician that Aristophanes came up against. Alcibiades, once Pericles' ward, began to lay claim to Pericles' political mantle during the 420s. He was elected general for 420/19 BC, and was to be re-elected for at least four of the next five years, before going into exile in 415 BC.[10] The stories about Alcibiades' role in the theatre suggest that it would have been wise to make any attacks on him covert. Alcibiades struck a rival *choregus* "before the audience and judges" ([Andoc.] 4.20–21), he went to the Record Office and "expunged with his wetted finger" an indictment against the comic poet Hegemon of Thasos (the officials were afraid to renew the charge "for fear of Alcibiades"; Ath. 9.407c), and members of "the circle around Alcibiades" intimidated the judges to prevent Aristophanes from winning first prize for *Clouds* in 423 BC (Arg. *Nu.* 5 Coulon), His belligerence went beyond this; he once hit his future father-in-law "as a joke" (Plut. *Alc.* 8.1), he beat up a schoolmaster for not possessing the works of Homer (*ibid.* 7.1), and in a fit of anger had killed one of his servants with a club (*ibid.* 3.1).[11] All this in a society that was characteristically not given to exceptional violence, and where self-restraint was the officially honoured norm.[12] Cleon might have been coarse and abrupt and a politician to be feared, but his usual course of action when crossed was to take legal proceedings; Alcibiades was prone to take direct action and to thump (or club to death) anyone who offended him.

---

10 Develin 1989, 142–50 (there is some doubt about a generalship in 418/17).
11 Alcibiades had the nickname εὐρυμέτωπος ("broadfaced": Poll. 2.43). On the supposed connection between a wide face and a tendency to aggression, see Carré, McCormick, Mondloch 2009.
12 Herman 2006, 184–215.

Alcibiades' Speech Defect; Legal Constraints on Comedy

Aristophanes' rival Eupolis clearly went too far in the *Baptae* when he drew Alcibiades' especial anger by "openly lampooning his τραυλότητα" (Tzetz. XIAi 89 Koster). τραυλότης was a speech defect whereby *rho* is pronounced as *lambda*: such a confusion could deliver meanings in Greek as different from each other as "Pirate" and "Pilot" in English. Alcibiades' speech disorder was thought by contemporaries, "to be full of charm, and to have added persuasiveness (πιθανότητα) to his discourse" (Plut. *Alc.* 1.6). Even today, "Many politicians and others dependent on public esteem go in for lisps, stutters and bizarre pronunciations ... and these afflictions may serve to make the sufferer more likeable".[13] Alcibiades' son later adopted both his father's distinctive gait and his mode of speech, presumably because it was to his social and political advantage to do so: κλασαυχενεύεται τε καὶ τραυλίζεται ("he bends his neck in an affected way and pronounces *rho* as *lambda*"; Archipp. *PCG* 48 *ap.* Plut. *Alc.* 1.8.). The speech condition is usually translated as "lisping", but traulism, or lambdacism might be more accurate.[14] Aristophanes spells things out in *Wasps*, where a slave says that in a dream he saw a certain Theorus with the head of a κόραξ (crow). Then (44–5) Alcibiades is supposed to have said to him τραυλίσας (lambdacizing):

> ὁλᾷς; Θέωλος τὴν κεφαλὴν κόλακος ἔχει
> "Do you see Theolus? He has the head of a flatterer".

He should have said:

> ὁρᾷς; Θέωρος τὴν κεφαλὴν κόρακος ἔχει
> "Do you see Theorus? He has the head of a crow".

Normally, lambdacism would not have been indicated in the text, as Quintilian explains: λαμβδακισμός, along with iotacism, a soft voice, and broad pronunciation "happen through sounds, and ... cannot be shown in writing because they

---

13 Sayle 1988, 10.
14 Alcibiades the younger, Demosthenes (Stanford 1967, 152, n. 10 for refs.) and Aristotle (D.L. 5.1) also shared the same speech impediment. For a discussion of the condition, see O'Neill 1980 (a reference I owe to the kindness of David Crystal). It is worth bearing in mind the relationship between childhood speech impairment and emotional disorders which often results in "destructiveness [and] temper tantrums": Baker and Cantwell 1982, 291–2.

are errors in speech and of the tongue" (Quint. *Inst. Or.* 1.5.32).[15]There are special reasons why the lambdacism is spelled out at *Wasps* 44–5, for they are spoken by an individual who is characterized as someone other than Alcibiades.[16]

Playwrights exploited the possibilities for double meanings presented by Alcibiades' speech mannerism. Sophocles was doing it as early as 438 BC,[17] and we find Aristophanes doing so from *Knights* onwards. Eupolis clearly upset Alcibiades' in *Baptae*, and not only does he seem to have been punished (Alcibiades having some of his friends "baptise" the poet in the sea),[18] but Alcibiades is said to have "passed a law to the effect that comedy should no longer be written openly, but figuratively" (Tzetz. XIAi 97–8 Koster). There may be some support[19] for this statement if, as seems probable, *Baptae* was performed shortly before the Sicilian expedition,[20] in legislation passed in 415 BC. The Decree of Syracosius stated that it should henceforth be illegal to lampoon people in the theatre by name (μὴ κωμῳδεῖσθαι ὀνομαστί τινα: Schol. Ar. *Av.* 1297; cf. Eup. *PCG* 220).

There has been much discussion of the meaning of Syracosius' legislation.[21] The absence from *Birds* of the names of any of those found guilty of parodying the Eleusinian Mysteries or the mutilation of the Herms, for example, has been taken as evidence for the law having applied to them: that these individuals should not be mentioned on the stage.[22] The reality may have been that Aristophanes was simply obeying the law in not mentioning by name the major figures who were being seriously lampooned. Aristophanes is in any case said to have been among those who practised symbolic satire after 415 BC (Tzetz. XIAi 99–100 Koster), and if his next extant play, *Birds*, was concerned with Alcibiades' exile at Sparta, the bamboozling of his hosts, and the seduction and impregnation of Agis' queen Timaea, then Aristophanes was simply obeying the law in lampooning Alcibiades "symbolically" and failing to mention him by name.

---

15 Cf. Ahl 1991, 96.
16 See further *Pericles on Stage*, 125.
17 *Sophocles and Alcibiades*, 27–8.
18 Tzetz. XIAi 89 Koster: "Baptise me on stage and I will soak you in salt water"; an authentic couplet: M. L. West 1972, 29–30; 1974, 17. On the tradition that Alcibiades drowned Eupolis, see p. 79, below.
19 The evidence is very uncertain: Halliwell 1991, 55–6.
20 Storey 1990; 1993.
21 E.g. Halliwell 1991, 54–66; Csapo and Slater 1995, 415–16; Trevett 2000; Bierl 2002; Cottone 2007.
22 Sommerstein 1986, 101–8, with references to earlier literature.

The κωμῳδούμενοι

Despite all the indications that Aristophanes was obliged to write figuratively, most scholars have chosen to take the most literal view of his plays, and since some 37 Athenians are mentioned in *Birds*, performed in the following year 414 BC, it has been suggested that the Decree of Syracosius was a dead letter, if it existed at all.[23] This has perhaps overlooked the possibility that Aristophanes had larger targets in mind; that he might have gone for the big fish, rather than the small fry—which is in fact what comedy was supposed to be about according to our only contemporary account. The Old Oligarch, probably to be identified with Xenophon the Rhetor writing in the later 420s BC,[24] states that the "kind of person who is κωμῳδούμενος ('lampooned') is usually ἢ πλούσιος ἢ γενναῖος ἢ δυνάμενος ('rich, or aristocratic, or powerful': [Xen.] *Ath. pol.* 2.18)"—and Aristophanes himself claims to attack οἱ μέγιστοι ("the most influential"): *Nu.* 549; *Ve.* 1030; *Pax* 751.[25] It will be taken as a working hypothesis in what follows that it was the truly "rich, or aristocratic, or powerful", such as Pericles ("aristocratic on both sides"; Plut. *Per.* 3.1), Aspasia (who probably came from "a distinguished Milesian family"),[26] Alcibiades (supposedly descended from Ajax on his father's side, and from Nestor and Alcmaeon on his mother's; Plut. *Alc.* 1.1; Paus. 2.18.7), his wife Hipparete (the daughter of "the richest among the Greeks": Isoc. 16.31), and Cleon, a wealthy tanner, and not the individuals who are mentioned along the way,[27] who were properly the κωμῳδούμενοι— fewer than a dozen, perhaps, in Aristophanes' surviving plays. The actual names of the principal targets of the comic writer remained concealed (and the names of "real" people are often employed to enhance the characterization), but the disguises were easily penetrable, in that the characterisations were based on the anecdotal traditions relating to the individuals in question. This explanation has the advantage of by-passing recent scholarship—much of it highly ingenious—on the Decree of Syracosius, if it existed; and if it did not, the essential point still remains.

---

23 E.g. Sommerstein 2002, 135.
24 Keen and Sekunda 2007; cf. Rosetti 1997; Forrest 1970, 1986 ("c. 424"); de Ste Croix 1972, 308–10 ("431–421"); Ostwald 1986, 182, n. 23 ("c. 430"); Hornblower 2000 ("the 4th century BC"); Mattingly 1997: ("414").
25 Cf. Heath 1987a, 42, n. 90.
26 Henderson 2000, 140, citing Laurenti 1988. For a valuable collection of sources relating to Aspasia, see Solana Dueso 1994.
27 Useful lists in: Holden 1902; Sommerstein 1996a; Storey 1998.

In addition, if a law restricting dramatic ridicule of citizens at Thurii (founded in 443 BC with considerable Athenian participation; cf. Diod. 12.35.2) το μοιχοὶ καὶ πολυπράγμονες ("adulterers and those who were overly active in political matters": Plut. *Mor.* 519*b*), points to similar legislation (or custom) at Athens,[28] then the contemporary public images of both Pericles and Alcibiades will have qualified them in both categories. Thus, "Pericles was much given to love affairs," (Clearch. *FHG* 2.314 *ap.* Ath. 13.589*d*), and Alcibiades was a serial pathic and adulterer. The political activities of neither need no gloss.[29] Aspasia too, whose popular image was essentially that of a prostitute (a characterization that was in all likelihood the result of comic invention generated by Pericles' enemies),[30] may also have qualified under both rubrics. At all events, she "figured large in the works of comic writers" (Did. *ap.* Clem. Al. *Strom.* 4.19.122; cf. Plut. *Per.* 24. 9–10).

A later source is in keeping with both the Old Oligarch and the Thurian law, but is a little more informative. The text of Platonius *On Different Kinds of Comedy* relies on a source that antedates Eratosthenes (3rd century BC)[31] and is short, but repetitive. It states variously that "The writers of comedies had licence to mock generals, dishonest jurors and those citizens who were avaricious or led a life of licentiousness" (Platon. 1.7–8), or that "The purpose of Old Comedy was as follows: to criticize generals, unjust jurors, and those who accumulate illicitly acquired wealth or who led a dissolute life" (*Ibid.* 49–52).[32] Once again, this strikes a familiar note so far as our principal κωμῳδούμενοι, Pericles, Aspasia, Cleon and Alcibiades, are concerned. Pericles, Cleon and Alcibiades (and Nicias, Demosthenes and Lamachus) were generals; Pericles faced accusations of maladministration of funds, and Alcibiades' name was often associated with pecula-

---

28 Henderson 1990; add Thuc. 3.34 (on the [re-] foundation of Notium in 427 BC, to which the Athenians "gave laws like their own").

29 See however e.g.: Levi 1980; Stadter 1989; Kagan 1990; Brulé 1994; Schubert 1994; Podlecki 1998; Azoulay 2014 (on Pericles); Hatzfeld 1951; Levi 1967, 131–45; Bloedow 1972; Forde 1989; Ellis, 1989; de Romilly 1993; Gribble 1999; 2012; Munn 2000; Rhodes 2011, *Sophocles and Alcibiades* (on Alcibiades).

30 Podlecki 1999, 115–7; Solana Dueso 1994, xvi-xvii; Henderson 2000, 140.

31 Perusino 1987, 74.

32 Perusino 1987, 92–5; cf. Mastromarco 2002, 205, n. 1, who also adduces Horace (*Serm.* 1.4.1–5) who says much the same thing: *Eupolis atque Cratinus Aristophanesque poetae/atque alii, quorum comoedia prisca virorum est,/siquis erat dignus describi, quod malus ac fur,/quod moechus foret aut sicarius aut alioqui/famosus, multa cum libertate notabant.* ("Cratinus, Aristophanes, and all/The elder comic poets, great and small,/If e'er a worthy in those ancient times/Deserved peculiar notice for his crimes,/Adulterer, cut-throat, ne'er-do-well, or thief,/Portrayed him without fear in strong relief". Trans. Conington 1882). Cf. Hooley 2007, 46–52.

tion, embezzlement or outright theft; and all three members of the Periclean household might reasonably be said to have acquired dissolute reputations— often exaggerated no doubt by comic invention.

Platonius also preserves an extremly valuable, but generally neglected, indication that the κωμῳδούμενοι were few in number. He says: "In Old Comedy, the masks were made to look like the κωμῳδούμενοι, so that before an actor spoke a word, the audience would recognise from the visual likeness who was being attacked" (*ibid.* 64–6). Platonius' testimony receives support from the fact that no mask-maker dared to make a portrait mask of Cleon for the performance of *Knights* (230–3); the implication being that portrait-masks were the norm. On this evidence, it is inherently unlikely that the κωμῳδούμενοι should have been the 300 "real people" whose names occur in Aristophanes' works,[33] for there would have to be a quick change of mask every time a different person was named (and quite how this might work in practice is difficult to conceive). Rather, the characterisation of the few rich, or powerful, or dissolute individuals that emerges from the text was already apparent to the audience, even before the characters spoke.[34] Friedrich Dübner noted with surprise in 1842 that he had not come across any earlier citation of Platonius.[35] It clearly takes time for fresh input into dramatic studies to seep into the mainstream.

In the light of these testimonia concerning Old Comedy, it is strange to reflect, for example, that the prevalent view of *Lysistrata*, famous for the "sex-strike" which underlies the plot, is that "very little of the satire is really topical ... there are only a few references to contemporary events and people".[36] Or that the "relative absence" of "ephemeral topicalities" from *Thesmophoriazusae* could be considered a distinctive feature of that play. *Thesmophoriazusae* is "not a political play and was never designed to be", in the words of a recent critic. "It is a drama about drama and about gender".[37] *Frogs* is generally thought to be "about" literature rather than politics, and *Ecclesiazusae* to be yet another play concerned with "gender", but with a socio-economic twist.[38] These judgements are all mistaken to some degree. While Alcibiades lived, the allusions to him in Aristophanes' plays were very topical, and reflected both his recent actions and what it was feared he might do. After his death, individuals based on him, like those based on Pericles, Aspasia and Hip-

---

33 Storey 1998.
34 Cf. Sidwell 1997, 255. This testimony is consistently overlooked. Storey 2003, for example, uses Platonius in discussing Eupolis' style, but has nothing on masks or κωμῳδούμενοι.
35 Dübner 1842, xiii.
36 Spatz 1978, 102.
37 Sommerstein 1994, 4, 12.
38 E.g. Taaffe 1993, 132–3, 136–8.

parete, became stock characters. The caricatures are now fixed, but members of Pericles' extended family continue to be an immensely rich source of inspiration. The plays all emerge as highly political, in that they dwell to a large extent on the lives of a small number of politically prominent Athenians. They may be read as elaborate but subtle allegories of contemporary or recent history. Characters based closely on Pericles play opposite an Alcibiades who is rendered "figuratively and not openly" in accordance with the regulations. It looks as though the law continued to be obeyed for many years. And if Alcibiades had indeed pushed for the Decree of Syracosius—assuming it existed at all—one wonders why he was so foolish, for censorship can be a very uncertain tool, and one that can rebound on its inventors.[39] Furthermore, it will be argued below that many of the names of real people who are specifically mentioned are simply vehicles for the further lampooning of the major targets. The latter, and not the individuals concerned, are properly the κωμῳδούμενοι.

It is a commonplace of Aristophanic scholarship that Alcibiades is apparently absent from comedy. A recent statement noting "the almost complete dearth of attacks by comic poets on one of the most controversial figures of the day: the flamboyant aristocrat Alcibiades"[40], is typical, and in the specific context of *Birds*, it was noted long ago that Alcibiades is nowhere mentioned by name.[41] This can only have been partly due to the difficulty of fitting Ἀλκιβιάδης into verse (cf. Critias 88 B 4DK), for his patronymic ὁ Κλεινίου ("son of Cleinias") could be (and usually was) employed instead (Tib. *Fig.* 35.10; Ar. *Ach.* 716). Scholarly surprise was due not only to the fact that Alcibiades was "rich, aristocratic and powerful", but that he was the most controversial individual of his age, having been "the leader of the dissolute younger generation";[42] having been elected one of the generals for the Sicilian expedition (a campaign he had done much to promote); having been suspected of involvement in the profanation of the Mysteries before the departure of the fleet; having been recalled from Sicily to stand trial; having jumped ship and gone into exile at Sparta; having advised the Spartans on the most effective ways to defeat Athens; having, so rumour had it, se-

---

39 For a well argued case that Alcibiades was not in fact especially bright, see Bloedow 1992.
40 Robson 2009, 179. Cf. de Ste. Croix 1972, 361: "Aristophanes makes surprisingly few references to the aristocratic Alcibiades"; Heath 1987a, 34: "Alcibiades appears surprisingly infrequently in Aristophanes and the fragments of other dramatists"; Halliwell 1991, 61: "Alcibiades, however surprisingly, does not appear to have been a particularly appealing butt for comic poets at any point in his career"; Hertzberg 1853, 303: "references made by Athenian dramatists to Alcibiades in the years 414–411 BC are only to be found in a very limited quantity". For specific references to Alcibiades, see Talbot 1963; Moorton 1988.
41 By Droysen 1835, 161–208.
42 Ehrenberg 1943, 104–5.

duced and impregnated Timaea, the wife of the Spartan king; having then fled to take refuge with the Persian satrap Tissaphernes before taking command of the Athenian forces on Samos; having returned to Athens in glory, and having died in exile again, in disgrace. He captured the imagination of friend and foe alike, electrifying Athenian drama, but one must look long and hard to find discussion of the evidence for this in modern scholarship relating to the Athenian stage, which largely resists any notion that plays might deal with day-to-day politics, and in particular with the career of individuals such as Alcibiades.

The Problem with Political Allegory

Birds provides a useful testing ground for theories of allegory in Greek drama, and there is nothing new in seeing the play as an allegory in which Alcibiades underlies the hero Peisthetaerus, but there is a widespread resistance today to any political reading at all.[43] Perhaps the most influential advocate of an allegorical reading was J.W. Süvern's study of 1827, translated into English in 1835,[44] but which is now generally dismissed as "a warning against eagerness to credit the play with an explicit political design."[45] Süvern was reacting against the view expressed by A.W. von Schlegel earlier in the nineteenth century: "that the 'Birds' was nothing more than the fantastic exuberance of poetic genius, soaring with light wing into an airy region of its own creation, but yet with a shrewd eye for the follies of a world from which it pretends to have shaken itself free."[46] Most scholars today adopt this position; Cedric Whitman went further, claiming that "the theme of the *Birds* is absurdity itself ... it is about meaninglessness".[47] The growing dislike for allegory was reinforced by the fact that by the second half of the nineteenth century the allegorists had apparently spun out of control, exemplified by the fact that by 1879 there were no fewer than 79 accounts of the *Tendenz* of the *Birds* on offer.[48]

Greek studies developed in northern Europe during the sixteenth and seventeenth centuries as a means of challenging the traditional authority of the

---

43 E.g. Whitman 1964, 169: "*Birds* is strangely free of political concerns. Cf. Konstan 1990, 187; Sommerstein 1987, 1; Dunbar 1995, 3–4. Arrowsmith 1973 and Sidwell 2009 are exceptions to the general trend. On the name Peisthetaerus, see p. 39–40, below.
44 Süvern 1827; 1835.
45 Dobrov 1990, 214; cf. Arrowsmith 1970, 7; Dunbar 1995, 4.
46 Merry 1904, 18, characterizing Schlegel 1809.
47 Whitman 1964, 179.
48 Süss 1911, 137, citing W. Behaghel.

Roman church. The Greek New Testament of Martin Luther was the weapon used to attack an institution whose spiritual claims appeared to rest on a Latin pun,[49] and there has long been a connection between Protestantism and Greek studies,[50] well epitomised by an observation of Thomas Mitchell, writing in the mid-nineteenth century: "Of that Book, which alone solves the enigma of the otherwise incomprehensible world in which we live ... it has pleased the Disposer of all things, that the most important portion of it should be written in original Greek, and that the rest of it should be found among us in translated Greek".[51]

Classical scholarship had begun in the Renaissance courtly tradition of cloaking secrets in the fabric of fables,[52] but by the end of the seventeenth and in the early eighteenth century there was a "a diminishing tolerance of error, an increasing demand for precision",[53] that led to the creation of the science of *Altertumswissenschaft* in early nineteenth century Germany. Its attendant specialization led to what its proponents believed to be an increased rigour in the treatment of ancient literature.[54] But a "science" that had begun as a defence of the Word of One God was perhaps ill equipped to understand a culture that worshipped many gods.

A complicating factor was philhellenism, which lined scholars up against an *ancien régime* that reckoned its descent from exiled Trojans. The Habsburgs for example reckoned their descent from Priam and Hector.[55] Courtly society had derived moral and ethical truths from emblem books and amused themselves with riddles, but these both lost their status under the new order.[56] Puns went the same way. Nowadays, it is axiomatic that "the pun is the lowest form of wit", but it was not always so. Shakespeare revelled in puns, as did Edmund Burke.[57] Dr Johnson abhorred them, and the Whig wit, the Rev. Sydney Smith had "very little to say about puns; they are in very bad repute, and so they

---

49 *"Tu es Petrus et super hanc petram aedificabo ecclesiam meam"*, inscribed around the base of the dome of St Peter's.
50 Lloyd-Jones 1982, 19; Bernal 1987, 193–4.
51 Mitchell 1836, iv. On Mitchell himself, see E. M. Hall 2007, 76–7.
52 Wind 1966.
53 R.H. Griffith 1945, 156.
54 Pfeiffer 1976; Wilamowitz-Moellendorff 1982; Bernal 1987.
55 Laschitzer 1888; MacDougall 1982.
56 See the Chronological Index in Heckscher, Sherman and Ferguson 1984, 81–90: emblem books published in the sixteenth century take up 2½ pages, seventeenth century 4, eighteenth century 1½, and the nineteenth less than 1. On riddles, see Bryant 1990, 51: "With the coming of the nineteenth century there began a decline in the esteem in which the riddle was held."
57 Tartakovsky 2009.

ought to be".[58] Ambiguity in ancient literature tended to be overlooked. "Hidden meanings" came to be disregarded, even derided.[59] Puns might be explained away as accidental; contrast Frederick Ahl, who has done much to rescue ambiguity in Greek and Latin literature: "The pun is not natural, it is an art form and thus not careless". [60] Such was the prejudice against puns that those of Aristophanes could be dismissed as "rarely sophisticated".[61] But then "few scholars are so Oedipal as to seek what they consciously do not wish to find."[62] While it is true that "tyrants and terrorists pun sparingly",[63] their opponents often find ambiguity to be an effective means of safe criticism. Allegory—and certainly political allegory—went out of scholarly fashion; it was only tolerated in the form of what De Quincey called "impersonated abstractions".[64]

Ambiguity in Greece

Ambiguity, by contrast, was very appealing to the ancients and in the appropriate contexts they would disguise (or enhance) fact with fiction. Plato's *Protagoras* provides a good example; the Abderite philosopher asks his audience whether they would rather he made his case μῦθων λέγων ("in the form of a myth") or whether he should go through it in a factual way (Pl. *Prt.* 320c). His listeners prefer the myth. Isocrates put matters very effectively in speaking of λογοὺς ἀμφιβόλους ("ambiguous words"):

> arguments the employment of which, when one contends in court over contracts for his own advantage, is shameful and no slight token of depravity but, when one discourses on the nature of man and of things, is fine and philosophical (Isoc. 12.240).[65]

Ambiguity might also exist in poetry. W.B. Stanford, writing in pre-war Trinity College, Dublin, amid the last vestiges of the *ancien régime*, and in the city of

58 S. Smith 1886, 241.
59 E.g. Dover 1958, 235; Friis Johansen 1962, 172.
60 Ahl 1988, 25; cf. Vendryes 1921, 209; Redfern 1984, 15.
61 Dover 1968, 96; cf. 2004, 242–3.
62 Ahl 1988, 21–3.
63 H.G. Hall 1984, 100.
64 De Quincey 1857, 13.281; cf. Newiger 1957; 2000; Hubbard 1998, 374.
65 Cf. Stanford 1939, 13.

those supreme wordplayers James Joyce and Myles na gCopaleen, was one of the few to recognize the fact:

> No *genre* of Greek poetry is entirely free from deliberate ambiguities, whether trivial puns, superstitious or sophistical etymologies, cryptic oracles, diplomatic evasions, cunning and deceptive equivocations, humorous or cacemphatic *doubles entendres*, unconscious foreshadowings of catastrophe, allusive phrases, associative meanings and vaguenesses, or any other of the manifold devices of ambiguity in its widest sense. Simpler lyric poetry had least of it, drama most.[66]

These devices might be employed in the service of political allegory in both serious and comic contexts. Bacchylides, for example, used the career of Theseus as a graceful tribute to Cimon, his family, and his exploits.[67] Sophocles reacted in his *Antigone* to his fellow-general Pericles' excesses following his victory over the rebellious Samians in 439. It was said that the bodies of the executed Samian leaders, after many indignities, were cast away unburied (Plut. *Per.* 28.2). Unburied bodies are, significantly perhaps, prominent both in this tale and in Sophocles' play. Sophocles was still being implicated in the harrowing events on Samos centuries later (Strab. 14.1.18), but he seems to have made his feelings felt in representing Pericles as the austere, unbending Creon.[68] Myth could also be exploited to foresee the future: in *Oedipus Tyrannus*, Sophocles imagines what sort of individual Alcibiades might turn into given his current tendencies (the inconsistencies and improbabilities become less disconcerting once we realise Sophocles was not concerned with the "discovery of the past in the present action of the play", as Bernard Knox once put it, but rather the "discovery of the *future* in the present action of the play"). Euripides, as we shall see in Chapters 4 and 7 and in Appendix 1, was a past master at interpreting recent historical events with a deft, allusive, touch. Myth could indeed be "readily adjusted or invented in the service of state, family or politics".[69]

The same "emphatic" approach to historical events and the individual's role in them was employed by writers for the Athenian comic stage. Instead, however, of graceful compliments, psychological analysis, or spin-doctoring, insults were the common coin. Wordplay, ambiguity and "emphasis" lent themselves admirably to a discourse on the nature of particular individuals, and were especially

---

66 Stanford 1939, 181–2.
67 Barron 1980; Francis 1990, 53–66. *Pericles on Stage*, xxiii.
68 See *Sophocles and Alcibiades* for this (13–33) and other examples of treating recent events in the guise of myth. On Creon, see further Vickers 2011b.
69 Boardman 1982, 1; cf. Francis 1980; 1990.

useful when those who were "rich, or aristocratic or powerful" were in the line of fire.

Aristophanes' Sophisticated Audience

The foregoing is by way of suggesting that Aristophanes' humour might be very clever indeed; but this raises questions concerning the nature of the original audience, and here we are on very uncertain ground. It has been said that the commentary on contemporary reception of late seventeenth century English drama is "so scrappy as to terrify any responsible scholar";[70] how much more wary should we be of the infinitesimally small testimony relating to Attic comedy: an anecdote about Socrates' not unfavourable response to *Clouds* (Psellus, *Or. min.* 7.84), and another about Alcibiades' claque preventing it winning first prize (*Arg.* 5 Coulon), and that is about it. Nothing is known about the audience other than that foreigners were allowed to attend performances at the Greater Dionysia. It is a matter of debate as to whether women attended. There is even an influential school of thought that maintains that Aristophanes was writing for peasants,[71] with a consequent lowering of expectations.

Aristophanes' puns, for example, are said to be "rarely sophisticated".[72] It would be good to be able to show unequivocally that the audience did in fact include those who were urbane and politically aware, fully capable of grasping numerous intricate allusions, but beyond pointing out that folk who sat through the existing canon of Greek drama (and much more) could not have been exactly stupid, it is impossible to be certain, and the scholiast who noted how "the jokes in comedy are witty and urbane" (Schol. Ar. *Nu.* 64) may have been exaggerating. Another example of the impoverishment of the classical past that has been perhaps even more damaging to a proper understanding of Aristophanes is the principle of "one thing at a time", according to which we should "not turn our attention to two different levels of humour operating simultaneously".[73] Without any firm evidence to the contrary, it is perfectly possible that Aristophanes' audience consisted of zombies, but better perhaps to see Aristophanes' humour working at as many levels as he could possibly get away with. It has been well said of the pun that it "brings in another level (or levels) of meaning to a text, and an author may exploit this second level in a single occasion, on several separate occasions,

---

70 Hume 1999, 119.
71 E.g. Dover 1972, frontispiece; cf. Storey 1997.
72 Dover 1968, 96; cf. Storey 1997.
73 Dover 1987, 241.

or continually. Puns, employed in a sustained and intricate manner, will allow him to narrate on several levels simultaneously".[74] Aristophanes was writing for an audience that included many who were alert to any nuance, equivocation or ambiguity; in short "sophisticated". Simon Goldhill has rightly criticised the view that the "requirements of performance before a mass audience preclude, or at any rate severely limit, the possibilities of complex, problematic or obscure expression in the tragic texts";[75] the same considerations apply to comedy.

Much of what is imputed by Aristophanes is at the level of gossip or tittle-tattle, and much may well never have actually occurred in real life. Some incidents or conceits in any case had their origins in the exaggerations of comic writers—frequently grounds for dismissing elements of the anecdotal tradition out of hand, but in the present context all to the good. But while the historicity of some of the events and imputations discussed here may be open to question, the historical significance of the fact that such things were said, joked about, or even believed, should not be overlooked. As G.M. Young once observed: "the real, central theme of History is not what happened, but what people felt about it when it was happening,"[76] and in the specific context of the Athenian anecdotal tradition, Barry Strauss notes that "The truth of [the anecdotes about Alcibiades' youthful adventures] hardly matters; much more important is that Alcibiades elicited them".[77]

Much of what is preserved in the anecdotal tradition is tittle-tattle, and the comic theatre will have served as an effective means of dissecting rumour and gossip. It will be taken for granted in what follows that if there is a prefiguration in comedy of a story preserved in the anecdotal tradition, then the two are related. Whether the prefiguration or the story has a basis in fact will not be my concern. All I hope to demonstrate is that there is a sufficiently large overlap between tales told about members of Pericles' extended family, and the plots and situations that occur in Aristophanes' extant plays to justify a belief in political allegory.

It was probably with good reason that Aristotle mentions Alcibiades in his analysis of the difference between poetry and history:

> The historian and the poet do not differ in that they use metrical or unmetrical language .... The difference is that the one tells of events that have happened, the other of such as might happen ... poetry expresses the universal, history partic-

---

74 Hutchinson 1983, 106.
75 Goldhill 1987, 58–9.
76 G.M. Young, cited in Marcus 1966, 111.
77 B.S. Strauss 1990, 122.

ulars. Now, "the universal" consists in describing the kind of things that a person of a certain character would say or do probably or necessarily .... An example of the particular is what Alcibiades did, or what was done to him (Arist. *Po.* 9.2–4).

There is a large literature on what this might mean,[78] but it is tempting to think that what Aristotle is implicitly saying is that the poet (he is speaking of the dramatic poet) shows the kind of thing that someone like Alcibiades might say or do, given his known propensities.[79] Sophocles seems in any case regularly to have done this,[80] and this is what the Antiochene polymath Libanius implied centuries later when he posed the rhetorical question: "What play did not include [Alcibiades] among the cast of characters? Eupolis, Aristophanes, did they not show him on the stage? It is to him that comedy owed its success" (Lib. *fr.* 50.2.21). Given the information available to Libanius (the libraries of late-Roman Athens and Antioch will have contained rather more primary literature than is available to us),[81] it is possible that he knew what he was talking about. The essential accuracy of Libanius' observation concerning Alcibiades will be another working hypothesis in what follows.

Polymorphic Characterization

Perhaps the most important phenomenon to have emerged from this research is what I have called "polymorphic characterization". This technique, which I believe Aristophanes to have exploited throughout his career, was a highly effective way of revealing different sides of a person's character, especially useful in the case of an individual as complex as Alcibiades who was compared in antiquity to Proteus, proverbial for changing his shape (Lib. *Decl.* 12.42), and a chameleon (Plut. *Alc.* 23.4). The closest modern parallels can be found in the world of the political cartoonist. In Matt Wuerker's *Standing Tall in Deep Doodoo: A Cartoon Chronicle of Campaign '92 and the Bush-Quayle Years*, for example, there are cartoons in which President Bush Sr is represented *i.a.* as the Environmental President (wearing a hippy bandana), the Ethics President (wearing a halo), the No New Taxes President (with sealed lips), the Voodoo Economist President (with a bone through his nose and grasping a chicken by the neck), the President of the World (dressed as Napoleon) and Globo Cop (looking like Arnold Terminator). Aristophanes would

---

78 E.g. M. I. Finley 1965; Armstrong 1998; Kagan 2005.
79 Cf. Else 1957, 313.
80 Vickers 2005b; 2005c; 2007b; *Sophocles and Alcibiades*; 2011b; 2012.
81 Cf. Norman 1960, 122–26; Cribiore 2007; Nesselrath 2012.

have put a selection of such characters on stage, sometimes interacting with each other, and sometimes playing opposite an assortment of equally varied caricatures of someone else.

The same technique was used by the psychotherapist and playwright Nikolai Nikolaivich Evreinov (1879–1953) in his *Theatrical Soul* (1912),[82] and it was also employed by W.B. Yeats, who adopted it from William Hale White, who had introduced "characters whose function it was to speak for another side of his own mind and test ironically the strength of his developing convictions".[83] "Polymorphic characterization" was by no means an Aristophanic invention, for it was in use as early the 430s BC.[84] The technique neatly provided a means of representing internal debate and soul-searching, for Greek drama, unlike Elizabethan, was not distinguished for its soliloquies. If Christopher Gill is correct, there was no such thing as a true Greek soliloquy;[85] polymorphic characterization bore the burden. One of Wuerker's conceits has a film in which Saddam Hussein stars as Hitler. In Aristophanic terms, Saddam, not Hitler (for all that his name was used), would be the κωμῳδούμενος. There might also be temporary role reversals in Aristophanes' plays, which would complicate the sophisticated comedy even further.

The Bush cartoons mentioned above are already dated, and serve as a reminder that Athenian comedy had an even shorter shelf-life; as Evelyn Waugh once put it, "except for political claptrap few forms of writing are as ephemeral as comedy."[86] Greek plays were written with a view to their being performed, in principle, only once. Any political allusions would have made sense at the time of performance, but their pertinence would have quickly faded from the collective memory. The broad outlines of the stock figures may well have retained their potency for some decades, however, but eventually even their original meaning will have been lost. Aristophanes was able to employ the members of his "Happy Family"—Mr Dicaeopolis the Periclean statesman, Mr Sausage-seller the up-and-coming Alcibiadean politician, Mrs Praxagora the Aspasian philosopheress—throughout his lifetime, but the practice does not appear to continue later in the fourth century. "The comic poets got tired of writing about [Alcibiades'] exploits" (Lib. *fr.* 50.2.23). Comedy changed its nature, as ancient critics noticed.[87] The way in which the content was put across by means of the Periclean *ménage* belonged to what has recently been called the "complex network of codes and signs" that were part of the

---

82 Carnicke 1991.
83 Daiches 1969, 97; Kiberd 1995, 446.
84 *Sophocles and Alcibiades*, 13–33.
85 C. Gill 1996, 204–26; cf. Waterfield 1996.
86 Waugh 1984, 564.
87 Cf. Nesselrath 1990; English 2005.

performance of an ancient play;[88] the traditions relating to these individuals may have been "distorted and fragmented in various ways", but they are "still recognizable and significant"[89] for the understanding of the plays we still have.

Recognition of the phenomenon of polymorphic characterization also helps to explain, indeed explain away, the problem of an apparent lack of continuity that is felt by some to disfigure Aristophanes' plays; for the principal targets are never absent from the stage. Aristophanes' plot construction has been variously described as "loose and faltering",[90] or "inconsequential".[91] But once polymorphic characterization is understood to be present, Aristophanes' plots can be seen to be tightly constructed rather than rambling and lacking in unity. Similarly, the "incongruences" and "trivial inconsistencies" that the playwright might have might have removed by a "stroke of the pen",[92] prove not to be "mistakes", but to reflect historical reality. Dunbar once wrote of "inconsistencies ... probably due to carelessness of a type common in Aristophanes";[93] Aristophanes is never inconsistent and is never careless, and it is one of the purposes of this book to demonstrate the fact.

Nor is it unreasonable to find echoes of Aristophanes in Thucydides, who will have known how to read such allegory, as we shall presently see. Aristophanes and Thucydides were not alone in apparently exploiting Alcibiades' influential personality, and other writers, notably Sophocles and Euripides, used material that was common coin even before Aristophanes came on the scene. Much of this is discussed elsewhere,[94] but the charge that Alcibiades "lay with his mother", recorded by a contemporary, will be taken up in Appendix 1. We cannot hope to catch every allusion made by ancient writers, but we are fortunate in that we possess something of the rich anecdotal tradition relating to the principal personalities whose policies, idiosyncrasies and scandalous activities are lampooned by Aristophanes.

---

88 Lada-Richards 1999, 11, n. 28
89 Bowie 1993, 6.
90 Norwood 1931, 302.
91 Henderson 1987, lx.
92 Süss 1954; Norwood 1931, 299; cf. Dover 1972, 44, 59–65.
93 Dunbar 1995, 11.
94 Cf. Vickers 1994, 2005b, 2005c, 2007b, *Sophocles and Alcibiades*.

Chapter 2

Wordplay; Pericles, Alcibiades and Aspasia on Stage

Wordplay, History and Ambiguity

It has been wisely said that "wordplay, and the study of it, can give access to the implicit",[1] and the way in which Aristophanes employs "emphasis" has already been indicated in Chapter 1. Although allegory, ambiguity, and puns are not respectable in some academic quarters, there are welcome signs of change. Walter Redfern, Frederick Ahl, Jonathan Culler, James O'Hara, and Derek Collins[2] have done much to create a renewed interest in wordplay as an important aspect of many literatures. Ahl's work in particular is of special significance in that it shows how extensive was the role of wordplay in both Greek and Roman society. Jeffrey Henderson has done much to elucidate the double meanings which were engendered by comic poets in the realm of obscene language,[3] and Ralph M. Rosen has shed new light on the origins of obscene usage in the genre of iambic abuse a century or so earlier.[4] John Barron and E.D. Francis have elucidated the political allegory of Bacchylides' Thesean dithyrambs,[5] and I have elsewhere suggested that Sophocles regularly plays in an allusive manner on contemporary events.[6] Benyamin Shimron has shown that "Herodotus ... smiles with a purpose", that he uses "sarcasm, wit, simple jokes ... irony [and] puns" to make more serious points.[7] Even Thucydides was not above punning,[8] and may even have lampooned Alcibiades' mode of speech.[9] Plato's *Cratylus* is a work which is based on wordplay of a kind that clearly went down well in the fifth or the fourth century BC,[10] and whatever its precise significance might have been, it was composed on the principle that ambiguity can be an efficient means of communication that can greatly enrich what is being said.

---

1 Redfern 1984, 26.
2 Redfern 1984; Ahl 1984; 1985; 1991; 2007; 2008; Culler 1988; O'Hara 1996; Collins 2004.
3 Henderson 1975; 1987; 1991.
4 Rosen 1988a; 1988b.
5 Barron 1980; Francis 1990, 53 – 64, *Pericles on Stage*, xxiii and see p. 13, above.
6 Vickers 2005b; 2005c; 2007b; *Sophocles and Alcibiades*.
7 See "The Uses of Humour" in Shimron 1989, 58 – 72; on seriousness in comedy: Henderson 1990.
8 Powell 1937, 103; Shimron 1989, 71.
9 *Sophocles and Alcibiades*, 121 – 3.
10 Cf. Sedley 1998.

It is against this background of the humour of ambiguity being used to make serious points that we should perhaps view Aristophanes' extremely complex, subtle and sophisticated wordplay. For puns *can* be serious, even though they have a playful reputation.[11] J.D. Denniston put matters very crisply in his study of Greek prose style: "Seriousness may also be present in the pun, a quality with which it is not commonly associated .... 'Punning' ... is an unfortunate description because it connotes for us a humorous intention, while by the Greeks it was frequently regarded as a means of attaining truth, or as aesthetically valuable in itself".[12]

One way in which Aristophanes generated double meanings was, as we have already seen, by exploiting Alcibiades' distinctive speech mannerism. The resulting words are not only Greek, but are entirely consistent with the anecdotal tradition relating to Alcibiades. The dramatic device was well known in antiquity: when the author of advice to the public speaker attributed to Hermogenes had to give an example of parody in Old Comedy, he chose Alcibiades' speech mannerism and the double meanings generated thereby ([Hermog.] *Meth.* 34). It is important to realise that such wordplay cannot occur accidentally; it is not inherent in the Greek language to deliver *doubles entendres* whenever there is a potential confusion of *rho* and *lambda*. There is thus no wordplay of this kind to be found in, for example, *Iliad* 1, *Agamemnon*, or *Dyscolos*. Nor is there any in *Acharnians*, a play Aristophanes wrote before Alcibiades' entry into politics (although his trendy vocabulary is mocked in *Banqueters* of 427 BC [Ar. *PCG* 205.5 – 6]). Lambdacism is not usually indicated in the text (see p. 4 – 5, above), but will have been added by the actor.

Aristophanes exploits other features of Alcibiades' mode of speech as well, notably his frequent use of καί ("and") to begin sentences, of paratactic constructions (sentences held together internally by means of "and"), and of the grammatical form known as the potential optative (an overly polite way of giving orders). These occur, as Daniel Tompkins has demonstrated,[13] in Alcibiades' speeches in Thucydides, a writer who regularly imitated the manner of speech of his speakers.[14] The application of Alcibiades' speech-patterns to Aristophanes provides us with an element of relative objectivity, or an "external control, evidence independent of our reading of the play."[15] A good example of such objectivity, discussed in *Pericles on Stage,* is the way in which the Alcibiadean Saus-

---

11 Cf. Mahood 1957, 164; Hutchinson 1983, 104.
12 Denniston 1952, 136.
13 Tompkins 1972.
14 [Hermog.] *Meth.* 31. Cf. Tompkins 1972, 37, and Francis 1991 – 93.
15 Cf. Heath 1987a, 8.

age-seller in *Knights* speaks at a rate of 7 initial καίs in 22 sentences; this—or so it was argued—will have been the model for the speech Thucydides puts into Alcibiades' mouth at 6.89–92,where there are 14 initial καίs in 44 sentences. It also quickly emerges that there is much to be said for the allegorical approach. Far from being an uncontrollable, amorphous mess, the resultant material possesses an internal consistency that can be controlled against the historical record, even when that record may be the result of an anecdotal tradition.

Alcibiades and Pericles

It is a widespread view that "Pericles' … death save[d] him from Aristophanes' relentless blows".[16] In *Pericles on Stage,* I suggested that such was not the case, and that the statesman's personality might be the basis for posthumous lampoons beyond his appearance as himself in Eupolis' *Demi* of c. 417–410 BC.[17] Although there was an Athenian law of apparently long standing forbidding verbal abuse of the dead,[18] it has been shown that "sufficiently striking examples [of comic denigration of the dead exist] to suggest that fear of legal prosecution was not operative."[19] I argued too that Cratinus' *Dionysalexandros,* the play that "satirized Pericles … by means of *emphasis*",[20] might also have been posthumous,[21] especially if *POxy* 2806, of which fr.1.i.6–7 makes mockery of premature births ("Your wives will bear all of you babies, five-month ones and three-month ones and thirty-day ones"), belongs to that play, as Eric Handley once proposed.[22] The allusion is clearly to the remarkably quick marriage (or cohabitation) of Aspasia and Lysicles after Pericles' death, and the birth of their son, Poristes (Plut. *Per.* 24.7), an association that may well have begun when Pericles was still alive.[23]

If so, the Spartan depredations alluded to in the plot-summary will have been those of 428 (Thuc. 3.1.1) or 427 (Thuc. 3.26.1), rather than earlier events.

---

16 Solomos 1974, 60.
17 On the date, see e.g. Braun 2000 (417); Telò and Porciani 2002 (410); Storey 2003 (417); Torello 2006, 145–65 (414).
18 Dem. 20.104; Halliwell 1991, 49.
19 Halliwell 1991, 51.
20 Cf. Schwarze 1971, 24; Handley 1982, 115; Revermann 1997, 199. Storey 2009 argues for 437 or 436, but has spoken of the possibility that the title of the play may have read Διονυσα-λέξανδρος ἤ [Σάτυροι], in which case, the play would date to 424 BC.
21 *Pericles on Stage,* 193–5: "Postumous parody in Cratinus' *Dionysalexandros*".
22 Handley 1982.
23 Cf. Stadter 1989, 237.

The practice of *idolopoeia* , whereby characters were brought back from the dead in order to make a contemporary point.[24] seems to have lasted until well into the fourth century, at least judging by *Plutus* (388 BC), the latest of Aristophanes' extant plays. There, the characters of the κωμῳδούμενοι have become stereotyped: since they are dead, their characterization partakes of the whole of the anecdotal tradition

It was argued in *Pericles on Stage* that the dead Pericles is the principal target of *Acharnians*, and that he continues to be a prominent κωμῳδούμενος in subsequent plays. Increasingly, however, he shares the limelight with the very-much-alive Alcibiades. Their relationship on stage reflects their relationship in real life. "Periclean" figures play a paternal role with respect to "Alcibiadean" ones, reflecting Pericles' quasi-paternal role with regard to Alcibiades. Thus in *Knights*, a "Periclean" figure is addressed by an "Alcibiadean" one as as "Father" and "Daddikins", and in *Clouds* and *Wasps* an "Alcibiadean" character plays the part of a son to a "Periclean" father. Indeed, for much of the nineteenth century and beyond it was not unusual to see Alcibiades "coming forward" in the character of Pheidippides in *Clouds*.[25] It is perfectly easy to see why, and the idea even appealed to Alcibiades' foremost modern biographer J. Hatzfeld, who only rejected it on the grounds that in no way could Strepsiades correspond to Alcibiades' physical father Cleinias.[26] There are, however, several reasons why he could correspond to Pericles, in whose house Alcibiades grew up, and who played the *de facto* role of a father.[27] The "heroic and frightening" nature of filial rebellion in the 420s BC, and "the claims of the young to an early assumption of their political patrimony"[28] are given added point by being shown on the stage in a personalized way. In *Peace* Alcibiades is to the fore, while "the Olympian" underlies the characterization—appropriately enough—of a god, albeit a minor one. In *Birds*, an echo of Pericles the leader of his people could be seen to play opposite a tyrannically-inclined Alcibiades. The conclusions of *Pericles on Stage* are summarized in Chapter 3.

In this book, we shall see that *Lysistrata* is as much concerned with the view that Alcibiades was aiming at tyranny, still prevalent in 411 BC, as it is with a sex-strike: the violent seizure of the Acropolis has not been given nearly enough at-

---

24 Aristid. 3.487; Hermog. *Prog.* 9; Aphth. *Prog.* 11. Cf. Aristid. 2.322 (on Pl. *Ep.* 8.355a [Dion]); Cratin. *PCG* 87 (Solon); Pl. *Mx.* (Aspasia and Socrates); cf. Loraux 1981, 471, n. 308.

25 E.g. Donaldson 1860, 185; Rennie 1909, 200.

26 Hatzfeld 1951, 34; cf. Turato 1972, 100; Ambrosino 1986–87, 103–4.

27 Loraux 1981, 467. B.S. Strauss 1990, 122. The precise relationship between Pericles and Alcibiades is uncertain: Thompson 1970 and Cromey 1984.

28 B.S. Strauss 1990, 118–9; cf. 1993.

tention of late. Lysistrata's masculine traits, noted by G. Mastromarco,[29] can be accounted for if she "comes forward" as an Alcibiades concerning whose "ambivalent sexuality"[30] the anecdotal tradition is replete. *Thesmophoriazusae* is concerned with the capture and imprisonment of the Kinsman at the hands of a barbarian, and closely reflects Alcibiades' capture and imprisonment by Tissaphernes late in 411 BC. Euripides' *Helen* and *Andromeda* are also probably concerned with Alcibiades' relations with Tissaphernes: not with his imprisonment at the satrap's hands, but with his more comfortable, but to the sceptical eye no more free, earlier sojourn in Tissaphernes' Carian paradise in 412 BC. The characterisation of Alcibiades as Helen appears to play on the famous beauty of both, as well as on Alcibiades' some-time effeminacy. Euripides seems to be well disposed towards Alcibiades and in effect argues for his forgiveness and return to Athens. None of the apparently positive elements are, however, quoted in Aristophanes' parodies in *Thesmophoriazusae*; these throw further invidious light on Alcibiades and the situation in which he had recently found himself as the plaything of a Persian satrap, for Tissaphernes may be insultingly represented as the Scythian Archer, his meanest possible barbarian analogue. Interesting possibilities arise from the Archer's chasing after the bawd Artemisia ("Artamouxia": 1201, 1214, 1216, 1223, 1225), and Tissaphernes' evident devotion to Ephesian Artemis at the very end of Thucydides' *Histories* (8.109.2).

Likewise, *Frogs* has long been viewed as a literary play, but it is probably no more "about" literature than *Animal Farm* is "about" agriculture. There is something else going on beneath the surface. We know from other sources that the play's success was due to the way Aristophanes pleaded the cause of political exiles, none of whom was more prominent than Alcibiades. Indeed, the tie-breaking question in the second half of the play is "What would you do about Alcibiades?" Aeschylus unexpectedly wins, an Aeschylus who, as we shall see, is probably characterized as Pericles. The likely implication is that if Alcibiades is indeed to return, he should carry out the cautious policies of his foster-father.

Aspasia plays a prominent role in *Ecclesiazusae*; she had probably also "come forward" as Myrrhine—playing opposite a Periclean Cinesias—in *Lysistrata*. She lies behind Praxagora in the first half of *Ecclesiazusae*, and polymorphically underlies the succession of Old Hags in the second. An interesting by-product of the possibility that it is a calque of Aspasia who proposes a communistic way of life is that the problem of Aristotle's naming Plato as the sole source of that same idea changes character. Aspasia also polymorphically lies behind Poverty and the Hag in *Plutus*.

---

29 Mastromarco 1997, 108–9.
30 Duff 2003, 97.

More characters in both *Ecclesiazousae* and *Plutus* are based on Alcibiades' wife Hipparete, and we might wonder why the women of the Periclean household should only appear as κωμῳδούμεναι in the late plays. I suspect that the answer lies in the fact that both women were dead (Hipparete in 407/6,[31] and Aspasia probably c. 390 BC),[32] and were thus not subject to the taboo on speaking of (presumably live) women "for good or evil", so eloquently expressed by Pericles (in a speech some said was actually composed by Aspasia).[33] Pericles is also omnipresent in these later plays, "coming forward" as the Proboulos and Cinesias in *Lysistrata*, as Euripides and Echo in *Thesmophoriazusae*, as Aeschylus and Heracles in *Frogs*, and as Blepyrus, Chremes, Blepsidemus and Chremylus in *Ecclesiazusae* and *Plutus*.

Pericles' Reputation

The live Pericles had been mercilessly satirized in his lifetime, notably by Cratinus (whose *Dionysalexandros* may be a posthumous lampoon, as noted above). It is, though, a large step from seeing the live Pericles satirized to having him lampooned when dead. What evidence do we have for posthumous parody? Eupolis is not exactly complimentary towards Pericles in his *Demi*, with its abusive references to his "bastard" son, his "harlot" wife (*PCG* 110), and the peculiar shape of his head (*PCG* 115). Eupolis also satirises Cimon (*PCG* 221). The but recently dead Cleon is explicitly lampooned in *Peace*, as we have already seen; and perhaps the best known example of the genre is the parody of Aeschylus and Euripides in *Frogs*, the one long dead, the other only recently departed (although, as we shall see later [in Chapter 10], the playwrights are masks for others).

Pericles today is a figure whom it is customary to regard with respect, not to say adulation,[34] but it is clear that there was a strong critical tradition in ancient historiography.[35] In *Pericles on Stage* I touched on some of the ways in which Pericles' reputation changed for the better in the nineteenth century, largely

---

31 Plut. *Alc.* 8.7; Isoc.16.45; Rodríguez Blanco 1987, 75.

32 Cf. Solana Dueso 1994, xxiv.

33 Thuc. 2.45.2; cf. Pl. *Mx.* 236b, Solana Dueso 1994, xxv-xxxv; and Gale 2000. See further, p. 164, below.

34 But see Vogt 1956; de Romilly 1963, 375: "the case [against him] is not quite new, as one can see from fifth-century evidence"; Bloedow 2000, 309; and Azoulay 2014.

35 Stadter 1989, xliii-xliv (on Plutarch's treatment of hostile testimony), lxii (on Stesimbrotus), lxxvi-lxxvii (on Duris of Samos); *Sophocles and Alcibiades*, 13–33 (on Sophocles).

through the efforts of George Grote (1794–1871). His contemporary William Mitford, writing in 1829, could still charge Pericles with having "deprav[ed] the Athenian constitution, to favour that popular power by which he ruled, and [having] reviv[ed] that pernicious hostility between the democratical and aristocratical interests, first in Athens, and then, by the Peloponnesian war, throughout the nation".[36] How different (and deliberately so) the Utilitarian Grote's tribute to a "life, long, honourable, and useful."[37] The tales preserved about Pericles give another, frequently salacious and sometimes brutal, side to his character (often ignored by Grote), and these underlie many of Aristophanes' plots and allusions.

Those used to the "plaster saint" image of Pericles will doubtless be repelled by some of the dirt Aristophanes throws at the dead statesman. The symptoms of the Plague, for example, are a constant motif (and one suspects that Plutarch's reference to ποικίλαι μεταβολαί ["varied symptoms"; Plut. *Per.* 38.1] is based on a knowing reading of the "emphasis" of Thucydides' description of the effects of the malady [Thuc. 2.49], placed as it is after Pericles' Funeral Speech [Thuc. 2.35–46] and shortly before the report of his final speech and Thucydides' appraisal [Thuc. 2.60–65]). Thucydides and Plutarch between them let us know what Pericles is supposed to have suffered from in instructive but reticent detail. In Aristophanes by contrast, there is much "cripple-teasing"[38] of a kind familiar from eighteenth century political cartoons.[39] In addition to mockery of Pericles' congenitally misshapen head, such Plague symptoms as sores and ulcers, blindness, forgetfulness, and the loss of the genitalia are distastefully employed as vehicles for criticism of Pericles' reputation (see Appendix 2). Small wonder that Cicero considered the attacks on Pericles in Attic comedy to be shameful (*de Rep.* 4.11).

Far worse, from the point of view of Pericles' reputation, are the constant allusions to his alleged mistreatment of Samian prisoners in 439 BC. According to the tale Plutarch tells (though he claims not to believe it himself), these unfortunates were tied to planks in the Agora at Miletus, and were left in the open for ten days before being beaten to death with wooden clubs, and their bodies cast away unburied (Duris *FGrH* 76 F 67 *ap. Per.* 28.2–3).[40] The source was Stesim-

---

36 Mitford 1829, 2.403.
37 Grote 1870, 2.432. The issues involved have since been explored in exemplary fashion by Vincent Azoulay (2014, 192–226).
38 A word I owe to the perverse genius of Barry Humphries.
39 E.g. Stephens and George 1870–1954; George 1961; Rodnan 1961; Atherton 1974; Brewer 1986. I owe these references to the late Roy Porter.
40 Grote, whose aim was to rehabilitate Pericles, omits the story of the punishment of the Samians altogether (1870, 5.292), as does duBois 1991—cf. Kagan 1990, 142, n. 2: "calumnies";

brotus of Thasos who (like Aristophanes in *Clouds*) wrote a "contemptuous review of the education and training of Athenian leaders".[41] Vincent Azoulay notes that "the Samian affair shows us a Pericles who resorted to unbridled violence", and recognizes "the existence of a tradition hostile to Pericles that emphasizes his intolerable cruelty". He sees in Herodotus' account of Pericles' father Xanthippus' cruel action at Sestos (9.120.4: the stoning to death of the son of the Persian satrap followed by the satrap's crucifixion σανίδι ["on a board"]) an implicit criticism of Pericles' own behaviour.[42]

There are indications that eyebrows were raised about the treatment of the Samian captures almost immediately at Athens: at the funeral ceremony for Athenians fallen at Samos, Cimon's sister Elpinice is supposed to have said to Pericles: "A fine exploit and one worthy of garlands, Pericles, to lose many of our brave fellow-citizens, not fighting with Phoenicians or Medes, as my brother Cimon did, but καταστρεφόμενος ('subduing' [or 'torturing']) our allies and our kith and kin" (Plut. *Per.* 28.5–6). For all that Plutarch affects not to believe the Samian story, in his *Parallel Lives* he compares Pericles' exploits at Samos with Q. Fabius Maximus' recapture of Tarentum, an event that gained Fabius a reputation for cruelty: *Fab*, 29.1; cf. 22.5.

I have argued elsewhere that *Antigone* reflects Sophoclean distaste for events in which he was still being implicated centuries later.[43] στρέφειν ("twist", "torture") occurs frequently in Aristophanic contexts where Periclean characters are being delineated, the most obvious one being Strepsiades' name in *Clouds*. Stories of torture do not necessarily have to be true, but the fact that they were told at all—and that they formed the basis of posthumous mockery—puts Pericles in a novel light, and raises questions as to whether his *auctoritas* depended upon respect generated by fear as much as upon admiration.[44]

In Aristophanes' plays, the debate across the generation gap is frequently conducted by means of figures evocative of popular images of Pericles and his ward

---

Podlecki 1998, 125–6: "exaggeration"; Mackenzie 1937, 233: "The character of Pericles contradicts such a story without discussion". For Meiggs 1972, 192, however: "... the substance of the story rings true". Stadter 1989, 258–9 also believes that archaeological evidence for *apotympanismos* "makes it likely that Duris' story is at least partially true". The most satisfactory solution to the problem is that of Landucci Gattinoni 1997, 231–4 who believes that Thucydides' silence in the matter can be accounted for by his wish to put Pericles in a favourable light, and that Duris' testimony comes from an independent Samian anti-Athenian source.

41 Stadter 1989, lxii, following Schachermeyer 1965.

42 Azoulay 2014, 59–60.

43 Strab. 14.1.18; Vickers 2007; *Sophocles and Alcibiades* 13–33.

44 Cf. Calder 1981; 2005, 28 on the traditions that Pericles arranged the deaths of Ephialtes and the Athenian herald Athenocritus.

Alcibiades. There can be little need to justify a concentration on Alcibiades, for a new awareness of his omni-presence on the Athenian stage—five of Sophocles' extant plays, for example, appear to be based on his extraordinary career[45]—should help to fill the lack felt by many scholars hitherto. Many of the characters in *Lysistrata* (411 BC), *Thesmophoriazusae* (410 BC), *Frogs* (405 BC), *Ecclesiazusae* (391 BC), and *Plutus* (388 BC) also appear to resonate with members of Pericles' extended family—Pericles himself, Aspasia, his sons, and especially Alcibiades, as well as Alcibiades' wife Hipparete. Such resonances continue even after the death of Alcibiades in 404 BC, in a nocturnal ambush in Phrygia.[46] But there is no reason why Alcibiades should not have continued to be ridiculed after his death especially as his son, Alcibiades Jr, was a person of some influence who traded on his father's reputation[47] (and doubtless similar considerations had applied to Alcibiades with regard to his foster-father).

Aspasia, too, came in for banter in *Acharnians* (at 527), and as we shall see, she is mercilessly lampooned in *Ecclesiazusae* and *Plutus*. We have no precise information concerning Aspasia after the death of Lysicles (with whom she had taken up after—or even before[48]—Pericles' death) in 428 BC, but the assumption is usually made that she and their son Poristes lived on in Athens.[49] The date of Aspasia's death is unknown, although guesses have been made.[50] Members of the audience at the time of the *Ecclesiazusae* and *Plutus*, if they remembered Aspasia at all, would have known her as an ageing woman with a past.

Aristophanes and Politics

In *Pericles on Stage* I expressed the view that speculation about Aristophanes' own political views[51] was irrelevant; or rather, whatever they may have been, that it is methodologically sounder, advantageous even, to ignore them, especially in the case of plays which—like *Acharnians* and *Knights*—won first prize. For

---

45 *Sophocles and Alcibiades.*
46 Robert 1980, 257–307; Briant 2002, 395, 928.
47 Generals came forward in his defence in a trial in 395 BC (Lys. 15); Archippus drew attention to the way in which Alcibiades Jr imitated his father's gait and diction (*PCG* 48 *ap.* Plut. *Alc.* 1.8). Cf. Loening 1987, 94–5, 136–7; Gribble 1999, 93–6.
48 Stadter 1989, 237.
49 Mähly 1853, 230; Bicknell 1982. On the historicity of Poristes, see p. 175, below.
50 For discussions of Aspasia's likely birthdate (not much earlier than 470), see Bicknell 1982, 245; Solana Dueso 1994, xiii, who (p. xxiv) believes she died in c. 390 BC; see p. ●000●, below.
51 Cf. Gomme 1962; for other views, see de Ste. Croix 1972; Fisher 1993; Spielvogel 2003.

unless some external factor intervened,[52] we can be reasonably sure that whatever the playwright might include with a view to winning the dramatic victory would have reflected the current outlook of a majority of Athenians. The judges were chosen by lot, and were thus likely to be as fair a cross-section of the Athenian body politic as anyone could have wished.[53] Now, however, I believe that Aristophanes' political standpoint can be established with some certainty, and that it was a firmly anti-Alcibiadean stance for most of Alcibiades' public career. This is how Aristophanes comes across in plays before *Frogs*, and this will have been his political position in a city where politics might often be very personal. Nowhere can I see evidence for Aristophanes having been a radical democrat.[54]

It is fruitless to attempt to assess the historical accuracy of allegations made about Pericles and Alcibiades. Much of the tittle-tattle may well have had its origin in the exaggerations of comic writers. For this study the sources of the anecdotes are largely irrelevant. This is a reasonable position so long as one is not attempting to establish historical truth, simply the early existence of a piece of gossip. The discussion of a typical example will help to elucidate the issues involved. The precise source of a story told by Frontinus of Pericles is, and will doubtless remain, a mystery,[55] and yet the tale would seem to bear upon Aristophanes' *Clouds*, but is rarely, if ever, brought into play in this context. It goes as follows:

> Pericles, when a thunderbolt struck his camp and terrified his soldiers, calling an assembly, struck fire by knocking two stones together in the sight of all his men. He thus allayed their panic by explaining that the thunderbolt was similarly produced by the contact of the clouds (Front. *Strat.* 1.11.10).

Pericles' practical mindedness and lack of superstition is diametrically opposite that of Strepsiades at *Clouds* 385, who is unwilling to believe in Socrates' explanation that clouds make a noise when they collide with each other (383–4). In *Pericles on Stage*, I argued on other grounds that the character of Strepsiades is a comic Pericles, and there can be no reason for not taking Frontinus' story as corroborative evidence for such a view. Even if the tale was made up after the performance of *Clouds* in order to illustrate Pericles' interest in natural philosophy (cf. Plut. *Per.* 6.1–3), Pericles is still there, and that is all that is necessary. Posthumous invention is, however, unlikely, and it is probably safer to

---

52 As in the case of *Clouds*: see p. 3, above.
53 Pickard-Cambridge 1968, 95–6. On the underlying principles of lottery, see Pope 1986; 1989.
54 As Sidwell 2009.
55 On what is known of Frontinus' sources, see Bendz 1963, 7–8.

think of it as the kind of story told about Pericles that Aristophanes used as the basis for his plot. Either way, the tale is Periclean in character.

If so, the Aristophanic example will also be an example of the comic technique described by Gilbert Murray, in which "a man from Aberdeen was represented as wildly scattering his money" in a twentieth century farce.[56] Aristophanes frequently takes a known characteristic of a historical individual and either exaggerates it, or unexpectedly reverses it. It has much in common with the second item in a list attributed to Hermogenes the rhetorician of the ways in which writers of Old Comedy made their audiences laugh, *viz.* παρὰ προσδο-κίαν ("by means of the unexpected"; [Hermog.] *Meth.* 34). Any such reversal has of course to be a complete one for it to work effectively.[57] It will henceforth be referred to as the "spendthrift Aberdonian principle" (apologies to present-day Aberdonians who are, as everyone knows, expansive and generous folk, but I take my cue from Aristophanes, who would never have been a devotee of political correctitude).

Our principal source of information concerning Pericles and Alcibiades is Thucydides, whose work was heavily utilized by Plutarch. In addition, however, Plutarch made substantial use of other contemporary sources.[58] A recent biographer has, moreover, said of the *Life of Pericles* that it possesses

> great value. Plutarch had an excellent library containing many works now lost to us, some written by contemporaries of Pericles and by men of the next generation. He read the inscriptions and ancient documents and saw paintings, sculptures, and buildings that no longer exist. When used with care, his work is an outstanding source of authentic information.[59]

Much the same might be said of Plutarch's *Life of Alcibiades*,[60] which quotes from contemporary playwrights, and writers such as Antisthenes, Antiphon

---

56 G. Murray 1933, 86.

57 Cf. Bracht Branham 1989, 40, citing Monaco 1963: "the comic metaphor (or simile), the description of X as Y when Y would seem categorically inappropriate, was a much-cultivated form of joke in antiquity".

58 Stadter 1989, lix; cf. lviii-lxxxv. Stadter's work serves as a corrective to the negative judgements of Plutarch of e.g. Beloch 1893, 21–2; Meinhardt 1957; Will 2003, v.

59 Kagan 1990, xii.

60 Cf. Russell 1972, 117–29; Hertzberg 1853, 7–15; Prandi 1992, 281–92 (on sources); Duff 2003 (on Alcibiades' childhood); Pelling 1992, 10–40; Rhodes 2011, 1–4. In general, cf. Levi 1967, 132: "The sources for the history of Alcibiades are of the best quality"; Bloedow 2011: "As a working hypothesis, one may accept Plutarch in many instances unless it can be demonstrated that he is actually incorrect". There is a useful collection of sources relating to Alcibiades in Rodríguez Blanco 1988.

and Lysias who knew Alcibiades personally. Other sources used by Plutarch include the work of later writers such as Satyrus and Duris of Samos. Another important text is the speech against Alcibiades attributed (though not universally) to Andocides: [Andoc.] 4. Some believe that this speech was written in 417 BC;[61] others that it is a literary forgery of the early fourth century BC, when two anti-Alcibiadean speeches wrongly attributed to Lysias were also composed.[62] Either way, it is a reliable source for gossip, if not for history. Plato is another rich source, especially for Alcibiades. The *Symposium*, for all that it was probably a literary contrivance,[63] encapsulates the essence of the man, and whether or not the two dialogues that bear Alcibiades' name are actually by Plato, they depend to a greater or lesser degree upon the anecdotal tradition.[64] In this context, Plato probably ranks as a historical novelist rather than a historian, but again, the truths of fiction can be more telling than those of purely documentary sources.[65] An unexpected by-product of this study of Aristophanes has been to open up the possibility that among contemporary writers who used Aristophanes' plays as source material were Thucydides and Xenophon. These will be discussed in more detail below. Xenophon has much that is relevant in the *Hellenica* and *Memorabilia*, and Isocrates and Demosthenes reflect a surprisingly favourable fourth century view of Alcibiades.[66] Libanius is a rich and as yet largely unexploited source of *Alcibiadiana*,[67] and much useful material is to be found in the works of later grammarians and encyclopedists.

A question of method arises here. It is considered bad form in some quarters to use evidence of this kind. "Late, therefore unreliable" is the mantra uttered by purists, some of whom even draw the line at using evidence from Plutarch.[68] Anecdotes come close to gossip and tittle-tattle.Some of the gossip preserved in our sources may not have been true, and much of the tittle-tattle may have been exaggerated, but much of it reverberated down the centuries, and some anecdotes only survive in late sources. Are these the expression of quintessential truths, distilled over centuries, or the products of later scholars intent on muddying

---

61 Schroff 1901; Raubitschek 1948; 1991; Furley 1989; 1996; Cobetto Ghiggio 1995.

62 Maidment 1941, 538–9; Andrewes in *HCT* 4.287–8; Edwards 1995, 132–5; Heftner 1995; 2001; Gribble, 1997; 1999, 154–8; *Sophocles and Alcibiades*, 125.

63 Blanckenhagen 1992; Sheffield 2001; Hunter 2004.

64 de Strycker 1942; Bluck 1953; Gribble 1999; Denyer 2001. On Plato's likely dependence on Aristophanes, see Brock 1990; Vickers 1994; *Sophocles and Alcibiades*, 153–75; pp. 176, 178, below.

65 E.g. Cobb 1986; cf. Duff 2003.

66 Cf. Bruns 1896, 489–530, 557–85.

67 Rendered the more accessible thanks to Schouler 1984, esp. 626–34; cf. Wolf 1954.

68 E.g. Hubbard 1998; Neer 2002. For recent eloquent criticism of the view "late therefore bad", see Piccirilli 1997,17–23; Rubel 2000, 116–7; 2014, 66–7.

the waters, or simply carelessness? It is sometimes difficult to tell, and each case must be treated on its merits. It must be said, however, that the anecdotes relating to Alcibiades are rarely fanciful, Alexander the Great having soon supplanted him in the imaginations of all but the learned.[69] Indeed, R.R.R. Smith sees in Alcibiades "a kind of proto-Alexander" and draws a neat parallel: "each was the most famous pupil of the most famous philosopher of their day (namely) Socrates and Aristotle".[70] It is wrong to brush late evidence under the carpet on principle, for the carpet has come to resemble an Alpine range.

The Text of Aristophanes

There is no suggestion here that the text of Aristophanes should be emended to incorporate the lambdacisms that may be lurking beneath the surface; simply that a recognition of their presence can often help to resolve textual problems. Nor should it be an issue that lambdacism or traulism is alluded to directly in our texts but infrequently;[71] the places where it is mentioned specifically are enough to establish the nature of a phenomenon that must have been a life-long affliction (or affectation) in Alcibiades' case.[72] We are fortunate to have even these, for they were not normally "shown in writing" (Quint. *Inst.* 1.5.32). Nevertheless, *lambdakismos* remained a powerful vehicle that enabled a writer to say two (or more) things at once, and the amount of material is overwhelming. Comparatively little, however, will be discussed in detail here, for such wordplay quickly becomes wearisome today.

The manuscript tradition relating to Aristophanes is unusual in that there is only one manuscript which contains all eleven of the extant plays, and which is also the sole source for one of them. This is the tenth century Codex Ravennas 429 (R), which only became widely known to modern scholars in 1796,[73] and whose status has been controversial ever since. The feature that has helped give R a bad name is the frequency with which elementary mistakes occur. It has earned comments such as "R is the worst manuscript I have read as regards

---

69 Cf. Stoneman 2008. The tales surrounding the death of Alcibiades, discussed by Perrin 1906, are an exception to the general rule.
70 Smith 1990, 139; cf. Vickers 2011a.
71 At Ar.*Ve.* 42–6; cf. *Nu.* 869–72, 1381–2; Archipp. *PCG* 48 *ap.* Plut. *Alc.* 1.8; [Hermog.] *Meth.* 34; Tzetz. XIAi 89 Koster.
72 Barrie Fleet kindly reminds me that the use of the middle τραυλίζεται at Plut. *Alc.* 1.8 indicates habitual action.
73 Clark 1871; Austin and Olson 2004.

accents",[74] or "[In R] punctuation-marks are scattered as if out of a pepper-caster".[75] This last from W.M. Starkie, who was ultimately inclined to "respect [the] accuracy of R", concluding that its errors "though numerous are mostly trivial".[76] In general, however, "if there is such a profusion of small mistakes, how much greater the chance of large ones", is the way one senses the game has often been played, with the result that the idiosyncratic readings and line assignments of R have often been granted little respect.

The nature of the small mistakes in R is perhaps significant, and most telling are the frequent spelling mistakes deriving from a confusion between *epsilon* and *eta*,[77] and between *omicron* and *omega*.[78] Until 403/2, *epsilon* and *omicron* served for both short and long vowels, but when the Ionic alphabet was officially adopted in the archonship of Euclid *eta* and *omega* were used for the long vowels.[79] Aristophanes (born c. 460–450 BC) will have learned to write using the old Attic alphabet, and it is reasonable to suppose that he carried on using it throughout his life (he died in or shortly after 386 BC). The errors in R are the kind we might expect to have been made by someone who was converting a text that had been written in the old Attic alphabet into the new Ionic alphabet. The most economical interpretation of the data is that the first, "Periclean", collection was still written in the Attic alphabet, and that a later version of this collection, by now full of misspellings and uncertain breathings and accentuation, provided the basis for the Codex Ravennas. R's relatively late appearance on the scene may also have contributed to the comparative neglect of its qualities: norms of Aristophanic textual criticism had been well established by 1796.

For many reasons, therefore, I propose in what follows to favour the readings and line allocations of R, as I did in *Pericles on Stage*. With all its faults, R preserves something of the authentic flavour of Aristophanes' political comedy. Most printed texts of Aristophanes resemble the horse designed by a committee; the Ravenna codex, by contrast, is the nearest we shall ever get to a thoroughbred.

---

74 Elliott 1914, xviii, n. 1.
75 Starkie 1909, 32.
76 Starkie 1909, lxxvii.
77 In *Plutus*, for example, at 26, 123, 134, 220?, 247, 248, 272, 355, 454, 470?, 611, 651?, 656, 660, 683, 716, 798, 836, 1006, 1097, 111.
78 In *Plutus* again: 8, 9, 40, 261, 263?, 384, 629, 687, 876, 1064?, 1102.
79 Woodhead 1967, 16–17; D'Angour 1999.

Chapter 3

Pericles (and Alcibiades) on Stage: The Story So Far

This chapter summarizes the findings of *Pericles on Stage*, which discussed the first six of Aristophanes' extant plays: *Acharnians* (425 BC), *Knights* (424 BC), *Clouds* (423 BC), *Wasps* (422 BC), *Peace* (421 BC), and *Birds* (414 BC), prior to embarking on an analysis of the remaining plays: *Lysistrata* (411 BC), *Thesmophoriazusae* (410 BC), *Frogs* (405 BC), *Ecclesiazusae* (391 BC), and *Plutus* (388 BC), as well as of some relevant plays of Euripides: *Ion, Helen, Andromeda,* and *Hippolytus. Acharnians* apart, all of Aristophanes' extant plays are as much concerned with Alcibiades as with Pericles.

Acharnians (425 BC)

Dicaeopolis "comes forward" as Pericles. His boorish and uncultivated personality, is made to harmonise with that of the people on whom Pericles depended for political support. Dicaeopolis' crude behaviour waiting for the assembly to start is a parody of Pericles' scrupulous civic mindedness. Dicaeopolis' selfish preoccupation with food and sex both parody and parallel two things for which Pericles was famous. The Athenian grain supply was never far from his mind, and "Pericles was much given to love affairs". In real life, Pericles had been criticized by the Acharnians and accused of cowardice; hence the jests at the cowardly Dicaeopolis' expense. The visit of the ambassador from Persia is a parody of Aeschylus' *Persians*, of which Pericles had been *choregus* in 472, and the Thracian scene plays on relations between Athens and Thrace towards the end of Pericles' life. Commentators have consistently overlooked the potential topical significance of the Acharnians' assertion that Spartans stand by "neither altar, nor trust, nor oath", which must allude to the Spartans' brutal destruction of Plataea two years earlier in 427 BC, an event that would have been unknown to Pericles (dead by 429), which is why it has to be forcefully brought to Dicaeopolis' attention. We may even see the seeds of Thucydides' own invention here. There are many jokes which play on Pericles' pointy squill-like head, of which he was extremely self-conscious: Dicaeopolis offering to place his head on a chopping board, like a vegetable; Dicaeopolis putting on a pointed Mysian cap.

The supposedly "loosely constructed" scenes in the second half of *Acharnians* can be seen, thanks to "polymorphic characterization", to have been written with verve and panache and in such a way that an audience that was aware of the innuendo, and had visual aids in the form of appropriate masks, could enjoy it as a fast-moving farce that serves to sustain the critical survey of Pericles' life and times. Thus the Megarian scene reflects on the Megarian Decree that Pericles had moved, and the encounter with the Sycophant imputes to Pericles a rise in the influence of political informers. There are allusions to the plague and Pericles' loss of his sons in the Dercetes scene, and the scene where a bridegroom asks for a ladleful of peace so that he can stay at home and screw, and his bride asks how she can make her husband's cock stay at home, is a commentary on Alcibiades' draft-dodging, his recent marriage, and his early infidelities. There are several more instances in *Acharnians* of matters which are also discussed by Thucydides and sometimes in remarkably similar fashion: the debate between Dicaeopolis and the Chorus of Acharnians, which closely resembles that between Pericles and his Acharnian critics; Dicaeopolis' coldness towards Dercetes recalling Pericles' bleakness towards bereaved relatives; the political effects of the Alcmaeonid curse; the intricacies of Thracian politics; details of the plague. It is tempting to regard these parallels as evidence for Thucydides (in exile from 424 BC) having used Aristophanes' plays as an *aide-mémoire* for the composition of his history.

Knights (424 BC)

Aristophanes expressly mentions *two* targets in *Knights:* "the Typhoon *and* the Hurricane", although this has gone unnoticed in recent criticism. The "Typhoon" must of course be Cleon, but "the Hurricane" is Alcibiades who is attacked in the person of Agoracritus, the Sausage-seller. Athens' recent political history is described in terms of a progression from a "hemp-monger", *via* a "sheepdealer", to a "tanner", generally agreed to reflect the historical Eucrates, Lysicles and Cleon. The "Sausage-seller", fresh on the scene, represents the latest entrant to Athenian politics. Alcibiades will have thus shared with Cleon the criticism that Aristophanes heaped on the new class of demagogues. To show Alcibiades as a "Sausage-" or "Dick-seller" was an exaggerated and invidious characterization playing on his well-known youthful adventure with an admirer, Democrates. The language of the Sausage-seller also includes many of Alcibiades' linguistic mannerisms observable in Thucydides, as does that of the Chorus of Knights, a brigade that Alcibiades had recently joined: another example of "polymorphic characterization". Alcibiades, unusually for Athenian speakers, often began his sentences with *kai*/and. In one speech, Thucydides gives him 14 initial *kai*s in 44 sentences; Aristophanes has the Alcibiadean Sausage-seller speaking at a rate of 7 initial *kai*s in 22 sentences; Thucydides' model is clear. The competition with Paphlagon over who could offer the most animals for sacrifice recalls Alcibiades' taste for animal slaughter. The accusation that the Sausage-seller is tainted by the Alcmaeonid curse has caused general puzzlement among critics, but Alcibiades' Alcmaeonid descent explains, indeed explains away, the problem.

There are Periclean resonances too. The way the Alcibiadean Sausage-seller addresses Demus at 725 as ὦ πατέρ ... Δημίδιον ("Father ... Demidion"; and cf. the "mockingly affectionate"[1] Δημακίδιον at 823) and at 1215 as ὦ παππίδιον ("Daddikins") suggests that Demus may be based on the historical figure of Alcibiades' foster-father Pericles (and he is being addressed by means of diminutives, frequently used by those who are trying to extract favours from Periclean figures, and a feature that may have been characteristic of Pericles' own way of speaking; see pp. 81, 127, 153, below). Demus displays plague-symptoms: forgetfulness and plague-sores, appropriate too if Demus is an analogue of an individual who had "exhibited many varieties of symptoms" of the Plague. When the Sausage-seller eventually wins the debate with Paphlagon (full of pertinent Alcibiadean allusions), he refines Demus, and announces that he has rendered him καλόν ἐξ αἰσχροῦ ("handsome instead of ugly"). On Alcibiadean lips, this would play on καλόν ἐξ Αἰσχυλείου ("handsome instead of Aeschylean"), and thus refers to a taste for the dramatic poet for whom Pericles had acted as *choregus*. In *Knights*, Alcibiades' boyhood entanglements, which Pericles had had the foresight to try to conceal lest his ward be deprived of citizen rights, are held up to both ridicule and scrutiny. The lampooning of Alcibiades' corrupt practices, of his grand ideas for overseas conquests, and of his probably opportunistic enrolment in the Athenian cavalry can scarcely have been intended to enhance his reputation. There is, however, a strong implication that Demus was partly to blame for the decline of standards in Athenian politics; if so, it is a charge laid against Pericles.

Clouds (423 BC)

It used to be the case that an equation was made between Pheidippides in *Clouds* and Alcibiades as a matter of course, but this has dropped out of scholarly fashion. The idea has much in its favour, but the picture is more complex. It was the impossibility of Strepsiades "coming forward" as Alcibiades' physical father Cleinias that led to the idea being dropped. The financially stretched Strepsiades, however, "comes forward" as Pericles, Alcibiades' penny-pinching foster-father,

---

1 Kanavou 2011, 56.

and Pheidippides as an amalgam of those who stood in a filial relationship to him: his son Xanthippus the spendthrift, and his foster-son Alcibiades who was even more casual with money and besotted by chariot-racing. The object of the education of father and son is to find clever arguments that will help Strepsiades evade his creditors, and they take lessons in philosophy towards this end. The whole conceit is a parody of Pericles' interest in philosophy, and "Socrates" is a portmanteau figure, an amalgam of aspects of Socrates himself, and of Damon, Pythocleides, Zeno, Diogenes of Apollonia, Protagoras and Anaxagoras, the philosophers in Pericles' circle. The dialogue between Strepsiades and Socrates depends on parodies of Periclean themes: Olympian Zeus, jury-service, the grain-supply, Periclean cowardice, dislike of Aegina, and in particular the Plague: the bed-bug scene closely parallels Thucydides' description of the symptoms (see Appendix 2); so much so that Aristophanes was probably his immediate source.

The way in which father and son affect allegiance to different social classes in *Clouds* has long been a problem, but if Pericles and Alcibiades underlie the main characters, the problem disappears. Pericles was well born, but Aristophanes assimilates his Periclean character to the social class with which Pericles deliberately chose to be associated. Alcibiades was less inclined than his guardian to adopt a democratic facade, and Aristophanes exploits to the full his true social position and his tastes for the pastimes of the aristocracy, in particular chariot-racing. The encounter between the Stronger and Weaker Arguments, which is not only a debate across the generation gap akin to those between Strepsiades and Pheidippides, but which also recalls a conversation between Pericles and Alcibiades reported by Xenophon, where Alcibiades speaks of force and lawlessness. The debate between the Stronger and Weaker Arguments is often taken to be an uncomfortable disruption between the slapstick scenes involving Strepsiades and Pheidippides earlier and later in the play, but by invoking the principle of "polymorphic characterization", we can see the Stronger Argument standing for Pericles, and the Weaker for Alcibiades; continuity is thus preserved. Again the dialogue is full of allusions to the anecdotal tradition relating to Pericles and Alcibiades. The subsequent slapstick includes a scene where Strepsiades is transformed into an Alcibiadean figure (1214–1302), a typical Aristophanic ploy, but one unrecognized here hitherto. This has the added benefit of retaining a single Creditor, rather than postulating—as is now customary—an unparalleled extra speaking actor. K.J. Dover wondered "why [*Clouds*] fared so badly"; one of the plot-summaries gave the answer long ago: it was members of "the circle around Alcibiades" that supposedly prevented the poet from winning first prize; Alcibiades had an axe to grind. Aristophanes' insight into the education and shortcomings of two leaders of Athens against both of whom charges of tyranny were made, will have been a highly appropriate primer to have given to a tyrant of Syracuse. Plato's account of such a gift appears in two versions of the anonymous *Life* of Aristophanes, but it is such an extraordinary and unexpected tale that commentators have ignored it, editors have expunged it, and the reference to *Clouds* is actually omitted from a recent English translation of the medieval Greek text.[2]

Wasps (422 BC)

In *Wasps*, Pericles and Alcibiades are again the recognizable pegs upon which Aristophanes hangs his humorous sallies at the contemporary scene, and the same dramatic techniques are employed. In the opening scene, the slaves Sosias and Xanthias respectively embody Periclean and Alcibiadean characteristics; then Philocleon and Bdelycleon are based upon Pericles and his ward; and, just as the chorus of cavalrymen in *Knights* reinforced the characterization of Alcibiades as the Sausage-seller, so the chorus of elderly jurors in *Wasps* serve as additional personifications of a Pericles who was later to be described by Eupolis as a speaker who "left his sting behind in his hearers". The dialogue between the Chorus leader and his young servant (who also "comes forward" as Alcibiades) thus enables, by means of "polymorphic characterization", the Periclean and Alcibiadean imagery to continue unbroken. Another technique employed by Aristophanes is role-transformation. In the discussion of *Clouds* we saw how Strepsiades adopted the *persona* of Pheidippides; the "Periclean" taking on many of the characteristics of the "Alcibiadean" figure. Towards the end of *Wasps*, the main characters again reverse roles for humorous effect, when Philocleon, who has throughout the play exemplified Pericles' practice of never attending a symposium, begins to behave (and speak) like a party-going Alcibiades. The play is not disjointed, as is sometimes claimed.

Peace (421 BC)

Aristophanes' attitude towards Pericles and his extended family is usually negative. In *Peace*, however, he changes tack and treats his Alcibiadean character Trygaeus with rather more respect. *Peace* takes the form of a patriotic appeal to an Alcibiades who was bitterly opposed to talk of peace, to change his

---

2 Lefkowitz 1981, 171.

view. To this end, Aristophanes uses various characters to reflect different aspects of Alcibiades' personality, notably Trygaeus who, after a flight to Olympus on the back of a dung-beetle, is slowly transformed into an increasingly more responsible and civic-minded individual. Trygaeus' estate is at Athmonia (190; cf. 919), a fact that is of fundamental importance in establishing a link with Alcibiades, since ἐπικαρπία Ἀθμονοῖ ("crops from Athmonia") appear in a significant position on an inscription listing the possessions of those who were convicted of impiety in 414 BC.[3] The inscription is lacunose, but the place where the relevant lines occur makes it likely that the estate in question belonged to none other than Alcibiades (or so the late David Lewis once assured me).

By 421 BC, Alcibiades was of an age to be eligible for public office, although he was not to be elected general until the spring of 420. This will account for the reference to a "would-be general" at *Peace* 450 and also explain why Trygaeus is shown as an older man, rather than as the young tearaway who had been the object of much criticism in earlier plays. Alcibiades' presence on the political stage was a fact that had to be accepted, but there was a hope that his excesses might be curbed.

Alcibiades also underlies the figure of War, who displays Spartan characteristics (Alcibiades had a Spartan name, had had Spartan nannies, and had recently tried to ingratiate himself with Spartan prisoners from Sphacteria). Pericles underlies the figure of Hermes, a deity who "led the souls of the dead down to Hades", who was "essentially the god of simple people", and who was "used by Zeus to run his errands":[4] appropriate for "the Olympian", who in life had depended for his political support upon the less sophisticated members of Athenian society, but who had been dead for seven years. There are more echoes (or rather, prefigurations) of Thucydides. It is also worth noting that the Chorus in *Peace* are generally recognized as displaying the kind of "polymorphic characterization" and metamorphosis that one would claim was to be found throughout Athenian comedy.

Birds (414 BC)

Birds is extraordinarily complex, and was written soon after it had probably become compulsory by law for playwrights to write allusive, oblique, satire. Older arguments are revived that Aristophanes was attempting to persuade the Atheni-

---

3 ML 79, lines 22–3; Pritchett 1953, 241.
4 Guthrie 1950, 90–1.

ans to discontinue the Sicilian campaign "by intimating ... by means of Cloud-cuckooland ... the disasters which the Spartans were going to inflict on Athens and Attica, if Decelea were to be fortified in their neighbourhood according to Alcibiades' advice", in the words of Jacques le Paulmier de Grentemesnil, writing in 1668. Pierre Brumoy's insight (1730; 1785) that *Birds* was set in Sparta has, moreover, considerable merit. The sanctity of Decelea in Spartan eyes, probably contributed to the long delay in actually carrying out Alcibiades' suggestion.[5]

The economy of Aristophanes' wit is such that he manages simultaneously to tell the tale of Peisthetaerus' exploits in the land of the Birds; to dwell upon Alcibiades' exile in Sparta; and to comment on Athenian politics past and present. The vehicles he employs to do this are, as ever, Alcibiades and—surprising as it may seem—Pericles. It is not difficult to see Peisthetaerus as an individual with strong Alcibiadean characteristics, and there is good reason to believe that the Epops was presented in the guise of a Spartan ruler (and Ephor), and the Chorus of Birds as Spartans. What is extraordinary is the way in which Aristophanes succeeds in additionally representing the Epops as a Pericles (who hated Lacedaemon) playing the part of a Spartan official. This ambiguity extends to the Chorus who, being nominally characterised as Spartans, are nevertheless beholden to a "Periclean" character. This enables Aristophanes to "lampoon", if not actually "defame", the Athenian *demos* in a way that was legally off limits. It is an extremely clever and intricate conceit.

Detailed arguments are to be found in *Pericles on Stage*, but there is one point that merits further discussion here, namely the hero's name. B.B. Rogers is one of the few to have maintained that if *all* the relevant ancient testimonia conspire to call him Πεισθέταιρος, they probably do so because that is what Aristophanes wrote.[6] The name was indeed probably meant to be ambivalent, if not polyvalent, combining the notions both of "persuasion" and "seduction". On the one hand, Alcibiades had in the past won over many cities to friendship with Athens through his persuasive gifts (λόγῳ πείσας),[7] while on the other, the youthful Alcibiades had been notoriously πεισθείς ("seduced") by his admirers (Plut. *Alc.* 3.1; 6.1). Nikoletta Kanavou detects a certain "flexibility of meaning" in the naming of Agoracritus (the Sausage-seller) in *Knights*: appropriate—or so one would claim—for an analogue of the mercurial Alcibiades. Agoracritus could mean mean both "the quareller in the Agora" and "the man approved by the assembly". We might invoke the principle of "flexibility of meaning" in

---

5 Salmon 1946, 13–14; *HCT* 4. 367.
6 Rogers 1906, viii-x.
7 Isoc. 16.21, and cf. Plutarch on the πιθανότης ("persuasiveness") of Alcibiades' speech: Plut. *Alc.* 1.6.

the ambiguity inherent in Peisthetaerus'name. Far from being out of place, the Πεισθ- element, nowadays condemned,[8] will have been a reminder of Alcibiades' less than savoury youthful escapades. Then there are likely puns on ἑταῖροι ("partisans") and ἑταίραι ("prostitutes").[9] For not only was Alcibiades' membership of a ἑταιρεία ("political club") well-known,[10] but he was notorious for consorting with prostitutes, "foreign or Athenian" at Athens in the 420s BC (Plut. *Alc.* 8.4), and whoever was available behind the "doors of prostitutes" at which "he used to break in" at Sparta where he was currently in exile (Ath. 13.574*d*).

★ ★ ★

Athenians penned within their city, committed to a policy of not going out to meet the periodic Peloponnesian invasions, may well have enjoyed Aristophanes' comic revival of their dead leader in the person of Dicaeopolis; at least *Acharnians* won first prize. It might fairly be said that *Acharnians* was "about" Pericles, but two of the other five plays discussed so far are more concerned with Cleon (*Knights* and *Wasps*) and all of them with the rise to power of Alcibiades, Pericles ward. This was a development that was viewed by many with increasing concern, a concern mirrored in the figures of the Sausage-seller, Pheidippides, Bdelycleon, Trygaeus and Peisthetaerus. In *Knights*, *Clouds*, *Wasps* and *Peace*, however, Pericles is revived in order to provide a contrast between the new values that Alcibiades personified, and those for which Pericles stood. But none of the characterizations—Demus, Strepsiades, Philocleon, Hermes or the Servant—suggest that Pericles was without blame for the current state of affairs, or that his public policies and private neglect had not contributed to contemporary problems. His resurrection as a contributory element in the Epops in *Birds* serves to put a shameful cast on Alcibiades' seduction of the Spartan queen Timaea, an action that might otherwise have done Alcibiades credit in Athens in 414 BC. Pericles' peculiarities, his tastes and even his virtues are made the vehicles of Aristophanes' satire. Commentators have taken too literally the statement of Thucydides' Pericles that "the living have their rivals and detractors, but when a man is out of the way, the honour and goodwill he receives is unalloyed" (Thuc. 2.45.1). The ancient reality, not to mention Thucy-

---

8 E.g. Dunbar 1995,128–9; Kanavou 2011,105–7.

9 Cf. the pun on ἑταιρῶν and ἑταίρων at Ath. 13.571e. Kanavou 2011 overlooks this element in the name.

10 Cf. Ostwald 1986, 537–550; Aurenche 1974; cf. Westlake 1989, 160: "throughout his career it was [Alcibiades'] practice ... to gather round himself a formal or informal *hetaireia* consisting of associates, including relatives, who would support him in his schemes".

dides' awareness of it, was probably rather different. Pericles' memory, as well as the reputation of Alcibiades, receive far from unalloyed honour and goodwill at the hands of Aristophanes.

The eleven plays of Aristophanes we have may well have been selected at a very early stage from the forty or more plays he wrote (i.e. the selection took place during the first half of the fourth century BC) with the express purpose of illustrating the role played in Athenian politics by Pericles and Alcibiades. The plays were selected, and arranged, by someone who knew well what the issues were, and how Aristophanes had elucidated—or obfuscated—them. The presence of a revised, and never performed version of *Clouds* in the collection might point to its having been put together by someone with privileged access to the material. We shall probably never know the precise agency, and it would be going beyond the evidence to suggest that this collection necessarily had anything to do with the gift that Plato made to the Syracusan tyrant Dionysius I, or with the discovery of a copy of Aristophanes' plays in Plato's bed after his death. The difficulties that the transcriber of a predecessor of the Ravenna codex seems to have had with letters of the old Attic alphabet (p. 32, above) do, however, point to that text being closer to something Aristophanes wrote than anything else we have, and there is a *prima facie* case for the selection we have having been put together not so very long after his greatest hit, *Plutus*, was performed in 388 BC.

Chapter 4

The Tragic Context: the Case of Euripides' *Ion*

And we shall presently turn to an examination of *Plutus*, Aristophanes' last extant play, but before we can approach this remarkable work it will be necessary to examine something of the interplay between writers for the tragic and comic theatre; since the genius of comedy was, according to the Socrates of Plato's *Symposium*, the same as that of tragedy (223*a*), this need not be a problem. Tragedians were every bit as concerned with everyday politics as were writers for the comic stage, and it will be necessary to establish this before discussing *Plutus*.

In order to enter the world of the political tragedian, we must clear away much scholarly rubble placed in our path by well-meaning but essentially misguided scholars. E.R. Dodds, for example, rendered a serious disservice with his oft-repeated dictum that "it is an essential critical principle that *what is not mentioned in the play does not exist*" (italics original).[1] He was writing within a tradition that pays more than lip-service to Wilamowitz's influential view that "no Sophoclean tragedy has any immediate connection with a contemporary event":[2] an equally dangerous doctrine so far as a proper understanding of Greek drama is concerned, but one that is still almost universally held; witness the recent volume *Sophocles and the Greek Tradition*, where but one of nearly a dozen essays even comes close to a discussion of political issues, and that only in the broadest sense, drawing parallels between pressures experienced by characters in tragedies and the deliberative apparatus of the Athenian *polis*.[3]

This is to overlook the fact that Sophocles had a career in politics that was longer than that of Pericles.[4] It is also to overlook the fact that politics in Athens was intensely personal; the institution that was ostracism, whereby individuals who were regarded as potential threats to the city were sent into a ten-year exile, is sufficient evidence of this. When Sophocles' fellow-citizens gathered in the

---

1 Dodds 1966, 40; 1973, 68; 1983, 180.
2 Wilamowitz 1899, 59: "Es ist auf das scharfste zu sagen, dass keine sophokleische Tragodie eine unmittelbare Beziehung auf ein Factum der Gegenwart enthalt":; cf. Muller 1967, 245: "Grundsatzlich muss jedes zeitgeschichtliche Moment an Conception und Durchfuhrung der sophokleischen Tragodien geleugnet werden" ("Any contemporary factor in the conception and implementation of the Sophoclean tragedies must be denied on principle").
3 E.M. Hall, 2009.
4 From being the leader of a choir of boys in 480 BC to being a *proboulos* in 412/11, *via* chairmanship of the board of *hellenotamiai* in 443/2, and generalships in 441/0 and in either 438/7 or 437/6.

theatre to celebrate the Great Dionysia, they did not settle back to enjoy escapist drama "with no immediate connection with a contemporary event". They instead watched plays that were very much engaged with current affairs, and which provided the opportunity for experimental politics, where policies could be debated, or prominent personalities have their motives held up to scrutiny in ways that would not have been possible in more conventional political meetings.

Aristotle gives us an important clue when he differentiates between history and drama: history was personal and dealt in particulars. The example he chose is "what Alcibiades actually did, or what was done to him" (*Po.* 1451*b*.11), whereas drama describes the kind of things that "a person of a certain character would inevitably say or do" given their known proclivities and predilections (*Po.* 1451*b*.8–9). It is not such a bold step to infer that drama might often be concerned with what Alcibiades had recently done, or might be expected to do, given what was known about him; elements which, however, naturally fall "outside the play". There is also Libanius' rhetorical question: "What play did not include Alcibiades among the cast of characters?" (Lib. *fr.* 50.2.21); for all that Libanius appears to be referring to comedy, his observation might easily apply to tragedy as well. In *Sophocles and Alcibiades*, I suggested that five of the seven extant Sophoclean tragedies deal with Alcibiadean themes.

The theatre was an effective way of bringing together individuals who might be absent from Athens, or even dead. The only way that the Athenian public could witness a debate between exiles, for example, was for it to be represented on the stage. Thanks to the universality introduced by the fact that everything was couched in mythical terms, debates could be conducted in a considerably freer manner than was possible on most other public occasions.

Not everyone has been blinkered in their approach to tragedy. Angus Bowie has, for example, recognised that Sophocles' *Philoctetes* of 409 BC shows the crippled hero evoking in the most exaggerated way the life of an exile currently led by Alcibiades.[5] It shows him debating with an Odysseus who is a thoroughly unpleasant individual. What Bowie did not notice is that the figure of Odysseus is based on Alcibiades' current *bête noire* Andocides, also in exile and as his own attempts at self-justification in *De Reditu* reveal, was unappealing in similar ways. It was also widely believed, and this would have been a significant fact so far as Sophocles and his audience were concerned[6], that Andocides was physically descended from Odysseus (Hellanicus of Lesbos *FGrH* 4 F 170b, Plut. *Alc.* 21.1). The sudden denouement of *Philoctetes*, where the tragic hero falls in

---

5 Bowie 1997.
6 Thomas 1989, 159–96.

with a proposal made by the *deus ex machina* Heracles, has long puzzled those who refuse to look outside the play.[7] It comes about, however, through the intervention of a Heracles who shares many features with Pericles as manifested in the historical tradition, and who in effect speaks with Heracles' voice. The reason for Philoctetes' immediate acquiescence is apparently that here at last was the respectability that Alcibiades had craved for so long: the mantle of Pericles was to be his. Sophocles himself only acquiesces in Alcibiades' return if he should carry out Periclean policies. Otherwise, his attitude towards Alcibiades is generally unfavourable; but his view of Andocides is worse.[8]

Odysseus also figures large in a play written, I believe, the year before *Philoctetes*, where he again "comes forward" as the shifty Andocides. His Alcibiadean opposite number is this time Ajax, from whom Alcibiades claimed physical descent (Pl. *Alc.* 1.121a); again a significant factor in the eyes of the ancients. Ajax's madness, impiety, hubris and untruthfulness all find parallels in Alcibiades' character, and there are numerous echoes within the plot and Alcibiades' recent experiences. These include a prize of valour won at Potidaea, his enmity with the Spartans, his responsibility for the deaths of 300 Argives in 412 BC, his sacrificing hundreds of animals at Olympia in 416 BC, his involvement in the massacre of the menfolk of Melos in the same year or his having taken a prisoner of war as his mistress and having a child by her. All of these elements lie "outside the play" but will have been part of any audience's appreciation of an *Ajax* performed in 410 BC.[9]

The characters of both Ajax and Odysseus are eventually subsumed in that of Teucer; It has been well said that "Teucer's qualities ... emerge as neither fully Odyssean nor completely Ajaxian".[10] Teucer's role in *Ajax* has caused scholarly puzzlement in the past, but once we see Sophocles making the case that things were so bad for Athens in 410 BC that sworn enemies should put their excesses behind them and unite in the face of adversity, it makes a certain sense. Another gain from looking "outside the play" is that the final lines of the Chorus are no longer banal, but are full of foreboding tinged with hope: "Mortals can understand many things when they have seen them; but before he sees them no one can predict how he will fare in the future" (1418–20; trans. Garvie). The Athenians were playing for high stakes in 410, and Sophocles was well placed to know how very high those stakes were. "The miserable condition of the Cho-

---

7 For a detailed account of many of the proposed solutions, see Visser 1998, 241–64.
8 See further, *Sophocles and Alcibiades*, 78–80.
9 *Sophocles and Alcibiades*, 47–58, and p. ●000●, below.
10 Hesk 2003, 125.

rus on campaign"[11] thus well encapsulates (and will have brought home to the audience in Athens) the current state of those Athenians encamped by the sea not far from Troy in the spring of 410 BC, unsure of how matters will develop under the command of an unpredictable Alcibiades. It was only by playing on what was public knowledge "outside the play", however, that Sophocles could put his points across.

Greek playwrights might, moreover, be venal, might be corrupt. This is a point that has largely escaped modern critics, but it did not escape Plato, who excluded "poetry" from his ideal republic probably for this very reason (tragic poets were his chief target: *Rp.* 595*b*.4, 597*e*.6, 598*e*.8, 602*b*.9, 605*c*.11, 607*a*.3; cf. 595*c*.1). It has been wisely said that "The poets are rhetoricians who are, as it were, selling their products to as large a market as possible, in the hope of gaining reputation and influence"[12] —but reputation and influence for their patrons, and presumably financial gain for themselves. Euripides had thus been in Alcibiades' pocket ever since he wrote a praise poem in honour of Alcibiades' Olympic victory of 416 BC.[13] Euripides obsequiously (and inaccurately) attributed first, second and third places to his patron. Thucydides subtly corrected the record, putting the fact that Alcibiades was placed first, second and *fourth* into the Olympic victor's own mouth in a speech to the Athenian assembly (6.16.2). Euripides' position was akin to that of Simonides, Pindar or Bacchylides with respect to their patrons. The poets traded their skills for riches. We only have one statistic, but it is a telling one: Pindar was paid 10,000 drachmas (= 43 kilos of silver) for verses in honour of Athens in the 470s BC (Isoc. 15.166; Pi. *fr.* 75 Snell). His Theban neighbour who was appointed to look after Pindar's house while he was away (Pi. *Pyth.* 8.58) was probably the curator of a choice collection of gold and silver vessels.[14]

It will not be surprising therefore to see Euripides after 416 putting the most generous interpretation on Alcibiades' actions, defending his reputation, and making a strong case for his forgiveness and return. Whether in his *Helen* of 411, his *Ion* of 409, or his *Bacchae* of 407/6 BC, there is a consistently pro-Alcibiadean line being pushed. Urgent political questions are being asked, and the views of those who were antipathetic towards Alcibiades, such as Sophocles, are being challenged. It will be argued in Chapter 7 that *Helen* reflects Alcibiades' sojourn at the court of the Persian satrap Tissaphernes in 412, and the plot, involving as it does a blameless Helen, is intended to put Alcibiades in a

---

11 Heath 1987b, 201.
12 Griswold 2007.
13 Page, *PMG* 755.5; Bowra 1960.
14 Vickers and Gill 1996, 102

good light. In *Sophocles and Alcibiades* I suggested that *Bacchae* pits a Dionysus who is "the dispenser of natural joys" against a Pentheus who is a "joy-hating Puritan";[15] a reflection of a struggle for power and influence that was taking place between an Alcibiades who was very prone to pleasure (πρὸς ἡδονὰς ἀγώγιμος; Plut. *Alc.* 6.1–2), and a Critias who was possessed of "a strong puritanical streak".[16] The play was written by Euripides during his stay in Macedon,[17] where he will doubtless have received accounts from Athens of Alcibiades' return: his triumphant arrival by sea, and his restoration and magnificent celebration of the Eleusinian Mysteries; he will have heard how the Athenians granted Alcibiades "not only all human, but divine honours" (Just. 2.5.4). The exaggeratedly enthusiastic image of the Asia from which Dionysus has just come (*Bacchae* 13–19) represents an imperial shopping list that Alcibiades was in the event unable to fulfil. These lines did, however, inspire the young Alexander, who must have been very much aware of his Alcibiadean model.[18]

Euripides *Ion*

It is in *Ion*, however, that we can best witness Euripides' challenge to Sophocles' less than complimentary treatment of Alcibiades' genealogy in *Ajax*, and see how he in effect rewrote the plot by providing a different ancestry. It is generally acknowledged that the Delphian setting and the principal conceit of the significance of the first person encountered on leaving the Temple of Apollo underlies the plotting of Aristophanes' *Plutus* performed in 388 BC, and which will be discussed in Chapters 5 and 6.[19] It has, however, been argued with some plausibility that the *Plutus* of 388 is a revised version of a play of the same name that was performed in 408 BC,[20] and I have argued elsewhere that such a play would have been based on an *Ion* performed in 409 BC, which was in turn a rejoinder to Sophocles' *Ajax* of 410 BC.[21] *Ajax* dwells on Alcibiades' genealogy, and to his detriment; whereas *Ion*, as we shall presently see, provides him with an entirely new family tree and also absolves him from a great many of his sins.

---

15 Dodds 1960, 128.
16 Ostwald 1986, 465.
17 *Pace* Scullion 2003 , whose arguments will be met in Chapter 10.
18 Vickers 2011a.
19 Rau 1967, 160–2.
20 Macdowell 1995, 324–7; Sommerstein 2001,28–33 is doubtful.
21 Vickers 2014b, 302–3.

The plot of *Ion* is complex, but the outlines may be summarised as follows: "Apollo ... has ravished Creusa, an Athenian princess, and by her engendered a son whom he intends to make king of Athens, father of the Ionian race, and patron of the Ionian colonies. The design of the god, known to the audience from the beginning, is not made manifest to the characters of the play until the end, when they depart praising him for his benevolence".[22] For all its occasional lightheartedness, the play is a serious treatment of issues that were central to Athens and its origins, as Arlene Saxenhouse, Froma Zeitlin, and Nicole Loraux have argued,[23] mediated however through the pressing requirements of Alcibiades' current situation.

We have already seen how Euripides might have been indebted to Alcibiades after his employment as an epinician poet in 416 BC. Alcibiades had entered seven teams in the chariot race and, being victorious, he entertained the whole crowd to a magnificent feast. He had already impressed and/or scandalised the crowd by parading Athens' official plate "as though it was his own" ([Andoc.] 4.29; Plut. *Alc.* 13.3)—an indication that he may have held office as guardian of the Athenian treasury at the time.[24] Euripides' *Ion* is in a sense as encomiastic as his Olympic verses in that it puts a positive, pro-Alcibiadean spin on every detail.

There is not of course a one-to-one match between the characters in *Ion* and their historical counterparts, or between the plotting and the historical situation, for Euripides is too clever for that. Quintilian called him *sententiis densus* (10.1.68) for good reason, since Euripides was the master of oblique reference, of allusive resonance. His work is indeed full of *sententiae:* saying one thing, but making it clear to a knowing audience that he meant something else. This may sound like special pleading; but what gives one confidence in pursuing a subject that is still essentially taboo is that it is fully consonant with the way in which I believe that many other extant plays of the last decade of the fifth century, whether by Euripides, Sophocles or Aristophanes, are plausibly exercises in political commentary, usually with Alcibiades in mind. As often, Euripides "manipulates" that infinitely flexible commodity, myth, to this end.[25]

---

22 Burnett 1962, 89.
23 Saxenhouse 1986; Zeitlin 1989; Loraux 1990; 1998.
24 See p. 87, n. 34, below.
25 Cf. Cole 2005.

Ion and Alcibiades

Why should *Ion* be set in Delphi? Not, I think, in order that Euripides "the rationalist" might vent his spleen at Apollo, although the case has frequently been made.[26] Rather, *Ion* is "a drama of mortals who have been chosen by a god as his instruments",[27] where a "strong emphasis is laid on divine direction behind human activities".[28] Euripides' aim is to give divine sanction from Apollo, reinforced by Athena, for Alcibiades' return and acquisition of power, and the choice of Delphi in this context is highly significant.

Alcibiades was an Alcmaeonid through his mother (Plut. *Alc.* 1.1; cf. Isoc. 16.25), and the Alcmaeonids had a special relationship with Delphi, expressed most vividly by their having contracted to build a new temple of Apollo there. They gained fame, and doubtless the gratitude of the temple authorities, by going beyond the contract and constructing the east and west facades in Parian marble instead of *poros* (Hdt. 5.62.2–3). The Chorus appear to allude to this benefaction in the opening lines of their first song, when they describe the glories of the διδύμων προσώπων ("twin facades": 188–9) of Apollo's temple. The reference is otherwise unmotivated, and has caused puzzlement in the past (e.g., " ... attention could scarcely be attracted by a feature common to almost every temple in Greece").[29]

Sophocles usually stresses Alcibiades' negative qualities, but Euripides does the opposite. There was a lot that was negative about Alcibiades and Euripides could scarcely conceal it. In fact he does not do so in *Ion*, but creates a series of small errors, slips and misunderstandings that recall Alcibiades' major sins, but which are serially forgiven or clarified in such a way that it might seem that the major transgressions should be set aside as well.[30] A minor example is to be found at the point where Creusa declares that Ion's behaviour in drawing attention to her tears is οὐκ ἀπαιδεύτως (247: "not impolite [literally 'not uneducated']"). Alcibiades was notoriously ἀπαίδευτος as his contemporary Antisthenes explicitly states (*fr.* 30 *ap.* Athenaeus 12.534c). In having us see a small breach of manners excused in this way, Alcibiades' spin-doctor is subliminally encouraging his audience to forget that Alcibiades was severely *maleducato*.

---

26 E.g. Verrall 1890, xvi; cf. Verrall 1895, 136–40; Norwood 1942, 113; Greenwood 1953, 80; Willetts 1958.
27 Burnett 1962, 94.
28 Wassermann 1940, 597.
29 Verrall 1890, 18.
30 Cf. Arnott 1978.

A major example of the phenomenon concerns slavery. There are indications that Alcibiades' maternal ancestor, the first Coesyra who came from Eretria,[31] may have been a slave (Schol. Ar. *Nu.* 64; *Pax* 451). Alcibiades is also said to have earned the nickname of δοῦλος ("slave") on account of his having deserted to the Spartans in 415 (Schol. Ar. *Pax* 451). And whether or not these traditions are valid, it was certainly the case that on entering the service of Tissaphernes Alcibiades technically became the δοῦλος of the Persian satrap (see Appendix 1, below). Euripides could not overlook stories of Alcibiades' servile origins or his recent slave status, but neutralizes them in a highly skilful manner. Ion's service is not to a satrap, but to Apollo, slavery to whom (cf. δουλεύσω ["I will serve as a slave"]: 182; τοῦ θεοῦ καλοῦμαι δοῦλος εἰμί ["I am called the slave of the god"] 132; 309; 327) is no disgrace. Hermes explicitly states (55) that Ion is the ταμίαν τε πάντων πιστόν (the "steward who is trusted above all") at Delphi; phraseology highly reminiscent of (and scarcely unconnected with) the reports we receive in Plutarch of Alcibiades' speedy emergence as the πρῶτος καὶ μέγιστος ("first and greatest")—and presumably πιστότατος ("most trusted")—member of Tissaphernes' court in 412 (Plut. *Alc.* 24.4; Appendix 1, below). When Ion understands from Xuthus that his birth may have been the result of a romp with a free-born woman (551–6) he is relieved to have escaped the charge of being of servile extraction (ἐκπεφεύγαμεν τὸ δοῦλον).

The Pedagogue takes up the burden of Euripides' spin-doctoring at lines 836 ff. when it seems to him and Creusa that Xuthus may indeed have had his purported fling with a woman who may after all have been enslaved (ἐκ δούλης τινὸς γυναικός: 837–8), and then dwells on what a shameful thing it is to bear the name of slave (854–5). In passing, Euripides makes a glancing allusion to another scandalous fact concerning Alcibiades that could not be glossed over, namely his having bought a captive slave woman after the sack of Melos in 416 BC, having taken her as a mistress, and having had a child by her. This was considered this to be "a lawless outrage" of a kind more often "seen on the tragic stage" ([Andoc.] 4.23). A memory of this event probably lies behind the Pedagogue's complaint that it is an awful thing to take the child "of some slave woman" into one's house (836–8). Ion is concerned that the recognition-tokens with which he is entrusted by the Pythian priestess may yet reveal that his mother was a slave (1382). Ion's freeborn status is eventually made clear, however, and without specifically saying so, Euripides in effect implies that so far as Alcibiades was concerned, it was time to "draw a line" under the slavery issue and "move on".

---

31 Shear 1963. For contemporary references to disgrace attached to a charge of slavery, see Hunt 2010, 110–11.

Alcibiades' greatest sin was impiety. It was for whatever he and his cronies had got up to at their wild parties that he was formally condemned by nearly all the Athenian priesthood in 415 BC. To present Alcibiades as the hyper-religious Ion, and to have him mouth sanctimonious phrases with apparent sincerity will have improved his public image no end; indeed, nearly all the Athenian clerisy absolved Alcibiades of his sins in 407 BC making it safe for him to return to Athens without fear of prosecution. Ion's status as the χρυσοφύλαξ ("steward of the plate") of the god (54) recalls Alcibiades' real, or usurped, role as the effective controller of Athens' official plate in 416 BC, and the σεμνὸν βίον ("holy life": 56) that Ion leads at Delphi was in marked contrast to whatever it was thought Alcibiades had done to earn almost universal condemnation. And references to βίος ("life") recur more than 10 times throughout the play (56, 383, 581, 624, 1013, 1135, 1295, 1600; cf. βίοτον and cognates: 326, 670, 766) as constant plays on part of Alcibiades' name. βία ("violence") and cognates (378, 437, 445, 1295) perform much the same role, but more insidiously, for they help charge the play with its undertow of violence: It has been well said that "In all the reaches of the play … there is violence and force".[32]

Alcibiades was perhaps best known by his patronymic ὁ Κλεινίου ("son of Cleinias"), and Euripides playfully refers to Athens throughout the play in terms that imply it is Alcibiades' own: κλεινῶν Ἀθηνῶν (30) and κλεινὰς Ἀθήνας (1038) ("glorious Athens"; cf. κλεινὸν … ἄστυ ["glorious city": 262] and Ion's κλεινὸς … πόνος ["glorious toil": 131]) all play on Alcibiades' patronymic. The Pythian priestess' declaration that Ion should go to Athens purified (καθαρός) and with favourable omens (1333) again absolves the hero of a sin (in this case a nonexistent one) in a way that somehow served Alcibiades' pressing interests, namely, to be forgiven and to return to his native city.

Ion's punctiliousness where religious matters are concerned is sometimes expressed in terms which recall the terminology of the Eleusinian Mysteries. When his fate has been halfway revealed, Ion declares that it has been a day of μακαρίων … φαντασμάτων ("blessed visions": 1354). μακαρισμός ("blessed happiness") was part of the culminating ceremony of the Mysteries.[33] The most memorable event of Alcibiades' brief stay in Athens on his eventual return in the summer of 407 BC, and for which he disastrously delayed his departure on campaign, was a magnificent celebration of the Mysteries at which "all who did not envy him said that he had performed the office of high priest in addition to that of a general" (Plut. *Alc.* 34.6), and at which Alcibiades was presumably himself

---

32 Wolff 1965, 177.
33 Richardson 1974, 313–14.

initiated.[34] If Euripides had been hinting at Alcibiades' likely religious policy should he be allowed to return to Athens, he could scarcely have done a better job.

Euripides elsewhere puts Alcibiadean policy statements in Ion's mouth. At 621–5 Ion, in a speech that has been called a "deliberately disturbing interruption" on account of its contemporary reference,[35] explicitly criticizes tyranny, the political sin above all that Alcibiades' enemies believed him to be in danger of committing. Ion would rather live as a happy citizen than as a tyrant (625–6). He also rejects wealth as a desirable end (629–32); Alcibiades was one of the wealthiest of Athenians,[36] but his indebtedness was a constant problem, as Thucydides notes (6.15.3; cf. 6.12.2). He notoriously lived beyond his already considerable resources. In future, is the message, his requirements will be μέτρια ("moderate": 632).

The list of Ion's current blessings includes the information that no "rough person pushes [him] off the road. For it is unbearable to give way and to yield to baser men" (635–7). If Alcibiades is in question, this otherwise unmotivated remark probably relates in part to the occasion when "still a child, he was playing at knucklebones with other boys in the narrow street (ἐν τῷ στενωπῷ), and when his turn came to throw, a loaded wagon was passing. He at first ordered the driver to stop his team because his throw was to take place directly in the path of the wagon. Then as the boor who was driving would not stop, the other children made way; but Alcibiades flung himself down on his face directly in front of the horses ..". (Plut. *Alc.* 2.3–5). Such Alcibiadean intransigence apparently contributed to Sophocles' Oedipus' encounter with Laius, again in a narrow way (στενωπός: *OT* 1399),[37] and both the anecdote and Sophocles' reworking of it will have contributed to Euripides' imagery here. A difficulty that has hitherto beset the study of *Ion* is the "inconsistency" in the hero's character; sometimes he is a naïve lad, at others a cynical politician. This is not "the obtrusive clanking of dramatic machinery" as Kevin Lee once put it[38] (we are dealing with Euripides after all), but it is rather an accurate rendering of an Alcibiades who was full of "many strange inconsistencies and contradictions", according to Plutarch (Plut. *Alc.* 2.1), who also remarks on "the unevenness of his nature" (*ibid.*, 16.9).

---

34 *Sophocles and Alcibiades*, 101–2.
35 Wolff 1965, 174.
36 See pp. 62–3, below for relevant testimonia.
37 *Sophocles and Alcibiades*, 34–46, following Musgrave 1800; Wunder 1831.
38 Lee 1999, 29.

It was remarked of Alcibiades that when he was "a young boy he lured husbands away from their wives, but when he was a young man he lured wives away from their husbands" (Bion *ap*. D.L. 4.49), and there are vignettes in *Ion* of a couple of perhaps relevant encounters. The attentions that Xuthus pays to Ion immediately after he exits the temple and believes him to be his son are of course paternal. Ion, however, does not take them in this way, but rather seems to view such expressions as "let me kiss your hand and let me fold your body in my embrace" (519) as endearments that have been taken to be homo-erotic in their intent[39] and which he rejects. Then, Alcibiades was greatly admired by ladies: "many women, even of high rank, sought after [him] for his beauty" (Xen. *Mem.* 1.2.24). If Ion was indeed based on Alcibiades, the lines that he addresses "a little brashly, perhaps"[40] on first meeting Creusa, praising her aristocratic deportment (237–40) and commenting on the tears that grace her well-born cheeks (241–6) perhaps evoke the kind of chat-up lines used by Alcibiades during his amorous adventures. That the remarks could be taken in this way is perhaps apparent from Creusa's assurance that they are not in fact out of place (247; see above); in some circumstances they might have been considered impudent. They were certainly inelegant, but since Euripides is writing, probably deliberately so. The repetition of σχῆμα ("appearance") at *Ion* lines 238 and 240 was criticised in antiquity, as ἀνασχετόν ("insupportable") according to the critic Pausimachus (*ap*. Phld. *Po*. 1, col. 90, 5–7),[41] but it was presumably deliberate, and intended to enhance the image of youthful clumsiness that Euripides so wittily imparts.

There are many other resonances in *Ion* with Alcibiades' public image. The entertainment of the guests in Delphi echoes Alcibiades' victory feast at Olympia.[42] Whoever wished to attend was invited to Ion's feast (1166–7); "the whole crowd" at Olympia was invited to Alcibiades' celebratory event (Ath. 1.3*e*). Constant references to Alcibiades' *axioma*—his "reputation" recall the way in which he was granted the ἀριστεῖον or the prize for valour at Potidaea in 431 BC on account of his ἀξίωμα "in the eyes of the generals" (Pl. *Smp.* 219*e*; D.L. 2.23; Plut. *Alc.* 7). Thucydides states that although Alcibiades was young by the standards of any other city, he was nevertheless influential on account of the reputation (ἀξιώματι [5.43.2]) of his forbears; later, Alcibiades is said to have been held in high esteem (ἀξιώματι [6.15.3]) by the citizenry; later still, Alcibiades claims to have "ordered everything in a style worthy (ἀξιῶς [6.16.2]) of [his] victory" at Olympia in 416 B.C. This is probably relevant to the references to ἀξίωμα (603)

---

39 Kaimio 1988, 37–8, n. 21.
40 Conacher 1959, 28.
41 Cf. Janko 2000, 283–95; Pickering 2003, 493–4.
42 See further Vickers 2014b, 310.

and οἳ τὰς πόλεις ἔχουσι κἀξιώματα ("those who hold the place of privilege:" 605 [trans. Verrall]) in Ion's long "political" speech, as well as to his final words, where he remarks how appropriate (ἄξιον: 1618) is the outcome.

Sophocles *Ajax* and Alcibiades

There may be rather more than a generalised allusion, however, to Alcibiades' *axioma* in the stress laid on the concept in *Ion*, if it was indeed performed soon after Sophocles' *Ajax*, a play that probably first saw the light of day in 410. The traditional dating to the 440s is now said to be "a misdating".[43] Hugh Lloyd-Jones regarded the play as a "mature masterpiece",[44] and I have argued that the character of its deceitful, unstable, hubristic, and impious hero contains exaggerations of relevant aspects of the character of Ajax's supposed descendant Alcibiades, and that such details as "the unsettled problem"[45] of Ajax's claim ἐθηλύνθην ("I was made female"; *Ajax* 651), or the full title of the play in Greek (Αἴας μαστιγοφόρος, or *Ajax the Whip-carrier*), might be respectively explained by Alcibiades' "ambivalent sexuality"[46] and the tradition that Alcibiades had himself once been whipped in controversial circumstances (Hermog. *Inv.* 2.4.37).

We might also take note of the fact that the few examples in myth or history of hereditary *aristeia* are the one that Ajax hoped for (in vain) in Sophocles' play, and the one that came to Alcibiades in 431 BC.[47] One of Alcibiades' forebears, a certain Cleinias son of Alcibiades, had also been granted such a prize at Artemisium in 480 BC (Hdt. 8.17). It was, as Thucydides points out, the reputation of his ancestors that contributed to Alcibiades' early success in politics. Sophocles was scarcely complimentary towards the putative model for Ajax, and his overall conceit depends for much of its success on the fact that Alcibiades was thought to be descended from the flawed Homeric hero (Pl. *Alc.* 1.121a). Alcibiades' reputation was no less flawed and he could clearly benefit from a new genealogy. This is what Euripides provides in *Ion*: an unsullied family tree where the hero is the son of Apollo. This move will also have airbrushed out Alcibiades' poor standing with Apollo if he did indeed lie behind the characterisation of Oedipus in Sophocles' plays. Euripides has also conspicuously altered the traditional genealogy of

---

43 Kennedy 2009, 113.
44 Lloyd-Jones 1994, 9.
45 Taplin 1979, 128.
46 Duff 2003, 96–97; and see further pp. 92, 109, 134, below.
47 Cf. Grégoire and Orgels. 1953; Grégoire 1955; cf. *Sophocles and Alcibiades*, 50.

the Ionians. In making Ion out to be their ancestor, he is serving the ends of his patron by implying that any imperial ambitions Alcibiades may have are justified on hereditary grounds (the interests of Athens' imperialism are secondary). Ionia had of course been Alcibiades' field of action in the years immediately preceding his return to Athens, and was intended to be again (see the imperial shopping list at *Bacchae* 13–19 referred to above, p. 46). There was, moreover, nothing new in the creation of convenient genealogies for political reasons. Myth was the province of poets and local historians who took advantage of the indeterminate nature of the genre "to adapt and manipulate the available material at will" as Guido Schepens and Jan Bollansée have recently put it.[48]

Pericles and Delphi

Euripides also manipulates Ion's earthly parents Xuthus and Creusa in such a way that their lives resonate with what we know about Pericles and Aspasia, a couple who played a parental role where the orphan Alcibiades was concerned. There is not a one-to-one relationship, but there is nevertheless a rough parallelism. It was Aspasia who came from abroad, like Xuthus, and it was Pericles who, like Creusa, sprang from deep aristocratic roots (being well born "on both sides": Plut. *Per.* 3.1). But Pericles famously slept around (being "much given to love affairs"), as did apparently Xuthus in his younger days (551–4). And Aspasia, like Creusa, probably had had a "clandestine" child; at least the talk of "babies, five-month ones and three-month ones and thirty-day ones" in Cratylus' *Dionysalexandros*, a play which, according to the plot-summary, satirized Pericles by innuendo, arguably relates to her speedy marriage to Lysicles[49] to whom she bore a son soon—very soon—after Pericles' death.[50]

Xuthus' first words on entry (401–2) are a prayer to Apollo; Pericles always prayed before speaking in public (Plut. *Per.* 8.6). Xuthus' first statement on emerging from the temple is that it is a fitting (πρέπουσα) start to what he wants to say to address Ion as his son; a hallmark of Pericles' ascendency was πρέπουσα ("what is fitting"); Pericles is in fact the only speaker in Thucydides to use the word πρέπον (at 1.144.2; 2.36.1; cf. 2.36.4).[51] Xuthus' apparently homo-erotic approach to Ion (519), discussed above, was perhaps an ironic allusion to Pericles' denunciation of pederasty when he chided an inappropriately

---

48 Schepens and Bollansée 2004, 60; cf. Calame 2003.
49 *Pericles on Stage*, 194, following Handley 1982.
50 Stadter 1989, 237.
51 Tompkins 1972, 189.

aroused Sophocles with the words "a general ought to keep not only his hands clean, but his eyes" (Plut. *Per.* 8.7; Cic. *Off.* 1.40; Val. Max. 4.3. ext.1). Xuthus' injunction to Ion to "kill, then burn me" (527) suggests that it was Alcibiades who had performed the rites as next of male kin at Pericles' funeral in 429 B.C. Pericles' older legitimate sons had themselves died in the plague, Pericles Jr will have been too young, and it is difficult to think of who else might have officiated (if so, it will have been an act that also served to inflame Alcibiades' political ambitions). There may be an oblique allusion in Xuthus' claim not to know how Ion arrived at Delphi—ἀμηχανῶ (448)—to the μηχαναί ("siege engines") that Pericles had used to good effect at Samos (Plut. *Per.* 27.3). Xuthus' supposed "fidelity as a husband"[52] will have had a hollow ring about it if Pericles is indeed in question, for in addition to his other extra-curricular activities, rumour had it that Aspasia entertained respectable women with whom Pericles had affairs (Plut. *Per.* 32.1).

Pericles had, moreover, famously visited Delphi, at the end of the Second Sacred War in 447 B.C. Donald Kagan put things very well: "Pericles, ... in his prime at about forty-five years of age, marched an army to Delphi, restored its control to the Phocians, and regained the *promanteia* for Athens".[53] We can hardly doubt that Pericles, a victorious general "in his prime" and a "King of the Satyrs" (Hermipp. *PCG* 47.1 *ap.* Plut. *Per.* 33.8) "much given to love affairs" (Clearch. *FHG* 2.314 *ap.* Ath. 13.589d), conspicuously made the most of the female talent available. It was also about this time that the infant Alcibiades arrived in Pericles' household at Athens. There is more than even "rough parallelism" going on here. Alcibiades had long laid claim to Pericles' political mantle, but with little real success. Athena's injunctions to Ion at the end of the play seem to imply that Alcibiades' dream will come true. He will be placed in a position of authority (on θρόνους τυραννικοὺς ["tyrants' thrones"], no less; Pericles' ascendancy was regarded by his critics as a tyranny in the tradition of the Peisistratids). Ion will be εὐκλεής ("well-famed": 1575) throughout Greece, an epithet that recalls the name of "far-famed" Περικλῆς. This notion is reinforced with the prediction that the Ionians named after Ion will also possess κλέος ("renown": 1588). Sophocles makes a similar play on the names of both Pericles and Alcibiades at *Philoctetes* 1422: out of his πόνοι ("troubles"; a word that Thucydides' Pericles employs five times in his last formal speech (2.62.1, 62.3, 63.1, 63.3, 64.6) he will make a εὐκλεᾶ ("illustrious") ... βίον ("life"). *Philoctetes* was probably performed in the same year as *Ion*, perhaps at the same dramatic festival. Here too, Alcibiades appears

---

52 See Lee 1999, 221 on line 546.
53 Kagan 1990, 124; cf. Thuc. 1.112.5; *FGrH* 328 F 34 [Philochorus]; Plut. *Per.* 21.

to have been made the heir to Pericles' political mantle, by a Heracles who —or so I have argued—is lightly disguised as Pericles himself.[54]

Aspasia the Ionian

The plotting, as we have seen, provides rough parallels between Creusa's lot and that of Aspasia (whose Athenian status was in reality inferior to that of her autochthonous consort);[55] and the legitimacy and citizen rights of Pericles Jr, her son by Pericles (and who was politically active around the time *Ion* was performed: Hellenotamias for 410/9 [ML 84.8], and perhaps elected general for 409/8 B.C.),[56] will have added interesting resonances. Although everyone "lives happily ever after", Creusa is scarcely a role model mother, having twice tried to kill Ion (criticism of the case once made for an equation between Aspasia and Medea may have been misplaced)[57] Creusa successfully concealed her clandestine child; Aspasia clearly did not, if Cratinus is any guide.

The plotting aside, there are a few direct indications in the text suggesting an identification of Creusa with Aspasia. Thus, Creusa's praise of the doors (εὐωποὶ πύλαι: 1611; πύλας: 1613) of the house of her divine lover recalls Aspasia's activities at the door of Pericles' house: Pericles never went in or out of his house without embracing and kissing Aspasia passionately (Plut. *Per.* 24.9; cf. Ath. 13.589e). Within the larger picture, granted that "the overt purpose of the drama is to proclaim the Apolline parentage of Ion and the Ionians",[58] it is somehow appropriate that the contemporary analogue of Ion's mother should have been an Ionian. In the summer of 412 B.C., moreover, Alcibiades had been involved in the defence of Miletus, Aspasia's native city, against a combined Athenian and Argive attack (Thuc. 8.26.3). Alcibiades was also said to be "a friend of the leading men of Miletus" (Thuc. 8.17.2), and the association may go back to the days of the ostracism of Alcibiades' grandfather (of the same name) who

---

54 *Sophocles and Alcibiades*, 67–68, 78–80; and see p. 55 above.
55 Bicknell 1972, 245–7.
56 Develin 1989, 169.
57 Konishi 1986, 50–52 (for); Wilkins 1987, 8–10 (against).
58 Burnett 1962, 92

probably spent his exile there, married into the Milesian aristocracy, and brought Aspasia to Athens on his return.[59]

* * *

Ion thus represents an attempt by Euripides to render Alcibiades' public image more acceptable, an urgent political issue for many in 409 B.C.; and his propaganda will have contributed to Alcibiades' triumphal return in 407 B.C. Euripides cleverly glosses over his patron's less attractive features and substitutes piety for impiety, potential statesmanship for less than patriotic achievement, and above all forgiveness and reconciliation for discord and disharmony. In making the Alcibiadean Ion a descendant of Apollo, he effectively challenges Sophocles' critical approach of the previous year that had been predicated on Alcibiades' supposed descent from Ajax. Euripides' optimism was misplaced, however, for although Alcibiades did make a brief come-back, and did indeed clear his name with most of the religious authorities, his career was henceforth to be on a downward trajectory, and beyond the skills of even the most adept practitioner of the arts of the spin-doctor. For this is what Euripides' play amounted to; but just as Euripides was challenging Sophocles' harsh judgement of Alcibiades, it is not too difficult in the light of the plotting and characterization of *Plutus* of 388 to think of Euripides' venality and obsequiousness having been challenged in turn by Aristophanes in a *Plutus* attacking Alcibiades in 408 BC.

---

[59] Bicknell 1972, 245–47; Solana Dueso 1994, xiv-xv; Henry 1995, 10–11; *Pericles on Stage*, 177–8.

Chapter 5

Happy Families: *Plutus* i

Plutus concerns an encounter with the blind deity Wealth by a citizen of Athens, who takes him to a shrine of Asclepius to be healed. Once his sight is restored, Wealth proceeds to enrich the good and impoverish the bad. The plotting of the opening scene owes much to Euripides' *Ion*,[1] where as we saw in Chapter 4, the Delphian setting was itself largely dependant on Pericles' visit there at the end of the Second Sacred War in 447 BC. It was an Alcibiadean figure that the Periclean Xuthus first encountered on emerging from Apollo's temple at Delphi, and this will doubtless have informed the similar scene in *Plutus* (and especially in a version performed in 408, for *Ion* was probably performed the year before, in 409 BC). In *Plutus* too, a Periclean figure (Chremylus) encounters an Alcibiadean one (Wealth). The reasons for such identifications will be explained in detail presently.

Plutus has had an indifferent press of late, being variously described as "weak",[2] a "bloodless performance interesting chiefly for its place in the history of literature"[3] or even "ugly".[4] It is even deliberately omitted from a recent introduction to the works of Aristophanes.[5] In earlier ages, however, it was the most popular of Aristophanes' surviving plays by far. *Plutus* is preserved in 148 manuscripts, and occupies the first position in the Ravenna and Venetian codices.[6] Earlier critics may well have had a point, for *Plutus* is arguably one of the most ingeniously crafted examples of Aristophanes' dramatic art. At least the features that supposedly disfigure it recede once we realise that the characters in it, both major and minor, are polymorphic renditions of Pericles, Aspasia, Alcibiades and his wife Hipparete. The play is firmly based on the memory of specific individuals, their achievements, quirks and foibles; it is not an Athenian collective fantasy,[7] or simply a satire on utopian ideals.[8] The individuals on

---

1 Rau 1967, 160–2.
2 Sommerstein 1984, 315.
3 G. Murray 1933, 199.
4 L. Strauss 1966, 295.
5 Robson 2009.
6 Lord 1963, 104, who gives details of the other extant plays as follows: *Clouds* (127), *Frogs* (76), *Knights* (28), *Birds* (18), *Acharnians* (14), *Wasps* (10), *Peace* (8), *Lysistrata* (8), *Ecclesiazusae* (7), *Thesmophoriazusae* (2).
7 Cf. McGlew 1997, 52.
8 Konstan and Dillon 1981, 379, n. 10.

whom the original characterization was based were no longer alive and so the humour is more generic than in earlier plays (apart from *Ecclesiazusae*). The whole range of the anecdotal tradition relating to these targets was at Aristophanes' disposal, and their characterization has become crystallized. Comedy, by 388 BC, had by law—or custom—to satirize in an oblique fashion, enigmatically; solve the riddle, and *Plutus* becomes a fast-moving, hilarious, farce.⁹

The κωμῳδούμενοι

Pericles and members of his household underlie the characters in *Plutus*; or at least this will be the working hypothesis of the next two chapters. Polymorphic characterisation enables Aristophanes to keep the κωμῳδούμενοι on stage throughout. In this way, different aspects of the characters and reputations of the principal targets can be explored. For example, Pericles lies behind not only Chremylus and Blepsidemus, but also the Honest Man, the Sycophant, and the Chorus of Countrymen, who all echo in one way or another aspects of the anecdotal tradition relating to Pericles.

The names and identities of the Periclean figures are easily accounted for. Chremylus' name, like that of Chremes in *Ecclesiazusae*, is derived from χρέμπτομαι ("clear one's throat", especially "before making a speech": LSJ, *s.v.* and cf. Ar. *Th.* 381), a word that is said to be "akin" to χρεμετίζω that had connotations of "any loud noise" or "thunder" (LSJ *s.v.*). Pericles was renowned for his oratory and owed his "Olympian" nickname to the thunder and lightning of his eloquence (Plut. *Per.* 8.4; cf. Ar. *Ach.* 531). "Blepsidemus" involves "peering" and does indeed suggest "an old man with poor eyesight";¹⁰ it is but one of many examples of Aristophanes' cripple-teasing the memory of Pericles with allusions to symptoms of the Athenian Plague (cf. Thuc. 2.49.2: "redness and inflammation of the eyes"; see further Appendix 2).

The Honest Man—the Δικαῖος ἀνήρ—is an appropriate dramatic analogue of the "Olympian", for not only was δίκη ("justice") a concept closely linked with Zeus,¹¹ but δικαιοσύνη ("honesty", "incorruptibility") was, as we shall frequently be reminded, a virtue for which Pericles was renowned, and which is said to have been one of the pillars of his public conduct (Plut. *Per.* 2.5). A similar con-

9 I thus concur with Olson 1990, 242 in seeing *Plutus* as a "final sophisticated Aristophanic masterpiece", but for different reasons.
10 Sommerstein 1998, 168.
11 Cf. Lloyd-Jones 1983; Ostwald 1986, 143–4.

ceit lies behind the naming of Dicaeopolis in *Acharnians*.[12] Sycophants, or politically correct informers, had flourished under Pericles, and to show him as one,
recognisable both from his speech patterns and presumably the mask he wore, is
somehow appropriate. Although Pericles was of aristocratic descent, Aristophanes often adapts his Periclean characters to the social class with which he
chose to be associated. Dicaeopolis is one such, as is Philocleon; here the Chorus
of Countrymen take on the role. They will, moreover, have well reflected the interests of an individual who had his ancestral estates at Cholargus outside the
city.

Alcibiades is represented by another range of characters: by Carion, Wealth,
the Young Man, Hermes and the Priest of Zeus. In each case there is a logic to the
characterization. In the case of Carion it has been well said that there is something distinctly unservile about him "even if we allow for comic licence",[13] and
the explanation may well lie in the possibility that the model was not really a
slave at all, in the accepted sense of the word. While the slave's name, meaning
"the Carian" clearly recalls the source of many slaves in classical Athens, and
"the lot of a Carian" was a proverbial expression for "enslavement",[14] it was
also a highly appropriate means of evoking an Alcibiades who may have been
of servile descent (see pp. 49, above and 185, below) and who had technically
been a slave in Caria, albeit in the most luxurious circumstances. When he
fled from the Spartans in 412 BC, Alcibiades took refuge at the palace of Tissaphernes (Plut. *Alc.* 24.4) near Magnesia-on-the-Meander in Caria. We learn that
"having given himself, for safety's sake, to Tissaphernes, the satrap of the
king", Alcibiades immediately became the "first and greatest" member of his entourage (Plut. *Alc.* 24.4). In Persian terms Alcibiades' position was that of a δοῦλος ("slave"), and was to be again when during his second exile he was granted
an annual income of fifty talents by the Persian satrap Pharnabazus (Nepos,
Alc. 9). This is all discussed in greater detail in Appendix 1. Not only was Alcibiades' sometime slavery well known to Greek contemporaries, but it was also
to be the source of other dramatic treatments, notably Euripides' *Ion*, as we
have just seen. Caria was also the scene of Alcibiades' successful fundraising

12 *Pericles on Stage*, 58–9.
13 Cartledge 1990, 71. Cf. Sommerstein 2001, 24–5: "Aristophanes ... takes some pains to establish [Carion] as one who had become a slave relatively late in life and retained much of the
mental outlook of a free man."
14 Three Carian slaves (a Κάρ, a Κὰρ παῖς ["a Carian boy"], and a Καρικὸν παιδίον ["a Carian
lad"] were among those belonging to a certain Cephisodorus sold off in 415: *IG* I³ 421.38–
46; ML 79.

in 408 BC, when he sent 100 talents to Athens (Xen. *Hell.* 1.4.8, 11) raised, it has been suggested, by selling "a great mass of captives" into slavery.[15]

Other characters in whose guise Alcibiades "comes forward" include (i) the Μειράκιον ("Young Man"); a suitable analogue for an Alcibiades whose political advent had been notoriously precocious,[16] and who was being criticised on account of his relative youth as late as 415 BC, when he was already 37 (Thuc. 6.18.6; cf. 6. 12.2); (ii) Hermes, for whose appearance it was said that "contemporary and later sculptors used the features of Alcibiades" (Clem. Alex., *Protr.* 4.53.6); and (iii) the Priest of Zeus, who well reflects an Alcibiades who slaughtered "a great number of sacrificial animals" at the Altar of Zeus in the precinct at Olympia after his victory in 416 BC. There were enough beasts to feed the whole crowd (Plut. *Alc.* 12.1; cf. [Andoc.] 4.30; Thuc. 6.16.2; Ath. 1.3*e*). It will have been a memorable occasion.

Even—or rather especially—Wealth is characterised as Alcibiades. This is indicated by an expression he uses in his opening lines—Ἐγὼ μὲν οἰμώζειν λέγω σοι ("I tell you to groan": 58), after Carion has just asked him who he is in an extremely insulting manner (56 – 7). This would appear to relate directly to an anecdote told about Alcibiades preserved in a late medieval text: "Alcibiades, when some low type insulted him, said: "I will not tell you to groan, since you are not worthy of it" (οὐδ᾽ οἰμώζειν σοι λέγω ὡς οὐδὲ τούτου ἀξίῳ ὄντι: *Gnom.Vat.* 119). The expression οἰμώζειν λέγω σοι is otherwise unparalleled in the surviving sources, so far as one can discover,[17] and it would seem to allude to the dictum of Alcibiades (an individual who was very much aware of his own ἀξίωμα ["worth, fame, reputation"], as we saw in the last chapter [p. 52–3, above]), that was sufficiently well known to the audience for Aristophanes to exploit it in order to characterize Wealth the minute he opened his mouth (although the audience will presumably already have been primed by an appropriate mask and the actor's gait). The conceit is underlined by Chremylus half-repeating the expression in the following line (59) σοι λέγει τοῦτ᾽ ("he is saying this to *you*"), and then commenting on how harsh and crude had been Carion's initial enquiry (60), thus reinforcing the recollection of the involvement of "a low type" in the original encounter. The lateness of the source of the anecdote need not concern us. The *Gnomologium Vaticanum* is apparently acceptable when it

---

15 Munn 2000, 165.
16 Cf. Develin 1985.
17 Although the Kinsman, another analogue of Alcibiades, is made to allude to the same incident at *Th.* 248 (p. 139, below).

comes to the study of Epicurus,[18] for all that it dates from the fourteenth century. There is no reason why its testimony should not be acceptable here.

There are many reasons, moreover, for believing that blind Wealth is additionally characterised as a Spartan deity, and it is surprising that this has hitherto escaped the notice of commentators, for although Wealth was blind anywhere, he was thought to be more blind at Sparta than anywhere else (Plut. *Lyc.* 10.4).[19] If a Spartan Wealth indeed "comes forward" as Alcibiades the characterisation will have added a highly appropriate layer of meaning, for Alcibiades' name was Spartan, acquired through traditional family ties (Thuc. 8.6.3), and he had even had Spartan nannies (Plut. *Alc.* 1.3 [Amycla]; Schol. Pl. *Alc.* 1.121d [Lanice]). Then, while in exile at Sparta, not only had he supposedly succeeded in seducing, and impregnating, a Spartan queen, but chameleon-wise had taken to Spartan ways so well that it was said of him: "In Lacedaemon ... he was just such a man as Lycurgus trained ... fond of exercise, frugal and severe" (Plut. *Alc.* 23.6; 23.5). Alcibiades is elsewhere lampooned as a domineering Spartan, in *Peace*, and "comes forward" as Menelaus in *Helen* and *Thesmophoriazusae* (Chapters 7 and 9). Wealth's οἰμώζειν ("groan"; 58) is not only characteristically Alcibiadean, but it well evokes the punishment once inflicted by the Spartans on the Messenians and immortalised by Tyrtaeus (δεσπότας οἰμώζοντες: Tyrt. 7 [West]). The Spartans, like Wealth, were surly: "anger" and "sour looks" were the normal reaction even to one's neighbour at Sparta (Thuc. 2.37.2). The first few lines that Wealth speaks (58, 62, 71), with their clipped language, are distinguished moreover by a certain laconism of expression.[20] Wealth's dirty condition (cf. αὐχμῶν: 84) again smacks of Sparta, whose inhabitants were notorious for their filth (cf. Pl. Com *PCG* 124.2; Ar. *Lys.* 279–80), and there are other indications of Wealth's Spartan status, as we shall presently see.

To show Alcibiades as Wealth, too, was somehow fitting, for despite his periodic indebtedness there were occasions when Alcibiades was very rich indeed. His inheritance (of 100 talents: Lys. 19.52) was one of the largest of which we hear. On entering politics he was said to be possessed of τοῦ τε γένους καὶ τοῦ πλούτου ("noble birth and wealth": Plut. *Alc.* 10.3; cf. Diod. 13.37.2). Aelian preserves a story of Socrates bringing down to earth an Alcibiades τετυφωμένον ἐπὶ τῷ πλούτῳ ("full of over-weening pride on account of his wealth": *VH* 3.28), and for Constantine Porphyrogenitus Alcibiades was ἐν δὲ εὐγενείᾳ καὶ πλούτῳ πρῶ-

---

18 E.g. Arrighetti 1960; Warren 2004.
19 Cf. Hodkinson 1994, 183–4.
20 Cf. Francis 1991–3; Tompkins 1993.

τος Ἀθηναίων ("in birth and wealth the first of the Athenians": *De virt. et vit.* 1.232)—a financial assessment which at times was probably true. His wife Hipparete was the daughter of Hipponicus, "the richest among the Greeks" (Isoc. 16.31). Alcibiades' wealth would have provided a highly appropriate basis for the underlying conceit of *Plutus*.

Aristophanes had thankfully never heard of "Dover's Law" concerning ancient comedy: "the principle of 'one thing at a time'", according to which we should "not turn our attention to two different levels of humour operating simultaneously".[21] Instead, Aristophanes' humour can operate at several levels, and the Alcibiadean Wealth's blindness must owe an additional debt to Sophocles' *Oedipus Tyrannus*, a play that had held up to obloquy Alcibiades' immorality (contemporaries said that he slept with his mother), his habitual belligerence, and his tyrannical ambitions, and in which the tragic hero famously blinds himself.[22] There will of course be those who would see this as the log that brings any wigwam crashing to the ground; better, however, to regard it as the kingpost that supports the rest of the argument: it is the way to achieve an Alcibiades in need of a cure for his blindness. The characterisation is complex, subtle, and—dare one say it?—sophisticated.

Aspasia lies behind Poverty. Pericles was utterly devoted to Aspasia; not only did he embrace her warmly whenever he left the house or came home (Plut. *Per.* 24.9; cf. Ath. 13.589e), but he had supposedly expended the greater part of his wealth on her (Heraclid. Pont. *fr.* 59 *ap.* Ath. 12.533c). It is therefore ironic (or an example of the "spendthrift Aberdonian" principle) to have the Periclean Chremylus and Blepsidemus, to whom she had been a companion "for many a year" (437), driving her from "every land" (430). Poverty is described as ὠχρά ("pallid": 422) in appearance, which probably alludes to Aspasia's role as a philosopher, a σοφίστρια no less (Schol. Ar. *Ach.* 527).[23] Philosophers, along with shoemakers, were generally thought to be pale (e.g. Luc. 44.1.2; Ar. *Nu.* 1016–7; *Ec.* 385–7). Poverty is said to have a wild and tragic expression (424–5); Aspasia probably lies behind the figure of Phaedra in *Hippolytus*,[24] and doubtless others.[25] Poverty is taken to be a πανδοκεύτρια ("the manageress of a low-class hotel": 426); Plutarch clearly believed that Aspasia supported herself by running a brothel (Plut. *Per.* 24.5; cf. Ar. *Ach.* 527). Blepsidemus' fear of

---

21 Dover 1987, 241.
22 Musgrave 1800, 1.289; Wunder 1831, 94; Vickers 2005b; *Sophocles and Alcibiades*, 34–45.
23 She thus occupies a prominent position in Raphael's *School of Athens*: Haase 2002.
24 B.S. Strauss 1993, 166–75; Vickers 2000; Appendix 1, below.
25 Including Eurydice in Soph. *Ant.* and Jocasta in *OT*: *Sophocles and Alcibiades*, 24–5, 44–5; and Creusa: Chapter 4.

Poverty (440 – 44), moreover, will have reflected a real concern on the historical Pericles' part for domestic economy. The "women of his household", doubtless including Aspasia, criticised "his exact regulation of his daily expenses, which allowed none of the superfluities common in great and wealthy households, but which ma[d]e debit and credit exactly balance each other" (Plut. *Per.* 16.5).

Aspasia also "comes forward" as the Hag towards the end of the play, but this manifestation will be discussed in its place (and in Appendix 1). To complicate matters even further, one character might adopt another's characteristics (with role-reversal of a kind not unparalleled in Aristophanes).[26] In *Plutus*, the Periclean Chremylus is the subject of just such a transformation at 322, when he adopts the characteristics of Alcibiades. This is clear from the beginning of Chremylus' speech, when he declares that he rejects old-fashioned greetings in favour of something "up-to-date". The word he uses—ἀσπάζομαι ("I greet you warmly": 324)—is one that had been "up-to-date" some decades earlier (cf. Eur. *Hipp.* 102; Ar. *Nu.* 1145; *Av.* 1378), a fact that has much exercised commentators. If, however, Aristophanes is showing us a conversation in effect between Pericles and Alcibiades (and there are echoes in their dialogue of material we know about from the anecdotal tradition), we are perhaps to think of an encounter that supposedly took place in the past; the greeting also plays on Aspasia's name. While Chremylus is temporarily in Alcibiadean mode, moreover, the Wife of Chremylus "comes forward" not as Aspasia, but as Hipparete, Alcibiades' wife. This will be explained in greater detail below. If the characters in *Plutus* can be accounted for in this manner, problems of continuity and inconsistency are no longer an issue. The play has another, straightforward, logic that is governed by the known—or rumoured—relationships of the κωμῳδούμενοι to each other.

It was far from the case that the individuals who are the principal butts of *Plutus*—Pericles, Aspasia, Alcibiades and Hipparete—had been forgotten since their deaths. Pericles is remembered by Plato (though less than favourably), and he is much to the fore in Thucydides, who may have actually composed his *Histories* as late as 396/5 BC.[27] As we shall see in Chapter 11, Aspasia was the subject of philosophical dialogues by Antisthenes and Aeschylus of Sphettus, and figures large in Plato's *Menexenus*, not to mention Aristophanes' *Ecclesiazusae*. Alcibiades' significance was being actively debated by Isocrates (11.5 – 6), Polycrates, Speusippus (*Ep. Phil.* 10) and later on by Demosthenes (21.143 – 50): discussions which "show the extent to which Alcibiades became

---

26 E.g. the scene at the end of *Wasps* where the Periclean Philocleon adopts the *persona* of an Alcibiadean Bdelycleon.
27 Munn 2000; *Sophocles and Alcibiades*, 139, 151.

a rhetorical symbol in the fourth century, a figure from the great days of Athens".[28] Hipparete will have been remembered as the sister of Callias (c. 450–370 BC) who was busy working—or playing—his way through his fortune, and as the mother of Alcibiades Jr who had already done so by the time of *Plutus*. She will, moreover, have been still alive at the time of a first *Plutus*, performed in 408.[29]

If Pericles, Aspasia, Alcibiades and Hipparete are indeed the historical figures who underlie the characters in *Plutus*, their presence may be accounted for if we consider the "occasion" for the theme of the play to be the poverty of Athens, self-evident in 408, but also attested by Andocides (3.36) in 391, and later on by Isocrates (15. 142) and Xenophon (*Vect.* 1.1), in that the theme could be driven home more vigorously by lampooning the individuals through whose agency it could reasonably be supposed that Athens had been reduced to her sorry condition. There is nothing exceptional in seeing Pericles' extended family being held up to ridicule, especially as they had become part of Aristophanes' standard repertoire. It was also safer, and more economical, to go for old enemies, rather than make new ones (cf. Platon. 1.21–34).

The Opening Scene

Now that we know what to look out for in the opening scene, *viz.*, likely echoes of Alcibiades in Carion and Wealth, and of Pericles in Chremylus, we can understand many of the resonances. Thus, Carion's statement that "a man's body belongs not to himself, but to the buyer" (6–7), sounds like a wry reference to an earlier stage of Alcibiades' career when Aristophanes lampooned him as a "Sausage-" or "Dick-seller" in *Knights*,[30] evidently evoking a boyhood entanglement which Pericles chose to conceal lest his ward be deprived of civic rights (Plut. *Alc.* 3.1). Then, not only does Carion's master follow a blind man (13–15), but forces (προσβιάζεται: 16) his slave to follow behind as well. This is but one of many plays, in *Plutus* and elsewhere, on the βία ("force") element in Alcibiades' name. We saw Euripides employing such word-play in *Ion* (p. 50, above), and we might compare the conversation between Pericles and Alcibiades reported—or carefully contrived—by Xenophon in the *Memorabilia*. There, Alcibiades speaks

---

28 Gribble 1999, 91.
29 She died in 407/6 BC: Plut. *Alc.* 8.7; Isoc.16.45; Rodríguez Blanco 1987, 75.
30 *Pericles on Stage*, 100.

of force and lawlessness; where the stronger obliges the weaker … by force (βια-σάμενος: 1.2.43 – 4; and cf. βίαν [44], βία [45], βία [46] in the same conversation).

Chremylus states his belief that Carion is the member of his master's household who is κλεπτίστατος ("most inclined to be thieving": 27). Perhaps thievery amongst one's charges was an occupational hazard of slave-ownership, but this was also a wholly accurate appraisal of an Alcibiades who had stolen plate and livestock from his admirers (Plut. *Alc.* 4.4; Schol. Luc. 20.16), and who had been accused of stealing the Athenian public plate at the Olympic celebrations of 416 BC ([Andoc.] 4.29), and of embezzling 200 talents at some time between 412 and 404 BC (Lys. 14.38). Indeed so much was Alcibiades' name associated with theft that when Stephanus the Grammarian wanted to cite an example of τὸ εἰκός ("what is likely"), he chose "that Alcibiades is a thief who operates by night" (*in Rhet.* 1357a36).

Chremylus' claim by contrast to be θεοσεβής ("god-fearing") and δίκαιος ("honest": 28) carries certain Periclean resonances, not least his "Olympian" status and reputation for δικαιοσύνη ("honesty").[31] Chremylus reveals that he has been to Delphi to ask if his surviving son might change his τρόπους ("ways") and become a "rogue, a criminal and rotten to the core" (37), since such people succeed in life. These lines are full of significant echoes if Pericles and those who stood in a filial relationship to him are in question. Alcibiades, towards whom Pericles played a quasi-paternal role,[32] was in any case the very embodiment of roguery. Pericles' relations with his oldest son Xanthippus were less than happy (Plut. *Per.* 36.4), and Pericles' surviving son Pericles Jr was perhaps aiming at being elected general in 409/8[33] and if so was doubtless projecting an image of a worthy citizen; relevant if we are dealing with a revision of a play first performed in that year. Then, Alcibiades' own son, who had had a vicious childhood, had but a few years before our *Plutus* gained a reputation for being all the things in Chremylus' list (Lys. 14. 23 – 9)

The person Chremylus has been following, τουτωί ("this fellow": 44) will, if he is based on Alcibiades, have walked in an exaggerated version of the latter's mincing gait which was striking enough to be evoked by means of limping figures such as Oedipus or Philoctetes,[34] and which was still well known in the Athens of 388 BC from Alcibiades Jr's having adopted it (Archipp. *PCG* 48 *ap.* Plut.

---

31 Plut *Per.* 2.5; cf. Stadter 1989, 193.
32 Loraux 1981, 467; B.S. Strauss 1993, 134; *Sophocles and Alcibiades*, 152.
33 Develin 1989, 169.
34 See *Sophocles and Alcibiades*, 34 – 46, 59 – 81, 95 – 103, 110 – 11.

Alc. 1.8).[35] What the god plainly means is that Chremylus' son should adopt the ἐπιχώριον τρόπον ("manner of the country": 47), but on the lips of an actor speaking in Alcibiadean fashion, ἐπιχώριον would have sounded as ἐπιχώλιον, a play on χωλός ("limping"), again a conceit with a long pedigree.[36] The comic business would have drawn exaggerated attention to Alcibiades' "funny walk".

Pericles' nick-name "the Olympian" may have contributed to Chremylus' semi-quotation of the address to Zeus by the Chorus in Aeschylus' *Agamemnon* (160: Ζεύς, ὅστις ποτ' ἐστίν ["Zeus, whoever he may be"]) when he states that Wealth should say "whoever he may be ..." (53: ὅστις ποτ' ἐστίν). Chremylus' requirement that Wealth should also say what he needs (54: ... καὶ τοῦ δεόμενος) may also have a Periclean resonance, for it will perhaps have recalled the payment "for a necessary purpose" (Plut. *Per.* 23.1) that "caught the Athenian imagination".[37] It related to a famous occasion when Pericles had made a disputed payment which then became proverbial: ὥσπερ Περικλέης εἰς τὸ δέον ἀπώλεσα ("As Pericles put it 'I lost it for a necessary purpose'": *Paroemiogr.* 1.80.3), and which Aristophanes frequently exploits (see pp. 72–3, 81, 127, 133, 142, 154, below). Carion's abrupt enquiry of Wealth (56–7) is met with an equally abrupt response, albeit one with both an Alcibiadean and a Laconian reference, as we have just seen (p. 61, above). The Spartan image is intensified in the next few lines: after Wealth's next harsh response (62), Carion says "δέχου ('receive') the man" (63), perhaps playing on the Δέχας ("Receptory"), the name of the public prison at Sparta where malefactors were strangled (Plut. *Agis* 19.6). The oath by Demeter (64) may also have a special point in that Alcibiades had notoriously been condemned for having offended that goddess.

Wealth Declares Himself

At 81, Chremylus, who has just been to Delphi, swears by Apollo and "the gods and demons", then as an afterthought adds "and Zeus" (81–2)—amusing if he indeed "comes forward" as "the Olympian". "How did you come by your affliction?" he asks solicitously of Wealth (86)—as indeed the dramatic analogue of one who had suffered from a plague-induced eye condition might well have done. "It was

---

35 Gribble 1999, 72–3 compares Ar. *Ve.* 1168–71 σαυλοπρωκτιάω, "a word which suggests a wanton or effeminate walk" (cf. LSJ *s.v.* σαῦλος). One might speculate that a limp was the result of the severe wound that Alcibiades received at Potidaea in 432 BC (Plut. *Alc.* 7.3–4).
36 Apart from Sophocles, cf. Eur. *Ba.* 21 (*Sophocles and Alcibiades*, 110–11) and Ar. *Th.* 782, discussed p. 143, below.
37 Stadter 1989, 229–30.

Zeus who did it, from jealousy of mankind (87)", comes the reply: a slap in the face for a potential "Olympian". Wealth's claim that in his youth he only visited "the honest, the wise, and the orderly" (89) is, if he is a mask for Alcibiades, highly ironic, for Alcibiades' youth was notoriously debauched, and spent in the company of insincere flatterers. Wealth states that the reason why he was rendered blind was "ἵνα μὴ διαγινώσκοιμι ('so that I might not distinguish')" the good from the bad (91). Most editors since Aldus have silently emended the Doric διαγινώσκοιμι of many manuscripts to the Attic διαγιγνώσκοιμι, oblivious to the possibility that Aristophanes might have been deliberately putting a Doric form into the mouth of his laconising Wealth. Chremylus, who might be thought to have inside knowledge, observes that it was only through the well-born and honest (i.e. people like Pericles) that Zeus was honoured at all (94).

Chremylus begs Wealth to stay with him (101–5), claiming that he will not find a better man at τοὺς τρόπους ("ways")—"Apart from me" adds Carion: an allusion perhaps to Alcibiades' singular education in ἔργων τρόπους ("ways of doing things") at the hands, if that is the word, of the women of Abydos, as soon as he came of age (Antiph. *fr.* 67 Blass *ap.* Ath. 12.525b). Chremylus promises help to cure Wealth's ὀφθαλμία ("eye-trouble": 115): something with which a post-plague Pericles would have been entirely familiar. Wealth, however, does not want to see again, and this displeases Chremylus. He upbraids Wealth in terms that in fact sum up the popular image of Pericles. ὦ δειλότατε πάντων δαιμόνων ("Oh most cowardly of all the gods": 123), he says; Pericles had gained something of a reputation for cowardice himself as a result of his cautious attitude at the beginning of the Archidamian War (cf. Plut. *Per.* 18.1; 18.2–4; 19.3; 20.3–4; 21, and 38.4).[38] The reference to τὴν Διὸς τυραννίδα ("the tyranny of Zeus": 124) alludes perhaps both to Pericles' "Olympian" status, and to the fact that his authority was frequently characterised by contemporaries as a tyranny (e.g. Plut. *Per.* 12.2). It is possible that μικρὸν χρόνον ("for a short time:" 126) reflects that aspect of Pericles' manner of speaking that Thucydides caught with such expressions as περὶ βραχέως ("for a small matter") or διὰ μικρόν ("for a trifle") (1.140.4–141.1), and which Aristophanes frequently lampoons by employing diminutives.[39] And for a Periclean character to be shown proving that the power of Zeus was less than that of a mini-god (128 ff.) will have been diverting.

Carion became a slave διὰ μικρὸν ἀργυρίδιον ("on account of a little bit of money": 147). If it is indeed Alcibiades speaking, the monetary allusion may well be to Alcibiades' virtual enslavement by Tissaphernes, undertaken in part for

---

38 Cf. Stadter 1989, 210.
39 See pp. 81, 127, 153, below.

self-protection, and in part in an attempt to secure Persian funds for the war against Sparta (cf. Thuc. 8.53–4, and p. 147 below). Alcibiades personally was all too often without wealth (cf. διὰ τὸ μὴ πλουτεῖν [R]: 148), in particular in 415 as a result of his "devotion to horseracing and other pleasures which outran his means" (Thuc. 6.15.3; cf. 6.12.2).

The Periclean resonances of 147 will have served to set up the next poke at the statesman's memory—at least as it was preserved in the popular mind. Chremylus speaks of Corinthian ἑταίρας who have no time for poor men, but if a rich man comes along they offer him anal intercourse (151–2). Pericles was much given to love affairs as we have frequently seen, and among his conquests was one Chrysilla of Corinth (Telecl. *PCG* 47 *ap.* Ath. 10.436 f). It was also popularly believed that Alcmaeonids (such as Pericles) felt constrained to "punt from the Cambridge end" on account of their ancestral curse.[40]

Carion then states (153–4) that boys do the same τἀργυρίου χάριν ("for the money" or, "for the silver") not from affection. Even if he did not actually receive payment for the services he is supposed to have rendered his admirers, Alcibiades had certainly broken into the house of his would-be lover Anytus to steal half the gold and silver vessels in the dining room (Plut. *Alc.* 4.5–6). Chremylus observes that only rent-boys did it for payment; the nobler sort did not ask for money. When asked what *they* did it for, Chremylus replies "A good horse or a pack of hounds". It is amusing then to have (the Alcibiadean) Carion say (knowingly?) that "they are ashamed to ask for money, and conceal their vice with [another] name" (158–9) in that Alcibiades had numerous flatterers fawning over him (Plut. *Alc.* 6.1), was mad about horses, notoriously kept a hound (whose tail he had cut off), and had spent a youth steeped in unnatural vice.

Chremylus lists the crafts that depend on Wealth. All of them, shoemakers (162), the worker in bronze, the carpenter (163), the goldsmith (164), occur in the list of trades encouraged by Plutarch's Pericles as a means of spreading the city's wealth among the citizenry (Plut. *Per.* 12.6). Carion interrupts with more scurrilous avocations that also depend on Wealth: footpads and robbers (165). Then the dialogue develops an even more personal tone, and Chremylus and Carion mention trades which have a special reference in the context of the historical Pericles and Alcibiades. "The fuller", says Chremylus (166): Alcibiades' extensive wardrobe will have involved a good deal of business with fullers.[41] "The washer of sheep-

---

40 Thanks are due to Robin Osborne for bringing this curious fact to light in an as yet unpublished lecture. For further details of the phenomenon itself, with pictures, see Milne and von Bothmer 1953. For further Aristophanic allusions, see pp. 71, 137, and 176, below.
41 The Alcibiadean Euaeon (Ar. *Ec.* 408–426) thus speaks of fullers in the context of cloaks: p. 169, below.

skins" replies Carion: an allusion to Lysicles the sheepseller (Plut. *Per.* 24.6), who may well have begun to associate with Aspasia before Pericles' death, and whom Socrates always addressed in terms of "sheep" and "fleeces" (D. Chr. 55.22); if so, the allusion will have been insulting addressed to a Periclean figure. "The tanner" says Chremylus (167); if we are now in the realm of Athenian politicians, an allusion to the tanner Cleon, Pericles' enemy (Plut. *Per.* 33.8) and Alcibiades' rival for Pericles' mantle in the 420s. "The onion seller" replies Carion: a reference to Pericles himself, or rather to his pointy head, of which he was extremely self-conscious (Plut. *Per.* 3.4–7). So far so good; each item in the list can be accounted for in terms of the recorded experiences, political or personal, of either Pericles or Alcibiades. If the next line was intended to hurt an Alcibiades, "through you the adulterer caught *in flagrante* gets plucked" (168), it must relate (whatever the precise nature of the punishment meted out)[42] to the amorous career of one who "when a young man, lured wives away from their husbands" (Bion *ap.* D.L. 4.49).

Wealth professes ignorance of all this (169), but his interlocutors go further, describing how the Great King depends on Wealth, how the Assembly meets on his account, and how he fills triremes (all of which, however, resonate with Alcibiades' career: it was on a journey to go and meet the Great King in 404 that Alcibiades met his death [Nep. *Alc.* 8–9], the Athenian Assembly certainly met on his account [e. g. Plut. *Alc.* 33.2], and not only did he fill many triremes, but he was extremely choosy about those on which he sailed himself [Lys. 21.6–7]). Then follow some topical contemporary references (173–80), before Wealth is described in terms which can easily be taken as relating to Alcibiades—he to whom Old Comedy owed its success (Lib. *fr.* 50.2.21): "Quite alone, you are the sole cause of all good and evil" (182–3). For several years, Alcibiades when alive was—like Wealth—indeed the prime mover of Athens' fortunes, for good or bad (recall "they love him, they hate him, they cannot do without him." Ar. *Ra.* 1425). Wealth's presence ensures success in battle (184–5); Alcibiades had "many victories both by sea and land" (Plut. *Alc.* 40.2) but was a notorious absentee from Athens' penultimate disaster at Arginusae (Plut. *Alc.* 36.6). Had he actually participated, victory would probably have been with the Athenians.

No one has enough riches, Wealth is told (187–8). There follows a litany of things of which it is possible to have a sufficiency (190–2). Chremylus' list consists entirely of commodities with Alcibiadean connotations: ἔρωτος ("love" or "Eros": 190 [see pp. 96, 108, 176, 185, below]; μουσικῆς ("music"): the teenaged Alcibiades had single-handedly rendered *aulos*-playing unfashionable at Athens (Plut. *Alc.* 2.5–7); τιμῆς ("honour": 191): Alcibiades in 415 seduced Timaea, a queen of

---

42 Discussed at some length by Sommerstein 2001, 144–6.

Sparta (Plut. *Ages.* 3.1–2); ἀνδραγαθίας ("bravery"): Alcibiades was said to have been "by far the most outstanding citizen in daring" (Diod. 13.37.2), while for Pliny he was "the bravest of the Greeks" (*HN* 34.12); φιλοτιμίας ("love of honour": 192): appropriate for Alcibiades in any case, but he is said to have stated that he did not seduce T̲i̲m̲aea out of *hubris*, but φιλοτιμούμενον ("seeking after the honour") of placing his own descendents on the throne of Sparta (Duris *FGrH* 76 F 76 *ap.* Plut. *Alc.* 32.2); στρατηγίας ("generalship"): Alcibiades had been general on numerous occasions (in 420/19, 419/18, perhaps in 418/17, in 417/16, 416/15, 415/14, 411/10, 410/9, 409/8, 408/7, and 407/6).[43]

Carion interposes with a series of comestibles. Just as the other catalogue seemed to reflect Alcibiadean interests, the contents of this list probably bear upon two things in which it was well known that Pericles was interested, *viz.* food and sex: ἄρτων ("bread": 190), τραγημάτων ("sweets"), πλακούντων ("flat-cakes": 191), ἰσχάδων ("dried figs"), μάζης ("barley-bread": 192), φακῆς ("lentil soup"). If this is indeed the case, the first item is clear: "bread" will relate to Pericles' involvement with the Athenian grain supply (e.g. Schol. *Ach.* 548). There is no direct evidence linking Pericles with "lentil soup", but the Periclean Philocleon in *Wasps* is made to consume quantities of it (*Ve.* 811, 814, 918, 984). The other items are all expressions with sexual overtones: τράγημα ("munchies": 190),[44] πλακοῦς ("phallus": 191),[45] ἰσχάς ("female member"),[46] μᾶζα ("shit-cake": 192).[47] Together they effectively summarise what it was popularly believed consenting Alcmaeonids got up to in private.

When Chremylus describes an existence where a man with thirteen talents has a consuming desire for sixteen, and given sixteen, he wants forty, he completes the catalogue with a double pun on Alci̲b̲iades' name: οὐ βιωτὸν αὐτῷ τὸν β̲ίο̲ν [R] ("life is not worth living": 197).[48] Chremylus' outline well corresponds to what we know of Alcibiades' financial conduct. When, for example, he married Hipparete, the daughter of a "man of great wealth and noble birth", she came with a dowry of ten talents. When she gave birth to their first child, he demanded and received an additional ten "as if he had made a previous agreement to that effect" (Plut. *Alc.* 8.3). Small wonder that Wealth (who might

43 Develin 1989, 142–8.
44 Henderson 1991, 144.
45 Henderson 1991, 129, 144, 160.
46 Henderson 1991, 118.
47 Henderson 1991, 194, 200–01.
48 The same expression is employed, again in a potentially Alcibiadean context, by the Hag at 969.

by now be thought to have a special insight into Alcibiadean ways of doing things) says that Chremylus has hit the nail on the head (198).

At 222 Carion is sent off to fetch Chremylus' fellow farmers. He duly leaves, drawing attention to his distinctive gait (καὶ δὴ βαδίζω: 227) as he goes. Chremylus invites Wealth, with flattering words, beneath his roof. Wealth is to fill the house with riches καὶ δικαίως κἀδίκως ("by fair means or foul": 233)—an indifference that is diametrically—and Aberdonically—opposed to Pericles' constant concern for δικαιοσύνη ("honesty", "incorruptibility": Plut. *Per.* 2.5).

Wealth is reluctant, citing two examples that once again have familiar resonances if Pericles and Alcibiades are in the frame. His stay with a φειδωλόν ("miser": 237–41) who kept his wealth hidden underground is perhaps an exaggerated version of both Pericles' public and private economy. In the Funeral Speech, Thucydides makes Pericles state that while the Athenians love the beautiful, yet they do so μετ' εὐτελείας ("thriftily": Thuc. 2.40.1), while at home, his son could not bear his father's ἀκριβείαν ("stinginess": Plut. *Per.* 36.2) nor could the women of the household (Plut. *Per.* 16.5). The other kind of ménage was that of a ne'erdowell (242) πόρναισι καὶ κύβοισι παραβεβλημένος ("dissipated with whores and dice": 243). Alcibiades was forever patronising "prostitutes foreign or Athenian" (Plut. *Alc.* 8.4), while his son, who emulated his father's vices, had but recently κατακυβεύσε ("diced away") his fortune (Lys. 14.27).

Chremylus promises (210) to restore Wealth's sight; Pericles, as we have seen, will have had something of an insight into optical ailments and their treatment. When Wealth hears that Phoebus Apollo knows of Chremylus' plan he utters a word of warning: ὁρᾶτε ("look out")—or perhaps pronounced ὀλᾶτε (cf. Ar. *Ve.* 45). Do not φρόντιζε ("concern yourself") says Chremylus (215); φρόνημα was "a fundamental attribute of the Plutarchean Pericles".[49] Chremylus assures Wealth that he will work things out "even if δέη ('it should be necessary') for me to die" (216). Not only was Pericles actually dead, but there may be another allusion here to Pericles' proverbial loss "for a necessary purpose" (see p. 67, above). Carion says he will do the same (217); Alcibiades was dead too. Chremylus' fellow-farmers, whom Carion is sent to fetch, are δίκαιοι ("just men")—an indication that they too may, polymorphically, be Periclean. And just in case this point is missed, it is reinforced by a reference to ἄλφιτα ("flour" or "daily bread": 219); Pericles had been responsible for the erection of the στοὰ ἀλφιτόπολις ("flour-market") at the Piraeus (Schol. Ar. *Ach.* 548). Chremylus' desire to give his fellows an equal share in what Wealth has to offer is entirely in keeping with the democratic façade that Pericles had found it expedient to adopt.

---

49 Stadter 1989, 75.

Wealth has never met a μετρίου ἀνδρός ("moderate man": 245) maintains Chremylus (245), nominating himself. Chremylus admits that he is more φειδόμε-νος ("parsimonious"; 247) than anyone else; we have just noted how Pericles' popular image was identical. Chremylus could spend money freely, whenever it δέῃ ("should be necessary": 248): perhaps yet another allusion to Pericles' "necessary purpose", and to his lavish expenditure from the public, rather than his private, purse. He wants to go indoors, to introduce Wealth to his wife and his only son (249–50): perhaps Aspasia and the younger Pericles are meant. The latter was in the public eye when Pericles begged the Athenians to allow him to be enrolled as a citizen against both the letter and spirit of Pericles' own citizenship law (Plut. *Per.* 37.2–5); he also perhaps stood for public office in 409/8 BC, when the first *Plutus* was performed. Chremylus' son is second in his affections only to Wealth (251).

Wealth's reply πείθομαι ("I am persuaded": 251) may have carried an "em-phatic" meaning, for persuasion was one of the things for which Alcibiades was famous, having won over many cities to friendship with Athens through his persuasive gifts (λόγῳ πείσας: Isoc. 16.21),[50] or perhaps it was a reminder of the youthful Alcibiades having been persuaded by flatterers (Plut. *Alc.* 6.1). Chremylus' question "why should one not tell the truth to you?" addressed to Ca-rion (252) perhaps alludes to Alcibiades' cavalier attitude to the truth that Plu-tarch put in a nutshell in describing him as πανοῦργος ἐν τῇ πολιτείᾳ καὶ ἀνα-λήθης ("a tricky and untruthful politician": *Alc.* 41.1). Carion then arrives with the Chorus of Countrymen, who are τοῦ πονεῖν ἐρασταί ("lovers of toil": 254). This must be shorthand for "Pericles' cronies", for the word πόνος ("blood, sweat and tears") was apparently such a prominent feature of Pericles" oratory that Thucydides artfully packs his last speech with several examples of the expres-sion, as we saw above in the context of *Philoctetes* 1422.[51]

---

50 And cf. Plutarch on the πιθανότης ("persuasiveness") of Alcibiades' speech: Plut. *Alc.* 1.6.
51 Thuc. 2.62.1, 62.3, 63.1, 64.3, 64.6; cf. Boegehold 1982, 154–5. For Thucydides' Sopho-clean models, see *Sophocles and Alcibiades*, 17, 67, 78.

Chapter 6

Home Economics: *Plutus* ii

When Chremylus returns (at 322), after the Chorus of Countrymen have sung their song, a transformation has taken place, and he has adopted quite another persona. There can be no doubt about this (although the change is generally overlooked by commentators), since it is specifically remarked on by Blepsidemus when he says "How much you have changed your ways from before" (365). The part he now plays is that of an Alcibiades. He greets Blepsidemus with ἀσπάζομαι ("I greet you warmly": 324), a pun on Aspasia's name, as we saw above. Chremylus' guests come συντεταμένως κοὐ κατεβακευμένως ("earnestly and not slothfully": 325), affected words of a kind Alcibiades was criticised for using as early as 426 (Ar. *PCG* 205.6–7). He asks that they become συμπαραστάται ("assistants": 326). συν- compounds are often used to denote membership of *hetareiai*—the political clubs that flourished at Athens in the later fifth century, to which Alcibiades was known to belong.[1]

There is yet more to learn from these συν- compounds, however, for the Ravenna manuscript preserves readings that may be significant. Those in the lines to be spoken by the Alcibiadeanizing Chremylus are spelt with the Ionic (and more up-to-date) *sigma*. Earlier in the play, when Chremylus was in Periclean mode, his lines have the older Attic *xi*: e.g. ξύμμαχοι (218), ξυγγεώργους (223); with Wealth's συμμάχους [R] at 220 neatly—and perhaps significantly—in between. This distinction may well be an important one, but it is one that is often lost in "one size fits all" editions where modern editors know better than the ancients. It was said by those who had heard both speak that Pericles' voice resembled that of Peisistratus (Plut. *Per.* 7.1), and this doubtless applied to his diction as well. Peisistratus, and consquently Pericles, will have used the more archaic ξυν-, whereas Alcibiades (and Alcibiadeanizing characters) will have tended to use "the parvenu συν-".[2]

Chremylus' Alcibiadean persona is reinforced at 332–4, when he announces Blepsidemus' arrival in terms which probably recalled Alcibiades' customary mode of speech. If Chremylus has been fully assimilated into his new role, he will have pronounced the ὁρῶ in καὶ μὴν ὁρῶ ("And now I see") as ὁλῶ, and an audience thus forewarned, on hearing the name Βλεψίδημον ("he who peers at the public") will have understood Πρεψίδημον ("he who is seemly

---

1 Aurenche 1974; Ostwald 1986, 537–50; Westlake 1989, 160.
2 Dunkel 1982, 56.

with the public"), an allusion to Pericles' having claimed to stand for τὸ πρέπον ("what is seemly"; cf. Thuc. 1.144.2; 2.36.1; 2.36.4):[3] the name is an appropriate one to give to another manifestation of Pericles.[4]

Chremylus describes the new situation in terms which possess the crazy logic of an Alcibiades trying to sell the Sicilian campaign to the Athenians (350–1). Blepsidemus smells a rat and voices his mistrust. The whole scheme, he says, is οὐδὲν ὑγιές ("unsound"). The word ὑγιές is frequently on the lips of Periclean characters: cf. 355, 356, 362, cf. 364, and it may be a glance in the direction of the miraculous incident during the construction of the Propylaea which resulted in the erection by Pericles of a statue of Athena Hygieia (Plut. *Per.* 13.13; *IG* I³ 824). Blepsidemus thinks (356–8) that Chremylus may have stolen precious metal from Apollo; Alcibiades purloined some of Athens' public plate (normally in the keeping of the goddess) for his Olympic celebration in 416 (Lys. 14.38), and Pericles was suspected of having conspired with Pheidias to embezzle gold from the chryselephantine statue of Athena (Plut. *Per.* 31.2–5). Chremylus counters at 366 with the sort of rough insult we last heard on Carion's lips: μελαγχολᾷς ("you are crazy"; cf. μελαγχολῶντ': 12).

Blepsidemus' suggestion for dealing with the matter is full of Periclean resonances. He wants (377–9) to do things ἀπὸ σμικροῦ ("for a trifle"): the Periclean "brevity" mannerism that we have already noted (p. 68, above). He also wants the task to be done before the whole city knows about it and observes that cash will stop up the orators' mouths. In attempting to hush things up Blepsidemus is behaving rather as Pericles did when Alcibiades ran away to the house of an admirer, and Pericles chose not to announce the fact publicly, lest it harm Alcibiades' reputation (Plut. *Alc.* 3.1). At 380–1, Chremylus suggests that Blepsidemus would like to spend three minae and λογίσασθαι ("charge for") twelve. This is perhaps a reference to Alcibiadean embezzlement, with an additional allusion to Pericles' difficulties in rendering his accounts, when Alcibiades supposedly suggested that Pericles should not be looking to a way to give an account (ἀποδοῦναι ... λόγον), but how not to do so (Diod. 12.38.2–3). Blepsidemus predicts (382–5) an image of a suppliant in the dock with his wife and children; the picture is not unlike that of Pericles appearing in court in defence of Aspasia (Aeschin. *ap.* Plut. *Per.* 32.5; cf. Ath. 13.589e), a report which may itself have been the fruit of comic invention.[5]

---

3 Cf. p. 146, below.
4 And it bears out Olson 1992, 306–9 on the importance of the "late" naming of comic heroes.
5 Wallace 1994.

Poverty

A proposal to have Wealth's sight restored (401–12) is about to be put into action when Poverty appears (415). In Aristophanes' game of Happy Families, she is characterised as Aspasia. There are several suggestive features, her pallid complexion, her tragic expression, and the charge of running a low class hotel, as we have seen (p. 63, above). Blepsidemus' fear of Poverty, moreover, reflects the historical Pericles' concern for domestic economy (Plut. *Per.* 16.5; p. 64, above).

There may also be an implicit reference to Thucydides here. We have already seen several instances of Thucydides' reliance on Aristophanes for details of his plotting, when the historian seems to have used the work of the playwright as an *aide-mémoire*. What we may have here is influence the other way round: the use of the historian by Aristophanes. Alternatively, Thucydides was relying on a copy of a 408 *Plutus*. If the *Histories* were, as it has recently been suggested, only written in 396–5, and immediately deposited in the Metroon or Public Record Office,[6] then Thucydides' works would have been in the public domain, and available for interested parties to consult. The *Menexenus* of *ca.* 385 has been taken as evidence for Plato having known Thucydides' writings,[7] and we can hardly expect Aristophanes to have ignored them. Either way, Thucydides' Pericles on the subject of poverty ("To admit to poverty is no disgrace: what is really disgraceful is not to διαφεύγειν ['flee'] from it" [Thuc. 2.40.1])[8] has much in common with the idolopoeïïc embodiments of Pericles and Alcibiades trying to flee from Poverty in *Plutus* (cf. φεύγομεν: 441). Thucydides' Pericles also spoke of "putting off" the evil day "in the hope, natural to poverty, that a man, though poor, may one day become rich" (Thuc. 2.42.4). To base Poverty on Aspasia would have been amusing, and especially so if in reality she had been instrumental in the composition of the Funeral Speech in which Pericles' observations occur (Pl. *Mx.* 236a-b); even more so if Pericles had indeed spent most of his wealth on Aspasia (Heracl. Pont. *fr.* 59 *ap.* Ath. 12.533c).

Poverty has never been ἀδικουμένη ("wronged") by Chremylus and Blepsidemus (457, cf. 428, 459, 460); the allusion being again to Pericles' reputation for δικαιοσύνη ("honesty"). Chremylus' reply at 461 contains more loaded language,

---

6 Munn 2000, 327; *Sophocles and Alcibiades*, 151–2.
7 Kahn 1996, 28.
8 Cf. Dem. 18.256: "No sensible man ... ever turns poverty into a reproach"; Missiou 1992, 38–9.

if ἐκπορίζομεν refers to Poristes, Aspasia's son by Lysicles (Schol. Pl. *Mx.* 235e).[9] Poverty is more than willing to δοῦναι λόγον ("give an account of herself": 467); another allusion, no doubt, to Pericles' difficulties in rendering his own accounts (ἀποδοῦναι λόγον: Diod. 12.38.2), as well to as Aspasia's reputation for philosophical debate. She had won renown as a teacher (διδάσκαλος: Pl. *Mx.* 235e; Ath. 5.219b); compare Poverty's καὶ σύ γε διδάσκου ("and you learn [what I have to say]": 472), and that Chremylus and Blepsidemus have to "learn" her truths (477).[10]

The ensuing debate (at 489–618) involves Chremylus in Alcibiadean mode, supported by the Periclean Blepsidemus, putting forward an argument which is diametrically opposed to the attested attitudes of the historical Pericles. In similar fashion, what Poverty says is greatly at variance from what we can deduce from the sources about Aspasia: she must have been one of the women in Pericles' household who complained that he was a skinflint, and who were in favour of greater expenditure (Plut. *Per.* 16.5). It is in any case unlikely that, as a wellborn Ionian, that she was abstemious (cf. Hdt 5.50; Ath. 12.523*f*-524c). It is an extreme manifestation of the "spendthrift Aberdonian" principle. Political economy takes second place to the major underlying conceit. (There is one possible context, however, in which the historical Aspasia might be thought of as having concerned herself with the Athenian economy: namely, the occasion when an exceptional property tax had been levied on the Athenians in 428, raising 200 talents, just before Lysicles' fatal fund-raising expedition to Caria in 428 [Thuc. 3.19.1]. If Aspasia was Lysicles' teacher in statesmanship, as was widely believed, hers may have been the brains behind these revenue-raising ventures.) The sophistic nature of Poverty's arguments[11] is, however, wholly in keeping with Aspasia's reputation as a σοφίστρια ("philosopheress": Schol. Ar. *Ach.* 527).

The passage at *Plutus* 527–534, where Poverty lists the luxuries which will cease to be available should everyone be rich, includes allusions to elements of not simply the anecdotal, but the historical, tradition relating to Alcibiades — (i) beds, (ii) perfumes and (iii) "richly woven *himatia* dyed with dazzling colours".

---

9 Poristes' existence as a historical figure has been doubted by some, e. g. Stadter 1989, 237; Kahn 1996. Solana Dueso 1994, xiii suggests that the name may have been an invention of the comic stage. Plutarch perhaps puns on "Poristes" at *Per.* 24.2 when he introduces Aspasia to his narrative: καιρὸς διαπορῆσαι μάλιστα περὶ τῆς ἀνθρώπου ("It is an excellent time to discuss this problematical woman").

10 McGlew 1997, 40. Cf. the Aspasian Jocasta's δίδαξον κἄμ' ("teach me too") at *OT* 697: *Sophocles and Alcibiades*, 45.

11 Cf. Olson 1990, 235–6, n. 44.

(i) Details of Alcibiades' beds were inscribed on a stele set up near the Eleusinion in the Athenian Agora in c. 414 where the confiscated property of those who had been found guilty of impiety was listed. Among the goods mentioned were: a χαμεύνη παράκολλος ("a low bed with only one end to it") and a κλίνη ἀμφικνέφαλλος (or more properly ἀμφικέφαλος [LSJ]: "a bed with cushions at both ends": Poll. 10.36), as well as leather, linen and woollen pillows (Poll. 10.38), all "belonging to Alcibiades"—information still freely available in the second century AD, and doubtless well known to Aristophanes' audience in 388 BC.

(ii) When in Sparta, Alcibiades adapted himself to his surroundings so well that one would never have believed he had ever laid eyes on a μυρεψόν ("*parfumier*": Plut. *Alc.* 23.3). The implication is that in other contexts perfumes might have figured large.

(iii) Alcibiades' rich garments were his most striking trademark; his *himatia* were the equivalent of Imelda Marcos' shoes. Whenever he served as *choregus*, he would enter the theatre wearing a πορφυρίς ("purple garment"), which "was admired not simply by the men, but by the women as well" (Sat. *FHG* 3.160 *ap.* Ath. 12.534c). We hear of him wearing a Milesian cloak (Μιλησία χλανίς: Plut. *Alc.* 23.4)—the best wool—and trailing his purple-dyed robe through the Agora (Plut. *Alc.* 16.1). Then, no fewer than 22 of his *himatia* were sold by public auction in 414.[12]

These allusions, in this combination, can only refer to Alcibiades.

The Visit to Asclepius

Chremylus' Wife is completely different in character from the Aspasian Poverty. She is passive, credulous and not very bright. By strict logic, if Chremylus "is" Pericles, then his "wife" should be Aspasia, but Chremylus has been temporarily transformed into an Alcibiades—which is why his wife is characterised as Hipparete, Alcibiades' long-suffering spouse. The daughter of Hipponicus, a man whose birth and wealth made him "a person of great influence and repute" (Plut. *Alc.* 8.1), Hipparete was "quiet and loving", as we have already seen. She appears elsewhere in Aristophanes' extant plays, for example: (i) in the scene in *Acharnians* where she shyly sends a message asking how she can get her husband's cock to stay at home (1040; p. 34 below), and (ii) in *Ecclesiazusae* where she lies behind both the somewhat ditsy Second Woman (the one who wishes that someone else could have spoken, while ἐκαθήμην ἥσυχος ["(she)

---

12 Pritchett 1953; 1956, 167, 190–210; 1961, 23.

sat quietly by"]), and the Girl who encounters the First Hag (see Chapter 11 below).

The Wife had been sitting in the women's quarters with desperate longing (642–3). Carion bids her bring some wine, that she might drink (he knows she likes a drop). Rogers intuitively translated τὰ πράγματα at 649 as "this striking business" wholly accurately, in that an Alcibiadizing Carion would have pronounced the word as πλάγματα, playing on πληγή ("blow"). The Wife later asks specifically that blows should not fall on her (651); Alcibiades had first made the acquaintance of Hipponicus, Hipparete's father, by striking him a blow with his fist (Plut. *Alc.* 8.1–3). Carion then says how first (πρῶτον, but presumably pronounced πλωτόν ["afloat"]) they took Wealth to the sea and bathed him there. This is surely an echo of the story that Alcibiades once took the playwright Eupolis (who had lampooned him in *Baptae*) and dipped him in the sea— a story that was later exaggerated so that Eupolis was said to have drowned.[13] The Wife's delight (657–8) that Wealth (a laconizing Alcibiades, recall) had been bathed in cold water may allude to the historical Alcibiades at Sparta, where not only had he been unfaithful to his wife, but had attracted criticism for having bathed in too much (cold) water (Plut. *Mor.* 235*a*). Again the poles of the wigwam circumscribe a kind of truth, if only the fruits of gossip rather than hard fact.

Aristophanes' blind or partially sighted characters are often cruel caricatures of a post-plague, bleary-eyed Pericles. Neocleides is one of them; he is twice taunted in this manner in *Ecclesiazusae* (see Chapter 11, below), and twice again in *Plutus*. Neocleides may well have been a real person, but it is Pericles and not Neocleides who is the κωμῳδούμενος. The first instance is at 665–6, where his name serves as a vehicle for in effect accusing Pericles of peculation on a widespread scale; the context is probably Pericles' reputation for incorruptibility, on the "spendthrift Aberdonian" principle. The second occurrence is at 715, where Carion describes how he saw Asclepius preparing a salve for Neocleides' eyes, which not only contained σκορόδων κεφαλάς ("heads of garlic": 718) but σχῖνον ("squill": 720); Pericles' pointy-headedness or schinocephaly was a constant cause of embarrassment to him, but of amusement to others (e. g. Plut. *Per.* 3.4–7: "The Attic playwrights called him 'squill-head'"). It will have been amusing too, to an audience conditioned to the finer points of cripple-teasing, to hear of the eyes of a Periclean figure besmeared with bitter

13 Cf. Nesselrath 2000 (who, however, seems to think that the story of the dipping was a "toned-down" version of a late tradition that Eupolis was drowned by Alcibiades; less likely, in my view).

balm (721), and then for him to be forced by Asclepius to refrain from attendance at assemblies (725); Pericles was notoriously keen on his civic duties (Plut. *Per.* 7.5). Once again, we have a cluster of features that can only refer to Pericles.

The god's treatment of Wealth by contrast, is gentle and considerate. His daughter Panacea covers his head and all his face with a φοινικίδι ("red sheet": 731), a significant item in terms of Alcibiades' history: when he was found guilty of the profanation of the Mysteries, "his property was confiscated, his name was put on a stele, and all the priests and priestesses were instructed to curse him. All ... except one duly did so, turning to the west and waving φοινικίδας ('red sheets')."[14] If there is a connection, then the clucking of the god (ἐπόπτυσεν: 732) perhaps plays on the ἐποπτεία, the highest grade of initiation into the Eleusinian Mysteries. The title of Ἐπόπται (those thus admitted) was bestowed on his friends by Alcibiades when they parodied the Mysteries in his house (Plut. *Alc.* 22.4), an allegation that had greatly contributed to his downfall in 415 BC. There is a widespread belief that the Mysteries were too sacred a business for them to be the subject of mockery on the stage, but this and other instances (the initiation scene in *Clouds*, the Epops in *Birds*, the profanation of the Hyacinthia, again in *Birds*)[15] suggest that this was not in fact the case. Such a reminder of Alcibiades' impiety would have been highly appropriate in 408, when the possibility of his return from exile was a hot political issue.

Wealth's speech on his arrival is replete with oblique allusions to Alcibiadean themes. The order in which he pays his respects implicitly (i.e. "emphatically") reveals his supposed priorities. καὶ προσκυνῶ γε πρῶτα μὲν τὸν ἥλιον ("And first I bow in adoration to the Sun" 771). There are two allusions to the Persian Empire in this line that commentators have overlooked. Proskynesis was the usual form of obeisance in Persia (e.g. Hdt. 1.134; Arr. *An.* 4.10–11),[16] and the Sun held a special place in the Achaemenid religion (e.g. Hdt. 7.54.2; Arr. *loc. cit.*). It was said of Alcibiades "when he came to the Persians, he so imitated their mode of life that they themselves greatly admired him" (Nep. *Alc.* 11.5). Only after Wealth has "played the Persian" does he pay his respects to Athens (772–3), but employing phraseology that makes it almost sound as though Attica were Alcibiades' own property: σεμνῆς Παλλάδος κλεινὸν πέδον ("the famous ground of holy Pallas"), where κλεινόν will again have played on Alcibiades' patronymic, ὁ Κλεινίου. Recall the similar word-play at Eur. *Ion* 30, 131, 262, and 1038 (p. 50, above).

---

14 Cf. D. M. Lewis 1966, 177 and 189.
15 *Pericles on Stage*, 35–6, 174, 187–8.
16 Briant 2002, 222–4. For Sophocles' use of the same metaphor in 409, see *Ph.* 533–4; *Sophocles and Alcibiades*, 73.

Wealth apologises for his past career, for the bad company he kept, and for having avoided those who were ἀξίους ("worthy") of his companionship (774–7). We do not know whether Alcibiades ever made such a speech on his return from exile in 407, but it was a fact often noted by his biographers that he kept bad company (e. g. Plut. *Alc.* 6.1–2). ἀξίους is a very pointed word, as we have noted in the context of Euripides' *Ion*, and it is carefully chosen so as to remind the audience of the tales of Alcibiades' ἀξίωμα ("social clout"). It was on account of his ἀξίωμα that Alcibiades was granted the prize for bravery at Potidaea in 431 over Socrates, who had really earned it (see pp. XII, 52 above), and Aristophanes is probably here "emphatically" alluding to this event. It was Socrates, moreover, who attempted to shield Alcibiades from bad company (Plut. *Alc.* 4.1), and it was Alcibiades who avoided his companionship (Plat. *Smp.* 216a-c). Plato also plays on Alcibiades' ἀξίωμα in making him confess to Socrates that "of all the admirers I have ever had, you are the only one who is ἄξιος of me" (*Smp.* 218d).

The Honest Man and the Sycophant

Wealth is only present on the stage for fifty of the remaining 956 lines of the play,[17] but the Alcibiadean persona he embodies is nevertheless present in various other characters: the Young Man, Hermes, the Priest of Zeus and, of course, Carion. Pericles still "comes forward", as the Honest Man and the Sycophant (and Chremylus, now back in Periclean mode), while Aspasia underlies the Hag. There are in fact three categories of scene involving the new arrivals in the second half of *Plutus*: the first scene with the Honest Man and the Sycophant is Periclean; the central scene (with the Hag, Chremylus and the Young Man) includes Aspasian, Periclean and Alcibiadean figures, while the last scene (with Hermes and the Priest of Zeus) balances the first, and is Alcibiadean. κωμῳδούμενοι are thus on stage all the time, and if they were appropriately masked (cf. Platon. 1.64–6), no one in the audience would have noticed any "lack of continuity".

Carion sings at 802–22 of the good fortune that has come everyone's way (or at least the way of honest folk). There then arrives a Δικαῖος ("Honest Man"), whose Periclean persona is quickly established by means of the diminutive παιδάριον ("young man" 823; cf. σκευαρίων ["little vessels"] at 839]).[18] The question as to what he needs (τοῦ δέει; 827) recalls Pericles' proverbial loss "for a necessary pur-

---

17 Sommerstein 2001, 27.
18 See further, pp. 83, n. 20, 127, 153–4, 159 below.

pose" (see p. 67, above). The Honest Man's experiences accurately reflect Pericles' political career: he squandered the public purse in the false hope that his generosity would be repaid in his hour of need. Then, in the realm of fantasy, Wealth has come to his aid, having recognised his virtues. The next arrival is a Sycophant, or informer, who reflects the negative side of Pericles, namely his tendency to πολυπραγμοσύνη ("political meddling"). Thucydides makes a delicate allusion to this by making his Pericles criticise ἀπραγμοσύνη ("political apathy"); here, we might compare the Sycophant's criticism of προβατίου βίον ("a sheep's life") at 922, which will not have been without an "emphatic" glance at Pericles' successor Lysicles, the "sheep-seller".

Pericles' tendency to repeat himself, which we shall often have occasion to note, helps to explain a feature of the Sycophant's language. This characteristic is lampooned in the degree to which the Sycophant says that he is unfortunate: three, four, five, twelve, 10,000 times (850–2), followed by the duplicated ἰοὺ ἰού. Then there is the repetition of closely related concepts: τεμαχῶν καὶ κρεῶν ("meat and flesh": 894), ὦ Ζεῦ καὶ θεοί ("O Zeus and gods": 898) and χρηστός... καὶ φιλόπολις ("virtuous and patriotic": 900). These are all in the same category as Thucydides' gentler lampoon: φρονήματι ("confidence") and καταφρονήματι ("a sense of superiority") at 2.62.3. Carion goes too far in nailing shoes to the Sycophant's face (942–3), though it is a characteristically violent and illogical action if Alcibiades is in question. Finally, the Sycophant's denunciation of Wealth as single-handedly overthrowing democracy (948–50)—a most serious charge—is a fair assessment of Alcibiades' political achievement. Anyone found guilty "was not only liable to the death penalty, but could be killed without trial and with impunity": [19] If the lines belonged to the 408 version of Plutus, it will show Aristophanes as having been vehemently opposed to Alcibiades' return.

Ménage à trois

The arrival of the Hag (959) marks the return of Aspasia to the stage, this time interacting with a dramatic analogue of Pericles with whom she appears to share the secrets of an illicit love-affair she has had with Alcibiades. The possible sources of the conceit are discussed in Appendix 1. Chremylus, who has reverted to his Periclean persona, is meant to be a stranger, but behaves in a very affectionate manner towards the new arrival, calling her by a diminutive μειρακίσκη ("young lady": 963); Pericles was very attentive towards Aspasia, and would kiss and caress her at every

---

19 Sommerstein 2001, 198.

opportunity. Chremylus' renewed Periclean status is clear from the repetition of ἐξε-λήλυθα ("I have come out": 965) and ἐλήλυθας ("you have come": 966), such repetitiveness being a Periclean marker, as will become very apparent later in this book (see pp. 85, 140–1, 144, 153, below). The subject of the Hag's complaint is made known to the audience, if not to Chremylus, by means of ἀβίωτον ... τὸν βίον ("life is not worth living"), which again puns on Alcibiades. Chremylus does not understand, but poses a question which establishes the characterisation of the Hag as Aspasia even more firmly. "Are you a συκοφάντρια ('she-sycophant'; 970)?" which recalls the roles of προμνήστρια ("matchmaker": Xen. *Mem.* 2.6.36), σοφίστρια ("philosopheress": Schol. Ar. *Ach.* 527) and perhaps πανδοκεύτρια ("brothel-keeper"; cf. *Plut.* 426), played elsewhere by Aspasia.

At 975 ff. the Hag confides in Chremylus the nature of her κνισμός ("itch"). She has the hots for a μειράκιον ("young lad"), who is πενιχρόν ("impecunious"), εὐπρόσωπον καὶ καλόν ("handsome and goodlooking": 976). Alcibiades' youth was a perennial issue, as we have seen, and at the time of any liaison—real or imaginary—with Aspasia he would have been young in any case); he was chronically short of money (e. g. Thuc. 6.15.3; cf. 6.12.2); he was famous for his physical beauty (e. g. Plut. *Alc.* 1.4; Ael. *VH* 12.14). The lad would beg money from her to buy a *himation* and shoes (983). Alcibiades' *himatia* were famous (see p. 78, above), and he also wore distinctive shoes called "Alcibiades" (Satyr. *FHG* 3.160 *ap.* Ath. 12.534c). The young man also wanted to buy a χιτώνιον ("little gown") for his sisters (984), and a ἱματίδιον ("little *himation*") for his mother (985).[20] We enter deep waters here, for it was said of Alcibiades by a contemporary that he was so debauched that "he lay with his mother, his sister and his daughter" (Antisth. 29*a* Caizzi *ap.* Ath. 5.220*a*; Lys. 14.29),[21] and even though the charge may well have been an invention of the comic stage, it provides an explanation for the young man's requests, and keeps Alcibiades' profligacy in the frame.

The respect that the young man showed for the Hag was immense: cf. ἐκνομίως (981) and ἐκνομιώτατα (992), literally "beyond the law". This recalls Thucydides' characterization of Alcibiades' personal conduct as παρανομία ("lawlessness" or even "perversion":[22] 6.15.4; cf. 6.28.2; Lys. 14.42). Adultery with a stepmother was

---

20 This (and χιτώνιον) must be the "wheedling" use of the diminutive: Ferguson 1977, 231. And are the χρυσιδάριον ("a little bit of gold"), ἱματιδάριον ("a little *himation*"), λοιδοριμάτιον ("a little insult"), and νοσημάτιον ("a little illness") in *Babylonians* (Ar. *PCG* 92 *ap.* Arist. *Rhet.* 1405b28) something similar?

21 See Vickers 2000; *Sophocles and Alcibiades*, 34–46, and Appendix 1, below.

22 Munn 2000, 120, 386.

much frowned upon.[23] ἐκνομίως is spoken by the Hag, and ἐκνομιώτατα by Chremylus, thus imputing a degree of mistaken complaisance on Pericles' part. Aristophanes shows Pericles as apparently complicit in his own cuckolding throughout the scene. When the nameless young man reportedly rejects the Aspasian Hag's overtures, it is with a tag of Anacreon's saying that the Milesians are not up to it any more (1002): highly appropriate in view of Aspasia's Milesian origins. τρόπους ("ways of doing things": 1003) probably alludes once again to Alcibiades' singular sex education at Abydos (see p. 68, above).

There are elements in what follows that can be associated with either Aspasia or Alcibiades: taken separately they are but poles, but collectively they constitute a wigwam. The young man would visit the Hag with a view to hearing her voice; Aspasia, who is said to have taught rhetoric to both Pericles and Lysicles, and who was lampooned as a nightingale in *Birds* and as Praxagora in *Ecclesiazusae*,[24] might well be thought of as having a distinctive voice. He would cheer her up when she was λυπουμένην ("distressed": 1010) with endearments: νηττάριον ("ducky") and φάττιον ("dovey": 1011), of a kind that might have more properly been addressed to Aspasia by Pericles. λυπουμένη, moreover, is the word Plutarch (who will have read—and understood—his Aristophanes)[25] uses to describe Hipparete's distress at Alcibiades' philanderings (Plut. *Alc.* 8.4). The reference to the young man's shoes (1012) again recalls Alcibiades' fashionable footwear. The Hag's complains that whenever her jealous boyfriend saw anyone looking at her in public, she was "beaten" (ἐτυπτόμην: 1015) all day long. The word may not simply carry the secondary secondary meaning of "banged",[26] but may also be a literal allusion to Alcibiades' propensity to violence and fisticuffs, as well as Aspasia's own readiness to throw a punch (hinted at at Pl. *Mx.* 236b-c). When the Young Man eventually arrives, there are not-so-concealed references (πορεύεται ["is coming"]: 1041 and ἀσπάζομαι ["I greet you"]: 1042) to Aspasia's son Poristes and, appropriately, Aspasia herself.

Chremylus joins in the abuse of the Hag in terms which are a farcical reversal of Periclean reality. The imagery in which she might go up in flames like an old funerary wreath[27] if a spark should fall on her (1053–4); her paucity of teeth (1058–9); her heavy make-up (1063–5), are insulting in any case, but their force would be greatly enriched if they came from a Periclean figure. The Young Man (who, if he

---

23 Barrett 1964, 12, n.1; cf. Watson 1995, 82, n. 115.
24 *Pericles on Stage*, 176–8 (nightingale), Chapter 11, below (Praxagora).
25 He seems to have had access to books on κωμῳδούμενοι: Stadter 1989, lxix-lxvi, 242, 297.
26 Henderson 1991, 172
27 Cf. *IG* III.1337; Alciphron 3.37 [2.35]; Eup. *PCG* 131; Ar. *Eq.* 729. The word is conventionally translated "harvest wreath", which misses the point.

"comes forward" as Alcibiades, must lambdacise) makes the accusation that Chremylus πειρᾷ ("is trying to seduce") the Hag (1067), but with a play on πηλ- ("knead") and τῶν τιτθίων ἐφάπτεται ("grabs her tits": 1067–8). The Hag protests at Chremylus' actions (1069); again highly amusing if it is an "Aspasia" rejecting the advances of a "Pericles". Chremylus repeats the charge that the Milesians are no longer any good (1074–5), and the Young Man offers to let Chremylus have the Hag as his own (1076–9). Chremylus' response (1080) is full of significant words: οἶδ' οἶδα τὸν νοῦν ("I know, I know what you are thinking"): Periclean repetition as well as an allusion to Νοῦς ("Mind") the nickname of Pericles' favourite philosopher Anaxagoras (Plut. *Per.* 4.6; Plat. *Phd.* 97b-d). οὐκέτ' ἀξιοῖς ("you do not think it worthwhile ...") will relate once more to Alcibiades' ἀξίωμα ("reputation").

If the Young Man lambdacizes, there will have been a splendid pun at 1082: "οὐκ ἂν διαλεχθείην ('I would not have anything to do') with someone who has slept through 13,000 suns/slept with 13,000 men". An audience attuned to lambdacism would have understood οὐκ ἂν διαρραχθείην ("I would not ejaculate").[28] There is another possible allusion to Alcibiades' ἀξίωμα at 1084, as well as to his boozing (Pliny included him in a list of the most famous topers of all time [Pliny *HN* 14.144; cf. Plut.; *Mor.* 800d]): "since you ἠξίους ('saw fit') to drink the wine, you ought to drink τὴν τρύγα ('the dregs')". Even more relevant is Alcibiades' characterisation as Trygaeus in *Peace*.[29] And when eventually they enter the house, Chremylus assures the Young Man that the Hag will οὐ βιάζεται ("not rape") him—a play on Alcibiades. The scene ends with the not merely complaisant, but blissfully unaware, Chremylus swearing ὦ Ζεῦ βασιλεῦ (redolent both of Pericles' "Olympian" status and the charges of kingship brought against him), and saying in effect how sweet it is that the γρᾴδιον ("little old lady": a diminutive) clings like a limpet to the Young Man—which puts the figure of Pericles who underlies Chremylus in an embarassingly stupid light.

Hermes and the Priest of Zeus

Hermes (on whose Alcibiadean associations see p. 61, above) is the next visitor (1099), and the dialogue between him and Carion is not calculated to flatter Alcibiades' memory. The humour is enhanced by the fact that both characters are based on him, the one the servant of Zeus, and the other the servant of the dramatic analogue of the "Olympian". Thus, when Hermes tells Carion to bring out

---

28 διαρρήγνυμι, pass. burst ... with passion: LSJ.
29 *Pericles on Stage*, 139–41.

everyone in the household, and places Carion way down the list between the dog and the pig (1103–6), he in effect demeans himself. When Hermes complains about the lack of offerings (1120–3), Carion knowingly remarks that even when Hermes did receive offerings in the past, he would wrong the donors; Alcibiades' admirers would shower him with gifts, but he would treat them shabbily (e. g. Plut. *Alc.* 4.5–6; Schol. Luc. 20.16). Hermes wants to ditch the gods and settle *chez* Chremylus on the grounds that things are better there. "Does desertion seem smart to you?" asks Carion (1150), to be told by Hermes that "My land is wherever one can do well" (1151). Athens' most famous deserter was Alcibiades, and he was famous for being able to make himself at home and "do well" anywhere (e.g. Plut. *Alc.* 23.4–6). Alcibiades' fickle character is well brought out by the suggestion that Hermes might be a στροφαῖον ("hinge-god"), a proposal that is milked for all its potential humour (1154) as it is being rejected. Nor does Athens need a Hermes παλιγκάπηλον ("double-dealing": 1156), a word which again well reflects Alcibiadean reality.[30] There is no need for a trickster or a leader either. Finally, Hermes suggests, and successfully, that he should become god of music and gymnastics; ironic in that Alcibiades had been less than brilliant at both; he had personally rendered the *aulos* unfashionable (Plut. *Alc.* 2.5–7) and was much more interested in chariot-racing than athletics (Isoc. 16.33).

There then arrives a Priest of Zeus whose opening line: Τίς ἂν φράσειε ποῦ 'στι Χρεμύλος μοι σαφῶς; ("Could someone possibly tell me where precisely Chremylus is?" 1171) is couched in terms that recall Alcibiades' use of the potential optative.[31] The Priest claims to be dying of hunger, since he has had nothing to eat, for all that he is the Priest of Zeus Soter. Alcibiades must have eaten his fill on the day in 416 when he famously won an Olympic victory and personally dedicated to Zeus "a great number of sacrificial animals" (Plut. *Alc.* 12.1; Andoc. 3.30; Satyr. *FHG* 3.160 *ap.* Ath. 12.534a), i.e. an opportunity for eating well.[32] The Priest's explanation for this unfortunate state of affairs, θύειν ἔτ᾽ οὐδεὶς ἀξιοῖ ("no one thinks it appropriate to sacrifice now") not only strikes an Alcibiadean sacrificial note, but alludes again to his ἀξίωμα. The Priest has had the same treacherous idea as Hermes (and Alcibiades all those years ago), namely to cut free from his traditional roots (1186–7). Chremylus then announces that Zeus has already come himself (1189). No need for scholarly fuss here; it is sim-

---

30 Cf. Plutarch's ἐπαμφοτερίζοντα τὸν Ἀλκιβιάδην: his propensity for double-dealing and general untrustworthiness (*Alc.* 25.7).
31 Tompkins 1972, 214, n. 58, and cf. pp. 102, 144, below.
32 See D. Gill, 1974, esp. p. 129.

ply a reference to the "Olympian" who lives in Chremylus' house in any case.[33] His epithet σωτήρ ("Saviour"), with its emphasis on safety and caution well reflects a Periclean policy that attracted criticism in public debate as well as satire on the comic stage.

The Finale

The farcical culmination is to place Wealth in the Opisthodomus of the Parthenon "where he was formerly installed" (1193). There are slight hints in the sources that Alcibiades was a Treasury official for, unless he held a position as "Schatzmeister auf der Burg",[34] how could he possibly have laid hands on the city's ceremonial plate for use at his elaborate Olympic celebration in 416 ([Andoc.] 4.29)? The sacrifices at Wealth's installation are to be of the meanest sort, however—both in contrast to Alcibiades' extravagance and in keeping with (or more likely, in perverse exaggeration of) Pericles' economical habits. Wealth does not in fact appear on stage; instead the Hag unexpectedly pops out, and is told by Chremylus to put some pots on her κεφαλῆς ("head"), and to carry them σεμνῶς ("respectably"). Pericles' head, it need hardly be repeated, was a constant object of fun for comic writers, and σεμνότης ("respectability") was one of the political virtues he constantly practised.[35] Aspasia's trade by contrast was said to have been in no way respectable (οὐδὲ σεμνή: Plut. *Per.* 24.5). Chremylus' promise that the Hag's Young Man will come in the evening is not only a final example of the Periclean character unwittingly collaborating in his own shame, but a reminder that the plot is really concerned with the ridiculous contortions that could still be achieved using the puppets Aristophanes had crafted over the years, rather than with economic theory as such. To the extent that there is an economic message, it is essentially a defence of traditional, rather than new, wealth in keeping with Aristophanes' earlier work;[36] it does not represent a radical change of view in favour of utopian socialism on the playwright's part.[37]

---

33 "The archetypal miser in this play is Zeus" (Sommerstein 1984, 332), and we have noted above (p. 72) how Wealth's reported stay with a miser at 237–41 evoked Pericles' reputation for parsimony.
34 Boeckh 1886, 252, in the context of Poll. 10. 126 (a puzzling reference to bronze weights dedicated on the Acropolis "in the archonship of Alcibiades").
35 Stadter 1989, xxxiii.
36 Lévy 1997, 212.
37 As Sommerstein 1984; Macdowell 1995, 334–5.

Aristophanes' witty conflation of the depressed condition of Athens in 388 with the stock characters of much of his preceding work is a dramatic *tour de force*. When the play is read as a fresh variation on old themes, problems of continuity melt away. Small wonder that *Plutus* was placed at the head of the plays included in the collection that has come down to us in the Ravenna codex. *Plutus* is the play that best introduces the *dramatis personae*, the members of the not-so-Happy Family who are the principal κωμῳδούμενοι in the plays we have. This is in fact what we learn from the sources: "many songs and jests were written about Pericles" (Plut. *Per.* 33.7–8); Aspasia "figured large in the work of comic writers" (Did. *ap.* Clem. Al. *Strom.* 4.19.122); and "what play did not include [Alcibiades] among the cast of characters? ... It is to him that comedy owed its success" (Lib. 5.644.5–7]).

Chapter 7

"The Woman of Old": Euripides' *Helen* and *Andromeda*

> Dictes moy ou, n'en quel pays,
> Est Flora, la belle Rommaine;
> Archipiada, ne Thaïs
> Qui fut sa cousine germaine;
>
> ....
>
> Mais ou sont les neiges d'antan?
> François Villon,
> *Ballade de dames du temps jadis*

We have already seen Aristophanes reacting to Euripides' pro-Alcibiadean propaganda in the discussions of *Ion* and *Plutus*. This chapter and the next are primarily concerned with three plays that were performed at the same celebration of the City Dionysia of 411 BC, namely Euripides' *Helen* and *Andromeda,* and Aristophanes' *Lysistrata*. Aristophanes was to parody *Helen* and *Andromeda* in *Thesmophoriazusae* the following year, and this will be discussed in Chapter 9. In *Birds*, it was Alcibiades' proposals that the Spartans should fortify Decelea in Attica that provided the basis for the plotting of the play, and Aristophanes showed him making the Spartans dance to his tune. Plutarch tells us how Alcibiades achieved this:

> The renown which he earned by [his] public services was equalled by the admiration he attracted to his private life; he captivated and won over everybody by his conformity to Spartan habits. People who saw him wearing his hair close cut, bathing in cold water, eating coarse meal, and dining on black broth, doubted, or rather could not believe, that he ever had a cook in his house, or had ever seen a perfumer, or had worn a mantle of Milesian purple. (Plut. *Alc.* 23.3).

Whether or not the tales of Alcibiades' involvement with Timaea, Agis' wife, were true, they were told and widely believed at Athens. For from the beginning of his exile, Alcibiades continued to exercise a "powerful hold ... on the Athenian imagination ... For while he was busily reconstructing a base of power among the Spartans, his visionary politics and theology were being played out in the Athenian theater".[1] Indeed, Athenian drama performed the function of experimental politics, where policies could be discussed, or prominent personalities supported or ridiculed in ways that would not be possible in more conventional political

---

1 Munn 2000, 124.

meetings, not least because some of the protagonists might be absent from Athens.

Euripides and Aristophanes played a prominent role in these developments. By 411 BC, Euripides was probably in Alcibiades' pocket, as we have seen. He had composed an ode in praise of Alcibiades' victory at Olympia in 416 BC (Plut. *Alc.* 11.3; Eur. 755.5 Page) and was presumably paid handsomely for it (see p. 45, above). And if Euripides was not paid (which is unlikely), he will have been closer still to Alcibiades than a client-patron relationship would imply.

What especially arouses suspicion is the fact that Euripides attributed first, second and third places to his patron; in fact, Alcibiades was placed first, second and *fourth* (Thuc. 6.16.2). To make matters worse, the winning team at Olympia did not belong to Alcibiades anyway, but "thanks to his influence with the judges of the games, Alcibiades stole this team and raced it himself" ([Andoc.] 4.26), taking "for himself the glory of the victory" (Diod. 13.74.3). This was a notorious scandal, and law-suits were still running twenty years later.[2] Given these circumstances, it is fair to regard Euripides as being now potentially sympathetic towards Alcibiades on the stage, as indeed *Helen* of 411 BC illustrates (and as Aristophanes definitely is not in *Thesmophoriazusae* of the following year, 410 BC).

Chronology

Some readers may well be puzzled by these dates, for the plays are now conventionally dated to 412 and 411 BC respectively. Everything hinges on the date of *Thesmophoriazusae*, for which, however, the relevant testimonia are contradictory and evenly balanced (see *HCT* 5, 184–93). Arguments will be presented in Chapter 9 in support of the view that *Thesmophoriazusae* was performed in 410 BC and that it closely reflects the events of the previous year, namely the imprisonment of Alcibiades by Tissaphernes late in 411 BC and Alcibiades' subsequent escape.

If *Thesmophoriazusae* were to be securely fixed in 410, there would be certain ramifications. If the play was performed at the City Dionysia of that year, this would free up the City Dionysia of 411 BC for *Lysistrata*, whose panhellenic theme is *prima facie* more appropriate for the Dionysian celebration, as even those who wish to force it into a Lenaean straightjacket admit.[3] There is a knock-on effect, too, with

---

2 Isoc. 16, cf. Vickers 1999; *Sophocles and Alcibiades*, 115–32.
3 E.g. Sommerstein 1977, 117.

regard to the *Helen* and the lost *Andromeda* performed "the year before" *Thesmophoriazusae*, and consequently in 411 rather than 412 BC, again presumably at the Dionysia. *Helen* and *Andromeda* too probably reflect recent events: this time, Alcibiades' somewhat more peaceful sojourn at the court of Tissaphernes which began towards the end of 412 BC, when, however, his existence—for all the luxury he enjoyed—was technically slavery (see Appendix 1, below). It will be argued in Chapter 9 that the Kinsman's captivity at the hands of the Scythian archer in *Thesmophoriazusae* resembles Alcibiades' later experiences, when he was imprisoned by Tissaphernes in 411 BC, too much to be coincidental. In similar fashion, Euripides' plotting follows, rather than prefigures, historical events.

Until recently, Euripides' *Helen* has bewildered commentators. "What are we to make of this play?" asked A.M. Dale.[4] "Rich but weak, brilliant and yet baffling" was the consensus at the beginning of the last century;[5] this view has only just begun to change, and A.C. Pearson's opinion that "no political bias is discoverable in the play"[6] has only recently begun to be effectively challenged. E. Delebecque and H. Grégoire, it is true, made some important observations regarding political allusions in *Helen*,[7] but these did not make much of an impression,[8] and since Delebecque considered that *Helen* was performed in 412 BC, many of his political analogies unfortunately miss the mark. Now, however, "recognizing Alcibiades in Euripides' *Helen* accounts for many of the singular aspects of that play". Thus Mark Munn in a discussion largely based on an earlier version of this chapter.[9] When Aristophanes parodies *Helen* he lampoons Alcibiades, as we shall see. It will be suggested here that Euripides too may have imbued the role of the heroine with Alcibiadean echoes, but rather than making fun of Alcibiades, makes out a case for his forgiveness and for his return to Athens. If so, this might explain both the unusual plot—in which Helen's reputation was rendered spotless, and Aristophanes' apparent antagonism towards Euripides in the following year.

---

4 Dale 1967, vii.
5 Verrall 1905, 43.
6 Pearson 1903, xvii.
7 Delebecque 1951, 338–346; Grégoire 1961, 11 ff.
8 Thus neither Dale 1967 nor Kannicht 1969 cites Delebecque's work, and Grégoire is usually only cited to be dismissed (e. g. Zuntz 1963, 156–8; Podlecki 1970, 417, 42; Segal 1971, 563).
9 Munn 2000, 132–3; cf. Vickers 1989a.

"Archipiada"

First, though, we must provide the framework within which Alcibiades could possibly be thought of in a feminine context. His "ambivalent sexuality"[10] is a constant theme of Plutarch's account of his career, from the charge made against the youthful wrestler that he bit his opponent "like a woman" (Plut. *Alc.* 2.3) to Alcibiades having been dressed for his funeral by his mistress Timandra in her own clothes (*ibid.*, 39.7). But our richest source concerning Alcibiades' complex sexuality (or more accurately, perhaps, the richest accumulation of material derived from the anecdotal tradition)[11] is to be found in the works of Libanius (he who once expressed the view that it was to Alcibiades that Old Comedy owed its success: Lib. *fr.* 50.2.21). He makes his Timon assert that "Alcibiades [was] in no way inferior to Omphale in his powers of seduction" (Lib. *Decl.* 12.17), and that "he is a sodomite at symposia and effeminate when drunk; he is ἀνδρόγυνος ('womanish') in the evening, changing his nature more than Proteus" (Lib. *Decl.* 12.42 [probably based on lines of a lost comedy: *CAF* 3.398.5]).[12] He also speaks of the youthful Alcibiades having run away from home to the house of an admirer; of his having taken a mistress when under age, "suffering terrible things, but performing worse", and boasting that "dressed in women's clothes ... he attended symposia undetected" [Lib. *fr.* 50.2.12–13]). If Alcibiades boasted of what he did, it will hardly have remained a secret, and I have argued elsewhere that his cross-dressing was a major contributory factor in Sophocles' decision in 439/38 BC to evoke the teenage Alcibiades on stage as Antigone.[13]

Libanius may have been writing much later than the events in question, but his account is borne out in part at least by other sources. Alcibiades' running away from home to the house of an admirer as a boy is related by Plutarch (*Alc.* 3.1), and now that we know of Alcibiades' sometime effeminacy we can make sense

---

10 Duff 2004, 9; Cf. Nussbaum 1986, 194 on "the sexual contradictions of Alcibiades' aspirations"; B.S. Strauss 1993, 171 on Alcibiades' "ambivalent gender"; and Moruzzi 2000, 143 on how "Alcibiades masked a consistent feminine masquerade".

11 Schouler 1984, 626–34; cf. Norman 1960, 122–26.

12 There was, as Martin Ostwald once reminded me, a medieval tradition that Alcibiades actually was a woman. Thus Alcibiades (or "Archipiada") appears in François Villon's *Ballade de dames du temps jadis* (p. 89, above), and the author of the pseudo-Aquinan commentary on the *De Consolatione philosophiae* of Boethius believed that "Alcibiades mulier fuit pulcherrima". Jean de Meun, author of the *Roman de la Rose*, speaks of "Alcipiadès" in the context of feminine beauty, and even Petrarch, it seems, may have thought of him as a woman. The question is fully discussed (though without any indication of possible pre-medieval sources) by Thuasne 1923, 624–43.

13 Vickers 2007; *Sophocles and Alcibiades*, 26–7.

of what had been a puzzling remark made by Plutarch elsewhere in the *Life of Alcibiades*. In elaborating on Alcibiades' ever changing character Plutarch compares him to a chameleon, "a creature which cannot, indeed, turn itself white, but Alcibiades never found anything, good or bad, which he could not imitate to the life ... In Lacedaemon you would say, looking at his appearance, 'It is not the son of Achilles, but Achilles himself'. He was just such a man as Lycurgus himself would have brought up, but if you examined his habits and actions more closely, you would say: 'It is the woman of old (ἔστιν ἡ πάλαι γυνή)'". (Plut. *Alc.* 23.5–6). The reference, from Euripides' *Orestes* (line 129), is moreover specifically to Helen and her "irrepressible vanity".[14] In the light of these stories, it is not difficult to see Alcibiades somehow underlying the figure of Helen. It is likely that Alcibiades had already been shown on the comic stage transgressing gender roles, perhaps in Eupolis' *Baptae* of 424–415 BC (though for several reasons 416 BC is perhaps the best date). Here we can at least probably see Alcibiades as "a transvestite devotee of the Thracian goddess Cotytto",[15] if not actually playing the part of the "coarse, lewd deity" herself. As we shall presently see, Alcibiades also underlies the principal character in *Lysistrata*, (Chapter 8), probably performed within a few days of *Helen* in the spring of 411 BC.

But to return to *Helen*. To begin with, let us establish a basis for a possible Helen/Alcibiades equation by examining a passage in which Euripides appears to play with extreme delicacy on some of Alcibiades' recent experiences. Not for nothing did Quintilian call Euripides *sententiis densus* ("the master of oblique allusion"; *Inst.* 10.1.68). Alcibiades was suspected of involvement in the mutilation of the Herms (Thuc. 6.28.2), statues sacred to Hermes the son of Maia (Apollod. 3.10). He was then recalled from Sicily (Thuc. 6.53.1), an island whose geography and customs will have been well known at Athens in 411 BC. At one time, "the younger Athenians" had been so enthused by Alcibiades with the prospect of Sicilian conquests that "many of them would spend their time ... drawing sketches of the shape of the island of Sicily (Plut. *Alc.* 17.4)". At one end of Sicily lay Drepana (modern Trapani) and at the other Syracuse, a city whose equivalent of ostracism was petalism (when olive leaves were used instead of *ostraka* [pieces of tortoiseshell,[16] or sometimes broken potsherds]: Diod. 11.87). After this, Alcibiades went to Sparta (Thuc. 6.88.9), whose most famous sanctuary was the Temple of Athena of the Brazen House (e.g. Thuc. 1.134.1). At *Helen* 241–5, Helen explains how she was carried away: the swiftfooted son of Maia

---

14 Munn 2000, 133.
15 Munn 2000, 133.
16 The primary meaning of the word is "ceratinaceous tissue", cf. Francis and Vickers 1988, 145–6, n. 20.

(τὸν ὠκύπουν … Μαιάδος γόνον) was sent to fetch her. He seized her as she was plucking (δρεπομέναν) fresh rose petals (πέταλα) on her way to the temple of Χαλκίοικον … Ἀθάναν ("Athena of the Brazen House"). This sequence seems consistently to follow the outlines of Alcibiades' story, from Athens to Sicily and on to Sparta. If it is not accidental (and Euripides was being uncharacteristically insensitive if it is), then perhaps we may be allowed to see echoes of Alcibiades in Helen elsewhere in the play.

Egypt

By 412 BC, Alcibiades was operating in Asia Minor in the Spartan interest, based at Magnesia-on-the-Maeander (Thuc. 8.50.3; cf. 48.1), a city that a couple of generations earlier had been the seat of another Athenian exile, Themistocles. But when he heard that a combination of Agis' hatred and the jealousy of "the most powerful and ambitious" of the Spartans had prevailed on the authorities to send instructions that he be killed, he took refuge with Tissaphernes, and immediately became the "first and greatest" member of his household. (Plut. *Alc.* 24.4). But why should residence at Magnesia be equated by Euripides with exile in Egypt? Partly perhaps on account of the tradition of a virtuous Egypt-based Helen in Stesichorus and Herodotus, and partly perhaps for the reason that Beaumarchais set his comedies in Seville, not Paris. There may, however, be other reasons. Until Alcibiades' arrival, the most important member of Tissaphernes' court will have been Tamos, *hyparch* of Ionia (Thuc. 8.31.2). This man was an Egyptian, from Memphis (Diod. 14.19.6). If Tamos was aggrieved at Alcibiades' prominence in Ionian affairs, a prominence which presumably eclipsed his own, this might account for the frequency of the word μέμφομαι ("complain") in *Helen*. It occurs six times: at 31, 462 and 453 (τί δὲ τὸ Νείλου μεμπτόν ἐστί σοι γάνος; ["Why do you complain of the pride of the Nile?"] – οὐ τοῦτ' ἐμέμφθην ["I did not complain of that, I complain of my own misfortune"]), 636, 1294, 1424.

Delebecque has well observed that when Euripides makes an allusion to current affairs, "he has no need to announce it with the voice of a herald; … a word, the tone of a phrase is enough to indicate to the spectator that behind what is shown, there exists something hidden, in keeping with the preoccupations of the day".[17] Euripides' sub-text shimmers with subtle nuances. Like Aristophanes, but for different reasons, he has to veil what he really wants to say. Proteus is a case in point. Alcibiades, it seems, was described by a contemporary writer as

---

17 Delebecque 1951, 23.

ὑπὲρ τὸν Πρωτέα τὴν φύσιν ἀμείβων ("changing his nature more than Proteus"; *CAF* 3.398.5.). Helen, already a possible allegory for Alcibiades, speaks of Proteus in line 4: Πρωτεὺς δ' ὅτ' ἔζη τῆσδε γῆς τύραννος ἦν ("When he lived Proteus was tyrant of this land"). If Proteus also refers to Alcibiades, and if Euripides was making a case for his forgiveness and return from exile, then it is highly significant that Proteus *was* a tyrant, in the past. The phraseology, in particular ὅτ' ἔζη, perhaps recalls a saying of Alcibiades datable to 415, when he heard that the Athenians had condemned him to death, he responded δείξω αὐτοῖς ὅτι ζῶ ("I'll show them that I live!" Plut. *Alc.* 22.4). The scholion to *Thesmophoriazusae* 922 explains ᾐγυπτιάζετ' ("Egyptianised") as ἐπανουργεῖτε· ὡς δὴ τῶν Αἰγυπτίων πανούργων ὄντων ("acted like scoundrels; the Egyptians being scoundrels"). In his appraisal of Alcibiades' career, Plutarch describes him as being consistently πανοῦργος ἐν τῇ πολιτείᾳ καὶ ἀναλήθης ("a scoundrel in politics and a liar" *Alc.* 41.1). For a virtuous Helen, who perhaps represents a bornagain Alcibiades, to speak of Proteus, perhaps the Alcibiades of old, as "king of Egypt" (5) may be another way of referring to Alcibiades' former villainy which had now to be kept at a distance, but which could never be concealed.

Love, Honour and Beauty

Athenaeus records a fragment of a comic writer who describes "Alcibiades, who lives a life of oriental luxury (ἁβρόν)[18] ... and whom Sparta wants to arrest as an adulterer (μοιχόν)" (*CAF* 3.398.3 *ap.* Ath. 13.574*d*). This doubtless refers to Alcibiades' supposed liaison during his Spartan exile with Timaea, the wife of Agis. As a consequence, so the story went, Timaea had a child by Alcibiades. The historicity of the affair has been denied, defended—and exaggerated.[19] The important point, however, is that true or false the story was told and widely believed soon after Alcibiades' departure from Sparta to Asia. If so, there may be a certain intentional irony in Helen's talk of leaving her "palace and marriagebed" (696) and her insistence that she had kept her bed undefiled (48, 795).[20] There may be irony too, and a punning reference to T̲i̲m̲aea, in the claim of

---

18 On the semantic range of ἁβρός, see Francis 1975, esp. 54, n. 24.

19 καὶ παρὰ Λάκωσι γενόμενος συνεγένετο τῇ τοῦ βασιλέως γυναικί τε καὶ μητρὶ καὶ θυγατρί ("Having arrived at Sparta, he lay with the wife of the king, his mother and daughter": Olymp. *in Plat. Alc.* 173): clearly a calque of Antisthenes' report of Alcibiades' relations with the women of his own family (Antisth. 29a Caizzi *ap.* Ath. 5.220*c*).

20 Delebecque 1951, 339–40.

Helen, another Spartan queen, to be τὸν πάλαι ... πόσιν τιμῶσα ("honouring my husband of old") towards the end of the prologue.

Delebecque has already argued that some fragments of *Andromeda* (performed as part of the same trilogy as *Helen*) appear to allude to Alcibiades and Timaea, and thereby to cast the royal house of Sparta in a bad light.[21] If so, the fact that Agis, king of Sparta had been occupying the Attic township of Decelea since 413—a policy actually instigated by Alcibiades (Thuc. 7.18.1)—will have added a certain relish. Delebeque notes in particular: "When mortals fall in love (ἔρωτα) and the object of their love is a noble being (ἐσθλῶν ... τῶν ἐρομένων) .." (Eur. *fr.* 138 Nauck), which he takes to be an allusion to Alcibiades' noble birth, and: "For myself, I refuse to have bastards, not because they may be inferior to legitimate children, but before the law their position is false; be careful not to have any" (*fr.* 141), the reference of which is fairly obvious if it relates to Alcibiades. Delebecque felt too that Alcibiades might have been intended by: "It was my youth which impelled me, and boldness stronger than my reason" (*fr.* 149). He did not, however, extract the full potential meaning from the lines "sur la puissance de l'amour" (*fr.* 138). Alcibiades was said to have attracted much criticism for having carried a shield adorned with an Eros wielding a thunderbolt (Plut. *Alc.* 16.1–2; cf. Ath. 12.534e), and the image is one that well expresses the essence of the man, even if Alcibiades' shield only existed on the stage;[22] There must have been good reason for a Roman patron to arrange for a portrait of Alcibiades as Eros to be painted on a wall of the Portico of Octavia (Pliny, *HN* 36.28) (We can gain an idea of the image in question from a chalcedony intaglio in the Antikensammlungen in Munich representing Eros with a thunderbolt).[23] Alcibiades' shield emblem, or at least his known attachment to Eros,[24] may well thus underlie Euripides' passage beginning σὺ δ' ὦ θεῶν τύραννε κἀνθρώπων Ἔρως ("O thou who art tyrant of both gods and men, Eros" (*fr.* 136; cf. ἔρωτα and ἐρομένων in *fr.* 138), and Alcibiades' relationship with Timaea, the references to τίμιος and τιμῶσι ("honour": *fr.* 136 *ap.* Ath. 12.561b-c). Such references are unlikely to be accidental if Alcibiades is in the frame.

Love and honour—arguably allusions to Alcibiades' Eros and to Timaea—are conspicuously absent from the extracts from *Andromeda* quoted and parodied by Aristophanes in *Thesmophoriazusae* (*TGF*² 392–404),[25] and we might well ask

---

21 *Ibid.*
22 Russell 1966, 45; Littman, 1970, 267–8.
23 Platz-Horster 1995.
24 Cf, Wohl 1999.
25 Cf. Gibert 1999–2000, 80.

why. While the old reckless and irresponsible Alcibiades may be a thing of the past, his womanising is one youthful characteristic that Euripides does appear to stress. To call attention to the stories of what Alcibiades had achieved in the very bosom of the family of the man currently occupying Decelea would both go down well with an Athenian audience and be an effective means of polishing Alcibiades' tarnished image.[26] Since Aristophanes' apparent object seems to have been to attack rather than to succour Alcibiades and to prevent him from returning to Athens, to have dwelt on one of the few things that most Athenians would find to his credit would have been counter-productive.

Aristophanes elsewhere drew attention to Alcibiades' amorous proclivities by calling a play *Triphales* ("He of the Triple [or All-Powerful] Phallus"),[27] the date of which is uncertain, but which was probably concerned with Alcibiades on account of references in the play to cities such as Chios, Ephesus and Abydos (Ar. *PCG* 556), for Chios and Ephesus were to be counted among Alcibiades' "handmaidens" whenever he travelled abroad (Ath. 12.534*d*), and Abydos was where he had learned sexual tricks from the women (Antiph. *fr*. 67 Blass *ap*. Ath. 12.525*b*). Elsewhere, Aristophanes makes the pretence that Alcibiades was born in the archonship of the otherwise unattested Phalenios "making fun on account of the phallus" according to the grammarian who preserves the fragment, in case we missed the point (Ar. *PCG* 554 *ap*. Hsch. *s.v.* ἐπὶ Φαληνίου). If Alcibiades does in fact underlie the character of Helen, the actor playing the part will have lambdacised the *rho*s in Πρωτεύς and τύραννος, thus preparing the way for the important wordplay in line 5, when he will have said Φάλον for Φάρον ("lighthouse"). If this were the case, then it would simply be another example of the phallic commonplace, and the topographical difficulty resulting from the fact that Egyptian Pharos is some distance from the waters of the Nile mentioned in the first line of the play, a difficulty which has greatly concerned some commentators, would become less pressing. Most editors these days prefer to drop line 5 altogether, but to do so would be to deprive the play of one of its grace notes.

Alcibiades' personal beauty was famous. "As to the beauty (τοῦ κάλλους τοῦ σώματος) of Alcibiades, it is not necessary to say anything except that it was equally fascinating when he was a boy, a youth and a man" (Plut. *Alc*. 1.4). He was ὡραιότατος καὶ ἐρασμιώτατος Ἑλλήνων ("the handsomest and loveliest of

---

26 Cf. *The Examiner* (22 February 1813) 123: "Cuckoldom has been a good joke from time immemorial".

27 Trans. Munn 2000, 104.

the Greeks" [Ael. *VH* 12.14]).[28] (And his son, Alcibiades Jr was also εὐπροσωπότα-
τος καὶ ὡραιότατος ["very attractive and handsome"], according to Xenophon's
Socrates [*Mem.* 1.3.10]). Although Helen's beauty was considerably more famous
than even that of Alcibiades, there are possible grounds for believing that a deliberate parallel is being drawn whenever Helen's κάλλος ("beauty") is mentioned (e. g. at 23, 26, 261, 304). Many men had died as a consequence of Alcibiades' policies (not least in Sicily—not to mention the Troad); there may be
an evocation of this in Helen's admission that the souls of many men perished
by the Scamander for her sake (52– 3). When Alcibiades was indicted *in absentia*
on a charge of sacrilege in 415, it was voted that all the priests and priestesses
should curse him publicly (καταρᾶσθαι: Plut. *Alc.* 22.5). This may be significant
in the light of Helen's complaint (54) that she is cursed (κατάρατος)—a point
taken up later in the play: "although Helen is the daughter of Zeus himself,
she is reviled throughout Greece as a traitor, as untrustworthy, unjust, impious,
(1137–59)".[29] Nearly all of these epithets could be equally applied to Alcibiades,
as well as her genealogy, for in addition to having been the ward of "the Olympian", he claimed physical descent from Zeus (Plat. *Alc.* 1.121a).

Theonoe, Piety and Purification; Teucer

Helen introduces Proteus' offspring Theoclymenus and Theonoe at lines 9–15.
She devotes very few words to Theoclymenus, but Theonoe is discussed at rather
greater length. G. Germain has argued that Euripides had in mind here Theano,
the priestess of Agraulos, who in 415 had refused to curse Alcibiades for having
profaned the Mysteries. He observes the close parallels between Theonoe's first
words (at 998) on announcing her decision to help Helen ("I am by nature and
inclination disposed to piety") and Theano's declaration on refusing to curse Alcibiades that it was to pray and not to curse that she had become a priestess.[30]
He could have added that it was in the shrine of Agraulos that young Athenian
men took the ephebic oath (Plut. *Alc.* 15.7), and that Alcibiades had once distorted the terms of this oath for his own ends.[31] Agraulos is occasionally referred to
as Aglauros (Dem. 19.303), and a popular confusion of *lambda* and *rho* (which
this time has nothing to do with Alcibiades) in this word may explain the de-

28 Cf. Plut. *Alc.* 4.1; 16.4; Pl. *Symp.* 216c-219e; *Prt.* 309a; Ath. 12.534c; Dio Chrys. 64.27; Gribble 1999, 39.
29 Juffras 1993, 51.
30 Plut. *Alc.* 22.5; Germain 1972, 268.
31 Siewert 1977, 108.

scription of the young Theonoe as τὸ μητρὸς ἀγλάϊσμα ("her mother's shining light": 11). Theonoe's first words of all, soon after the middle of the play at 865 ff., speak of the purification of a place that may have been polluted; they are expressed in generalities, but they may apply to Alcibiades.

When Teucer arrives on the scene, he appraises the palace he sees before him in terms which might be taken to describe the residence of Tissaphernes and Alcibiades: a house Πλούτῳ ἄξιος ("worthy of Plutus": 69; cf. 293 – 6); ἄξιος is frequently an Alcibiadean marker as we have already seen,[32] and this may well be the function it serves here. The reference to the god of Wealth, moreover, may have contributed to Aristophanes' conceit in *Plutus*, where as we saw in Chapters 5 and 6 the figure of Wealth appears to embody echoes of Alcibiades. Teucer then sees Helen, and immediately wants to kill her. It was once asked "Why is Teucer an exile so embittered that he longs to slay Helen at sight?"[33] The answer may well lie in the fact that an historical Teucer was among the individuals who had denounced those, including Alcibiades, who had profaned the Mysteries (Plut. *Alc.* 20.6). This Teucer was a resident alien who had himself participated in the events in question. He had gone into exile in Megara and only gave evidence in Athens under immunity from prosecution. "No sooner had Teucer denounced [the conspirators] than they fled the country".[34] It is a mutual hatred between traitor and betrayed that perhaps underlies the characterization of Teucer in *Helen*.

Menelaus

Aristophanes would appear to make his Menelaus in *Thesmophoriazusae* speak like Alcibiades, as we shall presently see (Chapter 9), and there are sufficient parallels between the way in which Euripides presents Menelaus in *Helen* and Alcibiades' recent history to suggest that any associations are not coincidental. It is scarcely surprising that such references—if indeed they are there—reflect Alcibiades' purely masculine qualities and interests. Alcibiades had spent part of his exile at Argos (Plut. *Alc.* 23.1; Isoc. 16.9) and part at Sparta, but was now unwelcome at both;[35] Menelaus is stated to be neither in Argos nor by the streams of the Eurotas (124), the river that runs through Sparta. In 416 BC Alcibiades entered seven chariot teams at Olympia, was victorious, and received many hon-

---

32 E.g. pp. 52 – 3, above.
33 Drew 1930, 188.
34 Andoc. 1.15; Aurenche 1974, 113; *Sophocles and Alcibiades*, 57 – 8.
35 Hatzfeld 1951, 207 – 8; Thuc. 8.45.

ours for his achievement, but already the seeds of his misfortunes were being sown: "even at this brilliant period of his life he incurred discredit, either by his own fault or through the spite of his enemies" (Plut. *Alc.* 12.2); Menelaus' first speech begins with a references to Pelops' victories in the Olympic chariot race, and to the misfortunes that had beset his descendants (386–92).

The Sicilian expedition of 415 BC had been enthusiastically promoted by Alcibiades (Thuc. 6.15; Plut. *Alc.* 17.2), and he had even induced the Argives and some Mantineans to join in (Thuc. 8.29; Plut. *Alc.* 19.4). When the departure of the fleet was held up on account of the charges of impiety that had been laid against him, Alcibiades found that he had the full support of both the sailors and soldiers. Nicias, the other influential commander, had been unwilling for the expedition to take place at all, and only participated with the greatest misgivings (Thuc. 6.8.4; Plut. *Nic.* 14). His excessive caution was probably the major reason for the expedition's ultimate failure. There may be a reference to all this in Menelaus' boast that he had been responsible for getting the greater part of the Greeks' armament to Troy (393–4), and that he had done so with the willing obedience of the troops involved, not πρὸς βίαν ("by force": 395–6); perhaps a play on Alcibiades. If so, there may be a special significance in the use of the word τύραννος ("tyrant": 395) to describe the authority he exerted.

The result of the Sicilian expedition had been the utter ruin of the Athenian forces: "... their sufferings were prodigious. Fleet and army disappeared from the face of the earth; nothing was saved, and of the many who went forth few returned home" (Thuc. 7.87.6). There may be an echo of these events, as Delebecque noted,[36] in Menelaus' lament for those that were lost at Troy, and his statement that the survivors brought the names of the dead back home (397–9). By 411, Alcibiades was longing to return home (e. g. Thuc. 8.47.1), but was unable to do so. Menelaus is said to be in the same situation (400–7). Alcibiades had now lost his earlier friends and was reduced to living in Persian Ionia; Menelaus is a friendless castaway on a foreign shore (408–9). The echoes resound.[37]

Alcibiades' extensive wardrobe has been mentioned already, including the *himatia* he left behind him at Athens (see p. 78, above). In exile in Sparta, however, he had adopted Laconian habits as we have just seen (p. 93, above), and lived relatively simply. By the time he reached Ionia on a Spartan ship, we might well assume that he was travelling light, at least by his former standards. Once installed, however, he became "luxurious (χλιδανός), frivolous and lazy"

---

36 Delebecque 1951, 323.
37 Burnett 1971, 83 perceptively compares Menelaus in the recognition scene to Xanthias at *Frogs* 414; see Chapter 16 below, where it is argued that he too probably "comes forward" as Alcibiades.

(Plut. *Alc.* 23.5). Menelaus is only dressed in rags saved from his ship, but is eager to describe the πέπλους χλιδάς ("luxurious robes") and λαμπρά τ'ἀμφιβλήματα ("splendid cloaks") he formerly wore. Menelaus' ragged appearance not only symbolizes "in a persistent and vivid way his temporary loss of identity and position",[38] but also Alcibiades' temporary embarrassment. Alcibiades had gone for help to the local representative of the Great King, Tissaphernes (Plut. *Alc.* 24.4) who, for all his parsimony, was a rich man. Menelaus' thoughts on approaching Theoclymenus' palace are recorded in detail: "Seeing this house surrounded by a frieze, and with majestic gates, I approached it. There is hope for sailors from a wealthy house (πλουσίον δόμον)" (430–3). The house in question had already been described earlier as "seeming to be worthy of the god of Wealth" as we saw, and as a royal enclosure (βασιλειά τ'ἀμφιβλήματα: 69–70)". Noteworthy, perhaps, that the word for "enclosure" is the same as that for "cloak". If there is any contemporary significance to be derived from this, it may be that an allusion is being made to Alcibiades' hopes to be reclothed at Tissaphernes' expense (as indeed he apparently was). If, moreover, the "royal enclosure" was Tissaphernes' satrapal palace, it will have contained the "garden full of meadows and health-giving waters which Tissaphernes had decreed should be called 'Alcibiades' .... [which] all men from that time forth spoke of by that name" (Plut. *Alc.* 24.7).

That such correspondences between life and art may not be wholly accidental is perhaps suggested by the speech patterns Euripides makes Menelaus employ. We have frequently had occasion to observe that Alcibiades' speeches in Thucydides are characterised by the frequent use of initial καί ("and"), and by the use of paratactic constructions.[39] The same is true of Alcibiades' conversation as reported by Plato (e. g. the καί-clusters at *Smp.* 220c and 220e). Vividness, swiftness and directness are some of the qualities that result from this practice (which is rare in other speakers).[40] Menelaus' speech at *Helen* 397–409 appears to incorporate the same phenomenon:

> *And* (καί) on the one hand can be counted those who are dead, on the other those who escaped safe from the sea to bear back home the names of the dead. But I have wandered wretchedly over the marine surging of the grey ocean ever since I sacked the towers of Troy, *and* (καί) craving to go home, I am not deemed worthy in the eyes of the gods to succeed. *And* (τε) I have sailed into every desolate and hostile landing-place in Libya; *and* (καί) whenever my native land draws near, a

---

38 Podlecki 1970, 404.
39 Cf. Tompkins 1972, esp. 204–214.
40 Tompkins 1972, 214.

wind blows me away, *and* (καί) never does a favourable wind fill my sail that I may come home. *And* (καὶ νῦν) now unfortunate, shipwrecked, bereft of friends, I am cast ashore in this land.

If Euripides did intend to show the manly and vigorous side of Alcibiades in the person of Menelaus, we might well expect to find examples of initial καί in his speeches, as indeed we do (here, and at 583, 591, 630, 658, 736, 741, 840, 950, 979, 1059, 1071, 1079, 1261, 1265, 1444). Another distinctive feature of Alcibiades' speech is said to be "the frequent ironic use of the potential optative".[41] It is interesting to note that Menelaus' first speech ends with just such a usage: τίς ἂν πυλωρὸς ἐκ δόμων μόλοι; ("could some gatekeeper possibly come out of the house?": 435). And further likely Alcibiadean allusions can be seen in the frequent play on our dubious hero's patronymic ὁ Κλεινίου ("son of Cleinias/Famous") in Menelaus' lines (e. g. 392, 453 ["Where is my famous (κλεινά) army now?"], 503). It is indeed the case that "the fame of the Trojan undertaking recurs too frequently to be accidental",[42] but the κλέος (845, 1603) is once again part of Euripides' subtle plot construction.

Theoclymenus

Proteus—so Helen told us in the prologue—had two children, Theonoe and Theoclymenus. There is some evidence, as we saw (p. 98, above) to suggest that Euripides equated Theonoe with Theano, the pious priestess who looked kindly upon Alcibiades. Theoclymenus seems to share many characteristics with another of Alcibiades' benefactors, *viz.*, "the sinister and enigmatic"[43] figure of Tissaphernes. The etymology of Tissaphernes' name is disputed, but one possible meaning is "Whose glory is in his lineage",[44] and Euripides may perhaps be alluding to this when he makes Theoclymenus declare on entering:

> Greetings, monument of my father. I buried you at the entrance of my house so that I could say: "Always on leaving or entering the house, Theoclymenus your son thus pays his respects, Father" (1165–6).

---

41 Tompkins 1972, 214, n. 58.
42 Podlecki 1970, 403, n. 11.
43 Westlake 1979, 35.
44 Stonecipher 1918, 65 (reading OP ciΘ[r]a ["lineage"] + farnah ["glory"]). (Mayrhofer 1973, 258 prefers *CiΘra-farnah-, "mit strahlendem Glanz").

We may perhaps see here a reference to a Persian practice for which evidence still survives in metropolitan Persis. Within the confines of the royal paradise at Pasargadae, but outside the palace buildings, stood—indeed stands—the tomb of Cyrus,[45] erected by Cambyses to honour his father. The monument would have been a prominent feature even in the days when the surrounding park was an arboretum, and the palace buildings were standing. It would be difficult to make a case that Euripides' alludes to Pasargadae (for all that craftsmen from Ionia worked there);[46] rather, that just as arrangements at the central court of the Persian empire were replicated in the satrapal courts,[47] the phenomenon of ancestral tombs—or perhaps cenotaphs—at the gates of Achaemenid palaces might have been familiar in Persian-ruled Asia Minor.

It was the Protean aspect of Alcibiades that seems to have appealed to Tissaphernes. "The barbarian being himself a lover of deceit and of crooked ways, admired his cleverness and versatility" (Plut. *Alc.* 24.5). Alcibiades was exceptional in this respect, for otherwise Tissaphernes was possessed of an "unrelenting hatred of all Greeks [that was] prominent at every stage of his career".[48] This attitude on the part of the satrap may in turn underlie references to Theoclymenus' dislike of Greeks (e. g. 155, 781). Theoclymenus is characterised as "a cruel despot, willing to break any law, human or divine",[49] and the way in which he is manipulated by Alcibiadean characters suggests that Euripides is indicating that Tissaphernes was somehow in Alcibiades' pocket. This was certainly the picture Alcibiades was trying to project as part of his campaign to return home, and a point that a sympathetic propagandist might be expected to enlarge upon.

In 412/411 BC the Spartans and Persians made three peace treaties: one in the summer of 412 BC, and the next in the winter of the same year, well after the arrival of Alcibiades at the court of Tissaphernes, and the third shortly before the Dionysia of 411 BC (*HCT* 5, 450 – 2), at which *Helen* was probably performed. The second treaty is "a document about *spondai* and friendship. *Spondai* generally imply the termination of hostilities, and it is possible that someone has woken up to the fact that Sparta and Persia have been at war with each other for seventy years".[50] This being so, it is interesting that the solemn agreement reached by Helen (a Spartan queen) and Theoclymenus (a barbarian ruler) is described in the terms σπονδὰς τέμωμεν, and even more interesting that immediately after-

---

45 Arr. *An.* 6.29.4–11; Stronach 1978, 24–43.
46 Nylander 1970; Stronach 1978, 22–3.
47 Briant 2002, 347.
48 Plut. *Alc.* 24.6; *Art.* 23.1; *Ages.* 10.5; cf. *Lys.* 4.2; Westlake 1979, 39.
49 Pippin 1960, 157.
50 D. M. Lewis 1977, 93, citing Amit 1974.

wards Helen performs an act of *proskynesis*, the regular form of obeisance before a Persian ruler.[51] She also says ἐπείπερ εἶ φίλος ("since you are a friend": 1237), which, if a contemporary reference is being made, may allude to Alcibiades' status as a "friend of the satrap"[52]. Indeed, the whole scene may reflect an Athenian view of the negotiations between Sparta and Persia.

The Phoenician fleet figured large in the negotiations between the Spartans and Tissaphernes in 412/411 BC. "Its first appearance is in discussions between Tissaphernes and Alcibiades (Thuc. 8.46.1) which may go back before the making of the second treaty ...".[53] In the event, as we have seen, the Phoenician ships did not get further than Aspendos, and Alcibiades claimed the credit for having persuaded Tissaphernes to keep them out of the Aegean (Thuc. 8.108.1). This, however, was to be months away. Early in 411 BC, when *Helen* was presumably still being written, "Alcibiades still continued his practices with Tissaphernes, whom he now sought to draw over to the Athenian interest" (Thuc. 8.52.1). The Phoenician fleet was still a threat, and was in fact mentioned in the third treaty with the Spartans, signed after March 29, 411 BC.[54] The vessel which Theoclymenus agrees to hand over to Menelaus and Helen is a Phoenician ship from Sidon (1272, 1412, 1451, 1531); there may be an allusion here to the impending danger and echoes of Alcibiades' promises to deal with it.

The Second Stasimon

By 412 BC, Alcibiades was living at Magnesia-on-the-Maeander, as we have seen (p. 60, above). Themistocles' descendants still had certain privileges there in Plutarch's day (Plut. *Them.* 32), and it is reasonable to suppose that Alcibiades enjoyed the society of a group of Athenians who had permanently medised. If, as seemed likely at one point, Alcibiades hoped to repeat Themistocles' submission to the Great King, Magnesia would have been a good place to make the right contacts (although it was to be another five years before he actually began to learn Persian: Ath. 12. 535e). If the Great King's promise to any Greek who wished to desert to him that he would be treated better than Themistocles belongs to

---

51 Briant 2002, 222–4. Cf. the *proskynesis* that the Alcibiadean Wealth performs at *Plutus* 771 (p. 80, above).
52 See Appendix 1, where it is argued that since Alcibiades was πρῶτος καὶ μέγιστος ("first and greatest") in the court of Tissaphernes he must inevitably have been his φίλος. On *philia* in general, see: Wiesehöfer 1980, 7–21; Tuplin 1987, 117; Briant 2002, 308, 923.
53 D. M. Lewis 1977, 106.
54 Andrewes in *HCT* 5.138.

this period (Plut. *Them.* 29), Alcibiades will have lived very comfortably at Magnesia (as Tissaphernes' naming a garden "Alcibiades" confirms).

Themistocles himself, while resident at Magnesia had escaped an assassination attempt thanks to the appearance in a dream of the "Mother of the Gods", and "having thus escaped from danger, he built a temple to Dindymene at Magnesia to commemorate the appearance of the goddess and appointed his daughter Mnesiptolema to be its priestess" (Plut. *Them.* 30). Strabo also speaks of the fifth century temple of the Mother of the Gods at Magnesia (14.1.40). This information might help to explain the hymn to the Mother of the Gods at *Helen* 1300 – 68, a hymn which has attracted such comments as "[it] is ... so absolutely irrelevant to the story, that some readers have actually supposed it to be an interpolation";[55] "a strange ode introduced for its own sake",[56] "all the ingenuity of minds learned and subtle has failed to discover adequate explanations",[57] and most recently, "the ode is only lightly attached to its context ... and the idea (1335 – 7) that Helen is in trouble because of the neglect of the goddess is without answering echo elsewhere in the play".[58] The possible Alcibiadean reference of this chorus, with its haunting image of a distressed Demeter, the deity whom above all Alcibiades was supposed to have offended, has already been proposed;[59] not "neglect" perhaps, but Euripides' subtle way of alluding to an episode in Alcibiades' career he could not overlook. If, moreover, we also take account of the cultic associations of Magnesia, Alcibiades' recent haven of safety, we may be on the way to explaining the inclusion of the hymn in Euripides' play, and to realising its central relevance and importance.

Shaving, Sacrifice and Sobriety

Alcibiades "let his hair grow long during a great part of his life" (Ath. 12.534c), but during his stay at Sparta, a city which was famous for still using iron currency,[60] he shaved his hair close (Plut. *Alc.* 23.3); there may be an allusion to these facts when Theoclymenus speaks of Helen's having taken the iron to the locks on her noble head at 1187 – 8 (cf. 1224). Alcibiades had attracted criticism at Sparta

---

55 Verrall 1905, 64.
56 Dale 1967, 147.
57 Decharme 1906, 314.
58 Kovacs 2002, 161.
59 Drew 1930, 188; Delebecque 1951, 341 – 2; Germain 1972, 268; Vickers 1989a, 62; Munn 2000, 132 – 3.
60 Plut. *Lyc.* 9.2; *Lys.* 17.3 ff.; *Mor.* 226c; cf. Laum 1925.

for bathing in a lot of water (Plut. *Mor.* 235*a*), the Spartans being unenthusiastic bathers (Xen. *Lac.* 2.4; Plut. *Lyc.* 50; *Mor.* 237*b*); this may lie behind Helen's invitation to Menelaus to come in and have a bath (1296), and her statement that "after all these years, he has had a bath in fresh water" (1383–4). Alcibiades is said to have been moved to tears by a sense of his own inferiority to Themistocles (Aesch. Socr. *Alc. fr.* 1 Kraus), in whose footsteps he had travelled during the years preceding *Helen*, and in whose city he was currently living; while we do not know quite when Alcibiades wept, Menelaus bursts into tears at *Helen* 455–7 and 990. Helen weeps, too, at 1189 and 1226. Such stress on tears may perhaps allude to Alcibiades' awareness of the reputation of his predecessor.[61]

Themistocles died at Magnesia, but in circumstances that were disputed even in the fifth century. Thucydides thought he died from an illness, but reports the view that he committed suicide (1.138.4). According to this, the "more melodramatic"[62] version, he committed suicide by drinking the blood of a bull he was sacrificing rather than betray Athens. There is a reference to this at *Knights* 83: "It is best to drink bull's blood (αἷμα ταύρειον πιεῖν)", and F.J. Frost has reasonably concluded that "we would assume, then, that the average Athenian, by the last quarter of the fifth century, had heard that Themistocles committed suicide by drinking bull's blood".[63] There may be a deliberate reminiscence of the tale in the Messenger's vivid account of the recalcitrant bull, reluctant to set foot on Menelaus' ship, but which is in the end heaved on board Ἑλλήνων νόμῳ ("Greek fashion": 1561). Not only does this mean "in the way it has been done properly from time immemorial",[64] but if there is a political secondary meaning, there may be a hint here of Alcibiades' turning his back on Persian ways and reverting to his ancestral norms. When the bull is eventually sacrificed, instead of recalling the memory of a man who is dead, Menelaus asks Poseidon that he and his wife be brought home safe ἐπ᾽ ἀκτὰς Ναυπλίας ("to the shores of Nauplia": 1586). Ἀκτή was, however, an archaic expression for Attica; if Helen and Menelaus together reflect different aspects of Alcibiades, then perhaps we can read into this a wish that Alcibiades should return home. Menelaus is also reported to have encouraged his men with the words ὦ γῆς Ἑλλάδος λωτίσματα ("O flowers of

---

61 Plutarch was very conscious of the similarity between both men's careers. For further parallels, see Podlecki 1975, 139, n.9; Schneider 1999, 23, n. 40; *Sophocles and Alcibiades*, 147–50. For Alcibiadean tears on account of his unfortunate situation in the summer of 411, see Diod. 13.41.5.
62 Podlecki 1975, 43.
63 Frost 1980, 227.
64 Ostwald 1969, 24.

Greece": 1593), but λωτίσματα may also play on Alcibiades' speech defect[65] (which is put to very clever—but for us distracting—effect in *Helen*). Alcibiades was considered by the Romans in the fourth century BC to be the bravest of the Greeks (Pliny, *HN* 34.12); if Menelaus' bravery in the ensuing seaboard battle as reported by the Messenger is any guide to the popular view of Alcibiades in action, one can see why.

The Dioscuri put Euripides' case very succinctly. Both Helen and Menelaus are to win eternal glory (and the reference to Acte at 1673 indicates their next, Attic, port of call). Even Theoclymenus is resigned to the outcome, and declares his belief in Helen's extreme sobriety and nobility (cf. σωφρονεστάτης, εὐγενε-στάτης: 1684, 1686). While Alcibiades' noble birth was unquestioned, it would have required immense goodwill to think of him as born again sober; this, how-ever, is what Euripides appears to have been attempting to achieve in 411 BC. If Alcibiades' recent history and present anomalous position does underlie *Helen* and *Andromeda*, then it would seem that Euripides argues the case for Alci-biades' return, his forgiveness and his restoration to the office of general. Herein lies the elusive seriousness of the play.[66] Euripides shows Alcibiades in the most favourable possible light, given the misdeeds and misunderstandings of the past few years. He seems to stress such topics as the embarrassment many thought Alcibiades had caused King Agis, Alcibiades' supposed influence with Tissa-phernes, and the promise that Alcibiades might be another Themistocles. Wheth-er or not Aristophanes was personally alarmed at this, he appears to have react-ed against such propaganda by using in *Thesmophoriazusae* Euripides' own plots to emphasize the more discreditable aspects of Alcibiades' recent history: his entanglement with the oligarchs, his imprisonment at the hands of Tissa-phernes, and his irresponsible lack of respect for hallowed custom. These ques-tions will be discussed in Chapter 9.

Andromeda

Helen is the only extant play from among those of Euripides produced in 411 BC. We know from Aristophanic scholia that *Andromeda* was performed on the same occasion, and enough fragments have survived for us to gain an approximate idea of the plot. Again, there is a heroine who escapes from captivity, and if *Helen* reflects Alcibiades' sojourn with Tissaphernes and his leaving him, then

---

65 Cf. *Suda* s.v. ῥωτακίζω: "make overmuch of the letter *rho*".
66 Cf. Podlecki 1970; Wright 2005.

the same will be true of *Andromeda*. One of the striking features is the way in which Perseus and Andromeda fall in love with one another, and John Gibert has well shown how popular was the Mills and Boon element—new to tragedy —with ancient audiences, and how it became a paradigm for those who were romantically smitten. Eros in *Andromeda* does indeed play "a conspicuously positive role",[67] but it is likely that it was the Eros that Alcibiades is said self-indulgently to have employed as his shield emblem.[68] In *Helen*, both Helen and Menelaus seem to "come forward" polymorphically as Alcibiades, and it is likely that this was also the case with Andromeda and Perseus: the one based on the "womanish" side of his character, the other on his bravery. Thus, to choose a couple of fragments which can probably be associated with Andromeda and Perseus respectively: (i) φίλαι παρθένοι, φίλαι μοι ("Dear maidens, dear to me": Eur. *fr.* 117) can be connected with Alcibiades' sometime effeminacy *via* Aristophanes' lampoon of the line as φίλαι γυναῖκες ... ("Dear ladies ...": *Th.* 574), in the mouth of the Alcibiadean pathic Cleisthenes (see p. 139, below). (ii) νεότης μ' ἐπῆρε καὶ θράσος τοῦ νοῦ πλέον ("it was my youth that impelled me, and boldness stronger than my reason": Eur. *fr.* 149), doubtless alluding to one whose "youth" was constantly an issue, and who was described by Plutarch as θρασύτατος ("extremely bold").[69] Perseus was in any case, like Helen, and as Alcibiades supposedly was, descended from Zeus (Plat. *Alc.* 1.120e).[70] As we have already seen, Alcibiades' genealogy played a significant part in another of Euripides' plays written during his exile, the *Ion* of a couple of years later (see Chapter 4).

---

67 Gibert 1999–2000, 80.
68 Cf. Delebecque 1951, 339–40, and pp. 185–6, below.
69 Plut. *Alc.* 44.2; cf. Delebecque 1951, 339–40.
70 On the importance attached to such genealogies, see Thomas 1989, 155–96.

Chapter 8

"Alcibiades is a Woman's Man": *Lysistrata*

The quotation in the title comes from Favorinus who said that "Eupolis, the comic poet, having learnt that Alcibiades was in the habit of committing adultery with the wives of citizens, said 'Alcibiades is a woman's man, apparently, as far as all the women are concerned, without actually being a man'," womanizing being somehow equated with effeminacy in ancient Athens.[1] We had occasion in the previous chapter to speak of the tradition of evoking Alcibiades on stage by means of female characters, and we noted part of Libanius' gloss on Alcibiades' conduct in a semi-fictional, but well-informed, speech where he makes Timon say that Alcibiades "appears noble in the Lyceum and knits his brows more than Protagoras or Gorgias, he is headstrong in the assembly and an orator beyond the Olympian, he is a sodomite at symposia and effeminate when drunk, he is ἀνδρόγυνος ('womanish') in the evening, changing his nature more than Proteus" (Lib. *Decl.* 12.42). We have also seen how the feminine side of Alcibiades' chameleon-like nature might be echoed in *Helen* and *Andromeda*, plays that happen to have been performed at the same celebration of the City Dionysia in 411 BC as *Lysistrata*.[2]

Such characterisation had its origin in Alcibiades' own youthful bravado, when he bragged that although a male he had "dressed in women's clothes ... and attended symposia undetected" (Lib. *fr.* 50.2.12–13). His "ambivalent sexuality"[3] will have been reinforced by contemporary gossip and dramatic invention,[4] and it thus becomes easy to see Alcibiades somehow underlying the figure of Lysistrata—quite how will be discussed below. Tales of Alcibiades in the women's quarters may well be "tittle-tattle", and some allegations may well have no actual historical basis, but if they have an apparent echo—or rather prefiguration—in Aristophanes then this may serve as sufficient justification for a belief that the stories were told at an early date.

---

1 Callanan and Bertini Malgarini 1986, cited at Pherecr. *PCG* 163 (which itself reads: οὐκ ὢν ἀνὴρ γὰρ Ἀλκιβιάδης, ὡς δοκεῖ, ἀνὴρ ἁπασῶν τῶν γυναικῶν ἐστι νῦν ["For though Alcibiades is not a man, as it would seem, yet he is today the one man of all the women" (trans. Munn 2000, 133)]); cf. Davidson 1997, 165 (whence the Favorinus translation).
2 On the date, see pp. 111–12, below.
3 Duff 2004, 96–7.
4 Such as Sophocles' evocation of such cross-dressing in *Antigone* of 438 BC: *Sophocles and Alcibiades*, 13–33.

While Alcibiades had had his admirers at Athens,[5] and did so again at the end of 412 BC (Thuc. 8.54.1), his extravagant and intemperate behaviour alienated substantial portions of the population (Plut. *Alc.* 16.2–5). In drawing attention to Alcibiades' less attractive characteristics, Aristophanes had a ready audience among people who had witnessed his "life of great luxury, the outrages he committed when drunk or in search of sexual satisfaction, and the θηλύτητας ('effeminacy') of his purple robes which he trailed through the Agora" (Plut. *Alc.* 16.1). Alcibiades' current affairs probably lie at the heart of *Lysistrata*, as we shall see. Every nuance of the plot hinges on what Aristophanes and his public knew of Alcibiades' career in general and his most recent activities in particular. And yet, in the recent past, allegorical allusions to Alcibiades in *Lysistrata* have been proposed only with the greatest diffidence,[6] and have been dismissed on the grounds that the passages concerned do not inevitably call him to mind, and that they need not do so to be dramatically effective.[7] It has even been observed that in *Lysistrata* Aristophanes "seems rather to forgo than exploit opportunities" to allude to Alcibiades.[8] It will be argued presently that Alcibiades is instead omni-present in the play, and that he is consistently lampooned. All is done allusively, however, for as we have seen (p. 5, above) Aristophanes is among those said to have practised symbolic satire after 415 BC (Tzetz. XIAi 99–100).

The question has been posed with regard to *Lysistrata* "Why does Aristophanes take women as spokespersons, and why does he have recourse to a means of action in doubtful taste?"[9] The answer to the first of these questions probably lies in Alcibiades' own inclinations and proclivities, his sometime effeminacy; the answer to the second may be found in the παρὰ προσδοκίαν principle ([Hermog.] *Meth.* 34) —what we have been calling the "spendthrift Aberdonian" principle—according to which audiences might be amused "by means of the unexpected". The last thing any Athenian would expect an Alcibiadean figure to be would be the moving force behind a sex-strike. It is akin to Euripides' basing the ultra-chaste Hippolytus on our doubtful hero—discussed below in Appendix 1; for Alcibiades was, if anything, the embodiment of unbridled lust. And whatever the precise date of the Andocidean speech *Against Alcibiades*, the speaker's statement that "Were I faced with

---

5 See e. g. his ἀξίωμα ("reputation") in 432 BC (Plut. *Alc.* 7.5); the delight of the populace at his first public act (Plut.*Alc.* 10.1–2); his gaining popularity and influence by means of his eloquence (Plut. *Alc.* 10.3–4); his ability to get "the Athenians to tolerate him, and always give his transgressions the mildest names, calling them youthful escapades and love of honour" (Plut. *Alc.* 16.4).

6 Sommerstein 1977; withdrawn: Sommerstein 1990, 2, n. 14.

7 Westlake 1980, 42, 47, 49, n. 32; Moorton 1988, 348.

8 Henderson 1987, xxiv.

9 Rosellini 1979, 26.

the task of describing at length [Alcibiades'] career as an adulterer, as a stealer of the wives of others, as a perpetrator of lawless acts in general, the time at my disposal would be all too short" ([Andoc.] 4.10), presumably reflects the view of many contemporaries.

The previous chapter did not dwell overmuch on the double meanings engendered by Aristophanes' exploitation of Alcibiades' speech defect. A spate of jokes based on a confusion of *lambda* and *rho* are distasteful to the modern reader; the wordplay to which Greek so readily lends itself[10] is generally overlooked. This chapter will by contrast dwell on such double meanings, the better to describe some at least of the fantastically ludicrous images that Aristophanes creates. Many of the *lambda*-generated puns serve to make Aristophanes even more Aristophanic than he is already. For example, the dildo at 109–110 is described as a σκυτίνη 'πικουρία ("a leathern aid"). σκυτίνη 'πὶ κουλεά, however, would mean "something leather for our cunts". It is important to remember too that such puns can work the other way as well, and that the listener can imagine a *rho* in a word that normally contains a *lambda*, and a double meaning can be created thereby. First, though, a few observations on the date of the play and on the likely inspiration for Aristophanes' conceit of the seizure of the Acropolis by women.

Alcibiades and Samos

The date of *Lysistrata* depends on where we place *Thesmophoriazusae*, and arguments will be presented in due course for seeing that play as a production of 410 BC. This would free the Dionysia of 411 BC for *Lysistrata*, and a date in April of that year would remove many of the difficulties associated with the visit of Peisander, the envoy from the "generals at Samos", to Athens in January and February of 411 BC (*HCT* 5.184–93). Thucydides' report can be taken at face value, without the contortions that a belief in a February date for *Lysistrata* renders necessary.

> Peisander and the other envoys who had been sent from Samos arrived at Athens and made their proposals to the people (ἐν τῷ δήμῳ). They said much in a few words, insisting above all that if the Athenians restored Alcibiades and modified their democracy they might secure the alliance of the [Persian] King and gain the victory over the Peloponnesians (Thuc. 8.53.1).

---

10 Stanford 1939; Ahl 1984; 1991; Chapter 1, above.

But both the reform of the democracy and the restoration of Alcibiades were anathema to many Athenians:

> There was great opposition to any change in the democracy, and the enemies of Alcibiades were loud in protesting that it would be a dreadful thing if he were to be permitted to return in defiance of the law. The Eumolpidae and Ceryces [the priests of the Eleusinian cult] called heaven and earth to witness that the city must never restore a man who had been banished for profaning the Mysteries (Thuc. 8.53.2).

Peisander faced the "violent expressions of indignation", and argued that the Athenians' only hope for the future lay in help from the Persians. Constitutional niceties were a luxury when the very existence of Athens was at stake. Thucydides makes him conclude his speech with the words "And we must restore Alcibiades, who is the only man living capable of saving us" (Thuc. 8.53.3). The outcome of the meeting was that "a decree was passed that Peisander himself and ten others should go out and negotiate to the best of their judgement with Tissaphernes and Alcibiades". So much was public knowledge. Far fewer will have known of Peisander's conspiring with the aristocratic clubs to overthrow the democracy, but "When he had completed all the necessary preparations and the plot was ripe, he and his colleagues proceeded on their voyage to Tissaphernes" (Thuc. 8.54.4) at whose court in Caria Alcibiades had been living since December 412.

Lysistrata thus suits the period after Alcibiades had been the object of renewed public scrutiny, when his critics had presumably not limited themselves to his acts of impiety, and when Peisander had described both publicly and privately Alcibiades' life of oriental luxury; but before reports of the abortive interview with him and Tissaphernes reached Athens, and before the anti-democratic plot resulted in the oligarchy of the Four Hundred in June 411 BC.[11] Euripides' Helen was written against the same background, but in support of Alcibiades' return to Athens, whereas Aristophanes takes a different view in Lysistrata. The play probably does therefore address the question of Alcibiades' recall,[12] and does so in ways that dwell on his tyrannical tendencies, on his dissolute way of life, and his current position with the satrap at Magnesia-on-the Meander.

---

11 Rhodes 1981, 406.

12 Pace Henderson 1987, xxiv, n. 7; Sommerstein 1990, 2, n. 14 (both favour a date of 411 BC for Thesmophoriazusae, and consequently date Lysistrata to February of that year). Contrast Russo 1962, 298; Wysocki 1988, 246, who sense the need to attribute Lysistrata to the City Dionysia of 411 BC.

Caryatids and Tyranny

Lysistrata is ultimately concerned with the establishment of peace between the various warring parties of Greece, but Aristophanes uses Alcibiades' personal history and known, or rumoured, tendencies and characteristics in order to make specific political points. A good example is the violent seizure of the Athenian Acropolis by Lysistrata and her cohorts. This is an act that has been played down, if not actually overlooked, by most scholars.[13] But before we examine this event and its implications, we should note another, related, phenomenon that should by any standards form part of the interpretation of *Lysistrata*, but never does. This is the Caryatid porch of the Erechtheum, which contains six strapping females who—irrespective of the date of construction of the building to which they belong—will have been admired and commented upon in much the same way as the visitors from Sparta, Boeotia and Corinth at 77–92. The date of the Erechtheum, however, is much disputed. There is no evidence at all for when it was begun, but many still accept a date arrived at on questionable stylistic grounds of the 420s. All we know for certain is that construction was in progress in 409/8 BC (*IG* I[3] 474–9), and that the Caryatids had been completed by then.

Vitruvius tells the story of how the inhabitants of Laconian Caryae, which had medised in 480 BC,[14] were punished. The men were put to death and the women sold into slavery, but were made to wear their finery in order to draw attention to their disgrace. Vitruvius' account—for which most scholars since Lessing have had little time[15]—occurs in a section near the beginning of his *De architectura* dealing with historical references in building decoration (1.2–4). It is a parade of Laconians who had famously sold out to Persia that is employed on the southern side of the Erechtheum—we must forget "Maids of Greece that might one day still be free", for that is simply nineteenth-century romanticism. The Caryatids' position bearing a heavy architrave is demeaning, and meant to be. Nor is there any indication that the inscriptions of 409/8 BC mark a resump-

---

13 Hulton 1972 and Munn 2002, 134 are exceptions.

14 Huxley 1967.

15 Lessing's argument for rejecting any association between architectural Caryatids and Vitruvius' story of Laconian Caryae, though influential, does not stand up to close examination. Winckelmann had identified a male statue with a rudimentary Corinthian capital on its head that he had seen in the courtyard of the Palazzo Farnese as one of the Caryatids of Agrippa's Pantheon mentioned by Pliny (Lessing [1925] 385–6; Winckelmann 1764, 387; Plin. 31.37). Lessing drew the implausible conclusion that since Winckelmann's "Caryatid" was male, then Vitruvius' account (referring as it did to female statues) must be fictitious, and everyone followed him; most recently Lesk 2005.

tion of work on the building; rather they are a graphic example of the detailed record keeping of the democracy that was restored while work was in progress.

I have argued elsewhere that the Erechtheum was begun in 412 and paid for with a tithe of the thousand talents put away in 431 BC (Thuc. 2.24.1), and kept in reserve until a real emergency occurred.[16] The priestess in charge of the cult (and the guardian of the money) was the Lysimache who may have contributed to the characterization of Lysistrata.[17] The occasion for including ladies of Caryae in a building begun in 412 will have been the peace treaty that Sparta made with the Persians in the summer of that year, reinforced by two further treaties, one in the winter of 412/11, and the third shortly before the Dionysia of 411,[18] when *Lysistrata* was probably performed. Treaties—σπόνδαι (literally "libations") would have been poured from φιάλαι ("libation bowls") of a kind still to be seen in the hands of the replicas of the Erechtheum Caryatids from Hadrian's Villa in Tivoli (those on the originals are worn away).[19] And the position of the Caryatid porch, overlying the foundations of the peristyle of the Old Temple of Athena which had been destroyed by the Persians in 480 BC, but whose ruins had been left as a visual memory of the outrage (it was still there, Kaiser Wilhelm Memorial Church-wise, in Roman times),[20] will have emphasized the visual message to any ancient visitor to the Acropolis. Moreover, if the work on the Caryatids—presumably carried out at ground level for any passer-by to see and comment upon —was in progress by the spring of 411 BC, then the statues would have provided a highly topical point of reference for Aristophanes' occupation of the Acropolis by women.

Mark Munn has noted that Lysistrata's name puns on Peisistratus and that she, like him, takes power by seizing the Acropolis.[21] He also connects Eupolis' parody of Alcibiades as Amphiptolemopedesistratus (*PCG* 424), with its implications of playing both sides together with overtones of tyranny, with Alcibiades and Lysistrata.[22] This is precisely the position adopted here. The capture of the Acropolis was indeed the tyrannical act *par excellence*, and the inclusion of such a deed in *Lysistrata* is more than merely comic "business". Not only was it the case that whoever

16 Vickers 1985; 2014a.
17 D. M. Lewis 1955.
18 *HCT* 5, 450–2, and p. 103, above.
19 Schmidt 1973, pls. 19–21, 26. The *phialai* are decorated with acorns, of a kind paralleled on Persian goldwork: Vickers 1984.
20 Ferrari 2002, esp. p. 22: "The maidens move forward in stately procession toward the site of the destruction".
21 Munn 2000, 134; cf. 389, n. 13.
22 Munn 2000, 334.

held the Acropolis held the mastery of Athens, but the most recent potential tyrant had been—indeed, still was—Alcibiades. He had been widely suspected in 415 of aiming at tyranny (Thuc. 6.15.4), and it was partly on this account, and partly because of his irregular private life, that he was not entrusted with sole conduct of the Sicilian campaign. Objections to his return were being made vociferously but a couple of months before the performance of *Lysistrata*, as we have seen, and we may well suppose that the danger of an Alcibiadean tyranny was among the arguments that were made.

Earlier, the tyrant Peisistratus had taken, and retaken, the Acropolis (Hdt. 1.59–60); the Spartan Cleomenes together with Isagoras had briefly seized it with a view to making the latter tyrant (Hdt. 5.72; 74); and it was the possession of oracles from the Athenian Acropolis which encouraged Cleomenes to try to reinstate as tyrant Hippias, Peisistratus' son (Hdt. 5.90–1). Then, in a suggestive passage Aelius Aristides states that "Pericles was an adornment to the city ... he never took thought for how he might exceed his rank, although he had more resources than Peisistratus. But he was like unto a man who holds the Acropolis (κατέχοντι τὴν ἀκρόπολιν) to preserve the laws and to benefit all men in common" (Aristid. 3.17). Pericles, moreover, was supposedly similar to Peisistratus in physical appearance (Plut. *Per.* 7.1), his followers were known as the New Peisistratidae (Plut. *Per.* 16.1.), and his adornment of the Acropolis was characterized by his enemies as an act of tyranny aimed at Greece as a whole (Plut. *Per.* 12.2). In *Lysistrata*, Aristophanes also uses the characteristically tyrannical act of the seizure of the Acropolis in order to recall the suspicions of tyranny harboured against Alcibiades.

The Opening Scene of *Lysistrata*

Alcibiades had been in exile in Sparta between 415 and 412 BC, when he was forced to take refuge in Asia Minor. Pompeius Trogus succinctly describes the situation: "Among the Lacedaemonians the abilities of Alcibiades had gained more envy than favour; and the chief men having formed a plot to kill him as their rival in glory, Alcibiades received intelligence of their design from the wife of Agis, with whom he had an intrigue, and fled to Tissaphernes, the satrap of king Darius, with whom he quickly ingratiated himself by his affability and desire to please" (Just. 2.4–5). An anonymous comic writer makes Alcibiades make the same journey as we have already seen: "Alcibiades, who lives a life of oriental luxury ... and whom Sparta wants to arrest as an adulterer" (*CAF* 3.398.3 *ap.* Ath. 13.574*d*). *Lysistrata* 1–3 and 7–8 cover the same ground in an economical and subtle fashion.

In the opening scene both Lysistrata and Calonice "come forward", poly-morphically, as Alcibiades, the one reflecting the decisive aspect of his person-ality, the other his tendency to βωμολοχία ("horseplay"), along the lines of Peis-thetaerus and Euelpides in *Birds*.[23] Doubtless they will have been equipped with appropriate masks (Platon. 1.64–6). Calonice's name (Καλονίκη) will have played in part on the καλλός ("beauty") for which Alcibiades was famous, and of which Euripides makes much in *Helen*, and in part on Alcibiades' "extremely strong de-sire to win and come first".[24] Calonice is Lysistrata's κωμῆτις ("neighbour"), but wordplay on κωμῆτης ("long-haired layabout"), will perhaps have reminded the audience of an Alcibiades who "let his hair grow long (κώμην) for the greater part of his life" (Ath. 12.534c). Calonice addresses Lysistrata in terms which recall one of Libanius' descriptions of Alcibiades: how when he appeared in the Ly-ceum, his brow was furrowed (τὰς ὀφρῦς ἀνεσπακώς) even more than those of Protagoras and Gorgias (Lib. *Decl.* 12.2.42), when she says: μὴ σκυθρώπαζ᾽, ὦ τέ-κνον· οὐ γὰρ πρέπει σοι τοξοποιεῖν τὰς ὀφρῦς ("Do not look so angry, my child. You should not knit your brows like a bow": 7–8). ὦ τέκνον is probably a means of recalling Alcibiades' notoriously youthful entry on the political stage (rather than an indication that Calonice is older than Lysistrata),[25] while if we allow Cal-onice to speak like Alcibiades, pronouncing *rho* as *lambda*, she will have said μὴ σκυτλώπαζ᾽. This is rich in additional resonance, for it plays on σκυτάλη, a spe-cial kind of coded Spartan message.[26] In apparently making Calonice enjoin Ly-sistrata not to "gaze at a Spartan letter", Aristophanes seems to allude to the in-structions that had been sent from Sparta to Ionia to execute Alcibiades, doubtless in the form of a scytale (Thuc. 8.45.1), and which had caused him to take refuge with Tissaphernes. τοξοποιεῖν in the following line seems to suggest as much, for the bow was the distinctive Persian weapon (e. g. Aesch. *Pers.* 147).

"But, O Calonice, I am grieved at heart", Lysistrata replies (9) and states that she grieves "over us women"—rather than women in general, since men "consider us to be πανοῦργοι": indeed "prepared to do any act however shameless", rather than merely "cunning" or "clever"[27] if Alcibiades is in the picture. For this was Al-

---

23 *Pericles on Stage*, 154–89.
24 Plut. *Alc.* 2.1; cf. Thuc. 5.43.2.
25 As Henderson 1987, 68.
26 "At Sparta, a *staff* or *baton*, used as a cypher for writing dispatches, a strip of leather being rolled slantwise round it, on which the dispatches were written lengthwise, so that when unrol-led they were unintelligible: commanders abroad had a staff of like thickness, round which they rolled these strips, and so were able to read the dispatches:—hence σκυτάλη came to mean a Spartan dispatch, Thuc. 1.131.1, *etc.*" LSJ *s.v.* 1; cf. Kelly 1985.
27 As Henderson 1987, 69.

cibiades' particular public image: witness the author of [Andoc.] 4 who is unrestrained in his criticisms of Alcibiades' shamelessness—of his embezzlement of the tribute, of his behaviour towards his wife and brother-in-law, of his imprisonment of the painter Agatharchus, of his attack on a rival *choregus*, of his fathering a child on a Melian slave, of his theft of a chariot team, and of his purloining of the Athenian official plate at Olympia. For Plutarch, moreover, Alcibiades was πανοῦργος ἐν τῇ πολιτείᾳ ("a scoundrel in politics": *Alc.* 41.1).

Lysistrata wants to put forward proposals for "a matter of considerable importance" (14). The Athenians will have heard Alcibiades making grandiose plans ever since he entered public life in the mid-420s; Aristophanes had often lampooned his μεγαλοπραγμοσύνη,[28] and few in the audience will have forgotten what happened the last time one of his schemes was adopted. Lysistrata thinks that the women are all asleep and will not come. Calonice encourages her to think that they will, but again her words evoke Alcibiadean images. Thus line 16

...χαλεπή τοι γυναικῶν ἔξοδος
It is difficult to leave the women's quarters

recalls a line of Eupolis' *Kolakes* of 421 BC:

Ἀλκιβιάδης ἐκ τῶν γυναικῶν ἐξίτω
Let Alcibiades leave the women's quarters[29]

—and the rest of the catalogue can be interpreted in a similar vein. One woman hangs her head in shame (ἐκύπτασεν· cf. Ar. *Eq.* 1354 and *Th.* 930) concerning her husband (17), another arouses a slave (18), another puts the little lad to bed, another bathes him and another gives him titbits to eat (19). The items in this list are in keeping with what we know about Alcibiades' activities with married ladies. "Many women, even of high rank, sought after Alcibiades for his beauty" (Xen. *Mem.* 1.2.24),[30] and some of them may have been embarrassed when their husbands found out. The reference to the bedding and bathing of the little lad may be another allusion to Alcibiades' prolonged youthfulness, as well as to his famous beds, sold off in 414 (Poll. 10.36–8), and to his apparent liking for bathing (Plut. *Mor.* 235a).

---

28 Cf. Plut. *Alc.* 6.4, and *Pericles on Stage*, 97–120; 154–180 (on *Knights* and *Birds*).
29 Eup. *PCG* 171 *ap.* Ath. 12.535a. Alcibiades seems to have spent a good deal of time in women's quarters in one way or another during his stay in Sparta. When he was not consorting with Timaea, he was in the habit of "breaking in at the doors of prostitutes" (Ath. 13.574d).
30 "In [Alcibiades'] case it was his seduction of other men's wives that crystallized most clearly the image of his sexual intemperance": Davidson 1997, 163.

At 33, Lysistrata's speech takes a more serious turn, and reverts to a commentary on Alcibiades' current concerns. "That there should no longer be any Peloponnesians", and Calonice understandably agrees, the Spartans having recently sent instructions that Alcibiades be put to death (Thuc. 8.54.3; Just. 2.4–5). "And that all the Boeotians should be destroyed" (34); an allusion perhaps to Agis' allies (Thuc. 8.3; 5) who were even now blocking Athens' overland communications as predicted in *Birds* (at 187–91); the intensity of the language is perhaps explicable by the Boeotians' involvement in the destruction of Plataea in 427 BC.[31] Calonice, however, continues with a reference to Boeotian eels, used as an image for a huge penis in *Acharnians* (888 ff.).[32] Lysistrata states "I will not ἐπιγλωττήσομαι ('bad-mouth') the Athenians" (37); Alcibiades had for the past few months been involved in extremely delicate negotiations with various groups of Athenians in the eastern Aegean (cf. Thuc. 8.54.8). ἐπιγλωττήσομαι, however, also smacks of the practices Alcibiades had picked up during his sex-education lessons in Abydos (Antiph. *fr.* 67 Blass *ap.* Ath. 12.525*b*).[33] "Listen to me" Lysistrata says, "if all the women come together here, the Boeotians, the Peloponnesians and us, we can unite and save Greece" (38–41).

At the time of the performance of *Lysistrata*, Alcibiades was under the protection of the Persian satrap Tissaphernes, living a life of great luxury, as we saw in Chapter 7. Alcibiades "outdid even the Persian in splendour and pomp" (Plut. *Alc.* 23.5), and reports would have reached Athens, if only from members of Peisander's delegation (cf. Thuc. 8.56). Other aspects of Alcibiades' current life of luxury and magnificence are alluded to in the two women's references to saffron dresses, to beautifying themselves, to perfume, to wearing long dresses and oriental slippers (43–8). Many items find parallels in what we hear about Alcibiades' supposed penchant for transvestism, his physical beauty, his use of perfumes, as well as the variety of "shoe of a striking pattern" that was called "Alcibiades" (Satyr. *FHG* 3.160 *ap.* Ath. 12.534*c*).

The women should have been present (54); they ought to have come sooner (55). "But that is the Athenians all over, doing everything later than they should" (56–7); if Alcibiades' point of view is being presented, the delay in prosecuting him in 415 BC may be intended (cf. Thuc. 6.29). That this might indeed be the case is suggested by the reference to the women from the Shore (Παράλων [58]) and from Salamis (ἐκ Σαλαμῖνος [59]): the *Salaminia* was the state vessel which had been sent to Sicily in 415 to bring Alcibiades back to Athens to face the charges

---

31 Thuc. 3.68; cf. Vickers 1995; *Pericles on Stage*, 73–6, and p. 35, above.
32 *Pericles on Stage*, 87–8.
33 Cf. Henderson 1991, 185–6 on *i.a.* τὸ γλωττοποιεῖν ["cunnilingus"]

of impiety; the *Paralus* was a similar ship which we know was operating in the eastern Aegean in 411 BC (Thuc. 8.73.5–6), and which may well have carried Peisander on his mission late in 412 BC to interview Alcibiades and Tissaphernes (Thuc. 8.54.2; 56).

Thus the scene is set for the oath taking—a procedure for which Alcibiades notoriously had little respect ([Andoc.] 4.39)—and the tyrannical seizure of the Acropolis. There is no reason to reject,[34] the association first made in modern times by D.M. Lewis between Lysistrata and Lysimache, the hereditary priestess of Athena who was certainly in office in 412 BC.[35] To satirise Alcibiades in the guise of a person who was arguably the most influential priestess in the city, a lady who—assuming the same individual is in question—possessed a sense of humour (Plut. *Mor.* 534c), and an individual who must have joined in the curses energetically uttered against Alcibiades in 415 BC, would have been both ironic and amusing. An Alcibiades cast in this manner would have embodied the comic principles described by Hermogenes, namely parody and the unexpected (Hermog. *Meth.* 34).

Lysistrata's masculine characterization

Nevertheless, there is something distinctively masculine about Lysistrata, and the point has been elaborated upon by Giuseppe Mastromarco.[36] Not for him the saccharine scholarship of C.H. Whitman: "Lysistrata is young and pretty, the role can be played properly only by an actress of singular grace and charm".[37] Rather, Mastromarco notes that from the start Lysistrata behaves in a masculine fashion, exercising such male prerogatives as calling a meeting, imposing her will, and "entertaining ideas rather than physical drives".[38] What he calls a clear "male characterization" emerges in particular in lines 1124–7, where he identifies a paradox in Lysistrata's claim ἐγὼ γυνὴ μέν εἰμι, νοῦς δ'ἔνεστι μοι ("I am a woman, but I can think"; 1124), for women were not thought by [male] Greeks to be intellectually endowed. The paradox disappears, however, if Lysistrata "comes forward" as Alcibiades. Moreover, Lysistrata's education ἐκ πατρός τε καὶ γεραιτέρων ("with my father and older men") would have been singular for a woman, but not for an Alcibiades some of whose philosophical discussions

---

34 As does Henderson 1987, xxxix.
35 D. M. Lewis 1955.
36 Mastromarco 1997, 108–9; cf. Kanavou 2011, 132 on Lysistrata's "masculine-like initiative".
37 Whitman 1964, 202.
38 Henderson 1980, 169.

with his foster-father are described by Xenophon (e. g. *Mem.* 1.2.40–46)—although they would be easy enough to infer. This education by males stands in distinct contrast to Aristophanes' Euripidean model, where Melanippe states that she had been educated by her mother (Schol. 1126; Eur. *fr.* 483). Lysistrata's male characterization is, moreover, underlined both by the epithet ἀνδρειοτάτη ("very brave") applied to her by the Chorus (1108), a word that is normally restricted to men,[39] and by the fact that she is inappropriately mentioned by name by men (1086, 1103, 1147).[40]

Then, at 98–9 there are indications that the Alcibiadean Lysistrata may be trying to speak like Pericles, in order no doubt to make herself sound more statesmanlike. She wants to ask τι μικρόν ("something small"), an expression that reflects an aspect of Pericles' manner of speaking caught by Thucydides with such phrases as διὰ μικρόν ("for a trifle") or the like (1.140.4–141.1; p. 83, above). And in the next line, τῶν παιδίων ("of your little ones") is a diminutive of a kind that Aristophanes frequently implies was characteristic of Pericles' manner of speech.

Lampito

If the principle of "polymorphic characterization" can encompass Lysistrata and Calonice as evoking aspects of the historical Alcibiades, is it not perhaps possible that it could stretch to include the Spartan Lampito as well? We have already had occasion to note Alcibiades' numerous Spartan connections: his Spartan name, his Spartan nannies, and his family's traditional Spartan *proxenia*. Two points should be borne in mind: that it is necessary to follow the readings of the Ravenna manuscript for sense to emerge, and that Lampito was famously the name of the mother of the Spartan king Agis, whose wife Timaea Alcibiades was widely believed to have seduced and got with child. As the daughter of Leotychidas II (ruled 491–476 BC), and both aunt and wife of Archidamus II (ruled c. 469–427 BC), not to mention the mother of Agesilaus II (ruled 400–360 BC), Lampito's name will have been well-known throughout Greece. As the fictional Lampito appears on the scene, Lysistrata greets her: "O dearest Laconian, greetings, Lampito. How your beauty (καλλός) shows ..." The announcement of the name will scarcely have been complimentary to the man who was currently in command of the Spartan garrison at Deceleia, and the reference to beauty is

---

39 Mastromarco 1997, 109; Foley 1982, 10; Taaffe 1993, 170, n. 37.
40 Kanavou 2011, 131–2.

in keeping with Alcibiades' reputation. ἄγχοις ("strangle": 81) will allude to the system of public execution at Sparta (see p. 67, above), and it should not be forgotten that Alcibiades had recently been condemned to death *in absentia* by the Spartans (Thuc. 8.45.1).

Lampito's opening words (81): μάλα γὰρ οἰῶ ναὶ σιώ (R) have regularly been emended by tidy-minded scholars oblivious to the possibility that Lampito may have been characterized as an Alcibiades speaking bad Laconian, as an Edward Heath might speak French. μάλα γαλοιῶ would sound rustic but might mean "I laugh a lot",[41] as did Alcibiades.[42] And although strictly speaking the article in the expression ναὶ τὼ σιώ is "essential",[43] its omission (as in R) would put across the idea that for all his intimacy with Sparta from earliest childhood, Alcibiades' Laconian was not very good. In exile at Sparta, Alcibiades was γυμναστικός ("fond of exercise": Plut. *Alc.* 23.5–6); hence, perhaps, Lampito's claim to γυμνάδδομαι ("practise gymnastic exercises"). But Aristophanes never lets slip the opportunity for "emphasis", and the kind of exercise he describes, ποτὶ πυγὰν ἅλλομαι ("I jump heel to buttocks": 82), was one recommended by doctors to induce an abortion;[44] the word is unmotivated unless, like the *bibasis* scene in *Birds* 659–63[45] reference is being made to queen Timaea's interesting condition.

Lysistrata prods Lampito like a sacrificial victim (84); sacrificing was one of Alcibiades' special interests,[46] and Aristophanes frequently alludes to the fact. The compact between the women is appropriately formalised with a sacrifice: not with an animal, but with an amphora of wine (196), a commodity of which both Greek women and Alcibiades were famous for being inordinately fond. Women's "liking for wine [was] common knowledge" in antiquity (Ath. 10.440e), and this is here coupled with Alcibiades' famous capacity for drink (Pliny *HN* 14.144; cf. Plut. *Mor.* 800d). If they fail to keep the terms of the oath, they will—ironically—only drink water in future (235–6). The three women who actually consume the wine are Lysistrata, Calonice and Lampito, as befits the three manifestations of the principal κωμῳδούμενος.

---

41 Cf. γελάω ("laugh"); γελοῖος ("amusing").

42 "Alcibiadean laughter" became proverbial for inappropriate behaviour (e.g. Sopater Rhet. Διαίρεσις ζητημάτων 8.127.

43 Wilamowitz 1927, 127.

44 Hippocr. *Nat. Puer.* 13.2; cf. Sommerstein 1990, 159.

45 *Pericles on Stage*, 168–9.

46 As a youth he sacrificed the most beautiful bulls of his admirers (Schol. Luc. 20.16); at an unknown date, he successfully proposed a decree providing for monthly sacrifices at the Temple of Heracles at Cynosarges: Ath. 6.234d-e; in 416 he took charge of the sacrificial arrangements at Olympia (Ath. 1.3e).

Generals at Samos

There is no intention here of treating *Lysistrata* in detail, but to do so sufficiently to show that the regular κωμῳδούμενοι: Alcibiades, Pericles (and Aspasia), underlie some at least of the characters. Pericles lies, in large part, behind both the Proboulos and the Chorus of Old Men who attack the Acropolis (254–705), by now occupied by the women. That what was by now a stock figure of Aristophanic comedy should be exploited as a Proboulos was both witty and appropriate. The Probouloi were a board of ten officials who had been appointed as a temporary emergency measure in 412/11 BC. One of them was the playwright Sophocles (Arist. *Rh.* 1419*a*.15),[47] who had been Pericles' fellow general at Samos in 441/40 BC, and whose name was even centuries later coupled with his in the context of the alleged cruel treatment of Samian prisoners (Strab. 14.1.18). This may explain the reference at 313 to "the generals in Samos" who might "supply wood (τοῦ ξύλου; cf. ξύλῳ 291, 307)". Not only was there a shortage of *matériel* felt by the Athenians stationed on Samos in 411 BC (a shortage which Andocides later claimed to have met "after the Four Hundred had seized power", i.e. a few months after the performance of *Lysistrata* [Andoc. 2.11]), but as we have often had occasion to note it was during the Samian campaign that the Athenians under Pericles were said to have executed Samian prisoners with wooden clubs (ξύλοις: Plut. *Per.* 28.2; cf. p. 25, above).

Sophocles was extremely old, and was probably about eighty-five in 411. Pericles, were he still alive, would have been nearly eighty. The characterization of both the Chorus of Old Men and of the Proboulos (which is a kind of portmanteau amalgam of the two) takes account of these facts; indeed, their age is exaggerated so that it is implied that they were around when Cleomenes the Spartan came to Athens in 508 (273–80), and that they set up the trophy at Marathon (285).[48] But whenever references are made to recent times, they seem to reflect the experiences, attitudes and incapacities of the elderly Pericles. The symbolism of the old men attempting ineffectually to take the Acropolis with their battering ram and crowbars has long been seen as sexual in nature,[49] but it is Pericles' tastes, his sickness, and his death, which provide the basis of much of the humour.

---

47 Cf. Foucart 1893; Wilamowitz 1893, 102, n. 6; Calder 2005, 219–20 (with further literature); Ahl 2008, 5–10; *Sophocles and Alcibiades*, 95–6.
48 Sophocles had led the Chorus of boys celebrating the victory at Salamis (*Vit. Soph.*).
49 Cf. Whitman 1964, 203, cited by Henderson 1991, 95–6.

It was illegal to cut down olive trees at Athens. The only exception was for use on a funeral pyre ([Dem.] 43.71).[50] The last time Pericles was seen by Athenians was as he went up in smoke, and the first two lines of the Old Men's Chorus, where reference is made to a freshly cut log of olive wood (254–5) must allude to such a pyre. The Old Men lament the fact that the women, a well-known evil, whom they used to tend in their home have seized the sacred image of Athena and taken "my Acropolis" and closed the Propylaea (260–5). These words make good sense from a Periclean standpoint: Pericles was guardian to Alcibiades and had taken him into his home; the Acropolis was in a very special way "his"; and the Propylaea, constructed in 437/6–433/2 BC, was one of the last great buildings of Pericles' political ascendancy (Plut. *Per.* 13.12). The plan is for the old men to besiege the Acropolis by surrounding it (266–7). Siege warfare was Pericles' speciality. At Samos that held out for nine months, he had built a wall around the city (Plut. *Per.* 27.1; cf. Thuc. 1.116.2), and made continuous attacks. He "prepared siege engines ... including those called κριούς ('rams') ... and by energetically besieging the city he pushed down the walls, and became master of the city" (Diod. 12.28.3; cf. Plut. *Per.* 27.3). Pericles was a pioneer of siege warfare in Greece, and his skills are apparently alluded to when the Old Men say "we will attack the gate κριηδόν ('like a ram': 309)."

This comes five lines before the reference to "generals at Samos," and while it tends to confirm the nature of the characterization, serious questions arise from the use of the expression ἀπὸ ψήφου μίας ("by a single vote": 270) when the Old Men say what they intend to do with the women. Condemnation *en bloc* by a "single vote," rather than on the basis of individual judgements, was highly irregular, and was to be an issue at the trial of the generals from Arginusae in 406 BC (Xen. *Mem.* 1.7.15); but this was well in the future and can have no bearing on *Lysistrata*. The same unconstitutional device was to be used by the tyrant Critias against the Eleusinians in 403 BC (Plut. *Lys.* 12.52). We might perhaps gather though from Aristophanes' phraseology that the unpleasant punishment supposedly meted out to "the trierarchs and sailors of the Samians" in 439, was not done on the basis of separate judgements, but in a mass trial at best. There is a reminder of the nature of this punishment when the Proboulos refers to τυμπανισμός (388): not simply "drumbeating" perhaps, but a word which resonates with ἀποτυμπανισμός ("crucifixion on a plank"), which is what is said to have happened to the Samian captives in 439 BC (Plut. *Per.* 28.2).[51]

---

50 The fine for illicit felling was 100 drachmas per tree.
51 Cf. Stadter 1989, 258–9; Vickers 2005–6; *Sophocles and Alcibiades*, 14–15. For the punishment, see Keramopoullos 1923; Bonner and Smith 1938, 279ff; *RE* Suppl. 7 (1940) 1606, 9ff (= Latte 1968, 400ff.)

The "single pyre" (μίαν πυράν: 269) which the Old Men will light may refer to Pericles' own, and talk of καπνός ("smoke": 295, 305, 311, 312, cf. 319) recalls the other scene where smoke (in itself an image of worthlessness: Schol. Ar. *Nu.* 252) figures large, *viz.*, the entry of the Periclean Philocleon through the chimney of his house.[52] The references to conflagration (269, 311) emphasize this notion. But the image of blowing on coals (293) in order to keep them alight also recalls the secondary, sexual, usage of "charcoal" in *Acharnians*.[53] And when one of the Old Men blows on his bucketful, the smoke leaps out at him like a κύων λυττῶσα ("bitch on heat"; cf. Pl. *Lg.* 839a, on λύττη ἐρωτικῇ) and δάκνει ("bites") his eyes. There may be a reference to Aspasia here, likened by Cratinus to a παλλα-κὴν κυνώπιδα ("bitch-faced paramour"; Cratin. *PCG* 259 *ap.* Plut. *Per.* 24.9): the insult is of the same order, if a trifle more exaggerated, but perhaps justified if Pericles did indeed undertake the Samian war to please Aspasia, as it was widely believed (Plut. *Per.* 24.2; 25.1). Wordplay on Λήμνιον ("Lemnian": 299) and λήμας ("pus": 301) perhaps alludes both to Pericles' placing of a hundred Samian hostages on Lemnos in 440 (Plut. *Per.* 25.2) as well as to his famous dictum regarding Aegina, which he likened to "pus (λήμη) in the eye of the Piraeus" (Plut. *Per.* 8.7). μηχανῇ at 300, moreover, recalls the μηχαναί ("siege-engines") for which Pericles was famous for bringing up against Samos (Diod. 12.27.3).

The names of the Old Men refer glancingly to Pericles. Aristophanes uses the names of real individuals, or invents fictitious names, in order the better to play on a known individual's traits and personal history. His technique here (and elsewhere) is akin to that involved in Theophrastus' Slanderer's derogatory genealogy of someone who had come up in the world. At first he was the son of Sosias (a servile name), but became the son of Sosistratus in the army, and when he had been entered in the citizen roll, he was the son of Sosidemus (Theophr. *Char.* 28.2). Aristophanes uses the names of real people to make similar, programmatic, points. Aristotle (*Po.* 1451*b*.13) happily calls such names τυχόντα ὀνόματα. It should be borne in mind that these are not the names of κωμῳδού-μενοι; Pericles is here the κωμῳδούμενος). Thus Draces at 254 may have been intended to evoke Dracontides, who (with others) moved the decree requiring Pericles to submit his accounts (Plut. *Per.* 32.3). Stummodorus (as the Ravenna manuscript has it) at 259 both plays on στύω ("have an erection") and Amphipolis on the Strymon founded under Pericles in 437/6 BC.[54] And the name of Philurgus is introduced at 266 presumably to reflect Pericles' love of both siege ma-

---

52 *Pericles on Stage*, 128–9.
53 Cf. Henderson 1991, 143, 177; *Pericles on Stage*, 70.
54 Thuc. 4.102; cf. Stadter 1989, 140–1; Vickers 2010.

chines[55] and public buildings. "Lycon's wife," who is the special target of the Old Men may, moreover, be an ironic allusion to Aspasia, in that an anecdote about Pericles has him carving an oracular response on a bronze wolf (λύκος) at Delphi (Plut. *Per.* 21.3). The "filthy, dirty, shaggy, unwashed Spartans" (279–80) will presumably have brought to mind the Spartans encamped at Decelea in Attica.

Cinesias and Myrrhine

Pericles comes on stage again in the person of Cinesias—Παιονίδης Κινησίας ("Mr Screw from Bangtown"; 852).[56] The name Cinesias was eminently suitable for one much given to "love affairs", in that κίνειν ("move") was synonymous with βίνειν ("bonk").[57] It will also have recalled the event for which Pericles was widely held to be responsible, namely the Peloponnesian War, which in the opening passage of his *History* Thucydides was to call the greatest κίνησις ("movement, disturbance, convulsion") ever to affect the Greeks (1.1.2). As in the case of Cinesias in *Birds*,[58] the characterization also alludes to Pericles' interest in music (a real Cinesias being the composer of dithyrambs). The Periclean reference is confirmed when Lysistrata declares that the new arrival's name is οὐ[κ] ... ἀκλεές ("not without fame": 863); not so much a reference to Cinesias as to "far-famed" Περικλῆς.

The name of Myrrhine, Cinesias' partner, was "evidently chosen for its sexual connotation", and the "skilful wheedling, teasing and coquettishness" are, as Henderson has rightly observed, "more characteristic of *hetairai* than wives".[59] This was Aspasia's perceived role, whether or not the analysis was accurate.[60] The primary concept in Myrrhine's name is μυρρίνη ("myrtle"), but μύρον ("perfume") cannot be far behind. This is a substance associated with luxurious living—as was Miletus (cf. Hdt. 5.50; Ath. 12.523*f*-524*c*), and one actually employed in the ensuing scene (946). There had once been a priestess of Athena Nike named Myrrhine,[61] and although her tenure of the post cannot have over-

---

55 Cf. Plb. 5.3.6: ἔργα καὶ μηχαναί.
56 Trans. Henderson.
57 Henderson 1987, 174 (citing Schol. Ar. *Lys.* 838). For Cinesias in *Lysistrata* (another Pericles surrogate), see Chapter 13, below.
58 *Pericles on Stage*, 182–3.
59 Henderson 1987, xli, 177.
60 Henry 1995, 28; Podlecki 1998, 110–17.
61 Mark 1993, 111–13.

lapped with the career of Pericles,[62] the very notion of a "woman on the Acropolis" might have brought to mind the "trysts with freeborn women" that Pheidias supposedly arranged for the statesman when ladies came to see work in progress on the great building projects (Plut. *Per.* 13.14). This behaviour on Pericles' part was the subject of comment on the part of comic poets, "who charged him with great profligacy" (*ibid.*) as, perhaps, here at *Lysistrata* 829–951.

If Strepsiades, whose characterization was also based on the personality of Pericles,[63] really complains of the extravagance of Aspasia at *Clouds* 49–55, then it may be significant that μύρον comes top of the list of his wife's luxuries. There may also be an allusion to the allegations of Periclean brutality on Samos when Lysistrata tells Myrrhine to "excite and στρέφειν ('torment')" her husband (839). στρέφειν recalls the remark of Elpinice to Pericles after his Samian triumph: "A fine exploit ... to lose many of our brave fellow-citizens, not fighting with Phoenicians or Medes, as my brother Cimon did, but καταστρεφόμενος ('torturing') our allies and our kith and kin" (Plut. *Per.* 28.5–6). Pericles' reply on that occasion is also recorded, and it bears directly upon the characterization of Myrrhine in *Lysistrata*. Pericles smiled calmly and quoted a line of Archilochus:

οὐκ ἂν μύροισι γραῦς ἐοῦσ' ἠλείφεο

"(If you had sense) you would not perfume yourself, since you are an old woman").[64] Aspasia (on whose behalf the Samian campaign was supposedly undertaken [Plut. *Per.* 25.1–2]), however, was not then an old woman,[65] and as a Milesian would doubtless have been an ardent user of unguents. The word used for "excite", ὀπτᾶν, is an apposite one if Pericles is in question. The word also means "to roast, fry, or toast", and Pericles' corpse had been thus disposed of on his funeral pyre in 428.

When Cinesias enters, his language is both amorous and full of likely allusions to Pericles. The σπασμός ("sexual excitement") that holds him in thrall (845), recalls the σπασμὸν ἰσχυρόν ("severe convulsion") which beset most victims of the plague at some stage or other (Thuc. 2.49.4). Pericles, who had actually recovered from the plague, will probably have experienced this symptom. His τέτανος ("hard-on") is as though he was being ἐπὶ τροχοῦ στρεβλούμενον ("tor-

---

62 The temple was only built in the 420s: D.W.J. Gill 2001.
63 *Pericles on Stage*, 26–9.
64 Plut. *Per.* 28.7; cf. Stadter 1989, 127.
65 Extrapolating from Bicknell 1982, 243–5, Aspasia will have been little older than thirty in 439 BC, and may well have been younger.

tured on the wheel" [846]), resuming the note that played on Pericles' reputation —in the eyes of some—for cruelty.

There is an interesting echo of the tradition that Pericles spent most of his wealth on Aspasia (p. 76, above) in Cinesias' willingness to pay all he has in order to lay hands on Myrrhine. Also somehow significant if the real-life Pericles' daily round is in question is Cinesias' description of Myrrhine's having "gone out from the house (ἐξῆλθεν: 866)", and his grieving when he "went in (εἰσιών: 867)", everything appearing desolate. The historical Pericles is said never to have gone in (εἰσιών) or out (ἐξιών) of his house without embracing and kissing Aspasia passionately (Plut. *Per.* 24.9; Ath. 13.589e). Cinesias is off his food; but the food is, significantly perhaps, σῖτος ("grain")—the supply of which was one of Pericles' principal concerns (Schol. Ar. *Ach.* 548).

Cinesias calls his wife: ὦ γλυκύτατον Μυρρινίδιον ("sweetest little Myrrhine": 872), employing the kind of diminutive that Aristophanes regularly puts into the mouths of his Periclean characters. And there are several more diminutives in the ensuing scene where Cinesias attempts in vain to persuade Myrrhine to make love to him: παιδίον (877, 880, 883, 906, 909: "baby"); Μυρρίνιον (906: "little Myrrhine"); χρύσιον (930: "goldie"). Myrrhine uses them as well: τεκνίδιον (889: "little child"); παιδίου (907); κλινίδιον (916: "little bed"; στρόφιον (931: "little bra"). Such use of diminutives helps both to characterize the actors, and to emphasize the lampoon of Pericles and Aspasia's love-making.

There are repeated allusions to the Periclean expression εἰς τὸ δέον ("for a necessary purpose": Plut. *Per.* 23.1) that had become proverbial in the dialogue between Cinesias and Myrrhine. Thus at *Lysistrata* 875. Myrrhine says "You call me, but you do not really need (cf. δεόμενος) me", and is answered by Cinesias: "What, not need (cf. δεόμενος) you? I am altogether destroyed" (876), which, if Pericles was in question, was quite literally true. The same conceit recurs at 926–7, when Cinesias refuses a pillow, saying "I do not δέομ' ('need') anything", and at 934 Cinesias again says "I do not δέομαι ('need') anything", all he wants to do is βινεῖν ("bonk"). The proverbial saying provides a constant refrain.

Finally, several questions arise from the terminology Aristophanes employs in this scene: can ἄνθρωπος, applied to Myrrhine at 936, be taken as the same kind of reference to Aspasia as ἡ ἄνθρωπος ("he-woman") in Plutarch (*Per.* 24.2) and Athenaeus (13.589e)? Is Myrrhine's mention of a προσκεφάλαιον (926: "pillow") a glancing allusion to the shape of Pericles' κεφαλή ("head")? Is her injunction to Cinesias to μέμνησό νῦν (931: "remember now") a reflection of the loss of memory Pericles will have suffered when he was afflicted with the plague? (cf. Thuc. 2.49.8). Can Cinesias' Myrrhine have evoked memories of the name of the wife of the tyrant Hippias (Thuc. 6.55.1)? Aspasia's position with regard to Pericles was analogous.

Lysistrata is full of similar resonances which appear to play on our likely κωμῳδούμενοι; but just as the dots in a *pointilliste* painting do not say very much individually, such passing allusions can easily be overlooked and left unnoticed. But when such resonances are seen as "emphatic" allusions, a cumulative picture emerges in which there is a pronounced overlap between both the historical and anecdotal traditions relating to Pericles, Aspasia—and even more frequently Alcibiades—and the plots of Aristophanes' extant plays.

Thus, Alcibiades and Pericles are once again the butts of Aristophanes' humour. Every allusion can be explained either in terms of Alcibiades' interesting position in 411, or of his "ambivalent sexuality"; in terms of the memory of Pericles' exploits on Samos in 439, and of the recent service as *proboulos* of his cogeneral Sophocles; and in terms of the roles played by prominent females such as the priestess of Athena, Lysimache, and the priestess of Athena Nike, Myrrhine, as well as by Pericles' mistress, Aspasia. Nor should *Lysistrata* cease to be a play studied for what it can tell us about the role of women in Greek society. For all that it has other objectives, the satire can only work if it invokes existing feminine stereotypes.

Chapter 9

Alcibiades in Gaol: *Thesmophoriazusae*

Thesmophoriazusae is one of Aristophanes' most amusing plays when read at
any level of understanding, but it will have been far more so to contemporaries
who were in a position to recognize and appreciate in detail the interplay of the
plot with the histories and idiosyncrasies of the likely κωμῳδούμενοι (who include Alcibiades, Pericles and Tissaphernes). To paraphrase, but to contradict,
a recent critic, it *is* a political play, and was designed from the very first to be.
It is no more a "drama about drama" than is *Midsummer Night's Dream* or *Ham-
let*, and Euripides' reputation as one who was inimical to women (cf. Ar. *Lys.* 283)
is a cover for something quite different.

The Date of the Play

The tone of *Lysistrata* is "sombre and anxious; there are tears even in its mirth",
while *Thesmophoriazusae* is "everywhere gay, light-hearted and playful". Such is
the assessment of B.B. Rogers, whose discussion of the date of the play still bears
re-reading. He notes that *Lysistrata* well reflects the mood that prevailed in Athens towards the end of 412 BC. There had been the defeat at Syracuse in the previous year, allies were falling away, and the prospect was gloomy. By the end of
411 BC, however, when *Thesmophoriazusae* was probably being written, "men's
minds were lighter and more buoyant, and hopes were once more entertained
that Athens might yet emerge in safety from the war". The oligarchic regime of
the Four Hundred had fallen, Alcibiades was once again on the Athenians'
side, and there had been naval victories at Cynossema and Abydos as a consequence.[1] Rogers was in good company, for arguments for a performance early
in 410 BC were first enunciated by Jacques le Paulmier de Grentemesnil in
1668, and taken up by P.P. Dobree, R.C. Jebb, J.P. Mahaffy, B.B. Rogers,[2] and Mil-
man Parry.[3] Today both P.J. Rhodes and Edith Hall lean towards a date of 410

---

1 Rogers 1904, xxviii–xxx.
2 Rogers 1904, xxxii–xlii.
3 Parry 1930, 141; 1971, 319.

BC.[4] Mark Munn (who also favours 410 BC) has stated the problem of the chronology of *Helen* and *Thesmophoriazusae* very well: "The evidence has been thoroughly reviewed by Alan Sommerstein (1977), who demonstrates that the decision ultimately rests upon our interpretation of the political circumstances alluded to, particularly in *Thesmophoriazusae* .... [A] date of 410, in the manifest failure of the Four Hundred, resolves all ... ambiguities [relating to 'any one of last year's councilors' each of whom 'handed over counsel to another' at 808–9]" and "the resulting date for Euripides' *Helen*, on the eve of oligarchy of 411, when both the recall of Alcibiades and the possibility of peace with Sparta was being mooted ..., makes eminent sense of the peculiar themes of recognition and reconciliation in that play, and of the retrospective parody of it the following year in *Thesmophoriazusae*."[5] The external evidence is very finely balanced, and the only serious impediment to a date of 410 BC, (Schol. *Ra.* 53 which states that *Andromeda* was performed in the eighth year before the *Frogs*, i.e. in 412 BC), disappears if we assume that the scholiast had the second performance of *Frogs* (in 404 BC) in mind.

Another problem is Schol. *Lys.* 963 that suggests some kind of relationship between Aristophanes' words in *Lysistrata* and those of Euripides in *Andromeda* (παρὰ τὰ ἐξ Ἀνδρομέδας "ποῖαι λιβάδες, ποία σειρήν"). Wilamowitz took this as meaning that Aristophanes was parodying *Andromeda*,[6] whereas Rogers (rightly: the operative word is παρά ["cf."]) thought that the scholiast meant "that the passages are parallel, and not that the one is a parody of the other".[7] As was suggested in Chapters 7 and 8, both plays were probably performed at the same dramatic festival, namely the City Dionysia of 411 BC.

---

4 Rhodes 1972, 185–6, 190; 1985, 185–6, 190, 308; E. M. Hall 1989, 53–4 (who adduces the oligarch Aristarchus' "barbarian archers" at Thuc. 8.98 as evidence for Scythian archers having been in the news in the summer of 411).

5 Munn 2000, 333–4; cf. Vickers 1989a. Those who favour 411 include: Wilamowitz 1893, 2.344; Croiset 1906, 238; Russo 1962, 298; Andrewes in *HCT* 5, 184–193; Sommerstein 1977, 112–3; 1994, 1–6; Gannon 1987, iv; Hubbard 1991, 187; Nesselrath 1996, 1123; Bäbler 1998, 168.

6 Wilamowitz 1893, 2.344; cf. Gibert 1999–2000, 90, n. 57.

7 Rogers 1904, xxxvii.

The dramatis personae

(i) The Kinsman

In *Thesmophoriazusae*, the Kinsman and Euripides are characterized as Alcibiades and Pericles respectively. If so, the one would naturally be the κηδεστής ("kinsman") of the other.[8] Rather more than half the play is taken up with the Kinsman's arrest, imprisonment and attempts to escape from a barbarian captor.[9] The plot closely reflects the imprisonment of Alcibiades by Tissaphernes and Alcibiades' subsequent escape. Had *Thesmophoriazusae* been performed in the spring of 411 BC (and the Kinsman have had nothing whatsoever to do with Alcibiades), the plot would be peculiarly predictive; too much so for the resemblance between it and Alcibiades' experiences to be coincidental. It is far simpler to assume a causal relationship between the historical events and the dramatic lampoon.

Given the numerous hints to the contrary, it is perhaps surprising that the Kinsman has been selected as paradigmatic of the thesis that "It is, simply, characteristic that—in a realist sense—Aristophanes' recreative figures have no effective past. Mnesilochus [i.e. the Kinsman] is, unquestionably, a figure that—in realist terms again—an audience knows very little about".[10] Rather, the audience will probably have known all too much. A likely characterization as Alcibiades can be immediately recognized from what are said to be "the few lines ... within the play that purport to allude to [the Kinsman's] personal history". But two instances are cited.

(i) The first is Euripides' "*bon mot* about Agathon (35)". The words bear closely on the anecdotal tradition relating to Alcibiades. The Kinsman affects ignorance of Agathon's identity to be told by Euripides "well you must have fucked him, though you might not know it".[11] It is clear from Plato's *Symposium* (supposedly attended by Aristophanes) that Alcibiades and Agathon were close. So much so, indeed, that at least one ancient commentator drew the inference that Alcibiades had the hots for Agathon: Alcibiades' arrival, where he drunkenly and noisily "asks where Agathon is, and demands to be taken to Agathon" (Pl. *Smp.* 212d) was taken by Athenaeus as τὸν Ἀλκιβιάδην ... λέγοντα ὅτι πασχητιᾷ ("Alcibiades declaring that he is consumed with lust": Ath. 5.187c). The image is reinforced by

---

8 Cf. Thompson 1970; Davies 1971, 18. Cromey 1984, 397 suggests that Alcibiades' mother Deinomache became Pericles' wife; if so, very much a "connexion by marriage" (LSJ s.v. κηδεστής).
9 E. M. Hall 1989, 39.
10 Silk 2000, 229; cf. Kanavou 2011, 146 on the Kinsman's "perplexing anonymity".
11 Trans. Henderson.

the Kinsman's words at 59 – 62, where he threatens the anal rape of both Agathon and his servant.[12] The servant's reaction "You must have been a ὑβριστής when you were young" (63) is peculiarly apposite if Alcibiades is in the frame, for "Alcibiades ... was of all Athenians, the most notorious for various types of *hybris*".[13]

(ii) The second "allusion to [the Kinsman's] personal history" is Euripides' injunction after his release that he should "make straight for his wife and kids" (1204 – 6). Far from being an example of a "bland lack of specificity",[14] this would appear to express both a generic (but not "bland") wish for Alcibiades to return home to Athens, and specifically to allude to Alcibiades' long-suffering wife Hipparete (Plut. *Alc.* 8.4) and her children, one of whom at least will probably already have been displaying delinquent tendencies (cf. Lys. 14.25 – 6 in the context of 406 BC: "[Alcibiades Jr] was sent for twice by Alcibiades, since his outrageous conduct was becoming notorious"). Alcibiades' abysmal relations with his wife had been a public scandal. She had been so upset at his prolonged absences in the arms of other women that she went to live with her brother, and while she was on her way to post a divorce petition, Alcibiades seized her by force, and then carried her home *via* the Agora (Plut. *Alc.* 8.5). Hipparete was still alive in 410, and only died in 407/6.[15] Far from being "inconsequentially specific",[16] this allusion to the Kinsman's personal history would have been hard-hitting stuff. There are in fact many more indications that the Kinsman might echo Alcibiades, as we shall see.

(ii) Euripides

Euripides may well be made fun of in *Thesmophoriazusae*, but he is not the principal κωμῳδούμενος in his role. This is strong meat, and perhaps the concept of what it took to be an Aristophanic κωμῳδούμενος needs to be spelt out again. According to our only well-informed source "the kind of person who is κωμῳδούμενος is usually ἢ πλούσιος ἢ γενναῖος ἢ δυνάμενος ('rich, or aristocratic, or powerful')"; ([Xen.] *Ath. pol.* 2.18; cf. p. 6, above). Euripides fell into none of these categories, and while we cannot be certain of his own views, it is likely that they are

---

12 See p. 176, 178, below for the suggestion that Epigenes' drunken and lustful arrival on stage at Ar. *Ec.* 946 and his expressed desire for anal intercourse (964) may have been Plato's model for *Smp.* 212d-e.
13 Fisher 1992, 461.
14 Silk 2000, 229.
15 Plut. *Alc.* 8.7; Isoc.16.45; Rodríguez Blanco 1987, 75.
16 Silk 2000, 229.

reflected in what his Theseus says in *Suppliants* where the rich are dismissed as useless drones: "There are three classes of citizens. The first are the rich, who are indolent and yet always crave more. The second are the poor, who have nothing, are full of envy, hate the rich, and are easily led by demagogues. Between the two extremes lie those who make the state secure and uphold the laws" (238–45). In Chapter 1 reference was made to a cartoon by Matt Wuerker in which Saddam Hussein was said to star in a film "as Hitler". In Aristophanic terms, it would be Saddam Hussein who was the κωμῳδούμενος, not Hitler. The audience would see Hitler, but understand Saddam Hussein, just as in Prokoviev's *War and Peace*, the audience see Napoleon, but understand Hitler. In *Thesmophoriazusae*, the audience would see Euripides, but understand Pericles. To represent one who was "much given to love affairs" as a woman-hater would be unexpected and amusing, akin to having the prosperous Milesian lady Aspasia lie behind Poverty in *Plutus* (pp. 76–8, above).

Euripides, who is given characteristics otherwise associated with Pericles, helps a Kinsman who embodies many characteristics of Alcibiades to resolve his problems. The characterization is effectively established in the first few lines of the play. Mention of Euripides' name (4) will have raised a laugh.[17] αὖθις φράσον ("say that again" (5) already plays on Pericles' tendency to repeat himself. Euripides' language in these lines is said to be ὑψηλότερον ("rather high-flown") by a scholiast; Pericles' oratory was characterized by "lofty intelligence" (ὑψηλόνουν: Plat. *Phdr.* 270a; Plut. *Per.* 8.2). The discussion of the things Euripides tells his Kinsman he needs must do, and what he needs to avoid (δεῖ: 5; δεῖ: 7; δεῖ, δέῃ: 8), is probably based on Pericles' proverbial loss εἰς τὸ δέον ("for a necessary purpose"; see p. 67, above). Then Euripides' speech about Ether, the Eye and the Sun (13–18) would appear to be a parody of Pericles' interest in natural philosophy in general, and his reaction to a partial eclipse of the Sun on 3 August 431 BC in particular, when he is said to have calmed the fears of a helmsman by holding his cloak over the man's eyes, and letting him know that there was no difference in principle between that and the solar eclipse itself.[18] Pericles' philosophical interests were the object of Aristophanes' wit in *Clouds*),[19] here they are described dismissively by the Kinsman as σοφαὶ ξυνουσίαι ("philosophical carryings-on": 21).

---

17 Cf. Olson 1992 (though here it is "early" rather than "late" naming).
18 Plut. *Per.* 35.2; for the date, see Stadter 1989, 320.
19 *Pericles on Stage*, 29–30.

(iii) Agathon

Nor is it the case that Agathon is the principal κωμῳδούμενος in *his* role either. Aristophanes appears to take advantage of Alcibiades's ambivalent sexuality, and his occasional cross-dressing, to make the effeminate playwright "come forward" as yet another manifestation of our doubtful hero. Euripides' announcement that "there lives Ἀγάθων ὁ κλεινός ['the famous Agathon']" is the giveaway line, with its play on Alcibiades' patronymic ὁ Κλεινίου ("son of Cleinias"). The Kinsman is made to profess ignorance—of himself and of Agathon who, it is implied, was but one of so many lovers that the Kinsman/Alcibiades has lost track. Agathon's servant comes out with "fire and myrtle branches" (37): the accoutrements for making a sacrifice, one of Alcibiades' favourite activities.[20] Agathon's activities are described in terms of shipbuilding and the casting of "a bronze statue" (52–7);[21] not simply echoes of the oar-spars and bronze that were currently being supplied to the Athenian forces in Samos (Andoc. 2.12), but of what Alcibiades (who was now in command of the Athenian forces there) was doing with the *matériel* in question. By the autumn of 411, Samos was the headquarters of the Athenian fleet, and all the building work hitherto done in the shipyards of the Piraeus was now carried out on the island.

The bronze was probably being put to an additional use beyond the Samian shipyards. In the second century AD, there could still be seen a "bronze statue (εἰκὼν χαλκῆ) of Alcibiades in the temple of Hera, dedicated by the Samians (Σαμίων ἀνάθημα)" (Paus. 6.3.15), of which it has been said that "the context shows that it was erected when [Alcibiades] had a strong fleet along the Ionian coast".[22] A likely occasion for such a dedication was Alcibiades' return from Phaselis to Samos in about September 411, when he announced that "he had prevented the Phoenician fleet from coming to the assistance of the enemy, and that he had made Tissaphernes a greater friend of the Athenians than ever" (Thuc. 8.108.1). If a bronze statue of Alcibiades was indeed being made during the winter of 411/10, we can be reasonably sure that the fact was known at Athens. The apparent concentration on bronzecasting in the language used at 18–19 by Euripides and the Kinsman and at 52–62 by Agathon's servant might thus be a deliberate allusion to the latest Alcibiades story. The word for "funnel" (χοάνη) (18–19) is also used for the vessel in which metal was melted in a foundry. The description of how Agathon went about the craft of writing is told in terms of bronzecasting: γνωμοτυπεῖ ("casts thoughts into a mould") (55), κηροχυτεῖ

---

20 See p. 121, n. 46, above.
21 Muecke 1982, 45. The craft metaphor is unusual in comedy: Harriott 1969, 96, n. 3.
22 Richter 1965, 1.105.

("moulds") in wax (56), and χοανεύει ("casts in a mould") (57) all seem to refer to the processes used in the craft of bronze sculpture.[23] If Aristophanes had Alcibiades' portrait statue in mind, this language would carry a rich secondary meaning, drawing attention to what might be considered by some to be a hubristic[24] course of action for a commander in the field to undertake—or to condone. It was, however, a practice that finds a contemporary parallel in the Persian Empire: we thus hear of a statue of Ariobazarnes, satrap of Phrygia 387–363/362 BC, being set up in the sanctuary of Athena Ilias at Sardis.[25]

(iv) The Scythian Archer

It is highly unlikely that the Kinsman's experiences on the Athenian stage as the captive of a barbarian prefigured Alcibiades' identical experiences at the end of 411 BC. In November of that year, Alcibiades went to visit Tissaphernes on the latter's arrival at the Hellespont, but rather than greeting him as an old friend (indeed as a φίλος, in the technical sense; see p. 104, above) as Alcibiades had hoped (given the lavish hospitality he had enjoyed some months earlier, and which had provided the basis for *Helen*; Chapter 7, above), Tissaphernes was not prepared to entertain Alcibiades' overtures and imprisoned him at Sardis until he escaped thirty days later (Xen. *Hell.* 1.1.9–10; Plut. *Alc.* 27.6–7, 28.1). The Kinsman's imprisonment and subsequent escape can only reflect this experience of Alcibiades. A Scythian archer—especially one as uncouth as this one[26] —was, it is true, a very far cry from the urbane and cultivated satrap Tissaphernes,[27] but from an Athenian point of view they both belonged within the parameters of the same barbarian stereotype, as does the πορμός/φορμόν ("Indian mat": 1007; cf. Hdt. 3.98) on which the Scythian squats. "In [the Scythian archer]", it has been well said, "are combined the cruelty and stupidity which the Greeks felt separated the Hellene from the rest of humanity, and he is portrayed not as a good-natured joke ... but as an intruder condemned to the outside".[28]

---

23 For accounts of the casting process, see Bol 1985; Mattusch 1996; Hoffmann and Konstam 2002.
24 Cf. the outrage expressed by "older men" at Athens when Aristophon painted Alcibiades with a personification of the Nemean games (Plut. *Alc.* 16.4–5), apparently shortly before 415; see further Schneider 1999.
25 Diod. 17.17.6; cf. Briant 1998, esp. 219–20; Paus. 7.6.6.
26 Well analysed by Bäbler 1998, 168–9; E. M. Hall 1989.
27 Westlake 1979, 35–41; 1981; 1985; Petit 1997; Wiesehöfer 2002; Briant 2002.
28 Long 1986, 107.

But Aristophanes was no stranger to invidious and exaggerated characterization: witness his treatment of Cleon in *Knights*, or of Socrates in *Clouds*.

The Interview with Agathon

Agathon's effeminate song is said to be unfunny,[29] but the humour will have lain in the parody of Alcibiades' recent luxurious confinement in Asia Minor (cf. "Asiatic lyre" and "Phrygian Graces": 120). "The metre of Agathon's song is largely Ionic ... appropriate for its general ethos of voluptuousness and effeminacy".[30] The Kinsman says how excited he is (130–3): tantamount to Alcibiadean narcissism if both "come forward" as Alcibiades. He then expresses amazement at the curious mixture of male and female attributes possessed by Agathon (136–43), who is addressed as νεανίσχ' ("young man": 134; contrast Agathon's "old man" at 146). Aristophanes provides a caricature both of Agathon's well-attested effeminacy and of Alcibiades' luxurious life *à la perse*. Athenian ambassadors visiting Tissaphernes (Thuc. 8.56) early in 411 BC must have brought back extravagant tales of life at the Carian court. Alcibiades conducted negotiations on the satrap's behalf, and it is difficult to believe that, ensconced as he was in an oriental paradise, he was not wearing Ionian garments—long flowing chitons—of a kind that had once been worn by aristocrats at Athens (Thuc. 1.6.3) but which were apparently considered effeminate by 410 BC (cf. 134–143). Where indeed was the cloak (χλαῖνα), where were the shoes (Λακωνικαί: 142)? Cloaks had been Alcibiades' speciality when he was in Athens, and he eschewed Laconian shoes, preferring his own "shoes of a striking pattern", which, like Tissaphernes' garden, were called "Alcibiades". Aristophanes gives us an exaggerated version of Euripides' picture in *Helen* of Alcibiades' Carian sojourn.

Alcibiades was famous for adapting to circumstances at will. Plutarch elaborates on his ability, chameleon-like, to oblige those he wished to please:

> At Sparta, he was devoted to athletic exercises, was frugal and reserved; in Ionia, luxurious, companionable, and indolent; in Thrace, always drinking; in Thessaly, ever on horseback; and when he lived with Tissaphernes the Persian satrap, he exceeded the Persians themselves in magnificence and pomp. Not that his natural disposition changed so easily, nor that his real character was so variable, but, whether he was sensible that by pursuing his own inclinations he might give offence to those with whom he had occasion to converse, he transformed himself

---

29 Muecke 1982, 48.
30 Dale 1968, 124; Muecke 1982, 48.

into any shape, and adopted any fashion, that he observed to be most agreeable to them. (Plut. *Alc.* 23.5).

It is this facility[31] that Aristophanes is lampooning as much as the historical Agathon's methods of composition, when he makes his Agathon say that he changes his clothing ἅμα γνώμῃ ("according to the way [he] feel[s]": 148). The references to "ways" (τοὺς τρόπους: 150; τῶν τρόπων: 152) in the context of empathy with women perhaps recall the singular education in ἔργων τρόπους ("ways of doing things") that the adolescent Alcibiades had received from the women of Abydos (see p. 68, above).

We shall discuss the Kinsman's aside to Euripides about Phaedra (153) in more detail in Appendix 1, but it will not perhaps come as a surprise by now to learn that it is probably a dig at Aspasia and is another example of Aristophanes' imputing unwitting cuckoldry to Pericles. There is something of the same in the next aside: "When you write about Satyrs, call me so that I can join in 'long and hard from the rear'."[32] Euripides had of course written about Satyrs (e. g. *Cyclops*), but there are also allusions here to Pericles' having won for himself, thanks to his amorous entanglements, the title of "King of the Satyrs", as well as to the preferred mode of sexual congress imputed to Alcmaeonids (see pp. 69, 71 above, and 178 below). An Ionian note is kept going with the reference to Anacreon, Alcaeus and Ibycus wearing oriental head-dresses (161–3), while the claim that they "moved as I do" (163) is perhaps an excuse for stage business involving an exaggerated version of Alcibiades' effeminate walk.[33] The statement that one must compose according to one's φύσις (167) brings to the fore an aspect of Alcibiades' public image that long exercised philosophers.[34] The Kinsman takes this at face value as dramatic criticism, but his line (168) about Philocles, Aeschylus' nephew, carries a very clever secondary meaning, for in the mouth of a lambdacizing Alcibiadean character αἰσχρὸς ὢν αἰσχρῶς ποιεῖ ("being ugly, he writes in an ugly manner") would play on Αἰσχύλειος ὢν Αἰσχυλειῶς ποιεῖ ("being Aeschylean, he writes in an Aeschylean manner"), employing wordplay that had already been used at *Knights* 1321 and *Clouds* 920;[35] and which was to be employed again at *Frogs* 1475 (see p. 158, below).[36]

---

31 Or, in reality, limitation: Vickers and Briggs 2007.
32 Trans. Sommerstein.
33 Cf. Gribble 1999, 72–3.
34 Cf. Bruns 1896, 512; Gribble 1999, 139; *Sophocles and Alcibiades*, 46, 64, 172.
35 *Pericles on Stage*, 117, 47.
36 For an earlier instance, see Soph. *Ant.* 5; cf. *Sophocles and Alcibiades*, 28.

Euripides wants to get on with his business, but imparts the information that he too was like Agathon when he was younger (172–3). It has been astutely said of these lines that "it is a standing joke that almost all successful *politicians* are former male prostitutes",[37] and Aristophanes is presumably having a cheap laugh at the expense of Pericles' memory. The Kinsman is shocked, but this in turn is a joke at Alcibiades' expense, for his early experiences certainly fell into the category in question. Euripides begins his speech with a quotation from Euripides' *Aeolus* which, however, contains a subtle reference to Pericles' mannerism of speech which Aristophanes often lampoons by means of diminutives, and which Thucydides characterised with expressions such as περὶ βραχέως ("for a small matter") or the like (1.140.4–141.1). "It is the distinguishing feature of a wise man to be able elegantly to compress many words ἐν βραχεῖ ('into few': 177)", says Euripides. He has, moreover, been struck by a new ξυμφορᾷ ("disaster": 179)— a word that Thucydides was to make his Pericles employ in the first sentence of his first speech (1.140.1). As we shall presently see, Thucydides certainly knew his *Thesmophoriazusae*.

Euripides tries to persuade Agathon to attend the Thesmophoria in his place. If he were to go himself, he would be easily recognised thanks to his beard. And while Euripides and Pericles, like most Athenian men, were bearded, Alcibiades, like Agathon, was usually not. Euripides' list of Agathon's characteristics (191–2) might apply equally well to Alcibiades; indeed were perhaps meant to do so. Agathon is said to be εὐπρόσωπος ("comely"): Alcibiades' physical beauty was famous (and provided the basis *i.a.* for his characterization as Helen, as we saw in Chapter 7). Agathon is said to be λευκός ("white"): so too will Alcibiades have been after living like a Persian (Persians' bodies were white since they "never took their clothes off," at least in public: Xen. *Hell.* 3.4.19). Agathon is said to be ἐξυρημένος ("clean shaven"): so too was Alcibiades at times (but not always, for otherwise his features could not have served as the model for Hermes [Clem. Alex. *Protr.* 4.53.6]), and extant portraits show him as beardless.[38] Agathon is said to be γυναικόφονος ("to have a voice like a woman"): might we not assume that Alcibiades' speech defect was considered to be effeminate? It was certainly thought to be childish (cf. Ar. *Nu.* 862). Agathon is said to be ἀπαλός ("soft, delicate"); so too would the current edition of Alcibiades have been, after living in Persian luxury (cf. *CAF* 3.398 *ap.* Ath. 13.574d). Agathon is εὐπρεπὴς ἰδεῖν ("easy on the eye"); so too was Alcibiades, judging by the attentions he received from admirers who were struck by τὴν λαμπρότητα τῆς ὥρας ("the brilliance of his beauty": Plut. *Alc.* 4.1;

---

37 Sommerstein 1994, 171.
38 Cf. Smith 1990, 139, pl. 9.4; 1991, 148–9, fig. 4; Richter and Smith 1984, 83, 196, fig. 46.

pp. 97–9, above). And both Agathon and Alcibiades might reasonably be thought of as having had reputations for ambivalent sexuality.

Agathon's response to Euripides is a quotation from the historical Euripides' *Alcestis* "You enjoy life; don't you think your father does too?" (194). This is a clever reversal of generations, for in this exchange it is Euripides who "comes forward" as the Periclean father, while it is Agathon who reflects the Alcibiadean son. The mutual insults concerning pathic sex (198–201) reflect equally upon the historical Agathon and Alcibiades. The reason why Agathon is reluctant to help Euripides is that he is afraid that the women will accuse him of stealing their νυκτερείσια ("knockturnal": 204)[39] activities. The Kinsman clownishly suggests that what he really means is to "be screwed" rather than to screw (205). Again appropriate for one who was "a sodomite at symposia and effeminate when drunk" (Lib. *Decl.* 12.42).

The Kinsman offers to help, and Euripides immediately takes him up on the proposal. "Take off your *himation*" (214), he says; *himatia* were items of everyday dress, it is true, but they were also very much part of Alcibiades' popular image. Then the Kinsman has to be depilated; elsewhere in Aristophanes (e.g. *Plutus* 168) depilation seems to relate to the punishment for adultery of a kind that Alcibiades may have undergone, or have been in grave danger of undergoing in view of his reputation for seducing married women. The Kinsman amusingly threatens to rush off to take sanctuary at a shrine whose clergy had cursed Alcibiades and condemned him to death in 414 BC, and compounds the point by swearing by Demeter, the deity whom Alcibiades had particularly offended. The depilation is so successful that the Kinsman is deemed to be εὐπρεπής ("attractive": 233); Alcibiades' σώματος εὐπρέπεια ("physical attractiveness") was among the qualities that encouraged the Athenians patiently to endure his excesses (Plut. *Alc.* 16.4). Invited to look in a mirror, the Kinsman sees Cleisthenes—an indication that when Cleisthenes comes on stage (at 574) he too is probably characterized as Alcibiades. Once singed, the Kinsman declares that he is καταπεπυρπολημένος ("wasted with fire"); is this perhaps one of Alcibiades' complicated words of a kind for which he was criticised in *Banqueters* (cf. Ar. *PCG* 205.6–7)? The Kinsman' οἰμώξεται τἄρ' ("will groan": 248) levelled at anyone who wants to wash his arse is certainly part of Alcibiades' attested idiolect, as we saw at *Plutus* 58 (p. 61, above).

The distribution of lines between speakers in the passage where the Kinsman is dressed in Agathon's clothes is disputed, but largely unnecessarily. If the line assignments of the Ravenna manuscript are followed, the problems disappear and the scene gains considerably in effect. Thus, if Agathon speaks line 253 (R), there

---

39 Trans. Sommerstein.

would be Alcibiadean cacophony if κροκωτὸν πρῶτον were pronounced κλοκωτὸν πλῶτον. If Euripides speaks line 254 (R) we have the likely dramatic analogue of one who was "much given to love affairs" swearing by Aphrodite; and of one who may well have lost his tackle as a result of the plague relishing the smell of a ποσθίου ("penis"), a diminutive, as often in the mouths of Periclean figures. At 261–2 there are successive references to a cloak, a bed and shoes: common enough commodities it is true, but all with particular Alcibiadean associations (see pp. 78 [cloaks], 78 [beds], 83 [shoes], above).

Euripides appraises the Kinsman with an expert Periclean eye, and approves of the transformation into womanhood. He reminds his kinsman to speak with an effeminate voice, and we might well guess that the Kinsman's reply πειράσομαι ("I will try": 268) was pronounced πειλάσομαι. The Kinsman insists on Euripides' swearing an oath to save him should things go wrong. The oath in question is a line from a Euripidean play, but is neatly in the names of deities close to Euripides and Pericles respectively, namely Aether and Zeus (272). The Kinsman says that this is equivalent to an oath by "the tenements of Hippocrates" (273); probably Hippocrates son of the Ariphron of Cholargus who happened to have been Pericles' fellow-guardian of Alcibiades (Plut. *Alc.* 1.2). While the precise point that is being made now escapes us (beyond the fact that the oath is deemed to be virtually useless), it clearly in keeping with the apparent drift of the play: that the κωμῳδούμενοι are usually members of Pericles' extended family. When Euripides swears by all the gods, The Kinsman revealingly flings at him lines (275–6) based on Euripides' *Hippolytus* 612: "It was my tongue that swore, and not my heart", a line spoken by Hippolytus who, it is becoming increasingly apparent, was again largely based on Alcibiades.[40] An Alcibiadean Kinsman would know all about perjury, hence the assurance demanded from a Periclean Euripides that there will be no cheating

The Festival, etc.

Let us pass quickly over the middle of the play, simply pointing out a few salient features. The prayers delivered by Critylla (295–311, 331–51) are, like the beginning of Dicaeopolis' rural Dionysia (Ar. *Ach.* 241–79), or Strepsiades' prayer before he enters the Phrontistery (Ar. *Nu.* 127) probably parodies of Pericles, who, "whenever he ascended the *bêma* to speak, would pray to the gods that nothing

---

40 B.S. Strauss 1993, 166–75; Vickers 2000; Appendix 1, below.

unfitted for the present occasion might fall from his lips" (Plut. *Per.* 8.6).[41] The Periclean characterization is immediately established by the repetition of Εὐφημία ἔστω at 296. The announcement of the business of the day (372–9) reflects regular procedure, but that Pericles is in the frame is perhaps apparent from the expressions in lines 381–2, for (i) σίγα, σιώπα ("be quiet, silence"), (ii) πρόσεχε τὸν νοῦν ("attend"), (iii) χρέμπτεται ("clears her throat [as orators do]") are all part of Aristophanes' Periclean repertoire and the reasons are easy to find, in: (i) Pericles' quiet endurance (σιωπῇ) in the face of adversity (Plut. *Per.* 34.1; cf. p. 152, below) as well as his apparent tendency to repetitiveness (ii) the centrality of Νοῦς ("Mind") in the teaching of Pericles' favourite philosopher Anaxagoras; (iii) χρέμπτομαι ("clear one's throat", especially "before making a speech": LSJ, *s.v.* and cf. Ar. *Th.* 381), is a word that had connotations of "thunder" (LSJ *s.v.*). Pericles owed his "Olympian" nickname to the thunder and lightning of his eloquence (Plut. *Per.* 8.4; cf. Ar. *Ach.* 531), and the conceit contributes to the Periclean characterization of both Chremes and Chremylus in *Ecclesiazusae* and *Plutus* (see Chapters 5–6, and 11).

Critylla's name is not actually revealed to the audience until line 898, but this "late naming" will have raised a laugh,[42] for Chrysilla of Corinth is the name of one of the many women with whom Pericles is supposed to have had an affair, a story we owe, moreover, to a writer for the comic stage (Telecl. *PCG* 47 *ap.* Ath. 13.589f). Critylla's patronymic, Ἀντίθεος is appropriate for "the Olympian", since the word means "equal to the gods" (LSJ *s.v.*), while her demotic Γαργηττόθεν (from Gargettus) will have evoked γαργαλισμός ("orgasm": cf. Ph. *de spec.* 3.11), appropriate again for one "much given to love affairs".

The First Woman's opening lines are full of likely Alcibiadean references, notably (i) φιλοτιμία ("ambition": 383) and (ii) προπηλακιζόμενας ("trampled in the mud": 386), and we are probably to take her, polymorphically, as yet another Alcibiadean manifestation. Alcibiades' ambition (i) needs no gloss, but the principal allusion here is perhaps to Alcibiades' seduction of Timaea, concerning which "Alcibiades himself stated that he did not seduce [her] out of ὕβρις, but φιλοτιμούμενον ('seeking after the honour') of placing his own descendants on the throne of Sparta" (Duris *FGrH* 76 F 69 *ap.* Plut *Ages.* 3.2). Then, (ii) προπηλακιζόμενος is a word elsewhere actually employed by Alcibiades (Plut. *Alc.* 37.2).[43] The First Woman is identical with the Mica over whose "baby" the Kinsman struggles (689–759), but which proves to be a wineskin; an appropriate image

---

41 And cf. Ar. *Ra.* 885 (p. 152, below).
42 On the phenomenon, see Olson 1992; Kanavou 2011, 12–13.
43 Although in his mouth it will perhaps have been understood as προπηρακιζόμενος "trampled in the shit"; cf. πῆραξον = ἀφόδευσον [excrement], Hsch.; *Sophocles and Alcibiades*, 161.

for likely polymorphs of the man who, as we frequently had occasion to note, was one of antiquity's most famous drinkers.

The Second Woman, meanwhile, probably "comes forward" as Pericles. Somewhat unexpectedly, perhaps, but apparently confirmed by the Chorus' reaction (459–65) to what he has to say. Their song is full of standard Periclean catchwords: (i) λῆμα ("spirit"); (ii) φρένας ("intelligence"); (iii) νόημ' ("mind"); (iv) οὐδ' ἀσύνετ' ("not unintelligent"); (v) δεῖ ("it is necessary"). For (i) λῆμα plays on Pericles' *bon mot* about Aegina being the pus (λήμην: Plut. *Per.* 8.7) in the eye of the Piraeus. (ii) The quality of Pericles' φρόνημα ("spirit") is frequently remarked upon by Plutarch.[44] (iii) relates once more to Anaxagoras. (iv) Thucydides was to call Pericles μὴ ἀξύνετος ("not unintelligent": 2.34.6). (v) Pericles' payment εἰς τὸ δέον ("for a necessary purpose") was proverbial.

In the speech itself (443–58) the audience would doubtless be alerted to the Periclean status of the speaker by mask and costume, so that the first word ὀλίγων ("[a] few [words]": 443) would raise a laugh, in that it falls into the category of words that Aristophanes regularly lampoons with diminutives, and to which Thucydides drew attention more subtly. The old woman makes garlands (448); Pericles introduced the custom of giving garlands to important visitors (Val. Max. 2.6.5). She has to rush off to the Agora; Pericles was never to be seen on any street except that which led to the Agora and the Bouleuterion. Her business concerns στεφάνους συνθηματιαίους ("garlands relating to a treaty": 458); Pericles speaks of ξυνθήκας ("treaties") in the Funeral Speech (Thuc. 1.144.2; cf. 145.1). I would claim a Periclean wigwam here.

Cleisthenes "comes forward" as another likely cross-dressing, effeminate, polymorph of the "son of Cleinias". Cleisthenes, like Agathon earlier, is not the κωμῳδούμενος—who, according to convention if not by law, could not be mentioned "by name". Cleisthenes' treachery is an embodiment of that of Alcibiades in recent years; but exaggerated, for even Alcibiades would scarcely have betrayed himself as Cleisthenes betrays the Kinsman. He is clean-shaven (575), he is woman-mad (576), and he claims to be a *proxenos* (576). Alcibiades' smooth visage and love of female company are well-attested, and in addition he was famously a self-elected *proxenos* of Sparta (Plut. *Alc.* 14.1; Thuc. 5.43.2). The women address Cleisthenes as ὦ παῖ (582), which may be yet another allusion to Alcibiades' precocious reputation.

---

44 Cf. Stadter 1989, 75.

Palamedes, Helen and Andromeda

Thesmophoriazusae is replete with apparent wordplay based on Alcibiades' speech defect, τραυλισμός, and there is even a direct allusion to his distinctive diction in the scene where the captive is made to re-enact part of Euripides' *Palamedes* (769–786). The comic hero is desperately trying to communicate with Euripides who has placed him in an awkward situation. He decides to copy Palamedes and write on oars. But there are no oars, so he uses instead votive wooden tablets that are somehow to hand. He carves the letters with care, but is moved to exclaim (780–1): Οἴμοι, τουτὶ τὸ ῥῶ μοχθηρόν ("Alas, what a really awful *rho!*"). There is indeed a *rho* in "Euripides", as the scholion reminds us, but there may be more involved here than that, for μοχθηρόν carries an undertone of depravity (LSJ *ad v.*), and would thus suit both the diction and the morals of Alcibiades. χωρεῖ, χωρεῖ ("Go on, go on"), the Kinsman enjoins the blade of his knife; or, if he does indeed pronounce *rho* as *lambda*, χωλεῖ, χωλεῖ ("limp, limp"): highly appropriate in a message to Euripides, whom Aristophanes elsewhere lampoons as the great χωλοποίος who was forever introducing lame heroes on the stage (cf. 24; Ar. *Ra.* 846).[45]

We saw that in *Helen* and *Andromeda* Alcibiades probably lay behind the characterization of the principal figures: Helen and Menelaus on the one hand, and Andromeda and Perseus on the other. The same seems to hold good for *Thesmophoriazusae*. To begin with, the Kinsman is already dressed in women's clothes, and says as much (851). He begins with a parody of the first lines of *Helen*, having again announced the fact to the audience (850). His interlocutor is Critylla who, as we have seen, is probably characterized as Pericles. Her "reactions throughout" are said to be "those of a person not acquainted with Euripides' *Helen*",[46] which is appropriate for an analogue of one who died long before its performance. She carries along the Periclean element, since Menelaus and Perseus "come forward" in the character of Alcibiades rather than that of Euripides. At 864–5, the Kinsman in the guise of Helen claims to have caused the deaths of "many souls by the streams of the Scamander", quoting *Helen* (52–3). In 410 BC Alcibiades was still operating in the Hellespont and Troad.

Menelaus, presumably wrapped in the same ragged clothing as in Euripides' play (and perhaps in seaweed), probably speaks κατ' Ἀλκιβιάδην. His first line (871) is taken straight from *Helen*; "Who holds sway over this imposing palace?"

---

45 And see *Sophocles and Alcibiades*, 77 and 110–11 on Soph. *Ph.* 1153 and Eur. *Ba.* 21.
46 Sommerstein 1994, 216.

he asks, but the next two lines are new. Is the local ruler one "Who might receive strangers (δέξαιτο) who have toiled in ποντίῳ σάλῳ ('marine tumult') in storm and shipwreck" (872); ποντίῳ σάρῳ, however, would mean "in seaweed" (cf. πόντοιο κακὸν σάρον: Call. *Del.* 225), which is not quite so elevated a concept. And let us also note the potential optative δέξαιτο, which is very much in keeping with the Alcibiadean characterization that Euripides (the real one) had been trying to establish at *Helen* 435. If the answer to Menelaus' question were to come from a lambdacizing Kinsman, he will have mispronounced Πρωτέως ("of Proteus") in such a way that it will have taken up the marine references of the previous couple of lines, for Πλωτέως would carry a meaning along the lines of "Sailorman". If Crytilla does indeed "come forward" as a Pericles, she will have known how to interpret Alcibiadean, which explains why she half-recognises what they are trying to say, although she takes it as a reference to Proteas, Pericles' colleague in the generalship in the late 430s BC (Thuc. 1.45.2; 2.23.2) and probably a member of his inner circle.[47] She is also made to repeat herself Pericles-wise at 880 (ληροῦντι λῆρον: "speaking foolish nonsense").

To see the Alcibiadean Helen and Menelaus expressing love for each other (902–16) must have been diverting, but their ploy fails, and their departure is impeded by Critylla. Euripides says ὑπαποκινητέον ("he will have to slip away": 924), employing a word whose stem lay behind the characterization of Pericles as Cinesias in *Birds* and *Lysistrata*. Euripides assures the Kinsman that he will bring his countless μηχαναί ("devices"; 927) into play in order to rescue him. This word has Periclean resonances, as we have seen, for it was Pericles' skill in the context of μηχαναί ("siege engines") that led to success at Samos. There are more echoes of Samos, and of Pericles' role within it, in the next few lines, for the Prytanis, who comes on stage with the Scythian Archer (929), seems to be characterized as a brutal Pericles, akin to the one who supposedly tied Samian prisoners σανίσι ("to boards") in the Agora at Miletus, left them in the open for ten days before having them beaten to death with wooden clubs, and their bodies cast away unburied (Plut. *Per.* 28.2). The Prytanis orders the Archer to fasten the Kinsman σανίδι ("to a board"; 931), a form of punishment which has been identified as *apotympanismos*,[48] the same as the punishment allegedly meted out to the Samians.[49] The Kinsman addresses the Prytanis asking a βραχύ ("small") favour in terms that recall the usage of figures who are characterized as Pericles, or by those

---

47 Cf. Kagan 1974, 55; Sommerstein 1994, 214.
48 Sommerstein 1994, 217.
49 Stadter 1989, 258–9; *Sophocles and Alcibiades*, 14–15.

who are trying to wheedle something out of them.[50] The authority of the Periclean Prytanis, moreover, probably reflects Pericles' likely introduction of Scythian policemen at Athens as a by-product of his activities in the Black Sea in c. 437 BC (Plut. *Per.* 20.1–2).[51]

At 1001, the Kinsman is dragged on stage clamped to his board, and then is tortured by the Scythian Archer, who soon goes off to get a mat on which to sit. The Kinsman then gets a hint from Euripides, dressed as Perseus, that he should pretend to be Andromeda, and since he is already tied up, this is a relatively easy matter. He then sings of his woes (1010–1055), until Echo makes herself heard. Like Euripides, Echo too "comes forward" as Pericles. It was a brilliant move on Aristophanes' part to lampoon Pericles' tendency to repetition in this way. Echo was an invisible character in *Andromeda*, and she almost certainly is in *Thesmophoriazusae* as well. The scholiasts certainly thought so, but objections have recently been made which can, however, now be easily met. "Inlaw [i.e. the Kinsman] addresses her at 1058 in a perfectly normal way, without any of the bewilderment one might expect if he had been greeted by a disembodied voice, and he also knows that she is elderly (1073)."[52] There would be no need for an Alcibiadean Kinsman to express bewilderment at hearing the distinctive (but disembodied) voice of Pericles, nor should Pericles' relative age be a surprise.

Echo and the Kinsman between them manage to enrage the Scythian (1056–97), before Perseus arrives on (or over) the scene. He carries the Gorgon's head, which the Scythian Archer topically takes to be the head of Gorgus, an individual who seems to have died in battle in the autumn of the previous year, in 411 BC.[53] One of the striking features of *Andromeda* was the way in which Perseus and Andromeda fell in love with one another, but it was the love of Alcibiades for himself,

---

50 Ferguson 1977, 231; *Pericles on Stage*, 145–6. Cf. the diminutive (ἀργύριον ["small coin"]) at 937.

51 The date of the appearance of the Scythian police force at Athens is said to be "obscure" (Bäbler 2005, 115)—although its continued existence can now be observed into the second half of the fourth century (*ibid.*, 118–19). Andoc. 3.5 dates the introduction to 446 BC, but this in the middle of a "scrambled series of half-truths," full of "puzzling and wildly inaccurate details" (Thomas 1989, 119–21). In the wake of Pericles' campaign, "the Black Sea region became part of the Athenian empire and, at the same time, more closely familiar to Athenians" (Braund 2005b, 99). While the references in Ar. *Lys.* 436, *Th.* 929 ff., and *Ec.* 259 attest the continued existence of the institution, they all occur in Periclean contexts (in terms of the fundamental premiss of this book), and this would seem to point to the Scythian police force having been one of the fruits of Pericles' Pontic activity in the early 430s. It was perhaps then that the 300 Scythians mentioned by Aeschines (2.173) were purchased.

52 Sommerstein 1994, 226–7.

53 *IG* I.950.54; cf. Sommerstein 1994, 230.

which is presumably why Aristophanes "refuses to recreate *Andromeda*'s strikingly positive conception of Eros".[54] Rather, it is lust of the basest sort that Aristophanes gives us, enhanced by the crude misapprehensions of the Scythian Archer. This is to put Alcibiades in a rather less favourable light than Euripides had done. Euripides (the dramatic poet) seems to support Alcibiades' return from exile, and thus puts the rosiest interpretation on his tastes and proclivities; Aristophanes holds them up to ridicule, and it is not until *Frogs* that he comes round to the view that Alcibiades might, after all, be Athens' saviour.

Thucydides' End

Euripides gradually resumes a Periclean persona, as he realizes that the Scythian is impervious to the tricks that he and the Kinsman try to play on him. Thus, the words that Aristophanes puts in his mouth at 1122: "to fall upon the bed and marriage couch" have been described as "a blatantly tautological expression of which one hopes that Euripides could never have been guilty".[55] No, but it is just the sort of repetitiousness that Aristophanes might impute to Pericles. Tissaphernes, like Pericles, was "not unintelligent", indeed may well have been even more acute. To represent him as a Scythian, whose barbarous nature could not possibly understand what Euripides might say to him (1129–31), would have been unexpected, but highly amusing. Euripides decides to try a πρέπουσαν μηχανήν ("more appropriate device"); Pericles claimed to stand for τὸ πρέπον ("what is seemly": cf. Thuc. 1.144.2; 2.36.1; 2.36.4 and p. 75, n. 3, above), and μηχανήν is probably yet another Samian allusion.

If the Kinsman does indeed embody Alcibiadean echoes, then his imprisonment at the hands of a barbarian and his subsequent escape can only reflect Alcibiades' experiences the previous year, when he was held captive at Sardis by Tissaphernes until he escaped a month later (Xen. *Hell.* 1.1.9–10; Plut. *Alc.* 27.6–7, 28.1).[56] There are distinct Persian allusions in the verses sung by

---

54 Cf. Gibert 1999–2000, 80. The supposed "rivalry" between Aristophanes and Euripides (*ibid.*, 87–91) is perhaps overplayed, and if it existed at all, it will have been political rather than literary. Wycherley 1946 bears re-reading, esp. p. 107: "... Aristophanes' attitude to Euripides was not based on hatred or even rigid disapproval; it is unjust to his appreciation of Euripides to impute such one-sided feelings to him—but on a subtle compound of love, amusement, and alarm".

55 Sommerstein 1994, 231.

56 And Aristophanes implicitly corrects Alcibiades' lie that his escape had been carried out with the cooperation of Tissaphernes (Plut. *Alc.* 28.1); cf. Briant 2002, 978.

the Chorus at 947–1000, while the Kinsman is off-stage being bound to the board by the Archer. They contain an invocation to τὴν τοξοφόρον Ἄρτεμιν ("bow-bearing Artemis"). The epithet τοξοφόροι was frequently applied to the Persians, and at the time of the performance of *Thesmophoriazusae* Persian coins bore images of archer-kings.[57] Early in 411 BC, Peisander the oligarch had gone to Ionia with a view to restoring Alcibiades and to persuading Tissaphernes to provide money to the Athenians, but came back empty-handed on both counts (Thuc. 8.53–4).[58] There may perhaps be an allusion to these transactions when Euripides offers to let the Scythian sleep with the dancing-girl if he gives him a drachma (1195). "Fine", says the Scythian. "Then hand over the money", says Euripides. But the Archer has no money and hands over a bowcase instead.

We learn from the very last, abrupt, sentence in Thucydides' *Histories* that when Tissaphernes went to the Hellespont in late 411 BC, he had just come from Ephesus where he had "offered sacrifice to Artemis" (Thuc. 8.109.1). Tissaphernes had the interests of Artemis very much at heart (cf. his instructions issued in 409 for "everyone to come to Ephesus, to the aid of Artemis" [Xen. *Hell.* 1.2.6]). Bow-bearing Artemis was invoked by the Chorus of *Thesmophoriazusae* at 970–1, as we have just seen. Euripides disguised as an old woman called Artemisia (1200) pretends to be the bawd of a dancing girl who greatly takes the Archer's fancy. He is so besotted with Artemisia's charge that he calls after her five times (1201, 1213, 1216, 1223, 1225) in his own, Persian-sounding,[59] fashion "Artamouxia" in the closing lines of the play. Not only would it appear that the Scythian's evident need to remain in contact with Artemisia is an allusion to Tissaphernes' sacrifice to Ephesian Artemis,[60] but that this is where Thucydides' Aristophanic source gave out. This is not to say that Thucydides might not have rounded off his account when the time came for revision; it is simply

---

57 E.g. Carradice 1987; 1988; Briant 2002, 213–4, fig. 17, 408–9; cf. Root 1991, 72: gold and silver archer coins "expressed a quintessentially Persian, Achaemenid, manifestation of imperial power".

58 A magnificent silver coin in the British Museum bearing a portrait that has been variously identified as Tissaphernes (Jenkins 1972, 103–4, figs 218–19) and Pharnabazus (Munn 2000, 164, fig. 4a-b, 397) is most plausibly seen as representing the Great King himself (Dusinberre 2000). It was probably minted to pay Greek rowers, for in addition to the legend ΒΑΣ (an allusion to the Great King), it bears an Attic owl and olive branch, which "starkly reminded the recipient that the source of his income was not Athenian, but Persian resources": Trundle 1999.

59 Cf. Kanavou 2011, 157.

60 On Persian involvement in cults of Artemis in Asia Minor, see Brosius 1998; Briant 2002, 1009.

that when his *aide-mémoire* ceased to function—a circumstance indeed "not of his choosing",[61] he stopped writing.[62]

---

61 Andrewes in *HCT* 5, 387.
62 I now withdraw an earlier suggestion (Vickers 1989a, 51–2) that it is a coincidence that Thucydides and *Thesmophoriazusae* end in the same way.

Chapter 10

Frogs: Nothing to Do With Literature

Or rather, "only incidentally to do with literature". The primary purpose of *Frogs* was to win Aristophanes the prize for comedy at the Lenaean festival celebrated in the first weeks of 405 BC. He achieved this by making a plea for domestic harmony at Athens. According to one of the plot-summaries, the play owed its success, and the unusual privilege of a repeat performance, to a patriotic appeal expressed in the Parabasis for those in exile to be allowed to return to Athens (*Arg.* 1 *Ra.* Coulon). These individuals now included Alcibiades amongst their number once again. Elsewhere, we learn that Aristophanes was granted the rare privilege of a wreath made from the sacred olive on account of the services he rendered to the city by what he said in *Frogs* about the ἄτιμοι ("those who had been deprived of civic rights": *Vit. Ar.* 28.39–43; 29.28–31 Koster).

Civic reconciliation was the note that Aristophanes struck so successfully, and which appealed to judges and audience alike. And yet, the interest in *Frogs* today is thought to lie in the literary contest between Aeschylus and Euripides which occupies most of the second half of the play; *Frogs* is viewed almost exclusively as an exercise in literary criticism. [1] It will be argued here that it is a political allegory, in which literature is a mask for something else.

Dionysus' Question

"What would you do about Alcibiades?" is the question Dionysus puts to Aeschylus and Euripides towards the end of *Frogs* (1422–6). Surprisingly, in most scholars' view, this is one of the few places in Aristophanes where Alcibiades is mentioned by name. But, as we have often had occasion to note, "the kind of person who [was] usually lampooned on the stage [was] rich, or aristocratic, or powerful" ([Xen.] *Ath. Pol.* 2.18), and there was legislation forbidding lampooning by name (Schol. *Av.* 1297). It would consequently be surprising to find Alcibiades mentioned "by name" any more than he is. The resolution of the plot of *Frogs* depends on the answers Dionysus receives to his question. But the plot itself is replete with apparent inconsistencies. Dionysus, desirous of bringing Euripi-

---

1 E.g. Radermacher 1954, 3: "*Frogs* is a literary comedy"; for Sommerstein (1996b, 1) one of the "central issues" of the play is "how to save Tragedy"; and for Habash (2002, 1) "Dionysus [in *Frogs*] is preoccupied with literary technique, style, and content".

des back to life, goes down to Hades where he finds himself judging a competition between Aeschylus and Euripides. He unexpectedly judges Aeschylus to be the winner, and brings him back with him. There are seemingly many loose ends, and there has been much scholarly discussion of such questions as: Why was Sophocles not involved in the dramatic competition? Why is the plot so apparently disjointed? Why does Dionysus seem to forget the purpose for which he went down to the Underworld in the first place?[2]

Attempts at finding literary reasons for these apparent inconsistencies have come to nothing. Or rather, there is such a wide range of explanations on offer that something must be awry. The key to these outstanding problems may perhaps lie somewhere else, in the political sphere. Arguments have been presented elsewhere in this book, not only for a strong political content in other plays of Aristophanes, but also for that political content to be put across by means of characters based on the personalities of Pericles and members of his extended family, in particular of his foster-son Alcibiades. *Frogs* is no exception to this pattern.

Pericles had been dead since 429 BC, but Alcibiades was still very much alive in 405 BC, and his future very much a political issue. He had been in exile successively in Sparta and Asia Minor after 415 BC, had won his way back into favour with the Athenians by 412 BC, had made a triumphant return to Athens in 407 BC, but at the time of the performance of *Frogs*, he was in exile again and had taken refuge in one of the strongholds in the Thracian Chersonese that he had thoughtfully prepared against such an eventuality. Deprived once again of his property in Attica, in the spring of 405 he was in as bad a position as he had been in the autumn of 415. He was to die, still in exile, at the instigation of his enemies in Athens and Sparta and by the agency of a Persian satrap, in the autumn of 404 BC.

Lions in the State and Aeschylus

Aeschylus' success in the competition is due in large part to the answer he gives to Dionysus' question concerning Alcibiades. He responds that one should not nurture a lion's whelp in the state, but if he be fully-grown, it were best to humour him (1431–3). In a little regarded passage, Valerius Maximus (7.2.7 [329.19]), a writer who often preserves valuable independent source traditions,[3]

---

2 Cf. Dover 1993.
3 Carney 1962.

attributes the dictum to Pericles. Why Pericles? It could be, as Kock and van Leeuwen suggested, that Eupolis had put the expression in Pericles' mouth in *Demi*.[4] But even if Eupolis does lie behind Aristophanes' conceit (which is, however, doubtful), Pericles is still there. The image is evocative, moreover, of the story of Agariste, Pericles' mother, who dreamt that she would give birth to a lion (Hdt. 6.131.2).[5]

Alcibiades grew up in the house of Pericles, who played—however indifferently—the *de facto* role of a father. It has even been suggested that Deinomache, Alcibiades' mother, was once married to Pericles.[6] Whether or not this was the case, Alcibiades could without difficulty be viewed as "a lion's whelp" with respect to a Periclean lion.[7] But the point at issue here is whether Aeschylus could plausibly be viewed as a mask for Pericles. What reasons could there be, apart from Valerius Maximus, for making such an association? Pericles had, of course, been the *choregus* of our earliest Aeschylean play, the *Persae*.[8] But there are also parallels drawn in the text of *Frogs* between the statesman and the playwright that probably go beyond any coincidental correlations. The loftiness of Aeschylus' diction (πυργώσας ῥήματα σεμνά: 1004) is cause for comment in *Frogs*. σεμνότης ("solemnity") was a political virtue practised by Pericles,[9] while Pericles' oratory was imbued with "lofty intelligence" (ὑψηλόνουν: Plat. *Phdr* 270*a*; Plut. *Per.* 8.2; cf. D.H. *Th.* 18). Aeschylus' loftiness of language in *Frogs* becomes exaggerated (ἐτερατεύετο ["talked marvels"]: 834; κομποφακελορρήμονα ["pomp-bundle-worded", LSJ]: 839); Pericles' exaggerated metaphors were famous; "that the dead in war were like the spring taken from the year, that the discordant Boeotians resembled old πρίνους ('holm-oaks') battering their limbs against one another, that he could see war sweeping forward from the Peloponnese".[10] The forcefulness of Aeschylus' language degenerates into violence (αὐθαδόστομος ["presumptuous in speech"]: 837; ἀθύρωτον στόμα ["unchecked mouth"]: 838; γηγενεῖ φυσήματι ["portentous conceit"]: 825; ἀγριοποιόν ["poet of savagery"]: 837); Pericles found the people "as a rule, willing to second the measures

4 *CAF* 1.279; van Leeuwen 1896, *ad loc.*
5 For the image, cf. Aesch. *Agam.* 717–36 and Pl. *Grg.* 483*e*. On Alcibiades' leonine characteristics, see Bloedow 1991; Munn 2000, 193–4; Duff 2003, 98–9; *Sophocles and Alcibiades*, 79, 162.
6 Cromey 1984, 385–401; Podlecki 1987, 111; Stadter 1989, 238.
7 Cf. the comparison Sophocles makes between the infant Eurysaces and "the whelp of a lioness forlorn" (Soph. *Ajax* 986); Eurysaces was Alcibiades' legendary ancestor: Plat. *Alc.* 1.121*a*; Cornford 1907, 186.
8 Broadhead 1960, 2.
9 Stadter 1989, xxxiii.
10 J. H. Finley 1942, 267; cf. Arist. *Rh.* 3.1407*a*.1–5; Plut. *Per.* 8.7.

which he explained to them to be necessary, and to which he asked their consent, but occasionally having to use violence, and to force them, much against their will, to do what was expedient" (Plut. *Per.* 15).

Such analogies might well be fortuitous and have as much as anything to do with the fact that when early "prose, especially oratorical prose, challenged the traditional superiority of verse, it also inherited the latter's attitudes and functions";[11] were it not that Aristophanes' Aeschylus is accused of shouting like a πρῖνος ("holm-oak": 859) ablaze, after he has been told to behave πραόνως ("temperately": 856). "Holm-oak" is not an especially common word, but "holm-oaks" are part of the very small certainly Periclean vocabulary (quoted above), and πραότης ("restraint") was the quality above all others that was associated with Pericles (Plut. *Per.* 2.5; 5.1; 34.1; 39.1).[12]

Aeschylus' silence when he first appears on stage, remarked upon (σιγᾷς: 832), and later reinforced by Euripides' attack on the openings of Aeschylus' plays (911–12), where a character would sit alone, in silence (σιωπῇ: 916), may relate to Pericles' quiet endurance (described by Plutarch as πρᾴως καὶ σιωπῇ [*Per.* 34.1]) in the face of much public criticism of his policy of retreating within the city walls during the Spartan invasions of Attica; there was also the occasion when Pericles sat all day in the Agora in silence (σιωπῇ), conducting business while some "low worthless fellow" berated him (Plut. *Per.* 5.2). As we have often noted, Pericles is said always to have prayed before speaking in public; hence, perhaps, the prayer Aeschylus makes "before [he] start[s]" (885). His prayer is to Demeter, who nurtured him and whom he asks to make him worthy of her mystic rites (886–7). Since Aeschylus was a demesman of Eleusis, this is not altogether unexpected, but there is a humorous point as well in that Aeschylus had once unwittingly betrayed the secrets of the Mysteries (Arist. *EN* 1111a.9). Pericles who saw to the restoration of both the shrine at Eleusis[13] and quite possibly of the Eleusinion in the Agora as well,[14] might plausibly be thought of as having been a well-known initiate,[15] and consequently as an individual who might be expected to take a close interest in Demeter's mystic rites.

---

11 J. H. Finley 1942, 287.
12 Cf. Stadter 1989, xxx-xxxi, xxxiii, 61, 78, 261, 314, 341, 347.
13 Plut. *Per.* 13.7; Shear 1966; Stadter 1989, 169–70; Camp 2001, 106–8.
14 Francis and Vickers 1988, 163; see too *IG* I³ 50, which records building "c. 435", probably at the Eleusinion ἐν ἄστει.
15 Aristotle describes a conversation with Lampon in which Pericles is as yet uninitiated (*Rh.* 1419a), but the date is uncertain; Plutarch records another discussion between Pericles and Lampon before 443 (*Per.* 6).

There are other phenomena common to Aeschylus and Pericles. One of the charges made against Aristophanes' Aeschylus is that he says things twice over (e.g. "here I come and hither I return" 1153; "I call upon my father to hear, to hearken", 1174). We have seen examples of Periclean repetition throughout this book, and we might suppose that the speeches composed by Thucydides and put into Pericles' mouth reflect individual traits. If so, the Prodican "assonances of thought and phraseology"[16] such as those that occur in Pericles' third speech (Thuc. 2.62.3): "Face your enemies not just with φρονήματι ('confidence') but with καταφρονήματι ('a sense of superiority')" might well be the kind of expression Aristophanes lampoons. Thucydides' words are said to "convey Pericles' characteristic intellectuality, and contrasted as they are with the far more usual statements on the unreliability of hope, give evidence of genuineness".[17] The conceit is very similar, as Dover rightly notes, to the scene at *Clouds* 658–93,[18] where the humour is again at Pericles' expense.[19]

Losing Little Oiljars

In *Pericles on Stage* it was suggested that various figures: Dicaeopolis, Strepsiades, Demus, Philocleon, Hermes, the Epops, Cinesias, were masks for Pericles. They all employed diminutives ending in –ιον, and it was concluded that the mannerism was probably part of the Periclean idiolect. A "sudden productivity" and a "rapid spread" of the word form that occurred during the second half of the fifth century,[20] seem to have coincided with diminutives in the mouths of "Periclean" characters in Aristophanes, of those apparently based on Aspasia, or of people asking favours of them.

This may help to throw new light on the most famous Aristophanic diminutive of all: ληκύθιον ἀπώλεσεν ("he has lost his little oil-jar"), which is spoken seven times by Aeschylus in capping Euripides' lines at 1208 ff. The word occurs three times in the introductory banter (1200, 1201, 1203), and nine times in the succeeding dialogue (1208–45). Without going too far into the likely meaning

---

16 Hornblower 1987, 94, cf. 120.

17 J. H. Finley 1967, 26.

18 Dover, 1993, 29.

19 Vickers 1993, 603–18; *Pericles on Stage*, 26–58. Sophocles makes his Periclean characters (e.g. Creon in *Antigone* and Heracles in *Philoctetes*) repeat themselves (*Sophocles and Alcibiades*, 18–19, 67, 78). Easterling (1974, 14) rightly saw Sophoclean repetition as somehow significant.

20 Petersen 1910, 139.

or meanings of ληκύθιον ἀπώλεσεν, it is surely relevant that the Periclean Dicaeopolis succeeded in causing another manifestation of Euripides much embarrassment with a string of diminutives in -ιον. After requesting the Mysian πιλί-διον (*Ach.* 439: "little pointy hat"), Dicaeopolis refers in succession to a βακτήριον (448: "little stick"), a σπυρίδιον (453: "little basket"), a κοτυλίσκιον (459: "little cup"), a χυτρίδιον (463: "little jar"), and a σπυρίδιον again (469). He requests these σκευάρια (451: "little things") from Εὐριπίδιον (404, cf. 475: "little Euripides"). The conceit in *Acharnians* clearly involves the poverty of Euripidean stage-props (in contrast perhaps to those Pericles provided for Aeschylus' *Persae*, parodied at *Acharnians* 61–125),[21] but whether this was the case with the twelve ληκύθια remains open to question. The same holds good over any connection with the Periclean dictum εἰς τὸ δέον ἀπωλέσα ("I lost it for a necessary purpose": *Paroemiogr.* 1.80.3) relating to the occasion when he was unable to account for public funds. (Plut. *Per.* 32.3; cf. *Clouds* 859).

A Periclean explanation of the ληκύθιον conceit in *Frogs* might, however, go as follows: Dover is probably on the right lines in seeing some kind of sexual innuendo. He identifies the ληκύθιον as a "penis", rightly deducing from 1203 that "fleece, flask and bag" must imply "pubic hair, penis and scrotum".[22] A feature of Aristophanes' earlier plays is the cripple-teasing of the memory of Pericles by means of somewhat distasteful allusions to the plague, of which the statesman experienced a "wide variety of symptoms", as a consequence of which his strength was undermined (Plut. *Per.* 38.1). We have a detailed account of these symptoms in Thucydides; the final one being "even if a person got over the worst, the plague would often . . . attack the privy parts . . . and some escaped with the loss of these" (Thuc. 2.49.8). There are numerous examples of plague symptoms, and in particular genital loss, employed by Aristophanes as a means of lampooning the late Pericles (see Appendix 2). The ληκύθιον scene in *Frogs* may well be another.

Exiles and Euripides

If Aeschylus "comes forward" as Pericles, Alcibiades can scarcely be far away. Alcibiadean figures consistently play opposite Cleonian or Periclean characters. The debate between the Stronger and the Weaker Arguments in *Clouds* is a case

---

21 *Pericles on Stage*, 63–7.
22 Dover 1993, 338.

in point.[23] The Stronger Argument represents an exaggerated version of old-fashioned Periclean values, while the Weaker expounds views more in keeping with
what we know about the historical Alcibiades. The Weaker Argument, moreover,
employs Alcibiades' speech mannerisms. For example, at *Clouds* 920, the Weaker
Argument tells the Stronger that he is repulsively αἰσχρῶς ("ugly"); lambdacized
this would play on Αἰσχυλειῶς ("Aeschylean")—which is both very much in
keeping with the attack being made on the values of earlier times, and presumably alludes to Pericles' choregic activity.

As we have already noted, *Frogs* owed its success to a patriotic appeal for
those in exile to be allowed to return. Alcibiades was by far the most prominent
among the exiles at the time, and even after Athens had fallen to the Spartans
later in 405 BC, "a vague hope prevailed among [the Athenians] that Athens
could not utterly be lost while Alcibiades was still alive" (Plut. *Alc.* 38.3). The
point was made "emphatically" in *Frogs* a few months earlier. The appeal on behalf of the exiles in the Parabasis of *Frogs* is made in terms that would inevitably
have brought Alcibiades to mind. His return to Athens in 407 BC had not been
accompanied by military success. The Athenians were turned against him by
his enemies and displayed their anger and ill feeling by replacing him with a
board of ten generals.[24] Despite this, Alcibiades was to show his willingness to
help within a few months of *Frogs* when he proffered advice to the generals at
Aegospotami. This advice was, however, rejected with contumely. πρὸς ὕβριν is
the expression Plutarch uses (*Alc.* 37.1); προπηλακισθείς ("trampled in the
mud") is how Alcibiades described it (*ibid.* 37.2; cf. p. 141, n. 43, above).

The phraseology of the Parabasis matches the situation that prevailed after
Aegospotami, and we might well assume that the second performance of *Frogs*
occurred at the next celebration of the Lenaea, early in 404 BC. It could in any
case scarcely have occurred at the Dionysia of 405 BC, for preparations for that
event will already have been well under way. The *terminus post quem non* for a
second performance will have been the death of Alcibiades that occurred later in
404 BC. "There should be no-one ἄτιμος ("treated with indignity") in the city"
(632), Aristophanes states; "the citizens should give up their anger (700), and
they should make use of all willing kinsmen (701) and ... whoever ξυνναυμαχῇ
('would fight at sea')". The description of the kind of person that had been insulted (cf. προυσελοῦμεν 730 [explained elsewhere as προπηλακίζομεν: *Suda*]), was
εὐγενής ("aristocratic", *contra* Dover), σώφρων ("temperate"), δίκαιος ("right-

---

23 *Pericles on Stage*, 43–52.
24 Plut. *Alc.* 39.2; Diod. 13.74.1 (who speaks of "the anger of the multitude" at Athens: 74.2);
cf. Xen. *Hell.* 1.5.16.

eous"), καλός and ἀγαθός ("gentlemanly"), and educated in παλαίστραις καὶ χοροῖς καὶ μουσικῇ ("wrestling schools, choruses and music"). These expressions all carry an Alcibiadean resonance. σωφροσύνη ("sobriety of conduct") and δικαιοσύνη ("a sense of what is just") were the virtues which Socrates attempted to instil in the young Alcibiades (Xen. *Mem.* 1.2.24); they were, however, virtues that Alcibiades had singularly failed to acquire. Similarly, it was absence from wrestling schools for which Alcibiades was notorious (Isoc. 16.33)—he preferred racehorses, just as his musical education was singular (Plut. *Alc.* 2.5–7). He was certainly aristocratic (Plut. *Alc.* 1.1), qualified as a "gentleman" (although lampooned for an apparent lack of gentlemanly qualities in *Knights*,[25] and had sponsored more than one chorus ([Andoc.] 4.20–1; Plut. *Alc.* 16.4). This conjunction of Alcibiadean resonances—a wigwamful—leaves little doubt but that Alcibiades would have been foremost in the minds of the audience. Since Aristophanes was putting a case for forgiveness, he puts a favourable, if ironic, spin on the allusions.

Aeschylus' foil in *Frogs* is Euripides, who "comes forward" this time as Alcibiades. Given Euripides' client relationship with respect to Alcibiades,[26] this would have been a highly appropriate characterization. It is another example of Aristophanes' highlighting the generation gap, putting a representative of old-fashioned, up against a personification of modern values. That Euripides is indeed marked out as Alcibiades is clear from Aeschylus' first mention of his rival at 840, where he uses terms which refer both to Euripides' mother's supposed interest in market gardening and to an Alcibiades who had once been compared to Achilles; at Sparta, Alcibiades was said to be "not the son of Achilles, but Achilles himself" (Plut. *Alc.* 23.6). Aeschylus addresses Euripides as ὦ παῖ τῆς ἀρουραίας θεοῦ ("O child of the goddess of the land": 840). ἄρουρα meant "arable land", which is the dig at Euripides' mother. The line as a whole, however, is a parody of ὦ παῖ τῆς θαλασσίας θεοῦ ("O son of the sea-goddess": Eur. *fr.* 885 Nauck); in effect "son of Thetis", thus equating Euripides with Achilles, and by extension with Alcibiades. The latter's role as a latter-day Achilles awaiting his recall to the flag is a recurrent theme in *Frogs*, as J.T. Sheppard once noted in an unjustly neglected article.[27] Euripides is made to quote five times from *Myrmidons*, demanding of Achilles why he does not come to the rescue (1264–5, 1266, 1271, 1275, 1277). It should, moreover, already be clear that if the regular Pericles/Alcibiades antithesis is handled by means of re-

25 *Pericles on Stage*, 97–120.
26 See p. 45, above.
27 Sheppard 1910.

flections on the life and works of Aeschylus and Euripides, then the problem of Sophocles disappears. No one watching the play in 405 BC would have given Sophocles much thought. Nor would the absence of any mention of Macedon have been a problem,[28] for Euripides "comes forward" as Alcibiades rather than the playwright. Nor would anyone have been disturbed by the recollection of a Euripides "coming forward" as Pericles in *Thesmophoriazusae* some years earlier; rather, they would have been amused and impressed by Aristophanes' versatility in handling his material.

Euripides' response to the question "What would you do about Alcibiades?" is unexpected in the light of the way in which the playwright had supported Alcibiades' cause in the past. In essence, he says "have nothing to do with him, he is selfish and treacherous".[29] But when we recall that it is really Alcibiades-as-Euripides speaking, it is another case of Aristophanes having Alcibiades condemn himself out of his own mouth; his reaction is amusingly unexpected.

Dionysus, Xanthias, Heracles

There remains the question of continuity. Aeschylus and Euripides are on stage only in the second half of the play. In Aristophanes' other plays, the κωμῳδού-μενοι: the "rich, powerful or aristocratic" who are satirised, are on stage throughout *via* the device of "polymorphic characterization", whereby figures representing different facets of the same individual could be on stage at the same, or different, times. How might this work in *Frogs?*

Dionysus' status as the "son of Zeus" (631) recalls Alcibiades' filial relationship with Pericles, the object of frequent Olympian comparisons. Dionysus is also called υἱὸς Σταμνίου (22: "son of Wine-jar"); the Alcibiadean Bdelycleon in *Wasps* was son of Καπνίου (151; "Smokey"). Both play on Alcibiades' patronymic: Κλεινίου ("son of Cleinias") (and the "wine-jar" will also have alluded to Alcibiades' liking for drink). Dionysus is "supple, fickle, wayward, panicky, opportunistic, and unscrupulous ..." who "changes like a chameleon":[30] in short, a fair caricature of Alcibiades. Dionysus' characterization is, of course, also based on what the average Athenian already knew about the wine-god, and we are now very well informed in this area.[31] Dionysus in *Frogs*, like his real-life model, probably pronounces *rho* as *lambda*. Two examples will suffice:

---

28 Cf. Scullion 2003.
29 Wycherley 1946, 103.
30 Stanford 1973, xxix-xxx.
31 Lada-Richards 1999.

at 184, he addresses Charon as follows: χαῖρ᾽ ὦ Χάρων, χαῖρ᾽ ὦ Χάρων, χαῖρ᾽ ὦ Χάρων ("Greetings, O Charon, greetings, O Charon, greetings, O Charon"). Lambdacised, χαῖρ᾽ ὦ Χάρων would render χαῖλ᾽ ὦ χαλῶν ("Greetings, O one who loosens his bowels" [cf. LSJ *s.v.* χαλάω, 8]). That this is not fortuitous is confirmed by Charon's reply, "Who is for the ἀναπαύλας ('rest-rooms': 185)?" Then, towards the end of the play, as the throne is awarded to Aeschylus and Euripides challenges the verdict, Αἰσχύλον occurs in two successive lines spoken by Dionysus: Αἰσχύλον δ᾽ αἱρήσομαι ("I choose Aeschylus": 1471) and ἔκρινα νικᾶν Αἰσχύλον ("I judged Aeschylus to be the winner": 1473). There is, however, a play on αἰσχρόν ("shameful"), with an invidious reflection on the victor. That this is so is confirmed by Euripides' claim that this is αἴσχιστον ("most shameful": 1474), to be capped by Dionysus' response τί δ᾽ αἰσχρόν (1475: "what is shameful?"), or—with lambdacism—a play on τί δ᾽ Αἰσχύλειον ("what is Aeschylean?"), using a joke of long-standing (see pp. 137, 155, above).

Xanthias is not, as someone once said, "the nearest we shall ever get to a real-life slave", for he too "comes forward", polymorphically, as Alcibiades. Both Xanthias and Dionysus represent in varying degrees the side of Alcibiades' character that had been used to good effect from the very start of his public career, namely his tendency to βωμολοχία ("clowning around": Plut. *Alc.* 40.3). Xanthias, like Dionysus, lambdacises. Awareness of this helps to remove a problem in the first line of the play (although commentators consistently overlook it). Xanthias ostensibly says to Dionysus: "Shall I tell one of the hackneyed jokes, master, the sort at which the audience for ever γελῶσιν ('laugh')". If Xanthias (and Dionysus) wore appropriate masks and costumes, and came on stage walking in the affected way in which Alcibiades did, the audience will have understood "Shall I tell one of the hackneyed jokes, master, the sort at which the audience for ever grow old?" playing on γεριῶσιν. The *double entendre* renders amusing a line that is otherwise bland. It also helps to explain why Dionysus a few lines later says that he comes away from a dramatic festival "more than twelvemonth older than [he] went" (18).[32] Xanthias had not, apparently, fought at Arginusae in 406 BC (191–2); no more had Alcibiades, who was a notable absentee, having been replaced as general by then.

What of Heracles, who is involved in a scene with the Alcibiadean Dionysus and Xanthias? He is not quite the same as the Heracles in *Birds* (who is a mask for Lamachus)[33] but he probably stands for Pericles. Aristotle lets us off the hook of having to explain "How can Heracles possibly stand for different characters?"

---

32 Trans. Rogers 1902.
33 Katz 1976; *Pericles on Stage*, xxvi-xxxi.

when he says that "all poets err who have written a Heracleid ... they imagine that, since Heracles was one, the plot should also be one" (Arist. *Po.* 1451a.19–27). There is in fact indirect evidence that Pericles was represented elsewhere on the Athenian stage as Heracles. Aspasia was called Omphale by either Cratinus or Eupolis (Schol. Plat. *Mx.* 235e); "Pericles", as Philip Stadter quite properly states, "would have been Heracles".[34] And I have argued elsewhere that the Heracles in *Philoctetes* "comes forward" as Pericles.[35] The Heracles in *Frogs*, moreover, says various things that recall Periclean themes: τίς ὁ νοῦς; Heracles asks at 47 (cf. 105). Νοῦς ("Mind") was, as we have often seen, a central concept of Anaxagoras, a philosopher close to Pericles. Heracles' stated dislike of Euripides (80–2) parallels that of the Periclean Dicaeopolis in *Acharnians*.[36] The two-obol fare (140) for Charon's boat recalls the jury-pay instituted by Pericles (Plut. *Per.* 9.3). Then there is the frequent use of diminutives ὠδελφίδιον (60: "little brother"), μειρακύλλια (89: "striplings"), θρανίου (121: "benchlet"), πλοιαρίῳ (139: "little boat"). Heracles may not be the only polymorph of Pericles, for if σκευάρι' (172: "little things") in Dionysus' address to the Corpse is an example of the "wheedling use" of the diminutive,[37] then the Corpse too may be another manifestation of the statesman. The Corpse drives a hard bargain; very much in keeping with Pericles' notorious tight-fistedness (Plut. *Per.* 16.3–4). Pericles was also dead.

A Chorus of Initiates is highly appropriate for both Pericles and Alcibiades. Pericles, as we have seen (p. 152, above), was probably an initiate himself. Alcibiades was involved in the popular mind both with the profanation of the Mysteries before 415 BC, for which he was condemned to death *in absentia*, as well as with a magnificent celebration of the Greater Mysteries in the summer of 407 BC: "It was an august and solemn procession, and all those that did not envy him said that he had performed the office of a high priest in addition to that of a general" (Plut. *Alc.* 34.3–7). The precise significance of the Chorus of Frogs remains a puzzle, but since they were, if the scholiast (Schol. *Ra.* 211) is correct, probably invisible and only relevant to a very short part of the action, this will hardly matter against the larger picture. Nor is the precise relationship clear between *Frogs* and Euripides' *Bacchae*, first performed at Athens after the writer's death in Macedonia, perhaps at the same celebration of the Lenaea as *Frogs*, or at the Dionysia a couple of months later. If, however, as some have ar-

---

34 Stadter 1989, 240.
35 *Sophocles and Alcibiades*, 67–8, 78–9, pp. 44, above.
36 *Pericles on Stage*, 76.
37 Cf. Ferguson 1977, 209–35.

gued, Aristophanes already knew details of the text of Euripides' play,[38] he will also have known its title. The Greek title of *Frogs*, *BATPAXOI*, may have played on *BAKXAI*.

Why Does Aeschylus Win?

Dover's workmanlike commentary on *Frogs* usefully isolates some of the reasons why the victory in the literary contest goes to Aeschylus.

> Lines 1482–99 tell us why Aeschylus has won; first in positive terms, then in negative. The first stanza congratulates him on ξύνεσιν ἠκριβωμένην (1483), εὐφρονεῖν (1485), and attributes his victory to his being συνετός (1490). [Euripides had earlier prayed to Ξύνεσις at 892f.]. The chorus's verdict is that Euripides was mistaken; it is Aeschylus who is superior in σύνεσις.[39]

Dover rejects the possibility that this σύνεσις ("intelligence") might be political: "The σύνεσις of Aeschylus must be his understanding of what works in the theatre ..". While this might be true up to a point (all the references to the dramatic poets have to make sense in literary terms), there are some clear Periclean and Alcibiadean allusions as well. Thucydides, whom we might regard as a shrewd judge of his contemporaries, was very sparing in applying the words συνετός and σύνεσις in the positive sense of "intelligent", "intelligence" to individuals. Alcibiades is strikingly absent from the list, and Edmund Bloedow has shown why.[40] Pericles was, however, numbered among the six fifth-century individuals that Thucydides considered to be intelligent;[41] but he is only admitted grudgingly, being merely deemed μὴ ἀξύνετος ("not un-intelligent").[42] It is, however, enough to account for a Periclean Aeschylus' victory in the intelligence stakes over an Alcibiadean Euripides. ἠκριβωμένην ("exact"), however, qualifies the "intelligence" in a pointed manner, for a cognate word was used to describe Pericles' exact regulation of his household expenses: εἰς τὸ ἀκριβέστατον. (Plut. *Per.* 16.5). Pericles, moreover, possessed an admirable φρόνημα ("disposition": Plut. *Per.* 39.1), an attribute which well corresponds to εὐφρονεῖν ("be well disposed"). The characteristics which Dover has so conveniently isolated—the wig-

---

38 E.g. Carrière 1966, 118–39; Cantarella 1974, 291–310.
39 Dover 1993, 20.
40 Bloedow 1992.
41 Who include Themistocles, Archidamus, Pericles, Brasidas, Hermocrates and Phrynichus.
42 Thuc. 2.34.6; Hornblower 1991, 124–5, 294.

wam he has unwittingly constructed—are all Periclean, and presumably carry a "political connotation" on that account.

The negative terms are similarly revealing. According to Dover, the list "tells us what Aeschylus did *not* do and thus by implication what Euripides did wrong":

> to sit by Socrates and talk (λαλεῖν), discarding poetry (μουσική) and leaving out what matters most in the art of tragedy. To spend time idly on theorizing (ἐπὶ σεμνοῖσιν λόγοισιν) and nonsensical quibbling (σκαριφησμοῖσι λήρων) is loony (παραφρονοῦντος ἀνδρός).[43]

They apply equally well to Alcibiades. He had been one of Socrates' most famous pupils, to the extent that the latter's tuition of Alcibiades (and Critias) was one of the charges specifically laid against him in 399 BC (Xen. *Mem.* 1.2.12). A quarter of a century earlier, Aristophanes had referred to Alcibiades in the same breath as a εὐρύπρωκτος καὶ λάλος "garrulous pathic" (*Acharnians* 716) and there is no reason to believe that he had become less talkative since. So far as μουσική is concerned, Alcibiades had been influential in making *aulos*-playing unfashionable among his younger contemporaries. (Plut. *Alc.* 2.5–7). If the word refers more specifically to "education" (as it can), Alcibiades was called by one of his contemporaries ἀπαίδευτος ("uneducated": Antisth. *fr.* 30 Caizzi *ap.* Ath. 12.534c), and a similar point was made about the Alcibiadean Pheidippides in *Clouds:* "He does not want to learn" (798).

Also in *Clouds*, Aristophanes had used Alcibiades' idle theorising with the sophists as a vehicle for satire. The unusual expression Aristophanes uses for "nonsensical quibbling" is close to one (διεσκαριφησάμεθα) employed by Isocrates (7.12) who was, like Alcibiades, greatly influenced by Gorgias (Cic. *De or.* 3.59).[44] Then, if Pheidippides was indeed largely based on Alcibiades, it may be significant that he, like the chorus in *Frogs*, uses the word παραφρονοῦντος—in speaking of his Periclean father's supposed madness at *Clouds* 884. Alcibiades' own mental health cannot have been much different; Sophocles makes much of his essentially irrational nature,[45] and Plutarch (who had access to far more sources than we do) describes Alcibiades' character as full of "many strange inconsistencies and contradictions" (*Alc.* 2.1). Again, the allegory is political. The literary content would not be there unless attention was

---

43 Dover 1993, 21.
44 On Alcibiades' relationship with Gorgias, see *Sophocles and Alcibiades*, 153–75.
45 *Sophocles and Alcibiades*, 29–30, 53–4; Vickers 2012.

being drawn to Alcibiades' less than satisfactory education[46] and its unfortunate political consequences.

But what is the larger picture of *Frogs?* Why should an Alcibiadean Dionysus reject an Alcibiadean Euripides in favour of a Periclean Aeschylus? If it relates to the possible return of Alcibiades to the Athenian fold, it would have been a delicate, and subtle, way of suggesting that if he were to return it should be to employ Periclean policies: of a kind actually spelt out at 1463–5, where Aeschylus recommends a concentration of Athenian forces on naval warfare, while allowing the enemy to invade Attica: identical with Pericles' advice at the beginning of the Peloponnesian War.[47] The accent on σωτηρία ("safety") towards the end of the play (e.g. 1419, 1433, 1436, 1448, 1458, 1501) is perhaps significant: taken together with the choice of Aeschylus, it amounts to a subliminal suggestion that Alcibiades, whom the Athenians "love yet hate" (1425) might still save Athens, albeit an Alcibiades more in tune with traditional values rather than those with which Aristophanes' Alcibiadeanising Euripides was thought to be associated. Any apparent approval of Alcibiades is thus highly qualified.

Aristophanes' appeal for an end to domestic strife, and for the return of the exiles, was probably directly responsible for the legislation of Patrocleides later in the year when the ἄτιμοι and other exiles were recalled. They did not actually return, however, until Athens was in the hands of the Spartans in the following April (Andoc. 1.80). These were not the circumstances in which Alcibiades would willingly come back to his native city. Soon afterwards, the conduct of domestic politics at Athens was seized by the Thirty, whose reign of terror lasted until early in 403 BC. The chief among these apostles of political correctitude was Critias, an individual whose name had until very recently been linked with that of Alcibiades. Whether or not they were ever truly close (and the evidence is ambiguous),[48] their relationship had certainly soured by 404 BC. Critias appealed to the Spartan admiral Lysander to have Alcibiades put to death as a danger to the Athenian state (Plut. *Alc.* 38.5–6; cf. Nepos, *Alc.* 10.1). At the additional urging of the authorities in Sparta, and probably with the active involvement of the local satrap, Alcibiades was killed in Phrygia in ignominious circumstances.[49] The lion's whelp had croaked.

46 And it really was unsatisfactory: Pericles entrusted Alcibiades' education to a Thracian slave who was "useless on account of his old age" (Pl. *Alc.* 1.122*b*; cf. Plut. *Lyc.* 15).
47 Thuc. 1.140–4; cf. Dover 1993, 75; Munn 2000, 430, n. 33; Azoulay 2014, 129.
48 See Ianucci 2002, 42–3; Wilson 2003; *Sophocles and Alcibiades*, 104–14.
49 Perrin 1906; Robert 1980, 257–307; Briant 2002, 395, 928 (and 618, 987 where it is suggested that an awareness on Alcibiades' part of Cyrus' plans for rebellion was a contributory factor in his assassination).

Chapter 11

Aspasia on Stage: *Ecclesiazusae*

Aspasia "figured large in the works of comic writers", wrote Didymus the Grammarian in the first century BC (Did. *ap.* Clem. Al. *Strom.* 4.19.122).[1] Aristophanes mentions Aspasia by name in a passage at *Acharnians* 516–539, where the outbreak of the Peloponnesian War is attributed to a row over two prostitutes belonging to her household. Plutarch, writing a couple of centuries after Clement, is able to name a few other instances: "in the comedies of the time, [Aspasia] is spoken of as the new Omphale and as Deianeira, and sometimes as Hera. Cratinus plainly speaks of her as a harlot ... and [Pericles'] bastard son is mentioned by Eupolis"—as is the shame he feels about his "harlot mother" (*Per.* 24. 9–10). These instances of Aspasia on the comic stage, which present her essentially as "a prostitute near the inner circle of power"[2] probably date to the fifth century.[3] The characterization is probably the result of comic invention, generated by those who wished to put Pericles in a bad light.[4]

Aspasia in the Fourth Century

Whatever the real state of affairs, it is the purpose of this chapter to suggest that Aspasia's presence on the Attic comic stage continued well into the fourth century. If such representations were posthumous, there are enough attested instances of *idolopoeia* (the device whereby characters were brought back from the dead in order to make a contemporary point) for this not to be an issue. Thus, Solon had been brought back from the dead in Cratinus' *Chirones*,[5] and Plutarch's aspersions on Pericles' "bastard son" and his "harlot mother" come from Eupolis' *Demi* of *c.* 417–410 BC, a play in which Miltiades, Aristides, Solon, and Pericles are recalled from Hades to help Athens. Pericles was long since dead by then, as indeed he was for all of Aristophanes' plays.

---

1 Ἀσπασίας γὰρ τῆς Μιλησίας, περὶ ἧς καὶ οἱ κωμικοὶ πολλὰ δὴ καταγράφουσιν ... (and he goes on to speak of her supposed influence over Socrates and Pericles).
2 Henry 1995, 28; Solana Dueso 1994.
3 Schwarze 1971; Mattingly 1977.
4 E.g. Wallace 1994, 147, n. 5; Henderson 2000, 140.
5 Cratinus, *PCG* 87; cf. Ogden 2001, 26.

Another well-known instance of *idolopoeia* involves Aeschylus and Euripides in *Frogs* (although, as we have seen, they are really masks for others); yet another involves Aspasia and Socrates. The dramatic date of Plato's *Menexenus* is 386 BC, and the dialogue represents Socrates (dead since 399 BC) quoting a funeral speech which he had heard the day before from the lips of Aspasia (presumably also deceased, but perhaps only recently)[6]—and which she forced him to commit to memory (236*b-c*). "She had been told that the Athenians were going to choose a speaker, and she repeated to [Socrates] the sort of speech which he should deliver, partly improvising, and partly from previous thought, putting together fragments of the funeral oration which Pericles spoke, and which she composed". (236*a-b*).

Plato's purpose in writing the *Menexenus* is much disputed; indeed, there is no agreement among scholars that it is actually by him.[7] For present purposes these issues are not directly relevant, but of all the explanations of *Menexenus* on offer, that of E. Bloedow seems the most acceptable: *viz.*, that it is a genuine work but one full of irony, incorporating an example of the kind of popular rhetoric of which Plato disapproved. He wishes to tar both Aspasia and Pericles with the same brush, in making them out to be co-architects of the sophistic movement. The work is a "vigorous and full scale attack on, not merely contemporary rhetoric, but on rhetoric in general and Sophistic rhetoric in particular".[8] At all events, Socrates regards Aspasia as surpassing Antiphon of Rhamnous as an instructor in rhetoric (Pl. *Men.* 236*a*), a speaker whom Thucydides considered to have given the best defence speech "of all known up to [his] time" (Thuc. 8.68.2).[9]

Antisthenes (*c.* 441–371 BC) wrote a philosophical dialogue called *Aspasia*. From the little that can be gleaned from fragments, it seems that Aspasia was presented in a poor light, and that the writer dwelt on her amorous relations, principally with Pericles.[10] The date is uncertain, but it is thought to antedate (but scarcely by much) another Socratic dialogue by Aeschines of Sphettus, also entitled *Aspasia*. This work, the first to mention Aspasia positively, was composed between 393 and 384 BC, although its action is set between 420 and 410 BC, at a time when Aspasia will have been an older woman, "perhaps a *graus*

---

6 Solana Dueso 1994, xxiv attributes the sudden appearance of works devoted to Aspasia to her death in c. 390 BC.

7 Loraux 1990, 228; Solana Dueso 1994, liv-lxix; Henry 1995, 33.

8 Bloedow 1975.

9 Cf. Rothwell 1990, 36.

10 Ehlers 1966, 30–33; Henry 1995, 30–32.

(crone)".[11] Socrates recommends her as a suitable teacher for the son of Callias (Aesch. Socr. *fr.* 17 [Dittmar]).[12] Elsewhere, Socrates is made by Xenophon to cite Aspasia praising honesty in courtship: the best matchmakers speak the truth about the parties they represent (Xen. *Mem.* 2.6.36). Then, in the *Oeconomicus*, Socrates offers to introduce Aspasia to his interlocutor as a reliable authority on the proper training of a good wife (Xen. *Oec.* 3.14.).

The precise dates of composition of the *Oeconomicus* and *Memorabilia* are difficult to establish, but whatever they were, it is clear that Aspasia was far from forgotten in the first half of the fourth century. It would be difficult to say that her memory was ignored at that time and yet, with few exceptions, the evident parallels between Aspasia and Praxagora in *Ecclesiazusae* (of 391 BC) have been passed over by scholars. Aspasia is not mentioned in the most recent commentary on *Ecclesiazusae*;[13] nor is Praxagora referred to in a recent biography of Aspasia;[14] nor, so far as I can tell, have the authors of these works been criticised for these omissions. It is not as though the equation is a new idea, or that it does not have obvious merits. R.G. Ussher saw Praxagora "in the enlightened tradition of Aspasia *Mx.* 236*b*",[15] Jeffrey Henderson sees "an element of the wily hetaira or Aspasia-figure" amidst other characteristics of Praxagora,[16] and Kenneth Rothwell devotes some excellent pages to "Praxagora and Aspasia", in which he lists some points of contact between the two:[17] "Both are capable orators: Aspasia would have given a speech had she the opportunity; Praxagora enacted what Aspasia aspired to". He cites an anecdote of Philostratus, according to which "it is said that Aspasia sharpened Pericles' tongue after the fashion of Gorgias" (*Ep.* 73); *Ecclesiazusae* is full of rhetorical figures of a Gorgianic nature: the frequency of antithesis, and the use of isocolon, and Praxagora actually learned the art of rhetoric by learning speeches by heart (ἐξέμαθον, *Ec.* 243–4), the method favoured by Gorgias for instruction.[18] Then, in recognition of her political influence, Aspasia was called τύραννος ("tyrant") by Eupolis (Eupolis *PCG* 294). Her "renown as a teacher (διδάσκαλος: Pl. *Mx.* 235*e*, Athenaeus 5.219*b*) resembles Praxagora's accomplishments in the *Ec-*

---

11 Henry 1995, 40–45.
12 Kahn 1996, 34 detects "an element of fantasy" here.
13 Sommerstein 1998.
14 Henry 1995.
15 Ussher 1973, 108.
16 Henderson 2000, 140.
17 Rothwell 1990, 92–5.
18 Rothwell 1990, 86–7, citing Arist. 183*b*.36.

clesiazusae: her task is to explain the new system, and she is repeatedly described as teaching or expounding (διδάσκειν 215, 514, 583, 662)".

Rothwell draws analogies between Aspasia and Praxagora at the erotic level,
too. "Aspasia, by profession, is knowledgeable in matters of *erôs*. Praxagora is a
housewife, yet she is hardly a model of restraint ... she has not committed adultery that we know of, but she certainly seems to know exactly how she would go
about it (522–26) .... Both are able to use their power, based on *erôs*, to achieve
their political ends. Aspasia used her allure to inspire politicians to become better orators ... Praxagora, by her performance as a *neaniskos*, and by offering laws
that do away with sexual barriers, makes the new society more attractive to Blepyrus and the Athenians". He also suggests that *Ecclesiazusae* is an elaborate
parody of Aspasia's role, well attested in the sources, as a matchmaker. "Aspasia
and Praxagora offer different solutions, but address a similar problem".[19]

A possible reason why there has been a general disinclination to make an
equation between Aspasia and Praxagora is that in her detailed study of Aspasia
in the Socratic tradition, Barbara Ehlers was reluctant to see Praxagora as anything other than the representative of Athenian matrons in general: "Praxagora
is the representative of her class; she is not a special type".[20] And yet, as Rothwell observes, "the similarities should not be overlooked". He goes on to note
that "the literary tradition of Aspasia flourished in the early fourth century", although the dates of specific works are uncertain. Aristophanes may have been
influenced by this tradition, or "Praxagora may have served as a model, or a further precedent, for the Aspasia depicted in Plato and Aeschines".[21] Rothwell's
points are substantial, and it is a pity that they have been overlooked.

Polymorphic Characterization

Additional arguments will be presented below that Aspasia does not simply underlie the character of Praxagora, but the series of Hags as well. Blepyrus and
Chremes reflect different aspects of Pericles, and Epigenes (and others) are
based on the popular image of Alcibiades. Alcibiades' wife, Hipparete, also
seems to come in for lampooning. If this were indeed the case, it would remove
what is often thought to be a major problem of continuity in *Ecclesiazusae*. Praxagora is on stage for only the first half of the play. Her absence after line 729 is

---

19 Rothwell 1990, 96.
20 Ehlers 1966, 46.
21 Rothwell 1990, 94–5.

said to be "surprising", and unparalleled elsewhere in Aristophanes' extant oeuvre.[22] Her absence supposedly means that there is "no clear thread of continuity binding the subsequent scenes".[23] But if, as in the other extant plays, the κωμῳδούμενοι are in effect on stage throughout then the problem is a non-existent one. The way this is achieved is again by means of "polymorphic characterization", whereby figures representing different facets of the same individual can be on stage at the same, or different, times.

Praxagora's name is a speaking one: "she who is effective in public meetings",[24] and Blepyrus ("he who peers") does indeed suggest "an old man with poor eyesight",[25] and the allusion is probably to one of the "variety of symptoms" that Pericles had experienced during the Athenian plague (see Appendix 2). His *neighbour* Chremes' name is based on χρέμπτομαι ("clear one's throat", especially "before making a speech": LSJ, *s.v.*), as we have already noted (pp. 59, 141 above on *Plutus* and Ar. *Th.* 381). So too the put-down of "the Olympian" inherent in a word that also had connotations of "any loud noise" or "thunder" (LSJ *s.v.*). Then, Epigenes means "'born after', i.e. 'young'".[26] Alcibiades' relative youth was a commonplace of comedy.

Pericles, Alcibiades

In order to explain how the characterizations of Pericles and Alcibiades might work in practice, let us look at the description of events in the Assembly. Blepyrus has trouble with his bowels at 326–371, and discusses details at some length with his neighbour. At 372, Chremes arrives, fresh from the Assembly, and describes what has taken place. Chremes notes that Blepyrus is wearing his wife's χιτώνιον (374). Blepyrus has already described it as a ἡμιδιπλοίδιον (318). In other plays, as we have seen, diminutives in –ιον are nearly always on the lips of Periclean characters, or of people asking favours of them. For both Blepyrus and Chremes to be made to employ such diminutives probably marks them both out as in some way Periclean; in fact they both act out characteristics which are exaggeratedly at variance with Pericles' own conduct: the "spendthrift Aberdo-

---

22 Sommerstein 1998, 26–7, n. 99.
23 Sommerstein 2001, 24.
24 Sommerstein 1998, 137; Kanavou 2011, 171..
25 Sommerstein 1998, 168; the explanation may indeed not "find support in the text" (Kanavou 2011, 172, n.773), but it can be accounted for by the pathology of the Plague, especially as it affected Pericles.
26 Sommerstein 1998, 218.

nian" principle in action, a standard convention in Old Comedy. The characters would in any case have been easily identifiable by the audience on account of their masks and distinctive voices (see p. 8, above). Blepyrus embodies ἀπραγμο-σύνη (he does not even know that there has been a meeting of the Assembly [376]; Pericles was public-spirited to a degree), while Chremes displays a lackadais-ical approach to his civic duties in arriving late at the Assembly (381; contrast the zeal of the Periclean Dicaeopolis in *Acharnians*).[27] Both swear by Zeus or invoke his name (373 [Blepyrus]; 377 [Chremes]; 378 [Chremes]; 390 [Chremes]; 433 [Blepyrus]; 438 [Chremes]; 439 [Chremes]), as befits individuals apparently based on one known to contemporaries as "the Olympian".

Chremes describes the proceedings in terms which bring to mind in turn Pericles, Alcibiades and Aspasia. The reaction of the populace to Neocleides, when he comes forward—gropes forward—to speak to the motion concerning the safety of the state, will have resembled that of the Athenian *demos* towards Pericles when he spoke in public after his illness, and when he was still out of favour. Characters based on the historical Pericles might be cripple-teased with references to plague-engendered eye trouble (e. g. p. 79 above; Appendix 2). For Chremes, himself a likely calque of Pericles, to describe Neocleides so heartlessly (397–403), is ironic; while for Blepyrus to add the suggestion that his eyes be dressed with a burning salve which includes a Laconian herb (404–7)—especial-ly galling to a Pericles—is to go even further.

The passage describing what Euaeon had to say has been misunderstood as an indication of "how desperate the state of Athens" was in 391 BC;[28] rather, it is probably the report of a speech supposedly made by a caricature of Alcibiades. Euaeon is said to have delivered a popular democratic speech: just the sort of thing Alcibiades did on many an occasion.[29] Euaeon was the name of a son of Aeschylus: an appropriate alias for the foster son of one who had been lam-pooned (in *Frogs*) as Aeschylus (Chapter 10). Euaeon, who is δεξιώτατος ("a clev-er chap"), is made to claim that he is clothed even though everyone could see that he was naked; Hans Christian Anderson *avant la lettre*. In the event, he is not quite so δεξιός, for all that Alcibiades was famously δεινότατος εἰπεῖν ("a clever speaker": Diod. 12.84.1; 13.68.5) not to mention δυνατὸς εἰπεῖν ("a power-ful speaker": Plut. *Alc.* 10.4). The audience can see through his claim that he is wearing a *himation* (410)—a garment with strong Alcibiadean associations, as we have often seen. Euaeon is out of pocket; Alcibiades, for all his wealth, was often

---

27 *Pericles on Stage*, 61.
28 Sommerstein 1998, 177; cf. B.S. Strauss 1986, 165.
29 He has been identified as Plato's "democratic man": Glover 1945, 58.

in debt. Four staters would see Euaeon right; staters figured in an anecdote concerning a resident alien who was one of Alcibiades' admirers, and who "was not rich". This man scraped together all he owned, "about a hundred staters", and begged Alcibiades to accept it. Alcibiades' attitude towards his admirers was usually high-handed, but on this occasion he pitied the man in question, refused his gift, and arranged for him to be enriched in a perversely complicated manner at a public auction of the right to collect taxes, and at the expense of the other bidders (Plut. *Alc.* 5). The plan Euaeon puts forward is equally far-fetched, namely to have fullers give clothes—specifically χλαίνας ("cloaks")—to the needy. Once again, Alcibiades was noted for his *chlamydes, porphyrides*, and *himatia*. Those without beds should sleep at the furriers. Alcibiades' beds were also in the public eye, beds and pillows "belonging to Alcibiades" having been auctioned in 414 BC (Poll. 10.38). Blepyrus comments that Euaeon's motion would have succeeded had he made an impractical proposal to give free grain to the poor: a suggestion which neatly combines Pericles' interest in the corn trade and Alcibiades' rash politics.

But then up jumps a young man, "pale (λευκός) like Nicias" (428). Commentators have made heavy weather of the identification of this Nicias, asuming that he must be a contemporary, alive at the time of the performance of *Ecclesiazusae*.[30] If, however, one Periclean figure is speaking to another, then it would be perfectly natural for the point of comparison to be the well-known fifth-century general, an individual who "shut himself up in his house and seldom stirred abroad" (Plut. *Nic.* 5.2), and who would as a consequence have been as pallid as any shoemaker or philosopher. We (though Chremes does not) know that the young man is Praxagora. She and her sisters win the day, having outvoted the rustic voters. Blepyrus approves of the opposition of the latter in terms which only emphasize his likely Periclean status: νοῦν γὰρ εἶχον, νὴ Δία (433: "they showed good sense, by Zeus"); not only swearing by "the Olympian's" tutelary deity, but alluding to the nickname Νοῦς ("Mind") of Pericles' favourite philosopher Anaxagoras. The young man/Praxagora (probably based on Aspasia) went on, according to Chremes, to call her husband Blepyrus (a likely Periclean figure) successively a rogue, a thief and an informer (435–39). The irony is intensified in that Chremes also probably "comes forward" as a Pericles. Chremes reports the arguments given in favour of women—their good sense (significantly perhaps, νουβυστικὸν), their eye for the financial main chance (441–2), their discretion, their trustworthiness and honesty (442–51); in short, their complete difference from men, performing good deeds,

---

30 E.g. Holden 1902, 76; Ussher 1973, 135; Sommerstein 1998, 178.

rather than acting as informers, carrying out prosecutions, or doing down the people (452–3).

It was furthermore resolved that Blepyrus (or "Pericles") should put the running of the city in their hands. This involves reading σε ("you") at 455, together with most of the manuscripts. R.G. Ussher read γε, on the grounds that "(a) the Assembly did *not* of course decree that he *personally* should hand over and (b) the jest from Chremes in this place is improbable (his σε joke clearly ended at 440)".[31] The truth perhaps lies in the opposite direction: and that Aristophanes' conceit does indeed involve a transfer of power to Praxagora from Blepyrus. Granted the premise that Praxagora is "Aspasia on stage", and that the man in Aspasia's life was Pericles, this is the obvious direction for power to go. Much recent criticism of *Ecclesiazusae* is couched in terms which imply that Aristophanes is making generalizations about all Athenians (e.g. "All differentiation disappears into the collective").[32] Rather, the humour is much more likely to have been specific, and aimed at the folk-memory of particular individuals who had dominated Athenian politics over several decades.

The prospect of his wife and the other women performing the civic duties he formerly carried out is met with a certain equanimity on Blepyrus' part. What does fill him with horror is the prospect of having to κινεῖν ("bonk") them (468). This is not so much an allusion to Pericles' famous tendency to "love affairs", as to his likely inability to keep Aspasia happy after he had recovered from the plague. As already noted, Pericles' genital loss will have made it likely that Aspasia sought solace elsewhere before Pericles' death.[33]

Aspasia, Alcibiades and Hipparete

Having thus established some of the parameters of Aristophanes' elaborate game of Happy Families, let us now examine the beginning of the play. In her opening speech, Praxagora (using paratragic language peculiarly redolent of Euripides' *Hippolytus*)[34] addresses a lamp in conspiratorial terms (1–16). She wonders where the other women are, and frets over details (17–27). Then, however, a light appears. "I will withdraw", she says, "in case the *person* who is approaching is a *man*" (μὴ καί τις ὢν ἀνήρ). As it happens, the First Woman who now

---

31 Ussher 1973, 139.
32 Zeitlin 1999, 177.
33 Stadter 1989, 237; pp. 54, 70, above.
34 On the likely Aspasian relevance of which, see Appendix 1.

comes on the scene (30 – 31)[35] is indeed probably characterised as a man, as Alcibiades, and so there is considerable point to the words Praxagora is made to say.

We have already seen, in discussions of *Helen*, *Andromeda* and *Lysistrata*, how Alcibiades might on occasion be lampooned in womanly form (see Chapters 7 and 8, above), and it is thus not too difficult to see Alcibiades underlying the figure of the First Woman. The identification would have been made clear to the audience by means of an appropriate mask (Platon. 1.64 – 6), and by the way she walked. We have already seen that Alcibiades' gait and diction were were so distinctive that his son imitated them; even Libanius (*Decl.* 12.2.18) refers to Alcibiades' βάδισμα ("gait"). The First Woman appears to draw specific attention to her "funny walk" with her opening words: ὥρα βαδίζειν ("it is time to walk"). "Funny talk" may be involved too, if that ὥρα were pronounced ὥλα. The First Woman's true masculine status is in any case indicated by the masculine participle at 31: no need for special pleading; no need for emendation.

Praxagora then calls upon the Second Woman (33 – 5) who again seems to be based on a recognisable individual: this time Alcibiades' wife Hipparete. Her husband is said to be a Σαλαμίνιος—Alcibiades was a well known "Salaminian" on two counts. On the one hand, he reckoned his descent from Eurysaces, the son of Salaminian Ajax,[36] and on the other had been famously sent for by the Athenian sacred vessel the *Salaminia* in 415 BC (Thuc. 6.53.1), and from whose escort he escaped at Thurii (Thuc. 6.61.6 – 7). Sailors who served on her were known as Σαλαμίνιοι (Poll. 8.116). The Second Woman's husband has been "rowing" her all night in bed (39), with perhaps a play on "driving", if ἤλαυνε, the usual word for driving a chariot (cf. Ar. *Nu.* 25), refers to Alcibiades' favourite daytime activity.[37] We have already seen how Alcibiades' beds had earned a certain fame, and the *himation* that the Second Woman has just snatched (40) evokes his well-known trademark. Hipparete was said to be a "quiet and loving" wife (Plut. *Alc.* 8.4), a characterization which well suits the shy and retiring Second Woman.

The First Woman interjects (41), saying that she can see more women coming, and if she does indeed "come forward" as Alcibiades, the first words of her speech are full of appropriate resonances. καὶ μὴν ὁρῶ ("And now I see"), she begins, employing an initial καί, and that ὁρῶ, if pronounced ὀλῶ, will recall ὀλᾶς at *Wasps* 45. The list of women who are arriving begins with a significant name which would appear to add considerable weight to the idea that Alcibiades

---

35 Ussher's distribution of parts is followed here.
36 Plut. *Alc.* 1.1; Davies 1971, 10 – 12; cf. *Sophocles and Alcibiades*, 47 – 58.
37 Schaeffer 1949 – 50.

and his wife are in Aristophanes' sights in these lines. "Cleinarete", a name otherwise unattested, far from being "uncomic in formation and meaning"[38] would neatly combine Alcibiades patronymic ὁ Κλεινίου ("the son of Cleinias") and the second half of his wife's name, Hipparete. And when the First Woman next speaks (46–8), there is another potential ὁρᾷς/ὁλᾷς confusion, and her next sentence begins καί μοι δοκεῖ ("And it seems to me")—with initial καί.

At line 57, Praxagora tells the women to sit down so that she might ask whether they have done what they undertook to do when they last met at a women's festival: ὡς ἀνείρωμαι ("that I might ask"), as the Ravenna manuscript puts it. "Ionic forms", says R.G. Ussher adopting an emendation to the Attic ἀνέρομαι, "are hardly to be tolerated here".[39] But if Praxagora "comes forward" as the Milesian Aspasia, then Ionic forms are only to be expected. The First Woman is first to reply. She has indeed done as was resolved, has let hair grow beneath her armpits, and has gone sun-bathing; ἐχλιανόμην ("I warmed myself") is what the manuscripts all say at 64, but Bergk's emendation ἐχραινόμην ("I touched myself") is often printed. Both are right, each in their own way, for an audience attuned to lambdacisation on hearing the one would understand the other. The First Woman has acquired a false beard (70); the fact that extant portraits of Alcibiades show him beardless may be relevant here (see p. 138, n. 38, above). The precise connotation of the reference to Lamias (or Lamios) at lines 76–81 is uncertain, but one would guess that it had something to do with Alcibiades' brush with the law in 415 BC, when he escaped the attentions of the public executioner (cf. 81: βουκολεῖν τὸν δήμιον). Talk of clubs (76, 78) may allude to the story of Alcibiades having killed one of his servants with one (Plut. *Alc.* 3.1). The Second Woman proposes to do some spinning while she waits (89–92), one of her reasons being that her παιδία ("kiddies") are naked. Hipparete's son Alcibiades Jr had recently been in the news when, in c. 395 BC, he was prosecuted for desertion, and described as πένης ("penurious": Lys. 14.44).

Praxagora puts her colleagues right, and tells them how to behave in the Assembly. If they undertake the "daring deed" (106), they will benefit the city. At present, "we neither row (θέομεν) nor race (ἐλαυνομεν)", employing words which refer on the one hand to Pericles' favourite sphere of activity, and that of Alcibiades on the other. "καὶ πῶς ('And how': n.b.the initial καί) will the womanly-minded band of women address the Assembly?" asks the First Woman at 110–11, over-egging her femininity. If it is indeed Alcibiades speaking, he gets an answer very much in keeping with the youthful indiscretions for which he was notorious: "They say that youths who are screwed the most tend to be the δεινοτάτους ('cleverest')

---

38 Sommerstein 1998, 141.
39 Ussher 1973, 82; cf. 85 *ad Ec.* 74–5 καθάπερ εἴπαμεν [R]: "doubtful Attic".

speakers". For women this comes naturally (114), but they must rehearse what they are going to say (117), at least those who have practised their talks (119: λαλεῖν). "Which of us does not know how to talk (120: λαλεῖν)?" replies the First Woman. Alcibiades had once been alluded to by Aristophanes in the same breath as εὐρύ-πρωκτος καὶ λάλος ("a garrulous pathic": *Acharnians* 716), a characterisation that well suits here. The scene that follows, where a hypercritical Praxagora puts the women through their paces, recalls Plato's fictional Socrates' being forced by Aspasia to memorize a funeral speech (Pl. *Mx.* 236*b-c*), very nearly hitting him in the process. This was, according to the author, but one of πολλοὺς καὶ καλοὺς λόγους ... πολιτικούς ("many more excellent political speeches") of hers that he could repeat (Pl. *Mx.* 236*e*).

The Second Woman, probably based on Alcibiades' wife Hipparete as we have seen, finds the whole business καταγέλαστον ("a joke": 125). Underlying this may be a reminiscence of the occasion when Alcibiades struck her father Hipponicus a blow with his fist ἐπὶ γέλωτι ("as a joke": Plut. *Alc.* 8.4). That the word certainly carried some significance is clear from the fact that Praxagora repeats it (126). Quite what may be the significance of the Second Woman's allusion to lightly grilled cuttle fish (at 126–7) is unclear, but a similar phrase occurs at *Acharnians* 1040 immediately before the Periclean Dicaeopolis interviews the best man and bridesmaid who have seemingly come from the wedding of Alcibiades and Hipparete. The bridesmaid appears to have shared some of Hipparete's modesty, for she whispers her request to Dicaeopolis (that the bride's husband's wandering sexual organs should stay at home).[40]

Praxagora asks who will address the meeting first (130). "I" says the First Woman, but having donned a garland assumes that she is at a symposium, and asks for a drink; not simply an allusion to women's "fondness for wine" (Ath. 10.440*e*), but it is surely relevant that Alcibiades was given to exceptionally heavy drinking (Pliny *HN* 14.144; cf. Plut.; *Mor.* 800*d*, and supposedly downed a wine-cooler at one go at the symposium immortalised by Plato [*Smp.* 213*e*]). Then, in a series of statements either beginning with or linked by καί (137, 140, 142, 143) the First Woman gives a dismissive account of democratic procedures, with their libations and prayers; it was for impiety that Alcibiades was condemned and cursed by most of the Athenian priesthood in 415 BC (Plut. *Alc.* 22.5). Praxagora bids the First Woman βάδιζε ("walk"; always significant in potentially Alcibiadean contexts) and sit down, for she is "no good": ironic if she stands for an Alcibiades who was δυνατὸς εἰπεῖν ("a skilful speaker"). The First Woman—based on an Alcibiades who was shown beardless in por-

---

40 *Pericles on Stage*, 95–6.

traits—expresses the wish that she had never worn a beard, and ends by saying δίψει ... ἀφαυθήσομαι (R: "I shall die of thirst"). That ἀφαυθήσομαι looks very much like one of the high-falutin' words that the young Alcibiades was accused of using (cf. ἀποβύσεται in Aristophanes' *Banqueters, PCG* 205.6–7).

Praxagora then asks if anyone else would like to speak, and the Second Woman volunteers. She has to be reminded that she should speak like a man, and rest her weight on her stick. We can take it that Hipparete was extremely ladylike, and that there was comic "business" in making her dramatic analogue manly. Hipparete, it will be recalled, was "quiet and loving" (Plut. *Alc.* 8.4). The Second Woman expresses the wish that someone else could have spoken so that she could sit and remain ἥσυχος ("quiet": 152). Not only may this allude to Hipparete's retiring nature, but there may be echoes too of Hesychia, the priestess produced by opponents of Alcibiades' war-party in 415 BC (Plut. *Nic.* 13.6). The Second Woman twice inadvertently betrays herself, to be scolded by Praxagora and dismissed.

Then Praxagora begins her own peroration, having prayed to the gods. We might compare Pericles' practice of always praying to the gods before he spoke in the Assembly (Plut. *Per.* 8.6).[41] She claims to have an equal stake in the country with members of her audience. Aspasia's non-Athenian status, however, meant that neither she nor her offspring enjoyed political equality with Athenians. This, and the difficulties that ensued, can be entirely attributed to Pericles' law that limited citizenship to those with an Athenian mother as well as an Athenian father. Praxagora's observations regarding the quality of Athens' statesmen, who are ἀεί ("always") unworthy (174–82) will have reflected as badly upon Pericles as any others. Her aspersions on Agyrrhius, who instituted payment for attendance at the Assembly, will have played on the memory of one who instituted payment for public service in the first instance. Lines 192–203 deal with politics of the 390s BC, and the First Woman's reaction is to say how ξυνετός ("intelligent") Praxagora is: ironic coming from the likely analogue of one who never earned such an epithet himself.[42] At 205–40 Praxagora makes a case for handing power over to the women, but not without a couple of specific Aspasian allusions. As we have frequently noted, on Pericles' death Aspasia had quickly taken up with one Lysicles, a sheepdealer, by whom she had a son called <u>Por</u>istes. The line

χρήματα <u>πορ</u>ίζειν εὐ<u>πορ</u>ώτατον γυνή

---

41 Ussher 1973, 99; cf. Sommerstein 1998, *ad loc.*
42 Bloedow 1992.

that Rogers translates as "For ways and means none can excel a woman", coming as it does after a description of how mothers look after their sons (233–5), would appear to make double reference to the son of Lysicles. These are not the only allusions to Poristes in Aristophanes (cf. pp. 77, n. 9, 84, above); together they tend to confirm that he really did exist despite his somewhat outlandish name (meaning "One who provides").

Speaking Names

Her speech is so impressive that Praxagora is asked how she learned to speak so well. It seems that she lived on the Pnyx together with her husband ἐν ταῖς φυγαῖς (243: "during the flights"). The allusion is doubtless to the accommodation of Pericles and Aspasia at the beginning of the Archidamian War. It was here that "hearing the speakers" she learned how to speak herself (244). In fact, tradition had it that it was Aspasia who taught both Pericles and Lysicles to speak in public (Pl. *Mx.* 235e; *Com. Adesp.* 122 *CAF* 3.431; Schol. *Acharnians* 527; Did. *ap.* Clem. Al. *Strom.* 4.19.122).[43] Aristophanes here cleverly imputes false modesty to Aspasia. The First Woman is impressed, and says how clever and σοφή ("wise") Praxagora is; Aspasia was said to be a σοφίστρια in addition to her other gifts (Schol. Ar. *Ach.* 527). Praxagora is then asked how she would deal with insults from Cephalus, in reality a potter politician, but bearing a name that will have recalled Eupolis' description of Pericles as the κεφάλαιον ("headman") of those in the Underworld (*PCG* 115) or Cratinus' Κεφαληγερέταν ("[the] head-gathering one" *PCG* 258; Plut. *Per.* 3.5)—both abusive allusions to Pericles' pointy cranium. Amusing too, to have an Aspasia call a Pericles crazy (250). Similarly, Neocleides may well have been a real individual, but as we have already seen in the discussion of the cripple-teasing at 397–406 (not to mention the Neocleides scene in *Plutus*), he is employed by Aristophanes as another likely analogue of Pericles in post-plague decrepitude. "What if Neocleides the blear-eyed should insult you?" asks the First Woman (254). Praxagora's answer "I shall tell him to look up a dog's arse" has long been a cause of mystification,[44] but when we recall (i) that according to Cratinus it was Καταπυγοσύνη (the personification of "anal intercourse")[45] who begat "Hera Aspasia the bitch-faced paramour"

43 Cf. Solana Dueso 1994, xxv-xxxv.
44 E.g. Ussher 1973, 110: "What the advice means (apart from the fact that it aims to be offensive) is obscure".
45 Stadter 1989, 241.

(*PCG* 259) and (ii) for reasons to do with their ancestral curse the Alcmaeonids supposedly favoured the "tradesmen's entrance", all is clear.

Hipparete, Aspasia and Alcibiades

The same kind of interaction between the principal κωμῳδούμενοι occurs in the scenes in the second half of the play, where the stock characters appear to be brought out again, but in different guises. In the first exchange, between the Girl and the First Hag (877–1044), the encounter evokes Hipparete (a lady who "was constantly insulted by her husband's consorting with foreign and Athenian prostitutes" [Plut. *Alc.* 8.4]) and an elderly Aspasia (the proprietress, in the popular mind, of a brothel: cf. Ar. *Ach.* 527). The Hag harps on Ionia (883, 918), and apparently draws attention to the Girl's lambdacization (e. g. μηρ-οῖς [902] and μήλοις [903]) by accusing her of going in for the "Big L" (920)[46]— "coming forward" as the wife of Alcibiades she was presumably thought to speak like him. Epigenes' arrival on stage, drunk and lustful (948) resembles nothing so much as Alcibiades' entry in Plato's *Symposium* (212*d-e*), and his expressed desire for anal intercourse (964) will perhaps have been another allusion to the public perception of the niceties of Alcmaeonid domestic life. His appeals to Eros (958, 966) recall the image, real or imaginary, that Alcibiades had controversially chosen for his shield emblem (see p. 96, above). His cries of ἀσπάζου με ("kiss me" 971, 974) play on Aspasia's name. His rejection of the dramatic analogue of a woman with whom the historical Alcibiades was popularly supposed to have had an quasi-incestuous relationship (Appendix 1) will have been amusing.

Epigenes' talk of ἀνάγκη ("necessity": 1029) invokes a word that was frequently on the tongue of Thucydides' Alcibiades.[47] The necessity in question is "Diomedean"; Alcibiades had entered a team of horses belonging to one Diomedes at Olympia in 416 BC as his own ([Andoc.] 4.26) and won the victory with them (Diod. 13.74.3). Ownership was disputed in 408 BC (*ibid.*), and again in c. 396 BC (Isocr. 16).[48] The image will thus have been a relatively topical one. The description of the funeral couch (which the First Hag chooses to interpret as a wedding bed) is full of likely Alcibiadeanisms. ὑποστόρεσαι ("strew"), the passage begins (1030); Thucydides makes his Alcibiades say in his speech before the Sicilian

---

46 Trans. Sommerstein.
47 Tompkins 1972, 189.
48 Cf. Vickers 1999; *Sophocles and Alcibiades*, 115–32.

campaign Πελοποννησίων τε στορέσομεν τὸ φρόνημα (Thuc. 6.18.4: "let us lay low
the pride of the Peloponnesians"), said by a scholiast to be an expression κατ' Ἀλκιβιάδην ("in the style of Alcibiades"). ὑποστόρεσαι comes close. In addition, the
succession of καίs (1030, 1031 [twice]) well evokes Alcibiades' paratactic manner
of speaking.

The reference to Oedipuses (1042) is significant. The Girl says that if Epigenes does go with the First Hag, who is old enough to be his mother, he will
fill the land with Oedipuses. The Oedipus plot seems at some stage to have
been appropriated in order to encapsulate the essence of a popular view of
the Periclean ménage.⁴⁹ The First Hag accuses the Girl of having said what
she did out of envy but, she says, τιμωρήσομαι (1044: "I will pay you back").
In the context of a squabble between an Aspasia and a Hipparete, this word
by itself was adequate revenge, for it will have placed the spotlight on Alcibiades' liaison with the Spartan queen T̲i̲maea (Plut. *Alc.* 3.1–2; Chapter 10,
above), a relationship that can hardly have pleased Hipparete. Small wonder
that Epigenes then spends four lines being as sweet as he possibly can be towards the Girl (1045–8).

Aspasia, Plato and Aristotle

Nearly all Athenians alive at the time of the *Ecclesiazusae* would have known Aspasia as an ageing woman with a past. The Second and Third Hags are further
manifestations of a progressively older (and more sickly) Aspasia. Space does
not permit fuller treatment here, but the reader should now be able to apply
the lessons learned above. (Similarly, it should now be easy to read the scene
between the Citizen and Chremes [730–876] as a discussion between two idolopoeïïc embodiments of Pericles: the one law-abiding to a fault, and the other all
too prepared to cheat the system; and the δεσπότης at 1128 ff.⁵⁰ will be simply
another polymorphic Periclean manifestation). The really interesting question
arising from *Ecclesiazusae*, however, is how is it that the regimen proposed by
Praxagora—the holding of property in common, the principal theme of the
play—so closely resembles that of the Guardians in Books 3 and 5 of Plato's *Republic*? Since the *Republic* was not composed until a decade or more later, there
is a major problem in that Aristophanes can scarcely have been caricaturing the
model Plato proposed.

49 See Vickers 2005b; *Sophocles and Alcibiades*, 34–46.
50 Cf. Olson, 1987.

A.H. Sommerstein has made a strong case for Plato having consciously adapted Aristophanes' schema at *Republic* 416d-465a-b. Not only does he demonstrate that the parallels are extraordinarily striking, but he notes that it is in this very part of the *Republic* that Socrates expresses his fears that his proposals might be ridiculed as comic fantasy (Pl. *Rp.* 452a-d).[51] This was a pre-emptive strike on Plato's part against potential criticism. Plato seems in any case to have been something of a devotee of Aristophanes, if we can take the scattered sources at face value. He gently ridicules him in the *Symposium*, but wrote an epigram "saying that the Graces, when looking for a temple that would never fall, found the soul of Aristophanes".[52] Moreover, he is said to have presented a copy of *Clouds* to a tyrant of Syracuse (who "wanted to know about Athenian government:" *Vit. Ar.* 28.46–8; cf. 29a.33–5 [Koster]),[53] and when Plato's bed was being tidied up after his death, his attendants supposedly found a set of Aristophanes' plays (Olymp. *Vit. Pl.* 5). Thucydides did not find Aristophanes too frivolous a source when he wrote his harrowing account of the Athenian Plague; indeed, as we have seen, Thucydides seems often to have used Aristophanes as an *aide-mémoire* when composing his histories (pp. 34, 36, 38, above; Appendix 2), down to the very last sentence (pp. 147–8, above). Plato, too, will have relied on Aristophanes in this manner. Simply staying within the confines of *Ecclesiazusae*, Epigenes' drunken entry at 948 could well have served as Plato's model for Alcibiades' arrival at *Symposium* 212d-e.[54]

But even if Sommerstein is fundamentally correct in his case that *Ecclesiazusae* "has been in the long run the most intellectually influential of all ancient comedies",[55] there is one loose end to clear up, namely the fact that Aristotle specifically named Plato as the only person to have proposed communal property, sex, and parentage (*Pol.* 1266a.31–36, 1274b.9–10). But now that Aspasia is in the picture, even this difficulty melts away. Plato will have known that his mentor's mentor lay behind the protagonist of Aristophanes' play. The issue is reduced to whether (i) in ignoring this fact Aristotle was simply being gentlemanly, taking at face value Pericles' dictum that "the greatest glory of woman is to be least talked about among men whether for good or bad"

---

51 Sommerstein 1998, 14.
52 G. Murray 1933, 189.
53 A scholarly hot potato: the reference to *Clouds* was omitted by Dindorf 1838; Dübner 1842; Lefkowitz 1981, 171.
54 And is the defiant τιμωρήσομαι that Alcibiades flings at Socrates (*Smp.* 213d) a barbed echo of *Ec.* 1044?
55 Sommerstein 1998, 17.

(Thuc. 2.45.2);[56] or (ii) Aspasia's contribution to world history (for good or bad) fell victim—Rosalind Franklin-wise—to Aristotle's misogyny; assuming of course that the historical Aspasia actually held the views expounded by Praxagora—which is far from certain.

---

56 Cf. Wiedemann 1983; Cartledge 1993. Thucydides must have been aware of the tradition that Pericles' Funeral Speech was actually written by Aspasia (cf. Pl. *Mx.* 236*b*, Solana Dueso 1994, xxv-xxxv; and literature cited by Gale 2000).

Conclusion

In the concluding remarks in *Pericles on Stage* I suggested that in his earlier extant plays Aristophanes dwelt, on the one hand, on the long shadow that Pericles cast over both Athenian politics and drama after his death and, on the other, on Alcibiades' rising star. Alcibiades' colourful career continued to provide inspiration even when he was in exile after 415 BC. His sometime effeminacy, coupled with fear of his tyrannical tendencies, underlie the plot of *Lysistrata*, and *Thesmophoriazusae* is concerned with the threat that Alcibiades might present to Athens' safety. *Frogs* by contrast considers the possibility that Alcibiades might be the city's saviour once things had become really desperate, but only if he were to pursue Periclean policies. In the two extant plays performed after Alcibiades' death, *Ecclesiazusae* and *Plutus*, the whole extended family, Pericles, Aspasia, Alcibiades and Hipparete, have become stock characters, and the plots have less of a topical touch and deal with themes that are more generic.

Several questions were left open at the end of *Pericles on* Stage: how does the case presented here change our overall assessment of Aristophanes as a poet and playwright? How does it alter our view of him as a commentator on, or participant in, Athenian politics? How should it cause us to re-assess the history of the last quarter of the fifth century BC? What questions of stagecraft does it raise? What does it tell us about the general sophistication and level of education of an Athenian audience? What can we now learn about the relationship between drama and political oratory? It was suggested there that the answers to such questions should await completion of a study of the rest of Aristophanes' plays, for only half of the evidence was in. We are now in a position to begin to answer some at least of these queries.

If the arguments presented above have any merit at all, the ramifications for Aristophanes as a commentator on Athenian politics are considerable. Now that the true κωμῳδούμενοι, in particular Pericles, Aspasia and Alcibiades, have emerged from the shadows, not only can we see that Aristophanes was an acute observer of the political scene, but we now also have a good idea of what his political views might have been. With the exception of *Peace* of 421 BC, where he tried in vain to win Alcibiades over, in the plays from *Knights* of 424 BC to *Thesmophoriazusae* of 410 BC Aristophanes' politics were to oppose Alcibiades at every opportunity. The plots of the plays written during this period depended entirely on what Alcibiades had been up to recently, whether it was his opposition to Cleon, his encouragement of the Spartans to fortify Decelea, or his relations with Tissaphernes. Euripides, by contrast, often puts a favourable spin on Alcibiades' activities (perhaps because his loyalties had been bought). When

Aristophanes parodies Euripidean plots he does so not for purely literary reasons, but to use the same material in order to make an opposite, anti-Alcibiadean, point. Athenian politics were personalised in a way that is perhaps alien to mature democracies; witness the way in which Thucydides son of Milesias had rallied opposition to Pericles in the 440s BC, and how that opposition had withered away once Thucydides had been forced into exile. Since Alcibiades' own mercurial politics were so fluid and fickle, it is little wonder that their Aristophanic antithesis should have been so difficult to pin down, and why there has been such a variety of proposals as to what Aristophanes' political views may have been.[1] Matters are not made easier when Aristophanes undertakes something of a U-turn with regard to Alcibiades in *Frogs* of 404 BC. The plea for the return of the exiles will have included Alcibiades, but the desired outcome was a return to a policy of Periclean caution.

It should also be noted that the practical effects of Aristophanes' satire amounted to very little. His appeal to Alcibiades to change his policy over the Peace of Nicias (in *Peace*) was a failure. His warnings of the dangers of Alcibiadean tyranny (in *Lysistrata*), and his rejection of the notion that Alcibiades should be encouraged to return from exile (in *Thesmophoriazusae*) fell on deaf ears, for Alcibiades was back in power in 407 (the fact that this was not to be for long was due to his own short-comings, not to anything Aristophanes had said: unless of course, Athenian mistrust can be attributed to a cumulative recollection of Aristophanic criticism). Even the appeal for the return of the exiles in *Frogs* failed in the case of Alcibiades. The only possible direct influences on policy that I have discovered Aristophanes having made are (i) an imputation that Alcibiades was avoiding military service in 425 BC (in *Acharnians* 1048–68) might have caused him to enroll in the brigade of knights by the following year, and (ii) his successful appeal for the return of political exiles in 404 BC.

How should this re-evaluation of Aristophanes cause us to re-assess Athenian history? It should not be necessary to insist on the paramount role played by Alcibiades in Athenian politics in the last quarter of the fifth century BC.[2] Nevertheless, as I know to my cost, there are some scholars out there who sincerely believe that "Alcibiades was not all that important". Unfortunately he was, and his centrality, whether in politics or the theatre needs to be universally recognised. It should also be noted that the anecdotal tradition deserves to be treated with greater respect than it has hitherto been granted in the name of "scien-

---

1 E.g. Gomme 1938; de Ste Croix 1972; Cartledge 1990; Fisher 1993; Spielvogel 2003; Sidwell 2008.

2 And recent accounts by Duff (2003), Gribble (1999; 2012), Munn (2000), and Rhodes (2011) (not to mention *Sophocles and Alcibiades*) make it even less necessary to spell things out.

tific" scholarship. Reckless scepticism is as damaging as thoughtless credulity, and more consideration should perhaps be given to tales that only survive in very late sources, especially if they appear to chime with something in fifth-century drama. The tales need not be true, but they may have something to say about what contemporaries accepted as gossip.

Innumerable questions of stagecraft are raised, whether at the level of actors' diction, or of comic business like "funny walks". There will have been many elements such as regional accents or lambdacism that are not in our texts, but which were added by the actors (because they "cannot be shown in writing" [Quint. 1.5.32], and rarely were). Actors' masks must have been immediately recognisable so that, for example, the fast-moving slapstick in the second half of *Plutus* would have been easily understood as the succession of would-be Pericleses, Aspasias and Alcibiadeses came on stage. The audience would not have had to rely on a close reading, or rather hearing, of the text alone to follow the plot. The likelihood that masks, once made, were kept in stock year after year will have provided a certain encouragement to repeat a limited number of κωμῳ-δούμενοι (and the less spent by a *choregus* on scenery and costumes meant more to be spent on the feast). And if the information in Platonius is essentially correct, it would appear that comedy in the early fourth century suffered from an increasing unwillingness on the part of potential *choregi* to sponsor performances that might cause offence to powerful individuals (Platon. 1.21–34). In such a climate, plays based on the Periclean household would have been relatively safe.

It has been unwisely said that "Aristophanes' puns are rarely sophisticated", and the suggestion has been made that his audience consisted mostly of peasants. The reading presented here does not thus demean Aristophanes, but shows him to have been working on the highest plane imaginable. His humour is crafted with immense skill and is extraordinarily sophisticated, working at several levels at once; there are no limits to his exercises in allegory. His audience will have been urbane, as befits the citizens of a city that came within an ace of becoming the mistress of the Mediterranean, and for whom the existing canon of Greek drama, and much more, had originally been written. At other times, these individuals would have heard speeches in the assembly or in the law-courts, and the content will have been akin to, though in a different register from, what was said in the theatre. For the theatre provided a means for the exploration of policies outside the more formal venues for political discussion. Its special contribution was the facility it gave for the public representation of individuals who, like Alcibiades, were absent from Athens for one reason or another. There could be a semblance of public debate between individuals who were not in town. Polymorphic characterization provided the means for public soul-searching (though usually in ways of which the principal κωμῳδούμενοι would not have themselves necessarily approved). The theatre was thus the venue for "experimental politics" where policies could be aired and considered, and perhaps acted upon later.

An awareness of the limited number of κωμῳδούμενοι will now enable us to interpret Plutarch's cryptic remarks when he explains why Old Comedy was not considered to be suitable after-dinner entertainment in his day. It was "too intense, too indecent", and "every person would need a grammar-teacher beside him, to explain who Laispodias is in Eupolis, and Cinesias in Plato [Comicus], Lampon in Cratinus, and each of the others made fun of in comedy, so that our dinner party would become a grammar-school, or the jokes would mean less" (*Mor.* 712a.7). What he probably meant was that it would be tiresome to have to explain that Laispodias had a bad leg and was thus considered by Eupolis to be an appropriate mask for an Alcibiades who was similarly afflicted (Eupolis' plays were in any case full of Alcibiades); it would hold up the conversation to have to explain why Cinesias, the dithyrambic poet who wore wooden stays and led a dissolute life might come forward as a Pericles who had instituted a dithyrambic competition, had allegedly used wooden clubs to execute prisoners, and whose private life was open to criticism; it would be boring (you know how it feels by now, Dear Reader) to have to explain that Lampon might have been another mask for a Pericles given to a certain degree of scientific scepticism. That Plutarch himself was probably aware of these categories is apparent from the fact that he had access to books on κωμῳδούμενοι.[3] When he adduces "the comic dramatists" as evidence for Alcibiades having been a "powerful speaker" (*Alc.* 10.4), we are now well placed to see what he meant. We are also in a position to see the essential weakness of Dover's claim that with very few exceptions "the rich anecdotal material" in the Andocidean speech ([Andoc.] 4) and in Plutarch's *Life of Alcibiades* "finds no echo in Aristophanes".[4] Aristophanes, like Eupolis, "openly lampooned" Alcibiades' speech impediment. It is therefore impossible to accept Dover's view that Aristophanes' characters "develop essentially through what they say without any help from the way in which they say it".[5] Likewise, Dover's assertion that it is "bizarre"[6] to see Thucydides and Xenophon having used Aristophanes as an *aide-mémoire* is itself far-fetched.

Even when specific attention was not drawn to the fact, constant use has been made throughout this book of the "wigwam argument", according to

---

3 Stadter 1989, lxix-lxvi, 242, 297.
4 Dover 1993, 371, who also asserts that "the *Baptai* of Eupolis seems to have been the only play in which [Alcibiades] was an important target".
5 Dover 1987, 248.
6 Dover 2004, 244. Contrast Westlake 1968, 8, 11 n. 5, 13 n. 1.

which "each pole would fall down by itself, but together the poles stand up, by leaning on each other; they point roughly in the same direction and circumscribe 'truth'". The working hypotheses, about polymorphic characterisation, about Aristophanic κωμῳδούμενοι, and about the essentially Periclean and Alcibiadean nature of the surviving corpus, seem to have survived unscathed. But rather than being left with a series of wigwams, I would claim that we have something else: *viz.*, a "big top" that needs to be taken into account whenever the three-ring circus of Aristophanic comedy is surveyed in the future.

Appendix 1

Alcibiades' "Servile Birth", Alcibiades' "Matrophilia": Inventions of the Stage?

"And some say that he was of servile birth", the tenth-century Byzantine lexicon known as the *Suda* informs us in the entry under "Alcibiades".[1] There can, however, have been few Athenians of the fifth century BC to whom such a judgement could have been ostensibly less applicable. More usually described as εὐγενείᾳ καὶ πλούτῳ πρῶτος Ἀθηναίων ("the first of the Athenians in birth and wealth": Diod. 13.37.2; cf. Plut. *Alc.* 10.3;), Alcibiades was not only supposedly descended from Eurysaces, the son of Salaminian Ajax on his father's side (Plut. *Alc.* 1.1; Pl. *Alc.* 1.121a), and from Megacles the Alcmaeonid on his mother's (Plut. *Alc.* 1.1; Isoc. 16.25), but he himself was said to have laid claim to descent from Eros, and by extension from Zeus. Such a pedigree can scarcely be said to equate to servile origins.

And yet, there was a tradition that Alcibiades' maternal ancestor, the first Coesyra who came from Eretria to marry Alcmaeon, and who was the mother of the first Megacles of whom we hear, was a slave (Schol. Ar. *Nu.* 64; *Pax* 451).[2] While this is difficult to reconcile with the report that the Eretrian Coesyra was "excessively well-born and rich" (ἥτις ἦν ὑπερβαίνουσα γένει καὶ πλούτῳ: Schol. Ar. *Nu.* 46), there is some, if slight, support in the equally unsure information the scholiast gives us that the Alcmaeonid Megacles son of Megacles was also lampooned as a slave (αὐτὸς δὲ διεβάλλετο ὡς δοῦλος: *ibid.*). Alcibiades is also said to have earned the nickname of δοῦλος on account of his having deserted to the Spartans in 415 (Schol. Ar. *Pax.* 451). It will be argued in what follows that these elements, if true, coupled with his residence at the court of Tissaphernes may well have contributed to a comic exaggeration of Alcibiades' real status (and if they were not, Alcibiades' Persian sojourn alone will have been enough to justify dramatic invention). As we saw above (pp. 49–50), Ion's concern lest his parents should have been slaves suggests that Alcibiadean slavery may have been an issue in 409 BC. The claim to descent from Eros may provide a useful model, for it has sometimes been claimed to have no basis in fact, and to have been the result of an invention of comic writers.[3] Alcibiades is said to have rejected his true ancestral shield emblem, and to have replaced it with an image

---

1 "καὶ ἐκ δούλων δὲ τεχθέντα τινες ἱστορήκασιν": *Suda* s.v. Ἀλκιβιάδης.
2 Shear 1963, 103–4.
3 Russell 1966, 45; Littman 1970.

of Eros brandishing thunderbolts, as we have frequently noted. True or false, the story must have reflected the essence of the man: Plato employed Alcibiades as the central figure in his *Symposium*, where the role of Eros figures large, and there was a painting of Alcibiades as Eros in the Portico of Octavia at Rome (see p. 96, above).

"He loved his mother"

The allegation made by Antisthenes (*c.* 441–371 BC) that Alcibiades was guilty of "lying with his mother, his sister and his daughter" (Antisth. 29*a* Caizzi *ap.* Ath. 5.220*a*; Lys. 14.29) may also have its origins in dramatic invention. Such an accusation is rarely laid against anyone, no matter how dissolute their lifestyle. It is true that Alcibiades and an uncle had celebrated Alcibiades' coming of age with a gap year in Abydos, where not only did Alcibiades learn "ways of doing things" from the women there (Antiph. *fr.* 67 Blass *ap.* Ath. 12.525*b*), but both uncle and nephew also shared the favours of a girl who subsequently gave birth to a daughter. Many years later, when they slept with this girl in turn, each would excuse his behaviour by saying that she was the daughter of the other (Lys. p. 346 Thalheim *ap.* Ath. 12.534*e*-535*a*; 13.574*d*; cf. Plut. *Alc.* 36.2). We know little or nothing about Alcibiades' sister (though something may emerge by the end of this appendix). It is the mother who attracts our interest. Are we meant to understand Deinomache, Alcibiades' physical mother, or the woman who shared the house of Pericles who, together with his brother Ariphron, stood *in loco parentis* after the death of Alcibiades' father Cleinias in 458 (Plut. *Per.* 1.1–2), namely Aspasia? The nature of the comic inventions that were generated by the relationship of Aspasia and Pericles (Plut. *Per.* 24.9–10) makes one suspect that Aspasia was in question. We owe to comedy the charge that Aspasia was supposedly responsible for the outbreak of the Peloponnesian War (Ar. *Ach.* 527), and it has often been noted that the story of Pericles' tears at the trial of Aspasia (Plut. *Per.* 32.5) may have its origins in a comic conceit;[4] Periclean tearfulness is certainly lampooned in *Wasps*, where Philocleon weeps over the line-up of puppies (978–9; cf. 882, 983).

But it is in tragedy that we find the broadest innuendo being made against Alcibiades and Aspasia. Oedipus has been discussed elsewhere;[5] here we are concerned with *Hippolytus*. Barry Strauss has demonstrated the manifold under-

---

4 Wallace 1994, 131, 148, n. 16.

5 Vickers 2005b; *Sophocles and Alcibiades*, 47–58.

lying similarities between the figure of Hippolytus in Euripides' extant play and those who stood in a filial relationship to Pericles, namely his son Xanthippus, his illegitimate son Pericles, and above all his ward Alcibiades.[6] The phenomenon is identical to the way Aristophanes established the portmanteau characterization of Pheidippides in *Clouds*, and may even have contributed to it. There, Xanthippus' inability "to bear his father's stingy ways" and his wife's "expensive habits", were coupled with Alcibiades' passionate interest in horses, his indebtedness, his keeping company with Socrates and sophists, and his diction. In the case of the *Hippolytus*, Strauss points out that the troubles of both households are ascribed to an inherited curse: "that of Theseus and Hippolytos is nameless (820, 1379–80), that of Pericles and his son [was] the infamous curse of the Alkmeonids .... Theseus accuses his son of sleeping with his stepmother; Xanthippos accused his father of sleeping with his daughter-in-law, [and] both sons, Hippolytos and Xanthippos, quarrelled bitterly with their fathers". Then, "both Theseus and Pericles had a well-loved illegitimate son (in Pericles' case it was his son Pericles)".[7] But, as with Pheidippides in *Clouds*, the characterization mainly depends upon Alcibiades. Strauss lists many of the parallels between Alcibiades and Hippolytus: a lack of respect towards older males, a love of horses, and a childhood in the household of a great political leader. Like Alcibiades, Hippolytus "appears in the company of young men and is sometimes seen as representative of them (*Hipp.* 967–70, 987)", he is a good orator (986–89), he is ambitious, and aspires to a famous name (1028, 1299) and to the "first place in the contests of the Greeks (1016)". Like Alcibiades, Hippolytus' "gender is ambivalent", he "disdains the common people (986), [and] does not hesitate to sing his own praises, announcing that no one will ever find a more *sōphrōn* (prudent, modest, virtuous) man than himself". Euripides opposes Hippolytus' absolute chastity to Alcibiades' notorious promiscuity, and Strauss believes that he may well have "enjoyed the humorous contrast between Hippolytos' un-Alcibiadean virginity and his other quite Alcibiadean characteristics".[8] Alternatively, there may have been a good practical reason for representing on stage the opposite of the true state of affairs: namely, that it would be difficult to challenge the imputation without drawing even more attention to it.

There are thus distinct parallels between the household in which Alcibiades grew up, and the one that Euripides delineates on the stage. Strauss was concerned with "fathers and sons" and restricted his analysis to the relationship be-

---

6 B.S. Strauss 1993, 166–75; overlooked by Roisman 1999, but not by Mills 2002.
7 The legitimacy of Pericles the younger was an active issue in *c.* 430 BC: Plut. *Per.* 37.5.
8 B.S. Strauss 1993, 247, n. 82.

tween Theseus and Hippolytus; but there are other resonances in the play. The head of the historical household was Pericles, of the fictional Theseus. Pericles' consort was Aspasia of Miletus, Theseus' Phaedra of Crete. There are several grounds for regarding Phaedra as a lightly disguised Aspasia (who had in any case been variously represented on the Athenian stage as Hera, Nemesis, Omphale, Chiron and Deianira,[9] not to mention Eurydice, Jocasta and Creusa).[10] Phaedra was of Cretan origin, but so too were the inhabitants of Miletus, Aspasia's native city (Paus. 7.2.5), and for Greeks, "a fictional relationship between peoples and cities had a very real significance".[11] Miletus was the foremost colonizer of the Black Sea, the Euxine, or "hospitable sea"; whence perhaps the Chorus' question to Phaedra regarding the mariner from Crete who has reached the εὐξεινότατον ("most hospitable") harbour (156–7). The Chorus' references to Hecate, the Corybantes, the Mountain Mother and Dictynna (142–6) neatly intertwine Asiatic and Cretan cults.

Phaedra's first spoken line (198), αἰρέτε μου δέμας, ὀρθοῦτε κάρα, does not simply mean "Lift up my body, raise up my head", but includes "emphatic" allusions to everything for which Aspasia was notorious. δέμας means the "male member" as well as "body", and is used as such by Plato Comicus when singing the praises of βολβοί ("bulbs"): τὸ γὰρ δέμας ἀνέρος ὀρθοῖ ("for a man's parts rise up") when he eats them (Pl. Com. *PCG* 189.10). ὀρθοῦτε κάρα ("raise up my head") continues the same idea. The choice of κάρα includes witty references to a prominent Periclean feature[12] and, in that κάρα was an Ionian word which not only meant "head", but also "sheep",[13] to both Aspasia's Milesian origins, and to her perhaps premature cohabitation with the "sheepseller" Lysicles.[14] The Ionian references continue in Phaedra's injunction (200) to her πρόπολοι ("attendants")[15] to take her εὐπήχεις χεῖρας ("beautifully armed hands"), if εὐπήχεις plays on παχύς ("plump")—and the expression is tautologous if it does not. Herodotus describes the exile of ἄνδρες τῶν παχέων ("men of substance" or "the fat") from Ionian Naxos to Miletus (Hdt. 5.30.1); and the "softness of the bodies" and σφρίγει ... βραχιόνων ("plumpness of the arms") of the effeminate men of

---

9 Maehly 1853, 215–8; Schwarze 1971.

10 *Sophocles and Alcibiades*, 24–5 (Eurydice), 44–6 (Jocasta), and Chapter 4, above (Creusa).

11 Cf. Orrieux 1988, 170, citing Louis Robert.

12 And cf. κεφαλῆς at 201—a Periclean catch-word. Guidorizzi 2006, 132 considers καραιέ at Cratin. *PCG* 118 to be an allusion "to the characteristically bulbous form of Pericles' head".

13 Hsch. s.v. κάρα· Ἴωνες τὰ πρόβατα. καὶ τὴν κεφαλήν ("[What] Ionians [call] sheep; and the head").

14 Cf. Stadter 1989, 237; Vickers 2000.

15 Perhaps itself an Ionian expression: cf. Xenoph. B1.18 West.

Abydos ("colonists from Miletus": Hermipp. *PCG* 57.6 *ap.* Ath. 12.525*a*) indicates what was a widespread view of Ionian luxury.

Aspasia's influence on Pericles was doubtless exaggerated.[16] It may be too that her alleged role as a confidante of Socrates went beyond the true facts. It may be merely a coincidence that Phaedra's complaint (199) that λέλυμαι μελέων σύνδεσμα φίλων ("the sinews of my limbs grow faint") somehow echoes Aspasia's claim that χαρᾶς ὑπὸ σῶμα λιπάνθη / ὑδρῶτι ("my body was suffused with the glow of joy") on hearing of Socrates' passion for Alcibiades (Aspasia fr. 1 West *ap.* Ath. 5.219*c*). It may be a coincidence that Euripides' Phaedra speaks of προμνήστριαι ("procuresses") (589), and that Aspasia was said by Xenophon to have proffered advice to Socrates concerning προμνηστρίδας ("matchmakers": Xen. *Mem.* 2.6.36). It may be a coincidence, too, that Socrates' reaction to Aspasia's encouragement is that, in Athenaeus' words, "he then κυνηγεῖ ("goes hunting"), having the Milesian woman as his instructor in love" (Ath. 5.219*d*),[17] and that there is much talk of hunting in the *Hippolytus*. But it can scarcely be a coincidence that Plato in the dialogue *Alcibiades* makes his Socrates quote Phaedra's "You heard this from yourself, not from me" (*Hipp.* 352) in a conversation with Alcibiades (Pl. *Alc.* 1.113*c*; cf. Schol.), nor that the conversation between Hippolytus and the Servant (88–120) is our earliest reflection of a Socratic dialogue.[18]

For all that Socrates is supposed to have tried to instil σωφροσύνη ("sobriety of conduct") in Alcibiades (Xen. *Mem.* 1.2.12; cf. Plut. *Alc.* 6), the way in which the Servant attempts to persuade Hippolytus that his devotion to chastity (cf. τὸ σωφρονεῖν at *Hipp.* 80) would be better diverted to a devotion to Aphrodite (101) well reflects the relationship between Socrates and Alcibiades in the tradition preserved by Crates. Hippolytus' assertion that "I ἀσπάζομαι ['greet'] from afar" the image of Aphrodite set at his doorway (πυλαίσι: 101–2) not only plays on Aspasia's name, but on Pericles' comings and goings, when "he kissed Aspasia amorously whenever he left the house or returned from the Agora" (Plut. *Per.* 24.9).[19] But it is Hippolytus, rather than Socrates, who goes hunting in Euripides' play and Phaedra, rather than Socrates, who conceives an unlawful passion. It would not be legitimate to argue from the evidence of the extant *Hippo-*

---

16 Schwarze 1971, 92; cf. Wallace 1994, 147, n. 5; Podlecki 1998, 101–117; Henderson 2000.
17 Cf. Plut. *Alc.* 6.1 (where Socrates ἐκυνεγεῖτο ["hunted"] Alcibiades down).
18 Note δαίμον' (*Hipp.* 99) and δαιμόνων (*Hipp.* 107) and Socrates' attachment to his δαιμόνιον (Xen. *Mem.* 1.1.2; Pl. *Ap.* 40*a*, etc.). Snell (1948; 1964, 47–69) senses Socratic resonances at *Hipp.* 373–90.
19 On wordplay between ἀσπάζομαι and Ἀσπασία, see Maehly 1858, 225; Podlecki 1987, 60, and pp. 74, 84, 176, above.

lytus that Alcibiades actually did have a sexual relationship with Aspasia. For the moment, let us adopt the position that it would have been possible years later to use the fiction that Aspasia had an unrequited passion for Alcibiades as the basis for an unworthy imputation that Alcibiades did commit adultery with his *de facto* stepmother. Whether or not there was a relationship between Aspasia and Alcibiades in real life, Euripides was implying by means of "emphasis" that there was. But not only did Euripides' conceit provide grounds for Antisthenes' claim that Alcibiades was guilty of matrophilia, but it also supplied the basis for Aristophanic humour well into the fourth century.

Until recently, it was universally believed that the extant *Hippolytus* was the second play of that name and that it was performed in 428. In a masterly article, John Gibert has now demonstrated that neither of these statements need be true.[20] Much criticism of ancient drama is characterised by a certain reckless scepticism; for once, however, scepticism has paid off, and we are now at liberty to consider the possibility that when we are told (i) that the lost play was characterized by τὸ ἀπρεπὲς καὶ κατηγορίας ἄξιον ("what is unseemly and worthy of criticism"), and (ii) that the second play "corrected" the first in such a way that pleased the Athenians and caused them to grant Euripides first prize, that the "correction" lay in getting the story—or the alleged story—straight, and that Phaedra did not conceal her passion for Hippolytus in the second play. There may even still be merit in the view, again once universally held,[21] that the epithet of the lost play, καλυπτόμενος or κατακαλυπτόμενος, referred to a scene in which Hippolytus veiled his head in shame at what Phaedra was proposing. This interpretation of the evidence is surely preferable to an explanation that the surviving play "won the prize by virtue of its morally improved heroine".[22] For matters to get this far on the stage, and if Euripides did indeed have Aspasia and Alcibiades in mind, there can be little doubt that it was popularly believed at Athens that any relationship was consummated. And whether or not it was in reality, this would be enough to provide a basis for Antisthenes' slander (and for Aristophanes' glosses, on which more below).

In both *Hippolytus* plays, Phaedra will have been a lightly disguised Aspasia. Phaedra—or Phaedras—are mentioned elsewhere in late fifth century literature. Gibert cites some, but not all, of them. One he omits to mention occurs at *Thesm.* 153, when the Kinsman says as an aside to Euripides:

οὐκοῦν κελητίζεις, ὅταν Φαίδραν ποιῇς;

20 Gibert 1997, 85–97.
21 Until questioned by Luppe 1994; cf. Gibert 1997, 95, n. 42.
22 Gibert 1997, 96 characterizing a view with which he disagrees.

Do you have her on top, when you write about Phaedra?

At one level, this is simply an enquiry—albeit a somewhat gross one—about Euripides' mode of composition, inspired by Agathon's need to empathize with his subject-matter; at another, it says something about the Periclean *ménage*. For in *Thesmophoriazusae*, as we saw in Chapter 14, the Kinsman and Euripides are characterized respectively as Alcibiades and Pericles. The Kinsman's enquiry at *Thesm.* 153 would additionally mean "Does she go on top when you have a go at Phaedra?" and for an Alcibiades to pose the question of a Pericles concerning a *de facto* Aspasia would involve an element of complicity that would scarcely have existed in real life, but which would have been amusing on the comic stage. In similar vein, if the Kinsman was based on Alcibiades, then he will have had inside knowledge into the way in which the Athens of the day was awash with Phaedras (*Thesm.* 545–8).

The other references to Phaedra are in *Frogs*, at 1043–4 and 1052. In this play, as we saw in Chapter 10, Aeschylus "comes forward" as Pericles and Euripides as Alcibiades. In such a situation, for Aeschylus to refer to Phaedras and Stheneboeas as πόρναι ("prostitutes") is tantamount both to Pericles' acknowledging Aspasia's guilt, and to his concurring with Eupolis' description of her as a πόρνη in *Demi* of a few years earlier (Plut. *Per.* 24.10), i.e. that she was an adulteress, and that he was a cuckold. It is perhaps for such reasons that Dionysus says to Aeschylus that "you yourself have suffered from the kind of thing you impute to women of long ago" (1048), and that Aeschylus agrees with Euripides when asked about the basic veracity of the latter's Phaedra (1052).

Servile Origins

But while this helps to suggest that Alcibiades and his proclivities provided subject matter for the stage, it does nothing to throw light on his supposed servile ancestry. If the traditions concerning Coesyra are genuine (and we are in no position to judge), they will be enough to account for the slur. There are, however, indications in comedy that there was another reason for regarding Alcibiades as having been himself a slave that will have served to reinforce the notion of servile origins. In *Pericles on Stage*, a case was made for *i.a.* the Sausage-seller in *Knights*, Pheidippides in *Clouds*, Bdelycleon in *Wasps*, Trygaeus in *Peace*, and Peisthetaerus in *Birds*, to have been (largely in the case of Pheidippides, and wholly in that of the others) based on Alcibiades. With the exception of the Sausage-seller, they are all characterised as relatively high-born. And from whatever rank the Sausage-seller may have emerged, he is subservient to no-one. There are, however, two very prominent slaves in Aristophanes' later extant plays, *viz.* Xanthias in *Frogs* and Carion in *Plutus*, both of whom display encouragingly Alcibiadean features, as we saw in Chapters 10, 5 and 6.

For present purposes, there is more meat on Carion. While his name ("the Carian") clearly recalls the source of many slaves in fourth century Athens (see p. 60, above), it was also a highly appropriate means of evoking a figure who was once technically a slave in Caria, even if the circumstances were of the utmost luxury. When he fled from Sparta in 412 BC, Alcibiades took refuge at the court of Tissaphernes (Plut. *Alc.* 24.4), situated near Magnesia-on-the-Meander in Caria.[23] According to Plutarch he gave himself (δοὺς ἑαυτόν) to the satrap. It was here that "the barbarian, being himself a lover of deceit and crooked ways, admired [Alcibiades'] cleverness and versatility" and enjoyed his company on a daily basis (Plut. *Alc.* 24.5). There were, however, good reasons of state for Tissaphernes' tolerating Alcibiades as a member of his household, for after the disaster in Sicily, the Persians began to take a renewed interest in Athenian affairs, and Tissaphernes played a double game, playing off the Athenians against their Peloponnesian enemies. Alcibiades was a useful pawn in such a situation.[24]

Plutarch's description of Alcibiades' position at Tissaphernes' court as πρῶτος καὶ μέγιστος ("first and greatest") is a highly significant piece of evidence in the present context, for it shows Alcibiades as one of Tissaphernes' πίστοι ("faithful/trusted [followers]"), if not actually the πιστότατος ("most trusted") of his entourage. The degree of trust that Alcibiades enjoyed in this role can be judged from the fact that he conducted the negotiations on Tissaphernes' behalf when an Athenian delegation visited Magnesia in 411 BC (Thuc. 8.56.2). πίστις ("trust") was the ruling principle of the Persian Empire, one on which status at the court of the Great King was based. Cambyses thus honoured Prexaspes because he was the πιστότατος of his Persian friends (Hdt. 3.30.3) and φιλία καὶ πίστις ("friendship and fidelity") was the hallmark of the relationship between Orontas and Artaxerxes II (Xen. *An.* 1.6.3).[25] The model was replicated in the satrapal courts where "arrangements were identical to those of the central court".[26] The relationship between ruler and ruled was characterized in Old Persian by the word *ba^ndaka*.[27] It is used in the Behistun inscriptions "to describe both subject and loyal peoples and those who supplied aid against rebels" and "the Akkadian

23 Briant 2002, 491.

24 Petit 1997.

25 Cf. Wiesehöfer 1980; Briant 2002, 324.

26 Briant 2002, 347.

27 Francis 1992, 349–50; Missiou 1993; Briant 2002, 324.

version uses a word (*qallu*) that comes from the vocabulary of slavery or depend-ence".[28] When rendered into Greek, the word δοῦλος ("slave") was generally used regardless of rank.[29] Thus, Cyrus the Younger was the δοῦλος of his brother Artaxerxes (Xen. *An.* 2.5.38).

The term was still remembered in the early Roman imperial period when priests of Apollo at Magnesia-on-the-Meander forged a letter (the "Letter to Ga-datas") from Darius the Great in order to gain for their temple privileges of du-bious antiquity.[30] When the author of the *de Mundo* describes Persian notables as οἱ πρῶτοι καὶ δοκιμώτατοι ("the chief and most distinguished men": [Arist.] 398*a*), they could, according to Briant, "all be considered 'slaves of the Great King'" (δοῦλοι τοῦ μεγάλου βασιλέως). Similarly, Alcibiades' position as πρῶτος καὶ μέγιστος at Magnesia made him the δοῦλος of Tissaphernes. This will have been quickly known at Athens when Peisander's delegation returned, and we can also assume that the Spartans, notionally tied to a programme of freeing the Greeks of Asia (a policy they paradoxically owed to Alcibiades),[31] made much of Alcibiades' current role as a slave. The gift of a garden called "Alci-biades" was part of this relationship between δεσπότης ("master") and δοῦλος, being akin to the way in which Themistocles (and others) were granted cities by the Great King to provide an income for as long as they qualified for it.[32] So far as Alcibiades was concerned, he had yet another period as the δοῦλος of a Persian master when, during his second exile, he took refuge with Pharnabazus "whom he so charmed ... that [the satrap] gave him Grynium, a stronghold in Phrygia", from which he received—like Themistocles—an annual income.[33] It was probably Alcibiades' encounters with satrapal court life that led to the creation of Alcibia-dean slave roles in Aristophanes, which come from towards the end of the extant oeuvre, and not before Alcibiades' bandakizations.[34]

---

28 Briant 2002, 324.
29 Rose 1957, 1.242.
30 ML 12.4; Briant 2003.
31 Seager and Tuplin 1980; Munn 2000, 388, n. 6.
32 Cf. Briant 1985.
33 Nep. *Alc.* 9.3; cf. Briant 2002, 618.
34 Cf. Eur. *Hel.* 1193, where Helen/Alcibiades actually calls Theoclymenus/Tissaphernes ὦ δέσποτ' ("Master"), thus confirming the impression that Alcibiades' visit was viewed as self-in-duced slavery.

Aspasia Again

There are many possible allusions to the anecdotal tradition relating to Alcibiades in the characterization of Carion, as we saw in Chapters 5 and 6. Likewise, we saw how the audience may have recognised Chremylus as Pericles. This being the case, the scene at *Plutus* 959 ff., between Chremylus and the Hag throws more light on the Phaedra problem alluded to above. The Hag is characterised as an Aspasia who interacts with the dramatic analogue of Pericles with whom she appears to share the secrets of an illicit love-affair she had with Alcibiades. This will have been the affair—real or imaginary—that lay behind Euripides' *Hippolytus* (where Theseus, Phaedra and Hippolytus "come forward" as Pericles, Aspasia, and [mostly] Alcibiades), and there is an echo of that play in ἡμαρτήκαμεν ("gone wrong") at *Plutus* 961, taking up a word that occurs in one form or another at *Hippolytus* 21, 320, 323 and 506. Chremylus' overly affectionate reaction to the Hag recalls, as we saw in Chapter 11, Pericles' canoodling with Aspasia. There are puns (ἀβίωτον ... τὸν βίον ["life is not worth living": 969]) on Alcibiades' name and the suggestion that the Hag might be a συκοφάντρια ("she-sycophant") places her firmly in the context of Aspasia the προμνήστρια ("matchmaker": Xen. *Mem.* 2.6.36), and σοφίστρια ("philosopheress": Schol. Ar. *Ach.* 527).

When the Hag confides in Chremylus (975 ff.) the nature of her κνισμός ("itch"), it is in terms that parody Phaedra's confidences to her Nurse, and we have seen in Chapter 11 how the catalogue of characteristic features that describe the Hag's lover neatly encapsulate those of Alcibiades' public image: his youth, his shortage of funds, his good looks. Unlike the extant *Hippolytus* (but perhaps like the lost one, in which the record was "corrected") there seems to have been a reciprocal relationship between lover and beloved (977–9). There are references to a *himation* and shoes (983), two Alcibiadean trademarks. It is at the point that the young man expresses a wish to buy a χιτώνιον ("little gown") for his sisters (984), and a ἱματίδιον ("little *himation*") for his mother (985) that Antisthenes' charge comes into play, and here at last that we encounter not just one sister, but a plurality. The fact that a love-gift was extracted from an Aspasia to give to one who seems to have been the youth's physical mother implies that Deinomache may have been in Antisthenes' mind as he wrote. But to argue from an Aristophanic fantasy to historical fact is a perilous route to take; best perhaps to be content with "gossip had it", that gossip was confused, and that that gossip may well have been an invention of the stage. At all events, we have both a possible source for Antisthenes, and an explanation for the young man's requests (not to mention a possible explanation for Euripidean—and other—"bad women").[35]

Clever Slaves

Once again, however, we have strayed from the other strand of this chapter: to judge whether or not there was not so much a grain of truth in the *Suda*'s reference to Alcibiades' possible servile ancestry, as a rational explanation for it. Coesyra may have played a part, but Xanthias and—especially—Carion will have contributed to the idea. Carion is the ancestor of a long line of clever and versatile slaves in later Greek and Roman comedy, a line moreover, that extends to Zero Mostel and Frankie Howerd, not to mention Olivia's Fabian, Jeeves,[36] and even Gromit. They will all have had their origins in the daily conversations in Caria between the "clever and versatile" Alcibiades (Plut. *Alc.* 24.5) and his barbarian master. *Plutus* was the most popular of Aristophanes' plays by far in later centuries,[37] perhaps because its humour was more generic than that of earlier works, in that it summarized the totality of the Periclean *ménage*, rather than dwelling on recent politics or fresh scandal. *Plutus* stands on the cusp between Old and Middle Comedy, at the beginning of the period just before Menander which was almost solely responsible for the formulaic characters of Greek or Roman New Comedy as we know them today.[38] These include slaves of various kinds: "hapless recipients of orders, ... smart-alec malcontents, and ... somewhat higher-level slaves who can function as their masters' confidants or advisers".[39] The seeds of all of them can be found in Carion, and a distant awareness that the famous Carion somehow stood for Alcibiades, perhaps coupled with the traditions concerning Coesyra, may well have contributed to the notion that "Alcibiades was of servile birth". If so, it will have been yet another instance of the potency of inventions of the comic stage, as well as a reminder of Alcibiades' central role in Athenian comedy.

---

35 Cf. Gibert 1997, 94–7.
36 "Mr Wodehouse, like Shakespeare, drew most of his characters from the upper class and their servants": Waugh 1984, 562.
37 Lord 1963, 104.
38 See Nesselrath 1990.
39 Rusten 2002.

Appendix 2

The Athenian Plague of 430–428 BC

There are several apparent references to the Athenian Plague in Aristophanes' surviving plays. They are usually introduced in order to cripple-tease the memory of Pericles, who was said by Plutarch to have suffered from "varied symptoms" (Plut. *Per.* 3.1). Pericles was to recover from an initial attack, before dying a few months later. The most extended and informative use of plague-imagery in Aristophanes is to be found in the bed-bug scene at *Clouds* 694–745, where Strepsiades' account of what the insects are doing to him closely parallel the symptoms described rather more fully by Thucydides. The truly remarkable fact is that the phenomena occur in the same order in both texts.[1] There are in any case enough parallels to construct another wigwam involving both Pericles and the Plague. Let us enumerate the various poles of such a structure:

(i) The bed-bugs are described as Corinthians; wordplay (on κόρεσι [699]) apart, there may be a connection with the fact that it was believed that the plague was introduced by the Peloponnesians (Thuc. 2.48.2).

(ii) The bugs are said to be devouring Strepsiades' ribs (711): one of the symptoms of the plague was that it quickly reached the chest (Thuc. 2.49.3).

(iii) Line 713 is usually taken to read: τοὺς ὄρχεις ἐξέλκουσιν ("they are dragging out my testicles"). The plausible suggestion has, however, been made[2] that (the differently accented) ἐξελκοῦσιν ("they are ulcerating") should be read instead. If so, there may be a connection with the report that the plague caused ἕλκωσις ("ulceration": Thuc. 2.49.6), albeit to the colon.[3]

(iv) The Ravenna and Marcian manuscripts invert lines 712 and 713, and thus give the symptoms in the order in which they are presented by Thucydides, a fact that bears witness to the inherent soundness of R. At 712 we learn that the bed bugs are draining Strepsiades' spirit: another symptom was severe diarrhoea (Thuc. 2.49.6).

---

1 Vickers 1991; 1993, 603–4..
2 By Blaydes 1890, 94, 411 (following Reiske).
3 And cf. the ἑλκύδρια ("little plague-sores") on the Periclean Demus' shins at Ar. *Eq.* 907.

(v) At 714 the bugs are said to be digging through Strepsiades' arse (καὶ τὸν πρω-κτὸν διορύττουσιν): in its final stages, the plague would "descend to the bowels" (Thuc. 2.49.6).

(vi) Strepsiades then claims that the bugs will kill him (715: καὶ μ' ἀπολοῦσιν): according to Thucydides, most died of exhaustion at this stage (Thuc.2.49.6).

(vii) Socrates tells Strepsiades not to feel hurt too much (716). "How can I not do so", replies Strepsiades, "When I have lost my money?" (718). Pericles had been fined between fifteen and fifty talents for his failure to take Epidaurus in the closing months of his life (Plut. *Per.* 35.4).

(viii) "When I have lost my complexion", Strepsiades continues, "When I have lost my life" (719); Pericles was dead.

(ix) "In addition to these evils, I sing on guard duty" (721); perhaps refers both to the Odeum (literally Song Hall) built under Pericles' direction (Plut. *Per.* 13.9 – 10), and to the Periclean policy of retreating within the city walls (Thuc. 2.13).

(x) "And I shall soon be lost altogether" (722); Pericles was dead.

(xi) The punch line of this Pythonesque little scene comes (at 734) when Socrates asks what Strepsiades has managed to get hold of: "Nothing except τὸ πέος ἐν τῇ δεξιᾷ ('my cock in my right hand')". Aristophanes has already (710 – 15) made more than half a dozen apparent references to the plague. If so, then this is evidently another one, and one that recalls Thucydides' final symptom: "even if a person got over the worst, the plague would often . . . attack the privy parts . . . and some escaped with the loss of these" (Thuc. 2.49.8). In the light of the plague-ridden lead-up, the scene must go beyond simply masturbation (as it is usually interpreted), and we might even envisage Strepsiades detaching and brandishing the large leather phallus with which comic actors were equipped.

This is all very distasteful, but the chances of these parallels being coincidental, in a play performed before an audience that had either witnessed or experienced similar symptoms but a few years earlier, are remote. For all that Thucydides had experienced the symptoms himself, these lines reinforce the view that he may have made use of Aristophanes as a handy means of recalling significant historical events,[4] especially if, as now seems likely, he actually composed the *Histories* as late as 396 – 395 BC.[5] Not only did the scene provide a useful checklist, but it even informed the tone of Thucydides' account. It was Pericles' preference for natural rather than supernatural explanations of physical phenomena that Aristophanes was lampooning. Thucydides is similarly concerned to attribute the Plague to natural, rather than divine causes.[6] His account of plague-symptoms will have been a discreet ("emphatic") way of describing the sufferings of a Pericles whose memory he wished to honour. Archaeologists have a dictum concerning features they excavate: "One stone is an accident, two stones are a coincidence, but three stones are a structure". I would maintain that the seven or more stones, the seven or more parallels between Aristophanes and Thucydides, amount to something too.

The feature that is present in Aristophanes but not in Thucydides, and which might throw new light on the pathology of the plague, is the involvement of insects. Otherwise, most of Aristophanes' other allusions to the plague elaborate upon one or another of the symptoms given in Thucydides' account. In *Acharnians* (425 BC), there are references to the loss of the privy parts (236 – 79, 802, 881 – 894), to forgetfulness (580, 963, 1050; cf. Thuc. 2.49.8), to eye problems (850, 1018 – 36; Thuc. 2.49.2), and to the heart (12, 485, 488);[7] In *Knights* (424 BC), the loss of the privy parts (1385) forgetfulness (732, 1041, 1339), ulceration (903), and eye trouble (909); in *Clouds* (423 BC), apart from the bed-bug scene, there are: forgetfulness (129 – 30, 414, 482 – 3, 631, 685, 854 – 5), and eye-trouble (946 – 7); in *Wasps* (422 BC), νόσος ("plague") (71 [twice], 76, 80, 87, 114) is made the basis for an elaborate conceit, and elsewhere in the play there are references to fever (284, 813; cf. Thuc. 2.49.2) and to βουβωνιῷ ("suffer[ing] from swollen glands") (277). In *Birds*, the Epops' bedraggled appearance is attributed to some νόσου (104). There are further allusions to genital loss at *Th.* 254, *Ra.* 1208 ff., and *Ec.* 468, and to eye-trouble at *Ec.* 397 – 403 and *Pl.* 115, 665, 716 – 22, not to mention in the choice of names for Blepsidemus ("he who peers at the public") and Blepyrus ("he who peers"). All these allusions are made in the context of characters who, like Strepsiades, are closely based on the historical Pericles. Periclean characters, it would seem, inevitably bring plague references with them. Such characters occur throughout the surviv-

4 Cf. Westlake 1968, 8, 11 n. 5, 13 n. 1.
5 Munn 2000, 292 – 329; *Sophocles and Alcibiades*, 139, 151.
6 Cf. Marshall 1990, esp. 169.
7 Where the Plague settled: Thuc. 2.43.5.

ing corpus; it is hardly the case that "Aristophanes in general avoided the plague", as has recently been argued. [8]

This is not the place to re-examine all the theories relating to the Plague, concerning which, it has been said, "more ink has been spilt in argument than there was blood shed in the Peloponnesian War".[9] Since *Pericles of Stage* was published, there have, however, been exciting new developments on the Athenian Plague front, including the discovery of a mass grave containing the remains of some 150 individuals buried in haste. The scanty grave goods point to the burial having occurred at the time of the successive outbreaks of the Plague (430 – 426 BC).[10] Analysis of microbial DNA in the dental pulp conducted in the molecular neurobiology laboratory of the Medical School of Athens University[11] suggests that "Typhoid fever almost certainly played a part in causing the Athens plague, either exclusively or in combination with another – and so far unknown – infection."[12] The methods used have been disputed,[13] and justified.[14] The dust has yet to settle.

All discussions prior to *Pericles on Stage* have been based on Thucydides' account alone. They need to be reassessed in the light both of the new scientific results, and of Aristophanes' evident interest in an event that had directly affected every member of his audience during the previous few years. While there is little that is new, that little may be enough to suggest that an insect-borne disease was believed to be in question. In *Clouds* in particular there is much talk of fleas (145 – 52), bed-bugs (37, 694 – 715), and gnats (156 – 65). Although lice are not mentioned in that play, they are elsewhere criticised as being among the stalest jokes of Athenian comedy (Ar. *Pax* 740), and were presumably a regular feature of everyday life ("lice, gnats and fleas" are markers of an impoverished existence at Ar. *Pl.* 537; cf. the "bed-bugs" at 541). But if lice were deemed unworthy vehicles for Aristophanes' humour, it would explain why Thucydides fails to mention insects in his sober and dignified account of the Plague. Insects are, however, recognised as vectors of typhoid fever, amongst other diseases,[15]

---

8 Mitchell-Boyask 2007, 38.
9 MacArthur 1961, 166. For bibliographical references to some of these theories, see e.g. Longrigg 1980; 1992; Sallares 1991, 244 – 56; Vickers 1991, 64, n. 1; Rubel 2000, 85; 2014, 201. Olsen *et al.* 1996 speak of 29 competing theories (and add Ebola); Cunha 2004 argues for Measles.
10 Baziotopoulou-Valavani 2002.
11 Papagrigorakis *et al.* 2006a.
12 Papagrigorakis 2006.
13 Shapiro *et al.* 2006.
14 Papagrigorakis *et al.* 2006b.
15 MacGregor 1918; Cirillo 2006; Vasan, Prabhu and Pandian 2008.

and the stress that is laid on insects by Aristophanes in *Clouds* may well be a reflection of the unpleasant—and infectious—conditions that prevailed in pla-gue-wracked Athens.

Appendix 3

Keith Sidwell's *Aristophanes the Democrat*

This book was essentially complete by 2008, and so I was not able to take account of Keith Sidwell's *Aristophanes the Democrat: The Politics of Satirical Comedy during the Peloponnesian War* (Cambridge, 2009). Nor can I do so now, for the simple fact is that I do not understand it. To engage with his argument would be akin to wrestling with jelly, for there is nowhere to get a grip. Sidwell is on the right lines, however, in perceiving that Aristophanes does indeed create caricatures of recognisable individuals, but the task of identification can be performed far more economically, via the families of Pericles and Alcibiades (as here).

Sidwell's identifications have been summarized as follows: "Babylonians: Dionysus = Cratinus; Acharnians: Dicaeopolis = Eupolis pretending to be Cratinus (sic); Eupolis' Noumeniai: Paphlagon = Cleon; Demos = Cratinus; Lamp-seller = Hyperbolus; Knights: Paphlagon = Cleon; Demos = Cratinus; Sausage Seller = Alcibiades; Cratinus' Pytine: Poet figure = Aristophanes; Wasps: Philocleon = Cratinus; Bdelycleon = Eupolis; Eupolis' Marikas: Marikas = Hyperbolus; Peace: Trygaeus = Eupolis; Clouds II: Strepsiades = Alcibiades; Pheidippides = Phaeax; Unjust Logos = Eupolis; Just Logos = Cratinus; Birds: Peisetairos = Critias; Thesmophoriazusae: Euripides' kinsman = Eupolis; Eupolis' Demes: Pyronides = Aristophanes; Frogs: Dionysus = Eupolis". And his argument has been criticised thus: "Tackling the famously elusive problem of Aristophanes' politics with conjectural interpretations of the fragments of Eupolis and Cratinus will strike most readers as a clear case of *obscurum per obscurius*".[1] Insofar as I can understand Sidwell's bewildering arguments, I tend to agree. Better perhaps to invoke Occam's razor, whereby among competing hypotheses, the one that makes the fewest assumptions should be selected.

---

1 Lefkowitz 2010.

Bibliography

Ahl, F. 1984. "The Art of Safe Criticism in Greece and Rome". *American Journal of Philology* **105**: 174–208.

Ahl, F. 1985. *Metaformations: Soundplay and Wordplay in Ovid and Other Classical Poets*. Ithaca NY and London: Cornell University Press.

Ahl, F. 1988. "Ars est ca(e)lare artem (Art in Puns and Anagrams Engraved)". In Culler 1988: 17–43.

Ahl, F. 1991. *Sophocles Oedipus: Evidence and Self-Conviction*. Ithaca, NY and London: Cornell University Press.

Ahl, F. 2008. *Two Faces of Oedipus: Sophocles'* Oedipus Tyrannus *and Seneca's* Oedipus. Ithaca NY and London: Cornell University Press.

Ambrosino, D. 1986–87. "Aristoph. *Nub*. 46 s. (Il matrimonio di Strepsiade e la democrazia ateniese)". *Museum Criticum* **21–22**: 95–127.

Amit, M. 1974. "A Peace Treaty Between Sparta and Persia". *Rivista storica dell' antichità* **4**: 55–63.

Armstrong, J. M. 1998. "Aristotle on the Nature of Poetry". *Classical Quarterly* n.s. **48**: 447–55.

Arnott, W. G. 1978. "Red Herrings and Other Bait: a Study in Euripidean Technique". *Museum Philologicum Londinense* **3**: 1–24.

Arrighetti, G. (ed.) 1960. *Epicurus. Opere. Introduzione, testo critico traduzione e note*. Turin: Enaudi.

Arrowsmith, W. 1970. *The Birds by Aristophanes*. New York, New American Library.

Arrowsmith, W. 1973. "Aristophanes *Birds*: the Fantasy Politics of Eros". *Arion* 1: 119–67.

Atherton, H. M. 1974. *Political Prints in the Age of Hogarth*. Oxford: Clarendon Press.

Aurenche, O. 1974. *Les groupes d'Alcibiade, de Léogoras et de Teucros: remarques sur la vie politique athénienne en 415 avant J.C.* Paris: Belles Lettres.

Austin, C. and Olson, S.D. (eds) 2004, *Aristophanes: Thesmophoriazusae*. Oxford: Oxford University Press.

Azoulay, V. 2014. *Pericles of Athens*. Princeton: Princeton University Press.

Bäbler, B. 1998. *Fleissige Thrakerinnen und wehrhafte Skythen: Nichtgriechen im klassischen Athen und ihre archäologische Hinterlassenschaft*. Stuttgart: B.G. Teubner.

Bäbler, B. 2005. "Bobbies or Boobies? The Scythian Police Force in Classical Athens". In Braund 2005a, 114–22.

Baker, L. and Cantwell, D. P. 1982. "Language Acquisition, Cognitive Development, and Emotional Disorder in Childhood". In *Children"s Language* 3, K. E. Nelson (ed.), 286–321. Hillsdale, NJ: Laurence Erlbaum Associates.

Barrett, W. S. (ed.) 1964. *Euripides Hippolytus*. Oxford: Clarendon Press.

Barron, J. P. 1980. "Bakchylides, Theseus and a Woolly Cloak". *Bulletin of the Institute of Classical Studies* 27: 1–8.

Baziotopoulou-Valavani, E. A. 2002. "Mass Burial from the Cemetery of Kerameikos". In *Excavating Classical Culture. Recent Archaeological Discoveries in Greece. Studies in Classical Archaeology* 1, M. Stamatopoulou and M. Yeroulanou (eds), 187–201. British Archaeological Reports International Series 1031. Oxford: Archaeopress.

Beloch, J. 1893. *Griechische Geschichte* 1. Strassburg.

Bendz, G. 1963. *Frontin Kriegslisten.* Schriften und Quellen der alten Welt 10. Berlin: Akademie-Verlag.

Bernal, M. 1987. *Black Athena* 1: *The Fabrication of Ancient Greece 1785–1985.* London, Free Association Press.

Bicknell, P. J. 1972. *Studies in Athenian Politics and Genealogy. Historia* Einzelschrift 19. Wiesbaden: Steiner Verlag.

Bicknell, P. J. 1982. "Axiochos Alkibiadou, Aspasia and Aspasios". *L'Antiquité classique* **51:** 240–50.

Biehl, W. (ed.) 1979. *Euripidis Ion.* Leipzig: Teubner.

Bierl, A. 2002. "'Viel Spott, viel Ehr!' – Die Ambivalenz des *onomasti kômôidein* im festlichen und generischen Kontext'. In *Spoudaiogeloion. Form und Funktion der Verspottung in der aristophanischen Komödie,* A. Ercolani (ed.), 169–87. Stuttgart-Weimar, J. B. Metzler.

Blanckenhagen, P. von 1992. "Stage and Actors in Plato's *Symposium*". *Greek, Roman and Byzantine Studies* **33:** 51–68.

Blaydes, F. H. M. 1890. *Aristophanis Nubes.* Halle: Orphanotrophei Libraria.

Bloedow, E. F. 1972. *Alcibiades Reexamined. Historia* Einzelschrift 21. Wiesbaden: Steiner Verlag.

Bloedow, E. F. 1975. "Aspasia and the Mystery of the Menexenos". *Wiener Studien* n.s. 9: 32–48.

Bloedow, E. F. 1991. "On Nurturing Lions in the State: Alcibiades' Entry on the Political Stage in Athens". *Klio* **73:** 49–65.

Bloedow, E. F. 1992. "Alcibiades 'Brilliant' or 'Intelligent'?" *Historia* **41:** 139–57.

Bloedow, E. F. 2000. "The Implications of a Major Contradiction in Pericles' Career". *Historia* **128:** 295–309.

Bloedow, E.F. 2011. "Pericles' Early Career". *Athenaeum* **99:** 279–98.

Bluck, R. S. 1953. "The Origin of the *Greater Alcibiades*". *Classical Quarterly* n.s. **3:** 46–52.

Blumenthal, H. J. 1983. "Aristophanes. *Frogs* 1437–65: Palamedes". *Liverpool Classical Monthly* **8:** 64.

Boardman, J. 1982. "Herakles, Theseus and Amazons". In D.C. Kurtz and B. Sparkes (eds.), *The Eye of Greece: Studies in the Art of Athens,* 1–28. Cambridge: Cambridge University Press.

Bobrick, E., 1991. "Iphigeneia Revisited: *Thesmophoriazusae* 1160–1225". *Arethusa* **24:** 67–76.

Boeckh, A. 1886. *Die Staathaushaltung der Athener,* 3rd edn. Berlin: Reimer.

Boegehold, A. 1982. "A Dissent at Athens *ca.* 424–421 BC". *Greek, Roman and Byzantine Studies* **23:** 147–56.

Bol, P. C. 1985. *Antike Bronzetechnik: Kunst und Handwerk antiker Erzbilder.* Munich: Beck.

Bonner, R. J. and Smith, G. 1938. *The Administration of Justice from Homer to Aristotle* 2. Chicago: Chicago University Press.

Bowie, A. M. 1993. *Aristophanes, Myth Ritual and Comedy.* Cambridge: University Press.

Bowie, A. M. 1997. "Tragic Filters for History: Euripides' *Supplices* and Sophocles' *Philoctetes*". In Pelling 1997, 39–61.

Bowra, C. M. 1960. "Euripides' Epinician for Alcibiades". *Historia* 9: 8–79.

Bracht Branham, R. 1989. *Unruly Eloquence: Lucian and the Comedy of Traditions.* Revealing Antiquity 2. Cambridge, MA: Harvard University Press.

Braun, T. 2000. "The Choice of Dead Politicians in Eupolis's *Demoi:* Themistocles' Exile, Hero-cult and Delayed Rehabilitation; Pericles and the Origins of the Peloponnesian War". In Harvey and Wilkins 2000: 191–232.

Braund, D. C. (ed.) 2005a. *Scythians and Greeks: Cultural Interactions in Scythia, Athens and the Early Roman Empire (sixth century BC-first century AD)*. Exeter: University of Exeter Press.

Braund, D. C. 2005b. "Pericles, Cleon and the Pontus: the Black Sea in Athens *c.* 440–421". In Braund 2005a, 80–99.

Brewer, J. 1986. *The Common People and Politics, 1750–1790s*. Cambridge: Cambridge University Press.

Briant, P. 1985. "Dons de terres et de villes: l'Asie Mineure dans le contexte achéménide". *Revue des études anciennes* 87: 53–71.

Briant, P. 1998. "Droaphernès et la statue de Sardes". In Brosius and Kuhrt 1998, 205–26.

Briant, P. 2002. *From Cyrus to Alexander: A History of the Persian Empire*. Winona Lake, IN: Eisenbrauns.

Briant, P. 2003. "Histoire et archéologie d'un texte: la *Lettre de Darius à Gadates* entre Perses, Grecs et Romains". In *Licia e Lidia prima dell'ellenizzazione. Atti del Convegno internazionale, Roma 11–12 ottobre 1999*, M. Gorgieri, M. Salvini, M.-C. Trémouille, P. Vannicelli (eds). Monografie Scientifiche, Serie Scienze umane e sociali, 107–144. Rome: Consiglio Nazionale delle Ricerche.

Broadhead, H. D. (ed.) 1960. *The Persae of Aeschylus*. Cambridge: University Press.

Brock, R. W. 1990. "Plato and Comedy". In Craik 1990, 39–49.

Brosius, M. 1998. "Artemis Persike and Artemis Anaitis". In Brosius and Kuhrt 1998, 227–38.

Brosius, M. and A. Kuhrt (eds.) 1998. *Studies in Persian History: Essays in Memory of David M. Lewis. Achaemenid History* 11. Leiden: Nederlands Instituut voor het Nabije Oosten.

Brulé, P. 1994. *Periclès: l'apogée d'Athènes*. Paris: Gallimard.

Brumoy, P. 1730. *Le théâtre des Grecs*. Paris: Chez Rollin père, etc.

Brumoy, P. 1785. *Le théâtre des Grecs*, second edition. Paris: Cussac.

Bruns, I. 1896. *Das literarische Porträt der Griechen im fünften und vierten Jahrhundert vor Christi Geburt*. Berlin: W. Hertz.

Bryant, M. 1990. *A Dictionary of Riddles*. London: Cassell.

Burnett, A. P. 1962. "Human Resistance and Divine Persuasion in Euripides' *Ion*". *Classical Philology* 57: 89–103.

Burnett, A. P. 1971. *Catastrophe Survived: Euripides' Plays of Mixed Reversal*. Oxford: Clarendon Press.

Caizzi F. 1966. *Antisthenis Fragmenta*. Milan: Istituto editoriale cisalpino.

Calame, C. 2003. *Myth and History in Ancient Greece: The Symbolic Creation of a Colony*. Princeton: University Press.

Calder, W. M. III. 1981. "The Anti-Periklean Intent of Aeschylus' *Eumenides*". In *Aischylos und Pindar: Studien zu Werk und Nachwirkung*, E. G. Schmidt (ed.), 217–23. Berlin: Akademie-Verlag.

Calder, W. M., III. 2005. *Theatrokratia: Collected Papers on the Politics and Staging of Greco-Roman Tragedy*, R. Scott Smith (ed.). Spudasmata 104. Hildesheim: George Olms Verlag.

Callanan, K. and A. Bertini Malgarini 1986. "Übersehene Favorin-Fragmente aus einer Oxforder Handschrift". *Rheinisches Museum* **129**: 170–184.

Camp, J. M. 2001. *The Archaeology of Athens*. New Haven: Yale University Press.

Campbell, D. B. 2005. *Ancient Siege Warfare: Persians, Greek, Carthaginians and Romans 546–146 BC*. Oxford: Osprey Publishing.

Cantarella, R. 1974. "Dioniso, fra *Baccanti* e *Rane*". In *Serta Turyniana*, J.L. Heller (ed.), 291–310. Urbana: University of Illinois Press.

Carney, T.F. 1962. "The Picture of Marius in Valerius Maximus." *Rheinisches Museum* n.F. 105: 289–337.

Carnicke, S. M. 1991. *The Theatrical Instinct: Nicolai Evreinov and the Russian Theater of the Early Twentieth Century*. Frankfurt: Lang.

Carradice, I. 1987. "The 'Regal' Coinage of the Persian Empire". In *Coinage and Administration in the Athenian and Persian Empires* 1, I. Carradice (ed.), 73–95, pl.10–15. British Archaeological Reports 343. Oxford.

Carradice, I. 1988. "The Dinar Hoard of Persian Sigloi". In *Studies in Greek Numismatics in Memory of Martin Jessop Price*, R. Ashton and S. Hurter (eds), 65–81. London: Spink.

Carré, J. M., C. M. McCormick, C. J. Mondloch 2009, "Facial Structure is a Reliable Cue of Aggressive Behavior". *Psychological Science* 20: 1194–1198.

Carrière, J. 1966. "Sur le message des Bacchantes". *Antiquité Classique* **35**: 118–39.

Carter, L. B. 1986. *The Quiet Athenian*. Oxford: Clarendon Press.

Cartledge, P. A. 1990. *Aristophanes and his Theatre of the Absurd*. Bristol: Bristol Classical Press.

Cartledge, P. A. 1993. "The Silent Women of Thucydides: 2.45.2 Reviewed". In Rosen and Farrell 1993: 125–32.

Cartledge, P. A. and Harvey, F. D. (eds.) 1985. *Crux: Essays Presented to G.E.M. de Ste Croix on his 75th Birthday*. Exeter: Imprint Academic.

Cirillo, V. J. 2006. "'Winged Sponges': Houseflies as Carriers of Typhoid Fever in 19th- and Early 20th-Century Military Camps". *Perspectives in Biology and Medicine* **49**: 52–63.

Clark, W. G. 1871. "The History of the Ravenna Manuscript of Aristophanes". *Journal of Philology* **3**: 153–60.

Cobb, R. 1986. *Promenades: a Historian's Appreciation of Modern French Literature*. Oxford: Blackwell.

Cobetto Ghiggio, P. 1995. *[Andocide] Contro Alcibiade: introduzione, testo critico, traduzione e commento*. Pisa: Edizioni ETS.

Cole, S. 2005. "The Manipulation of Tradition in Euripides' *Ion*". *Abstract of a paper delivered at the 2005 APA Annual Meeting* (http://www.apaclassics.org/AnnualMeeting/05mtg/abstracts/COLE.html).

Collins, D. 2004. *Master of the Game: Competition and Performance in Greek Poetry*. Hellenic Studies 7. Washington, D.C.: Center for Hellenic Studies.

Conacher, D.J. 1959. "The Paradox in Euripides *Ion*". *TAPA* **90**: 20–39.

Conington, J. 1882. *The Odes and Carmen Saeculare of Horace: Translated into English Verse*. London: George Bell.

Cornford, F. 1907. *Thucydides Mythistoricus*. London: Edward Arnold.

Coulon, V. and Van Daele, H. 1923–30. *Aristophane*. Paris: Collection Budé.

Craik, E.M. (ed.) 1990. *"Owls to Athens": Essays on Classical Subjects Presented to Sir Kenneth Dover*. Oxford: Clarendon Press.

Cribiore, R. 2007. *The School of Libanius in Late Antique Antioch*. Princeton: Princeton University Press.

Croiset, M. 1906. *Aristophane et les parties à Athènes*. Paris: A. Fontemoing.

Cromey, R.D. 1984. "On Deinomache". *Historia* **33**: 385–401.

Cropp, M., Fantham, E. and Scully, S.E. (eds) 1986. *Greek Tragedy and its Legacy: Essays Presented to D.J. Conacher*. Calgary: University of Calgary Press.

Crosby, M. 1949. "The Altar of the Twelve Gods in Athens". In *Commemorative Studies in Honor of Theodore Leslie Shear*, 82–103. *Hesperia*, Supplement 8. Princeton NJ: American School of Classical Studies at Athens.

Csapo, E. and Slater, W. 1995. *The Context of Ancient Drama*. Ann Arbor, MI: University of Michigan Press.

Culler, J. 1988. *On Puns: the Foundation of Letters*. Oxford: Blackwell.

Cunha, B. A. 2004. "The Cause of the Plague of Athens: Plague, Typhoid, Typhus, Smallpox or Measles?" *Infectious Disease Clinics of North America* **18**: 29–43.

Daiches, D. 1969. *Some Late Victorian Attitudes*. London: André Deutsch.

Dale, A. M. (ed.) 1967. *Euripides Helen*. Oxford: Clarendon Press.

Dale, A. M. 1968. *The Lyric Metres of Greek Drama*. 2nd edition. Cambridge: University Press.

D'Angour, A.J. 1999: "Archinus, Eucleides, and the Reform of the Athenian Alphabet". *Bulletin of the Institute of Classical Studies* **43**: 109–130.

Davidson, J. 1997. *Courtesans and Fishcakes: The Consuming Passions of Classical Athens*. London: HarperCollins.

Davies, J. K. 1971. *Athenian Propertied Families 600–300 BC*. Oxford: Clarendon Press.

Decharme, P. 1906. *Euripides and the Spirit of his Dramas*. New York: Macmillan.

Delebecque, E. 1951. *Euripide et la Guerre du Péloponnèse*. Études et commentaries 10. Paris: Klincksieck.

Denniston, J.D. 1952. *Greek Prose Style*. Oxford: Clarendon Press.

Denyer, N. (ed.) 2001. *Plato* Alcibiades. Cambridge: Cambridge University Press.

De Quincey, T. 1857. *Collected Works* 13. London: J. Hogg.

Develin, R. 1985. "Age Qualifications for Athenian Magistrates". *Zeitschrift für Papyrologie und Epigraphik* **61**: 149–59.

Develin, R. 1989. *Athenian Officials 684–321 BC*. Cambridge: Cambridge University Press.

Dobrov, G. 1990. "Aristophanes' *Birds* and the Metaphor of Deferral". *Arethusa* **23**: 209–33.

Dodds, E. R. 1951. *The Greeks and the Irrational*. Berkeley and Los Angeles: University of California Press.

Dodds, E. R. (ed.). *Euripides Bacchae*. Oxford: Clarendon Press, 1960.

Dodds, E. R. 1966. "On Misunderstanding the *Oedipus Rex*". *Greece and Rome* **13**: 37–49. Reprinted 1973 in E.R. Dodds, *The Ancient Concept of Progress and other Essays on Greek Literature and Belief*, 64–77. Oxford: Clarendon Press; 1983 in *Oxford Readings in Greek Tragedy*, edited by E. Segal, 177–88. Oxford: Clarendon Press.

Donaldson, J. W. 1860. *Theatre of the Greeks*, 7th edition. London: Longman and Co.

Dover, K. J. 1958. Review of Newiger 1957. In *Classical Review* n.s. **8**: 235–7.

Dover, K. J. (ed.) 1968. *Aristophanes Clouds*. Oxford: Clarendon Press.

Dover, K. J. 1972. *Aristophanic Comedy*. Berkeley and Los Angeles: University of California Press.

Dover, K. J. 1987. *Greece and the Greeks: Collected Papers* 1: *Language, Poetry, Drama*. Oxford: Clarendon Press.

Dover, K. J. (ed.) 1993. *Aristophanes Frogs*. Oxford: Clarendon Press.

Dover, K.J. 2004. "The limits of allegory and allusion in Aristophanes". In *Law, Rhetoric and Comedy in Classical Athens. Essays in honour of Douglas M. MacDowell*, D.L. Cairns and R.A. Knox (eds), 239–49. Swansea: The Classical Press of Wales.

Drew, D. L. 1930. "The Political Purpose in Euripides Helen". *Classical Philology* 25: 187–9.

Droysen, J. 1835. "Des Aristophanes Vögel und die Hermokopiden". *Rheinisches Museum für Philologie* 3: 161–208.

duBois, P. 1991. *Torture and Truth*. New York: Routledge.

Dübner, F. 1842. *Scholia Graeca in Aristophanem*. Paris: Didot.

Duff, T. 2003. "Plutarch on the Childhood of Alkibiades (*Alk.* 2–3)". *Proceedings of the Cambridge Philological Society* **49**: 89–117.

Dunbar, N. 1995. *Aristophanes Birds*. Oxford: Clarendon Press.

Dunkel, G. 1982. "σύν, ξύν". *Glotta* 60: 55–61.

Dusinberre, E.R.M. 2000. "King or God? Imperial Iconography and the 'Tiarate Head' Coins of Achaemenid Anatolia". In *Across the Anatolian Plateau: Readings in the Archaeology of Ancient Turkey*, D.C. Hopkins (ed.), 157–71. *The Annual of the American Schools of Oriental Research* 57.

Easterling, P.E. 1974."Repetition in Sophocles". *Hermes* **101**: 14–34.

Edwards, M. (ed.) 1995. *Greek Orators 4: Andocides*. Warminster: Aris & Phillips.

Ehlers, B. 1966. *Eine vorplatonische Deutung des sokratischen Eros. Der Dialog Aspasia des Sokratikers Aischines*. Zetemata 41. Munich: Beck.

Ehrenberg, V. 1943. *The People of Aristophanes*. Oxford: Blackwell.

Ellis, W. 1989. *Alcibiades*. London: Routledge.

Else, G.F. 1957. *Aristotle's Poetics: the Argument*. Cambridge, MA: Harvard University Press.

English, M. 2005. "The Evolution of Aristophanes' Stagecraft". *Leeds International Classical Studies* **4.3**: 1–16.

Ercolani, A. (ed.) 2002. *Spoudaiogeloion: Form und Funktion der Verspottung in der aristophanischen Komödie. Drama, Beiträge zum Antiken Drama und seiner Rezeption* 11. Stuttgart and Weimar: Verlag J.B. Metzler.

Fatouros, G. and Krischer, T. (eds) 1983. *Libanios*. Wege der Forschung 621. Darmstadt: Wissenschaftliche Buchgesellschaft.

Ferguson, C. A. 1977. "Baby Talk as a Simplified Register". In *Talking to Children: Language Input and Acquisition*, C. E. Snow and Ferguson (eds), 209–35. Cambridge: University Press.

Ferrari, G. 2002. "The Ancient Temple on the Acropolis at Athens". *American Journal of Archaeology* **106**: 11–35.

Finley, J. H. 1942. *Thucydides*. Cambridge, MA: Harvard University Press.

Finley, J. H. 1967. *Three Essays on Thucydides*. Cambridge, MA: Harvard University Press.

Finley, M. I. 1965. "Myth, Memory, and History". *History and Theory* **4**: 281–302.

Fisher, N. R. E. 1992. *Hybris: A Study in the Values of Honour and Shame in Ancient Greece*. Warminster: Aris and Phillips.

Fisher, N. R. E. 1993. "Multiple Personalities and Dionysiac Festivals: Dicaeopolis in Aristophanes' *Acharnians*". *Greece and Rome* **40**: 31–47.

Foley, H. P. 1982. "The 'Female Intruder' Reconsidered: Women in Aristophanes' *Lysistrata* and *Ecclesiazusae*". *Classical Philology* **77**: 1–21.

Forde, S. 1989. *The Ambition to Rule: Alcibiades and the Politics of Imperialism in Thucydides*. Ithaca, NY and London: Cornell University Press.

Forrest, W. G. 1970. "The Date of the Pseudo-Xenophontic Athênaiôn Politeia". *Klio* **52**: 107–116.

Foucart, P. 1893. "Le poète Sophocle et l'oligarchie des Quatre Cents". *Revue Philologique* **17**: 1–10

Francis, E. D. 1975. "Menandrian Maids and Mithraic Lions". *Glotta* **53**: 43–66.

Francis, E. D. 1980. "Greeks and Persians: The Art of Hazard and Triumph". In *Ancient Persia, the Art of an Empire, Invited Lectures on the Middle East at the University of Texas at Austin*, 4, D. Schmandt-Besserat (ed.), 53–86. Malibu, Calif.: Undena.

Francis, E. D. 1990. *Image and Idea in Fifth-Century Greece: Art and Literature after the Persian Wars*. London: Routledge.

Francis, E. D. 1992. "Oedipus Achaemenides". *American Journal of Philology* 113: 333–57.

Francis, E. D. 1991–93. "Brachylogia Laconica: Spartan Speeches in Thucydides". *Bulletin of the Institute of Classical Studies* 38: 198–212.

Francis, E. D. and Vickers M. 1988. "The Agora Revisited, Athenian Chronology c. 500–450 BC". *Annual of the British School at Athens* 83: 143–67.

Friis Johansen, H. 1962. "Sophocles 1939-1959". *Lustrum* 7: 94–288.

Frost, F. J. 1980. *Plutarch's Life of Themistocles, a Historical Commentary*. Princeton NJ: Princeton University Press.

Furley, W. D. 1989. "Andokides iv ('Against Alkibiades'). Fact or Fiction?" *Hermes* 117: 138–156.

Furley, W. D. 1996. *Andokides and the Herms: A Study of Crisis in Fifth-Century Athenian Religion*. London: Institute of Classical Studies.

Gale, X. L. 2000. "Historical Studies and Postmodernism: Rereading Aspasia of Miletus". *College English* 62: 361–386.

Gannon, J.F. 1987. *Aristophanes' Thesmophoriazusae: Commentary*. Bryn Mawr: Thomas Library, Bryn Mawr College.

George, M.D. 1959. *English Political Caricature 1793–1832: a Study of Opinion and Propaganda*. Oxford: Clarendon Press.

Germain, G. 1972. "Théano: Théonoè—sur un personnage d'Euripide". In *Studi Classici in Onore di Quintino Cataudella*, 259–73. Catania: Università di Catania, Facoltà di lettere e filosofia.

Gibert, J.C. 1997. "Euripides' *Hippolytus* Plays: Which Came first?" *Classical Quarterly* 47: 85–97.

Gibert, J.C. 1999–2000. "Falling in Love with Euripides (*Andromeda*)". In *Euripides and the Tragic Theatre in the late Fifth Century*, M. Cropp, S. Klee and D. Sansone (eds), 75–91. *Illinois Classical Studies* 24–5.

Gill, C. 1996. *Personality in Greek Epic, Tragedy and Philosophy: the Self in Dialogue*. Oxford: Clarendon Press.

Gill, D. 1974. "Trapezomata: A Neglected Aspect of Greek Sacrifice". *The Harvard Theological Review* 67: 117–137.

Gill, D. W. J. 2001. "The Decision to Build the Temple of Athena Nike. *IG* I^3 35". *Historia* 50: 257–78.

Gill, D. W. J. 2006. "Hippodamus and the Piraeus". *Historia* 55: 1–15.

Glover, T. R. 1945, *Springs of Hellas and other Essays*. Cambridge: University Press.

Goldhill, S. 1987. "The Great Dionysia and Civic Ideology". *Journal of Hellenic Studies* 107: 58–76.

Gomme, A.W. 1938. "Aristophanes and Politics". *Classical Review* 52: 97–109.

Gomme, A. W. 1962. *More Essays in Greek History and Literature*. Oxford: Clarendon Press.

Greenwood, L.H.G. 1953. *Aspects of Euripidean Tragedy*. Cambridge: Cambridge University Press.

Grégoire, H. and P. Orgels. 1953. "L'*Ajax* de Sophocle, Alcibiades et Sparte". *Annuaire de l'Institut de Philologie et d'histoire orientales et slaves* 13: 653–63.

Grégoire, H. 1955. "La date de l'*Ajax* de Sophocle". *Academie Royale de Belgique. Bulletin de la Classe des Lettres* 41: 187–98.

Grégoire, H. 1961. "Introduction". *Euripide* (Budé edition, vol 5). Paris: Les Belles Lettres.

Gribble, D. 1999. *Alcibiades and Athens: A Study in Literary Presentation*. Oxford: Clarendon Press.

Gribble, D. 2012. "Alcibiades at the Olympics: performance, politics and civic ideology". *Classical Quarterly* **62**: 45–71.

Griffith, R.H. 1945. "The *Dunciad*". *Philological Quarterly* **24**: 155–7.

Griswold, C. 2007. "Plato on Rhetoric and Poetry". *Stanford Encyclopedia of Philosophy* (http://plato.stanford.edu/entries/plato-rhetoric/).

Grote, G. 1870. *A History of Greece*, new edn. London: John Murray.

Guidorizzi, G. 2006. "Mito e commedia: il caso di Cratino". In *ΚΩΜΩΙΔΟΤΡΑΓΩΙΔΙΑ: intersezioni del tragico e del comico nel teatro del V secolo a.C.*, E. Medda, M. S. Mirto and M. P. Pattoni (eds), 119–135. Pisa: Edizioni della Normale.

Guthrie, W.K.C. 1950. *The Greeks and their Gods*. London: Methuen.

Haase, F.-A. 2002. "Aspasia—Historische Persönlichkeit und *fictio personae*. Schriftliche und bildliche Formen der Überlieferung einer Wissenschaft in Platons Dialog *Menexenos*, Raphaels Fresko *Schule von Athen* und in modernen Quellen". *Philologie im Netz* 19: 43–54 (www.fu-berlin.de/phin/phin19/p19 t2.htm).

Habash, M. 2002. "Dionysos' Roles in Aristophanes' 'Frogs'". *Mnemosyne* 4th series, **55**: 1–17.

Hall, E. M. 1989. "The Archer Scene in Aristophanes' Thesmophoriazusae". *Philologus* **133**: 38–54.

Hall, E. M. 2007. "The English-Speaking Aristophanes 1650–1914". *In Aristophanes in Performance 421 BC–AD 2007: Peace, Birds and Frogs*, E. Hall and A. Wrigley (eds), 66–92. Oxford: Legenda.

Hall, E.M. 2009. "Deianeira Deliberates: Precipitate Decision-making and *Trachiniae*". In S. Goldhill and E.M. Hall (eds). *Sophocles and the Greek Tradition*. Cambridge: Cambridge University Press.

Hall, H. G. 1984. *Comedy in Context: Essays on Molière*. Jackson, Miss.: University Press of Mississippi.

Halliwell, S. 1991. "Comic Satire and Freedom of Speech in Classical Athens". Journal of Hellenic Studies **111**: 48–70.

Handley, E. W. 1982. "*POxy* 2806: a Fragment of Cratinus?" *Bulletin of the Institute of Classical Studies* **29**: 109–17.

Harriott, R. M. 1969. *Poetry and Criticism Before Plato*. London: Methuen.

Harvey, D and Wilkins, J. (eds) 2000. *The Rival of Aristophanes: Studies in Athenian Old Comedy*. London: Duckworth and the Classical Press of Wales.

Hatzfeld, J. 1951. *Alcibiade: étude sur l'histoire d'Athènes à la fin du Ve siècle*, 2nd edn. Paris: Presses Universitaires de France.

Heath, M. 1987a. *Political Comedy in Aristophanes*. Hypomnemata 87. Göttingen: Vandenbroeck and Ruprecht.

Heath, M. 1987b. *The Poetics of Greek Tragedy*. Palo Alto, CA: Stanford University Press.

Heckscher, W. S. 1958. *Rembrandt's Anatomy of Dr. Nicolaas Tulp: an Iconological Study*. New York: New York University Press.

Heckscher, W. S. 1974. "Petites perceptions: an Account of Sortes Warburgianae". *The Journal of Medieval and Renaissance Studies* **4**: 101–34.

Heckscher, W. S., Sherman, A. B. and Ferguson, S. 1984. *Emblem Books in the Princeton University Library: A Short-title Catalogue*. Princeton, NJ: Princeton University Library.

Heftner, H. 1995. "Ps.-Andokides' Rede gegen Alkibiades ([And.] 4) und die politische Diskussion nach dem Sturz der 'Dreissig' in Athen". *Klio* **77**: 75–104.

Heftner, H. 2001. "Die pseudo-andokideische Rede 'Gegen Alkibiades' ([And.] 4)—ein authentischer Beitrag zu einer Ostrakophoriedebatte des Jahres 415 v. Chr.?" *Philologus* **145**: 39–56.

Henderson, J. 1975. *The Maculate Muse: Obscene Language in Attic Comedy*. New Haven, Conn.: Yale University Press.

Henderson, J. 1980. "*Lysistrate:* the Play and its Themes". *Yale Classical Studies* **26**: 153–218.

Henderson, J. (ed.) 1987. *Aristophanes Lysistrata*. Oxford: Clarendon Press.

Henderson, J. 1990. "The Demos and Comic Competition". In *Nothing to Do with Dionysus: Social Meanings of Greek Drama*, J. Winkler and F. Zeitlin (eds). Princeton: NJ: Princeton University Press: 271–313.

Henderson, J. 1991. *The Maculate Muse: Obscene Language in Attic Comedy*. 2nd edn. New York: Oxford University Press.

Henderson, J. 2000. "Pherekrates and the Women of Old Comedy". In Harvey and Wilkins 2000, 135–150.

Henry, M. M. 1995, *Prisoner of History: Aspasia of Miletus and her Biographical Tradition* New York: Oxford University Press.

Herman, G. 2006. *Morality and Behaviour: a Social History of Democratic Athens*. Cambridge: University Press.

Hertzberg, G. F. 1853. *Alkibiades. Der Staatsmann und Feldherr*. Halle: C.E.M. Pfeffer.

Hesk, J. 2003. *Sophocles* Ajax. London: Duckworth.

Hodkinson, S. 1994. "'Blind Ploutos': Contemporary Images of the Role of Wealth in Classical Sparta". In *The Shadow of Sparta*, A. Powell and S. Hodkinson (eds), 183–222. London: Routledge for the Classical Press of Wales.

Hoffmann, H. and Konstan, H. 2002. "Casting the Riace bronzes: Modern Assumptions and Ancient Facts". *Oxford Journal of Archaeology* **21**: 153–65.

Holden, H. A. 1902. *Onomasticon Aristophaneum*, 2nd edn. Cambridge: C.J. Clay.

Hooley, D. M. 2007. *Roman Satire*. Oxford: Blackwell.

Hopkins, K. 1978. *Conquerors and Slaves: Sociological Studies in Ancient History*. Cambridge: University Press.

Hornblower, S. 1987. *Thucydides*. London: Duckworth.

Hornblower, S. 1991–6. *A Commentary on Thucydides* 1–2. Oxford: Clarendon Press.

Hornblower, S. 2000. "The Old Oligarch (Pseudo-Xenophon's Athenaion Politeia) and Thucydides. A Fourth-century Date for the Old Oligarch?" In *Polis and Politics. Studies in Ancient Greek History Presented to Mogens Herman Hansen on his Sixtieth Birthday, August 20, 2000*, P. Flensted-Jensen (ed.), 363–79. Copenhagen: Museum Tusculanum Press.

Hubbard, T. K. 1991. *The Mask of Comedy: Aristophanes and the Intertextual Parabasis*. Ithaca, NY and London: Cornell University Press.

Hubbard, T. K. 1998. Review of Vickers 1997. In *Classical Philology* **92**: 370–75.

Hulton, A. O. 1972. "The Women on the Acropolis: a Note on the Structure of the *Lysistrata*". *Greece and Rome* **19**: 32–6.

Hume, R. A. 1999. *Reconstructing Contexts: the Aims and Principles of Archaeo-Historicism*. Oxford: Clarendon Press.

Hunt, P. 2010.*War, Peace, and Alliance in Demosthenes' Athens*. Cambridge: Cambridge University Press.

Hunter, R. 2004. *Plato's Symposium.* Oxford: Oxford University Press.
Hutchinson, P. 1983. *Games Authors Play.* London: Methuen.
Huxley, G. 1967. "The Medism of Caryae". *Greek, Roman and Byzantine Studies* **8**: 29–32.
Janko, R. 1984. *Aristotle on Comedy: Towards a Reconstruction of Poetics II.* London: Duckworth.
Janko, R. 2000. *Philodemus "On Poems" Book One.* Oxford: Oxford University Press.
Jenkins, G. K. 1972. *Ancient Greek coins.* London: Barrie and Jenkins.
Juffras, D. M. 1993. "Helen and Other Victims in Euripides' *Helen*". *Hermes* **121**: 45–57.
Kagan, D. 1974. *The Archidamian War.* Ithaca: Cornell University Press.
Kagan, D. 1990. *Pericles of Athens and the Birth of Democracy.* London: Secker and Warburg.
Kagan, D. 2005. "In Defense of History". NEH Jefferson Lecture.
    http://www.neh.gov/whoweare/kagan/lecture.html
Kahn, C. 1996. *Plato and the Socratic Dialogue.* Cambridge: University Press.
Kaimio, M. 1988. *Physical Contact in Greek Tragedy: a Study of Stage Convention.* Annales Academiae scientiarum Fennicae, ser. B, 244. Helsinki: Suomalainen tiedeakatemia.
Kanavou, N. 2011. *Aristophanes' Comedy of Names: a Study of Speaking Names in Aristophanes.* Sozomena: studies in the recovery of ancient texts, 8. Berlin/New York: de Gruyter.
Kannicht, R. (ed.) 1969. *Euripides Helena.* Heidelberg: C. Winter.
Katz, B. R. 1976. "The *Birds* of Aristophanes and Politics". *Athenaeum* n.s. **54**: 353–81.
Keen, A. and Sekunda, N. 2007. "Xenophon the Rhetor". In *Corolla Cosmo Rodewald*, N. Sekunda (ed.), 25–38. Gdańsk: Department of Archaeology Gdańsk University.
Kelly, T. 1985. "The Spartan Scytale". In *The Craft of the Ancient Historian: Festschrift C.G. Starr*, J.W. Eadie and J. Ober (eds), 141–69. Lanham: University Press of America.
Kennedy, R.F. 2009. *Athena's Justice: Athena, Athens, and the Concept of Justice in Greek Tragedy.* New York: Peter Lang.
Keramopoullos, A. D. 1923. Ὁ ἀποτυμπανισμός. Athens: Typographeion "Hestia".
Kiberd, D. 1995. *Inventing Ireland.* London: Jonathan Cape.
Knox, B. 1956. "The Date of the *Oedipus Tyrannus* of Sophocles". *American Journal of Philology* **77**: 133–47.
Knox, B. 1979. *Word and Action: Essays on the Ancient Theater.* Baltimore: Johns Hopkins University Press.
Konishi, H. 1986. "Euripides' Medea and Aspasia". *Liverpool Classical Monthly* **11**: 50–52.
Konstan, D. 1990. "A City in the Air: Aristophanes' *Birds*". *Arethusa* **23**: 183–207.
Konstan, D. and Dillon, M. 1981. "The Ideology of Aristophanes' *Wealth.*" *American Journal of Philology* **102**: 371–94.
Koster, W. J. W. 1975. *Scholia in Aristophanem* 1a. *Prolegomena de Comoedia.* Groningen: Bouma's Boekhuis.
Kovacs, D. 2002. *Helen; Phoenician Women; Orestes.* Loeb Classical Library. Cambridge, Mass.: Harvard University Press.
Lada-Richards, I. 1999. *Initiating Dionysus: Ritual and Theatre in Aristophanes'* Frogs. Oxford: Clarendon Press.
Landucci Gattinoni, F. 1997. *Duride di Samo.* Centro Ricerche e Documentazione sull'Antichità Classica Monografie 18. Rome: "L'Erma" di Bretschneider.
Lang, M. L. 1978. *Socrates in the Agora.* Princeton NJ: Princeton University Press.
Laschitzer, S. 1888. "Die Genealogie des Kaisers Maximilian I". *Jahrbuch der Kunsthistorischen Sammlungen des Allerhöchsten Kaiserhauses* **7**: 1–200.

Latte, K. 1968. *Kleine Schriften zu Religion, Recht, Literatur und Sprache der Griechen und Römer*, O. Gigon, W. Buchwald and W. Kunkel (eds). Munich: Beck.

Laum, B. 1925. *Das Eisengelt der Spartaner*. Braunsberg: Verlag der Staatlichen Akademie.

Laurenti, R. 1988. "Aspasia e Santippe nell'Atene del V secolo". *Sileno* **14**: 41–61.

Lee, K. (ed.) 1997. *Euripides, Ion*. Warminster: Aris and Phillips.

Leeuwen , L. van (ed.) 1896. *Aristophanis Ranae*. Leiden: A.W. Sijthoff.

Lefkowitz, M. 1981. *The Lives of the Greek Poets*. London: Duckworth.

Lefkowitz, M. 2010. Review of Sidwell 2008. In *Bryn Mawr Classical Review* 2010.10.62.

Le Paulmier de Grentemesnil, J. 1668. *Exercitationes in optimos fere auctores Graecos*. Leiden: ex officina Danielis, Abrahami & Adriani à Gaasbeeck.

Lesk, A.L. 2005. *A Diachronic Examination of the Erechtheion and Its Reception*, PhD thesis, University of Cincinnati.

Lessing, G.E. [1925]. *Schriften zur antiken Kunstgeschichte*, A. Schoene, J. Petersen, K. Borinski (eds). In *Lessings Werke: vollständige Ausgabe in fünfundzwanzig Teilen*, J. Petersen and W. von Olshausen (eds). 17. Berlin: Deutsches Verlagshaus Bong & Co.

Levi, M.A. 1967. *Quattro studi spartani e altri scritti di storia greca*. Milan: Istituto Editoriale Cisalpino.

Levi, M.A. 1980. *Pericle. Un uomo, un regime, una cultura*. Milan: Rusconi.

Lévy, E. 1997. "Richesse et pauvreté dans le *Ploutos*". *Ktema* **22**: 201–12.

Lewis, D.M. 1955. "Notes on Attic Inscriptions (II): xxii. Who was Lysistrata?" *Annual of the British School at Athens* **5o**: 1–12.

Lewis, D.M. 1966. "After the Profanation of the Mysteries". In *Ancient History and its Institutions: Studies presented to Victor Ehrenberg on his 75th birthday*, E. Badian (ed.), 177–91: Oxford: Blackwell.

Lewis, D.M. 1977. *Sparta and Persia*. Leiden: Brill.

Littman R. J. 1970. "The Loves of Alcibiades", *Transactions of the American Philological Association* **101**: 263–76.

Lloyd-Jones, H. 1982. *Classical Survivals: The Classics in the Modern World*. London: Duckworth.

Lloyd-Jones, H. 1983. *The Justice of Zeus*, 2nd edn. Berkeley and Los Angeles: University of California Press.

Lloyd-Jones, H. (ed.) 1994. *Sophocles: Ajax, Electra, Oedipus Tyrannus*. Cambridge, MA: Harvard University Press.

Loening, T. C. 1987. *The Reconciliation Agreement of 403/402 BC in Athens. Hermes Einzelschriften 53*. Stuttgart: Franz Steiner Verlag.

Long. T. 1986. *Barbarians in Greek Comedy*. Carbondale and Edwardsville: Southern Illinois University Press.

Longrigg, J. 1980. "The Great Plague of Athens". *History of Science* **18**: 209–25.

Longrigg, J. 1992. "Epidemics, Ideas and Classical Athenian Society". In T. Ranger and P. Slack, eds. *Epidemics and Ideas: Essays on the Historical Perception of Pestilence*. Cambridge: Cambridge University Press.

Lonis, R. (ed.) 1988. *L'Étranger dans le monde grec*. Nancy: Presses Universitaires de Nancy.

López Eire, H. (ed.) 1997. *Sociedad, Política y Literatura: Comedia Griega Antigua*. Salamanca: Logo.

Loraux, N. 1981. *L'invention d'Athènes: histoire de l'oraison funèbre dans la "cité classique"*. Paris: Mouton.

Loraux, N. 1990. *Les enfants d'Athéna. Idées athéniennes sur la citoyenneté et la division des sexes*. Paris: Editions du Seuil

Loraux, N. 1998. *Né de la terre. Mythe et politique à Athènes*. Paris: Editions du Seuil.

Lord, L. E. 1963. *Aristophanes; his Plays and his Influence*. New York: Cooper Square Publishers.

Luppe, W. 1994. "Die Hypothese zum ersten *Hippolytos*". *Zeitschrift für Papyrologie und Epigraphik* **102**: 23–39.

MacArthur, W.P. 1959. "The Medical Identification of Some Pestilences of the Past". *Transactions of the Royal Society of Tropical Medicine and Hygiene* **53**: 423–39 (the part dealing with the Athenian Plague reprinted in *Oxford Medical School Gazette* **13** [1961], 166–73).

MacGregor, M.E. 1918. "Insects as Carriers of Disease". *Transactions of the American Microscopical Society* **37**: 7–17.

MacDougall, H.A. 1982. *Racial Myth in English History: Trojans, Teutons and Anglo-Saxons*. Montreal: Harvest House.

Macdowell, D.W. 1995. *Aristophanes and Athens: an Introduction to the Plays*. Oxford: University Press.

Mackenzie, C. 1937. *Pericles*. London: Hodder and Stoughton.

Maehly, H. 1853. "De Aspasia Milesia commentariolus". *Philologus* **9**: 213–30.

Mahood, M. M. 1957. *Shakespeare's Wordplay*. London: Routledge.

Maidment, K. J. 1941. *Minor Attic Orators* 1. London: Heinemann.

Marcus, S. 1966. *The Other Victorians*. London: Weidenfeld and Nicolson.

Mark, I. S. 1993. "The Sanctuary of Athena Nike in Athens: Architectural Stages and Chronology". AIA Monograph n.s. 2; *Hesperia* Supplement 26. Princeton NJ: American School of Classical Studies at Athens.

Marshall, M. 1990. "Pericles and the Plague". In Craik 1990: 163–70.

Mastromarco, G. 1997. "La Lisistrata di Aristifane: emancipazione femminile, società fallocratica e utopia comica". In López Eire 1997: 103–16.

Mastromarco, G. 2002. "*Onomasti komodeîn* e *spoudaiogeloion*". In Ercolani 2002, 205–224.

Mattingly, H. B. 1977. "Poets and Politicians in Fifth-century Greece". In *Greece and the Eastern Mediterranean in Ancient History and Prehistory. Studies presented to Fritz Schachermeyr on the Occasion of his Eightieth Birthday*, K.H. Kinzl (ed.), 231–45. New York: de Gruyter.

Mattusch, C. C. 1996. *Classical Bronzes: the Art and Craft of Greek and Roman Statuary*. Ithaca: Cornell University Press.

Mayrhofer, M. 1973. *Onomastica Persepolitana. Das altiranische Namengut der Persepolis-Täfelchen. Sitzungsberichte der Akademie der Wissenschaften in Wien. Philosophisch-Historische Klasse* 286.

McGlew, J. 1997. "After Irony: Aristophanes' *Wealth* and its Modern Interpreters". *American Journal of Philology* **118**: 35–53.

Meiggs, R. 1972. *The Athenian Empire*. Oxford: Clarendon Press.

Meinhardt, E. 1957. *Perikles bei Plutarch*. Diss. Frankfurt.

Merry, W. W. 1904. *Aristophanes, The Birds*, 4th edn. Oxford: Clarendon Press.

Mills, S. 1997. *Theseus, Tragedy, and the Athenian Empire*. Oxford: Clarendon Press.

Mills, S. 2002. *Euripides: Hippolytus*. London: Duckworth.

Milne, M.J. and D. von Bothmer 1953. "Καταπύγων, καταπύγαινα". *Hesperia* **22**: 306–14.

Missiou, A. 1992. *The Subversive Oratory of Andokides: Politics, Ideology and Decision-making in Democratic Athens*. Cambridge: Cambridge University Press.

Missiou, A. 1993. "ΔΟΥΛΟΣ ΤΟΥ ΒΑΣΙΛΕΩΣ: the Politics of Translation". *Classical Quarterly* **43**: 377–91.

Mitchell, T. (ed.) 1836. *The Knights of Aristophanes*. London: John Murray.

Mitchell-Boyask, R. 2007. *Plague and the Athenian Imagination. Drama, History and the Cult of Asclepius*. Cambridge: Cambridge University Press.

Mitford, W. 1829. *The History of Greece*, new edn. London: T. Cadell.

Monaco, G. 1963. *Paragoni burleschi degli antichi*. Palermo: Palumbo.

Moorton, R.F. 1988. "Aristophanes on Alcibiades". *Greek, Roman and Byzantine Studies* **29**: 345–59.

Moruzzi, N.C. 2000. *Speaking through the Mask: Hannah Arendt and the Politics of Social Identity*. Ithaca NY and London: Cornell University Press.

Muecke, O. F. 1982. "A Portrait of the Artist as a Young Woman". *Classical Quarterly* 32: 41–55.

Müller, G. 1967. *Sophokles, Antigone*. Heidelberg: C. Winter.

Munn, M. 2000. *The School of History: Athens in the Age of Socrates*. Berkeley, Los Angeles: University of California Press.

Murray, G. 1933. *Aristophanes, a Study*. Oxford: Clarendon Press

Musgrave, S. (ed.) 1800. *Sophoclis tragoediae septem*. Oxford: Clarendon Press.

Neer, R.T. 2002. *Style and Politics in Athenian Vase-painting: The Craft of Democracy, ca. 530–460 BCE*. Cambridge: University Press.

Nesselrath, H.-G. 1990. *Die attische mittlere Komödie: ihre Stellung in der antiken Literaturkritik und Literaturgeschichte*. Untersuchungen zur antiken Literatur und Geschichte, 36. Berlin: de Gruyter.

Nesselrath, H.-G. 1996. "Aristophanes". *Der Neue Pauly* 1, 1122–30. Stuttgart: Verlag J.B. Metzler.

Nesselrath, H.-G. 2000. "Eupolis and the Periodization of Athenian Comedy". In Harvey and Wilkins 2000, 233–46.

Nesselrath, H.-G. 2012. *Libanios: Zeuge einer schwindenden Zeit*. Stuttgart: Anton Hiersemann Verlag.

Newiger, H.-J. 1957. *Metapher und Allegorie: Studien zu Aristophanes*. Zetemata 16. Munich: Beck. Reprinted 2000, *Drama, Beiträge zum Antiken Drama und seiner Rezeption* 10. Stuttgart and Weimar: Verlag J.B. Metzler.

Norman, A.F. 1960. "The Book Trade in Fourth-century Antioch". *Journal of Hellenic Studies* **80**: 122–26.

Norwood, G. 1931. *Greek Comedy*. London: Methuen.

Norwood, G. 1942. Review of Owen 1939. In *The American Journal of Philology* 63: 109–113.

Nussbaum, M. 1986. *Fragility of Goodness: Luck and Ethics in Greek Tragedy and Philosophy*. Cambridge: Cambridge University Press.

Nylander, C. 1970. *Ionians in Pasargadae: Studies in Old Persian Architecture*. Acta Universitatis Upsaliensis. Boreas 1. Uppsala: University Press; Almqvist & Wiksell.

Ogden, D. 2001. *Greek and Roman Necromancy*. Princeton, NJ: Princeton University Press.

O'Hara, J.J. 1996. *True Names: Vergil and the Alexandrian Tradition of Etymological Wordplay*. Ann Arbor: University of Michigan Press.

Olson, P.E., C.S. Hames, A.S. Benenson, and E. N. Genovese. 1996. "The Thucydides syndrome: Ebola déjà vu? (or Ebola reemergent?)". *Emerging Infectious Diseases* **2** (http://www.cdc.gov/ncidod/eid/vol2no2/olson.htm).

Olson, S.D. 1987. "The Identity of the δεσπότης at Ecclesiazusae 1128 f". *Greek Roman and Byzantine Studies* **28**: 161–66.

Olson, S.D. 1990. "Economics and Ideology in Aristophanes' Wealth". *Harvard Studies in Classical Philology* **93**: 223–242.

Olson, S.D. 1992. "Names and Naming in Aristophanes". *Classical Quarterly* n.s. **42**: 304–19.

O'Neill, Y.V. 1980. *Speech and Speech Disorders in Western Thought Before 1600*. Westport, Ct. and London: Greenwood Press.

Orrieux, C. 1988. "'Parenté' entre juifs et spartiates". In Lonis 1988, 169–91.

Ostwald, M. 1969. *Nomos and the Beginnings of Athenian Democracy*. Oxford: Clarendon Press.

Ostwald, M. 1986. *From Popular Sovereignty to the Sovereignty of Law: Law, Society and Politics in Fifth-Century Athens*. Berkeley and Los Angeles: University of California Press.

Owen, A.S. 1939. *Euripides, Ion*. Oxford: University Press.

Papagrigorakis, M. 2006. "Secret of Ancient Athens Plague is being Unravelled". *Kathimerini* English Edition, 21 January. (http://www.ekathimerini.com/4dcgi/news/content.asp?aid= 65444)

Papagrigorakis, M.J., C. Yapijakis, P.N. Synodinos and E. Baziotopoulou-Valavani. 2006a. "DNA Examination of Ancient Dental Pulp Incriminates Typhoid Fever as a Probable Cause of the Plague of Athens". *International Journal of Infectious Diseases* **10**: 206–214.

Papagrigorakis, M.J., C. Yapijakis, P.N. Synodinos and E. Baziotopoulou-Valavani. 2006b. "Reply to Shapiro et al.". *International Journal of Infectious Diseases* **10**: 335–6.

Pearson, A.C. 1903. *The Helena of Euripides*. Cambridge: University Press.

Pelling, C.B.R. 1992. "Plutarch and Thucydides". In *Plutarch and the Historical Tradition*, P. A. Stadter (ed.), 10–40. London: Routledge.

Perrin, B. 1906. "The Death of Alcibiades". *Transactions of the American Philological Association* **37**: 25–37.

Perusino, F. 1987. *Dalla commedia antica alla commedia di mezzo: tre studi su Aristofane*. Pubblicazioni dell'Università di Urbino, Serie di linguistica litteratura arte 8. Urbino: Università degli Studi.

Petersen, W. 1910. *Greek Diminutives in -ιον: a Study in Semantics*. Weimar: R. Wagner.

Petit, T, 1997. "Alcibiade et Tissapherne". *Les Études Classiques* **65**: 137–151.

Pfeiffer, R. 1976. *History of Classical Scholarship from 1300 to 1850*. Oxford: Clarendon Press.

Piccirilli, L. 1997. "Il primo caso di autodafé letterario: il rogo dei libri di Protagora". *Studi Italiani di Filologia Classica* [Ser. III] **15**: 17–23.

Pickard-Cambridge, A.W. 1968. *The Dramatic Festivals of Athens*, revised by J. Gould and D.M. Lewis. Oxford: Clarendon Press.

Pickering, P.E. 2003. "Did the Greek Ear Detect 'Careless' Verbal Repetitions?" *Classical Quarterly* **53**: 490–99.

Pippin, A.N. 1960. "Euripides' *Helen*: a Comedy of Ideas". *Classical Philology* **55**: 151–63.

Platz-Horster, G. 1995, "Eros mit den Waffen des Zeus: eine neue Chalcedon-Gemme in den Münchner Antikensammlungen". *Münchener Jahrbuch der bildenden Kunst* **46**: 7–24.

Podlecki, A.J. 1970. "The Basic Seriousness of Euripides' *Helen*". *Transactions of the American Philological Association* **101**: 401–18.

Podlecki, A.J. 1975. *The Life of Themistocles: a Critical Survey of the Literary and Archaeological Evidence*. Montreal: McGill-Queen's University Press.

Podlecki, A.J. 1987. *Plutarch: Life of Pericles*. Bristol: Bristol Classical Press.

Podlecki, A.J. 1998. *Perikles and his Circle*. London: Routledge.

Pope, M. 1986. "Athenian Festival Judges—Seven, Five, or However Many". *Classical Quarterly* 36: 322–6.

Pope, M. 1989. "Upon the Country—Juries and the Principle of Random Selection". *Social Science Information* **28**: 265–89.

Powell, J.E. 1937. "Puns in Herodotus". *Classical Review* **51**: 103.

Prandi, L. 1992. "Introduzione". In *Plutarcho, Vite parallele, Coriolano/Alcibiade*, 255–317. Milan: Rizzoli.

Pritchett, W.K. 1953. "The Attic Stelai". *Hesperia* **22**: 225–99.

Pritchett, W.K. 1956. "Attic Stelai, Part II". *Hesperia* **25**: 167–210.

Pritchett, W.K. 1961. "Five New Fragments of the Attic Stelai". *Hesperia* **30**: 23–29.

Radermacher, L. (ed.) 1954, *Aristophanes' "Frösche": Einleitung, Text und Kommentar*, 2nd edn. Vienna: In Kommission bei R.M. Rohrer.

Rau, P. 1967. *Paratragodia: Untersuchung einer komischen Form des Aristophanes*. Munich: Verlag C.H. Beck.

Raubitschek, A.E. 1948. "The Case Against Alcibiades (Andocides IV)". *Transactions of the American Philological Society* 79: 191–210. Reprinted 1991 in *The School of Hellas: Essays on Greek History, Archaeology, and Literature*, D. Obbink and P.A. Vander Waerdt (eds), 116–31. New York: Oxford University Press.

Redfern. W. 1984. *Puns*. Oxford: Basil Blackwell.

Rennie, W. 1909, *The Acharnians of Aristophanes*. London: Edward Arnold.

Revermann, M. 1997. "Cratinus' Διονυσαλέξανδρος and the Head of Pericles". *The Journal of Hellenic Studies* **117**: 197–200.

Rhodes, P.J. 1972. *The Athenian Boule*. 2nd edn, 1985. Oxford: Clarendon Press.

Rhodes, P.J. 1981. *A Commentary on the Aristotelian* Athenaion Politeia. Oxford: Clarendon Press.

Rhodes, P.J. 2011. *Alcibiades*. Barnsley, Pen and Sword Military.

Richardson, N.J. 1974. *The Homeric Hymn to Demeter*. Oxford: Clarendon Press.

Richter, G.M.A. 1965. *The Portraits of the Greeks*. London: Phaidon.

Richter, G.M.A. 1984. *The Portraits of the Greeks*. Revised edition, R.R.R. Smith (ed.). Ithaca: Cornell University Press.

Robert, L. 1980. *À travers l'Asie Mineur: poètes et prosateurs, monnaies grecques, voyageurs et géographie*. Bibliothèque de l'École française d'Athènes 239. Athens/Paris: École française d'Athènes/de Boccard.

Robson, J. 2009. *Aristophanes: an Introduction*. London: Duckworth.

Rodnan, G.P. 1961. "A Gallery of Gout. Being a Miscellany of Prints and Caricatures from the 16th Century to the Present Day". *Arthritis and Rheumatism* **4**: 27–46.

Rodríguez Blanco, M.E. 1988. *Alcibíades: Antología de textos con notas y comentarios*. Madrid: Ediciones de la Universidad Autónoma.

Rogers, B.B. (ed.) 1902. *The Frogs of Aristophanes*. London: George Bell.

Rogers, B.B. (ed.) 1904. *The Thesmophoriazusae of Aristophanes*. London: George Bell.

Rogers, B.B. (ed.) 1906. *The Birds of Aristophanes*. London: George Bell.

Roisman, H.M. 1999. *Nothing Is As It Seems: the Tragedy of the Implicit in Euripides'* Hippolytus. Lanham, Md: Rowman and Littlefield Publishers, Inc.

Romilly, J. de 1963. *Thucydides and Athenian Imperialism.* Oxford: Blackwell.

Romilly, J. de 1993. *Alcibiade, ou, Les dangers de l'ambition.* Paris: Editions de Fallois.

Root, M.C. 1991. "From the Heart: Powerful Persianisms in the Art of the Western Empire". In *Asia Minor and Egypt: Old Cultures in a New Empire*, H. Sancisi-Weerdenburg and A. Kuhrt (eds), 1–29. Achaemenid History 6. Leiden: Nederlands Instituut voor het Nabije Oosten.

Rose, H.J. 1957. *A Commentary on the Surviving Plays of Aeschylus.* Verhandelingen der Koninklijke Nederlandse Akademie van Wetenschappen, Afd. Letterkunde 64. Amsterdam: Noord-Hollandsche Uitgevers Maatschappij.

Rosen, R.M. 1988*a.* "Hipponax, Boupalos, and the Conventions of the *Psogos*". *Transactions of the American Philological Association* **118**: 29–41.

Rosen, R.M. 1988*b. Old Comedy and the Iambographic Tradition.* Atlanta: Scholars Press.

Rosen, R. and Farrell, J. (eds.) 1993. *Nomodeiktes: Greek Studies in Honor of Martin Ostwald.* Ann Arbor: Michigan University Press.

Rosetti, L. 1997. "Autore dell'Athenaion Politeia fu forse un socratico, omonimo di Senofonte erchieo?" In *L'Athenaion Politeia dello Pseudo-Senofonte*, M. Gigante and G. Maddoli (eds), 141–58. Naples: Edizioni Scientifiche Italiane.

Rothwell, K.S. Jr 1990, *Politics and Persuasion in Aristophanes'* Ecclesiazusae. *Mnemosyne* Supplement 101. Leiden: Brill.

Rothwell, K.S. Jr 2006. *Nature, Culture and the Origins of Greek Comedy: a Study of Animal Choruses.* Cambridge: Cambridge University Press.

Rubel, A. 2000. *Stadt in Angst. Religion und Politik in Athen während des Peloponnesischen Krieges.* Darmstadt: Wissenschaftliche Buchgesellschaft.

Rubel, A. 2014. *Fear and Loathing in Ancient Athens: Religion and Politics during the Peloponnesian War.* Durham: Acumen.

Russell, D.A. 1966. "Plutarch, 'Alcibiades' 1–16". *Proceedings of the Cambridge Philological Society* **12**: 37–47.

Russell, D.A. 1972. *Plutarch.* London: Duckworth.

Russo, C.F. 1962. *Aristofane, autore di Teatro.* Florence: Sansoni.

Rusten, J. 2002. Review of Nesselrath 1990, *Bryn Mawr Classical Review* 02.02.12.

de Ste. Croix, G. 1972. *The Origins of the Peloponnesian War.* London: Duckworth.

Sallares, R. 1991. *Ecology of the Ancient Greek World.* Ithaca NY: Cornell University Press.

Salmon, E.T. 1946. "The Belated Spartan Occupation of Decelea: an Explanation". *Classical Review* **60**: 13–14.

Saxenhouse, A. 1986. "Myths and the Origins of Cities: Reflections on the Autochthony Theme in Euripides' *Ion*". In *Greek Tragedy and Political Theory*, P. Euben (ed.), 252–273. Berkeley: University of California Press.

Sayle, M. 1988. "My friend Kim". *Spectator* 21 May: 9–12.

Schaeffer, A. 1949/50. "Alkibiades und Lysander in Ionien", *Würzburger Jahrbücher für die Altertumswissenschaft* **4**: 287–308.

Schepens, G. and J. Bollansée, 2004. "Myths on the Origins of Peoples and the Birth of Universal History". In *Historia y mito. El pasado legendario como fuente de autoridad. Actas del Simposio Internacional celebrado en Sevilla, Valverde del Camino y Huelva entre el 22 y el 25 de abril de 2003*, J.M. Morón, F.J. Javier González Ponce, and G. Cruz Andreotti (eds), 57–75. Málaga: Centro de Ediciones de la Diputación de Málaga.

Schlegel, A.W. von. 1809. *Vorlesungen über dramatische Kunst und Literatur* 1. Heidelberg: Mohr und Zimmer.

Schmidt, E. 1973. "Die Kopien der Erechtheionkoren". *Antike Plastik* **13**: 1–51, pls 1–56.

Schneider, W.J. 1999. "Eine Polemik Polemons in den Propyläen. Ein Votivgemälde des Alkibiades—Kontext und Rezeption". *Klio* **81**: 18–44.

Schouler, A. 1984. *La tradition hellénique de Libanius*. Lille/Paris: Atelier national reproduction des thèses. Université de Lille III/Belles Lettres.

Schroff, A. 1901. *Zur Echtheitsfrage d. vierten Rede des Andokides*. Inaugural dissertation, University of Erlangen. Erlangen: Hof- und Univ.-Bucherei.

Schubert, C. (ed.) 1994. *Perikles*. Erträge der Forschung 285. Darmstadt: Wissenschaftliche Buchgesellschaft.

Schwarze, J. 1971. *Die Beurteilung des Perikles durch die attische Komödie und ihre historische und historiographische Bedeutung*. Zetemata 51. Munich: Beck.

Scullion, S. 2003. "Euripides and Macedon, or the Silence of the *Frogs*". *Classical Quarterly* **53**: 389–400.

Seager, R. and C. Tuplin 1980. "The Freedom of the Greeks of Asia: on the Origins of a Concept and the Creation of a Slogan". *Journal of Hellenic Studies* **100**: 141–54.

Sears, E. 1990. "The Life and Work of William S. Heckscher". *Zeitschrift für Kunstgeschichte* **53**: 107–33.

Sedley, D. 1998. "The Etymologies in Plato's *Cratylus*". *Journal of Hellenic Studies* **118**: 140–54.

Segal, C. 1971. "The Two Worlds of Euripides' *Helen*". *Transactions and Proceedings of the American Philological Association* **102**: 553–61.

Selig, K.-L. and Sears, E. 1990. *The Verbal and the Visual: Essays in Honor of William Sebastian Heckscher*. New York: Italica Press.

Shapiro, B., Rambault A, Gilbert T.P. 2006. "No Proof that Typhoid Caused the Plague of Athens (a reply to Papagrigorakis et al.)". *International Journal of Infectious Diseases* **10**: 334–5.

Shear, T. L. Jr 1963. "Koisyra: Three Women of Athens". *Phoenix* 17:99–112.

Shear, T. L. Jr 1966. *Studies in the Early Projects of the Periklean Building Program*. PhD thesis, Princeton University. Ann Arbor: University Microfilms International.

Sheffield, F. C. C. 2001. "Alcibiades' Speech: a Satyric Drama". *Greece and Rome* **48**: 193–209.

Sheppard, J. T. 1910. "Politics in the Frogs of Aristophanes". *Journal of Hellenic Studies* **30**: 249–59.

Shimron, B. 1989. *Politics and Belief in Herodotus*. Historia Einzelschrift 58. Stuttgart: Steiner.

Sidwell, K. 1997. Review of Vickers 1997. In *Classical Review* **47**: 254–5.

Sidwell, K. 2008. *Aristophanes the Democrat: The Politics of Satirical Comedy during the Peloponnesian War*. Cambridge: Cambridge University Press.

Siewert, P. 1977. "The Ephebic Oath in Fifth Century Athens". *Journal of Hellenic Studies* **97**: 102–11.

Silk, M.S. 1980. "Aristophanes as Lyric poet". *Yale Classical Studies* **26**: 99–152.

Silk, M. S. 2000. *Aristophanes and the Definition of Comedy*. Oxford: Clarendon Press.

Smith, R. R. R. 1990. "Late Roman Philosopher Portraits from Aphrodisias". *Journal of Roman Studies* **80**: 127–55.

Smith, R. R. R. 1991. "Late Roman Philosophers". In *Aphrodisias 2: The Theater, a Sculptor's Workshop, Philosophers, and Coin Types*, R.R.R. Smith and K. Erim (eds), 144–58. *Journal of Roman Archaeology* Supplementary Series 2. Ann Arbor.

Smith, S. 1886. *The Wit and Wisdom of the Rev. Sidney Smith*, new edn. London: Longmans, Green and Co.

Snell, B. 1948. "Das frühste Zeugnis über Sokrates". *Philologus* **97**: 125–35.

Snell, B. 1964. *Scenes from Greek Drama*. Sather Lectures 34. Berkeley and Los Angeles: University of California Press.

Solana Dueso, J. 1994. *Aspasia de Mileto: testimonios y discursos*. Barcelona: Anthropos.

Solomos, A. 1974. *The Living Aristophanes*. Ann Arbor, MI: University of Michigan Press.

Sommerstein, A. H. 1977. "Aristophanes and the Events of 411". *Journal of Hellenic Studies* **97**: 112–26.

Sommerstein, A. H. 1984. "Aristophanes and the Demon Poverty". *Classical Quarterly* **34**: 314–33.

Sommerstein, A. H. 1986. "The Decree of Syrakosios". *Classical Quarterly* **36**: 101–8.

Sommerstein, A. H. (ed.) 1987. *The Comedies of Aristophanes 6. Birds*. Warminster: Aris and Phillips).

Sommerstein, A. H. (ed.) 1990. *The Comedies of Aristophanes 7: Lysistrata*. Warminster: Aris and Phillips.

Sommerstein, A. H. (ed.) 1994. *The Comedies of Aristophanes 8: Thesmophoriazusae*. Warminster: Aris and Phillips.

Sommerstein, A. H. 1996a. "How to Avoid being a Kōmōdoumenos". *Classical Quarterly* **46**: 327–56.

Sommerstein, A. H. (ed.) 1996b. *The Comedies of Aristophanes 9: Frogs*. Warminster: Aris and Phillips.

Sommerstein, A. H. (ed.) 1998. *The Comedies of Aristophanes 10: Ecclesiazusae*. Warminster: Aris and Phillips.

Sommerstein, A. H. (ed.) 2001. *The Comedies of Aristophanes 11: Wealth*. Warminster: Aris and Phillips.

Sommerstein, A. H. 2002. "Die Komödie und das 'Unsagbare'". In Ercolani 2002, 125–45.

Spatz, L. 1978. *Aristophanes*. Boston: Twayne Publishers.

Spielvogel, J. 2003. "Die politische Position des athenischen Komödiendichters Aristophanes". *Historia* **52**: 1–22.

Stadter, P. A. 1989. *A Commentary on Plutarch's* Pericles. Chapel Hill and London: University of North Carolina Press.

Stanford, W. B. 1939. *Ambiguity in Greek Literature*. Oxford: Blackwell.

Stanford, W. B. 1967. *The Sound of Greek: Studies in the Greek Theory and Practice of Euphony*. Berkeley and Los Angeles: University of California Press.

Stanford, W. B. (ed.) 1973. *Aristophanes Frogs*, 2nd edn. London: Macmillan.

Starkie, W. J. M. (ed.) 1909. *The Acharnians of Aristophanes*. London: Macmillan.

Stevens, F. G. and George, M. D. 1870–1954. *Catalogue of Political and Personal Satires … in the British Museum to 1832*. London: British Museum.

Stonecipher, A. H. M. 1918. *Graeco-Persian Names*. New York: American Book Company.

Stoneman, R. 2008. *Alexander the Great: A Life in Legend*. London: Yale University Press.

Storey, I. C. 1990. "Dating and Redating Eupolis". *Phoenix* 44: 1–30.

Storey, I. C. 1993. "The Dates of Aristophanes' *Clouds* II and Eupolis' *Baptae:* a reply to E.C. Kopff". *American Journal of Philology* **114**: 71–84.

Storey, I. C. 1997. Review of Vickers 1997, *Bryn Mawr Classical Review* 97.9.15.

Storey, I. C. 1998. "Poets, Politicians and Perverts; Personal Humour in Aristophanes". *Classics Ireland* **5**: 85–134.

Storey, I. C. 2003. *Eupolis: Poet of Old Comedy*. Oxford: Clarendon Press.

Storey, I. C. 2009. "On Looking Again at Kratinos' *Dionysalexandros*", *The Oliver Smithies Lectures 2009*, 1–24. Oxford: Balliol College.

Strauss, B. S. 1986. *Athens after the Peloponnesian War: Class, Faction and Policy, 403–386 BC*. London: Croom Helm.

Strauss, B. S. 1990. "*Oikos/Polis:* Towards a Theory of Athenian Paternal Ideology 450–399 BC". *Classica et Mediaevalia* **40**: 101–27.

Strauss, B. S. 1993. *Fathers and Sons in Athens: Ideology and Society in the Era of the Peloponnesian War*. Princeton: NJ: Princeton University Press.

Strauss, L. 1966. *Socrates and Aristophanes*. NewYork.

Stronach, D. 1978. *Pasargadae: a Report on the Excavations Conducted by the British Institute of Persian Studies from 1961 to 1963*. Oxford: Clarendon Press.

Strycker, E. de 1942. "Platonica I: l'authenticité du *Premier Alcibiade*". *Études Classiques* **11**: 135–51.

Studi ... Cataudella 1972. *Studi classici in honore di Quintino Cataudella* 1–3. Catania: Università di Catania, Facoltà di lettere e filosofia.

Süss, W. 1911. *Aristophanes unde die Nachwelt*. Leipzig: Dieterich.

Süss, W. 1954. "Scheinbare und wirkliche Inkongruenzen in den Dramen des Aristophanes". *Rheinisches Museum für Philologie* n.s. **97**: 115–59; 229–316.

Süvern, J.W. 1827. *Über Aristophanes Vögel*. Berlin: Ferdinand Dümmler.

Süvern, J.W. 1835. *Essay on "The Birds" of Aristophanes*, tr. W.R. Hamilton. London: J. Murray.

Taaffe, L.K. 1993. *Aristophanes and Women*. London: Routledge.

Talbot, J. F. 1963. "Aristophanes and Alcibiades". *Classical Bulletin* **39**: 65–8.

Taplin, O. 1979. "Yielding to Forethought: Sophocles' Ajax". In *Arktouros: Hellenic Studies, presented to Bernard M. W. Knox*, G. W. Bowersock *et al.* (eds), 122–9. Berlin: de Gruyter.

Tartakovsky, J. 2009. "Pun for the Ages". *New York Times*. Opinion 28 March (http://www.nytimes.com/2009/03/28/opinion/28Tartakovsky.html?_r=0).

Telò, M. and Porciani, L. 2002. "Un'alternativa per la datazione dei Demi di Eupoli". *Quaderni Urbinati di Cultura Classica* **72**: 23–40.

Thomas, R. 1989. *Oral Tradition and Written Record in Classical Athens*. Cambridge: University Press.

Thompson, W.E. 1970. "The Kinship of Perikles and Alkibiades". *Greek, Roman and Byzantine Studies* **11**: 27–33.

Thuasne, L. (ed.) 1923. *François Villon, Œuvres: édition critique avec notices et glossaire*. Paris: A. Picard.

Tompkins, D.P. 1972. "Stylistic Characterization in Thucydides: Nicias and Alcibiades". *Yale Classical Studies* **22**: 181–214.

Tompkins, D.P. 1993. "Archidamus and the Question of Characterization in Thucydides". In Rosen and Farrell, 99–111.

Torello, G. 2006. *Eupolis and Attic Comedy*. Diss. University of Nottingham.

Trevett, J. 2000. "Was there a Decree of Syrakosios?" *Classical Quarterly* **50**: 598–600

Trundle, M.F. 1999. "Identity and Community among Greek Mercenaries in the Classical World: 700–322 BCE". *The Ancient History Bulletin* **13.1**: 28–38.

Tuplin, C. 1987. "The Administration of the Achaemenid Empire". In *Coinage and Administration in the Athenian and Persian Empires: the Ninth Oxford Symposium on Coinage and Monetary History*, I. Carradice (ed.), 109–66. British Archaeological Reports 343. Oxford.

Turato, F. 1972. *Il problema storico delle Nuvole di Aristofane*. Padua: Antenore.

Ussher, R.G. (ed.) 1973. *Aristophanes Ecclesiazusae*. Oxford: Clarendon Press.

Vasan, P.T. , Prabhu, D.I.G. and Pandian, R.S. 2008. "Vector Competence of *Musca domestica* Linn. with Reference to the Virulent Strains of *Salmonella typhi* in Bus Stands and Markets at Madurai, Tamil Nadu". *Current Biotica* **2**: 154–60.

Vendryes, J. 1921. *Le langage: introduction linguistique à l'histoire*. Paris: Renaissance du Livre.

Verrall, A.W. (ed.) 1890. *The Ion of Euripides*. Cambridge: University Press.

Verrall, A.W. 1895. *Euripides the Rationalist*. Cambridge: University Press.

Verrall, A.W. 1905. *Essays on Four Plays of Euripides*. Cambridge: University Press.

Vickers, M. 1984. "Demus's Gold *Phiale* (Lysias 19.43)". *American Journal of Ancient History* **9**: 48–53.

Vickers, M. 1985. "Persepolis, Vitruvius and the Erechtheum Caryatids: the Iconography of Medism and Servitude". *Revue Archéologique*: 3–28.

Vickers, M. 1989a. "Alcibiades on Stage: *Thesmophoriazusae* and *Helen*". *Historia* **38**: 41–65.

Vickers, M. 1989b. "Alcibiades on Stage: Aristophanes' *Birds*". *Historia* **38**: 267–99.

Vickers, M. 1991. "A Contemporary Account of the Athenian Plague? Aristophanes *Clouds* 694–734". *Liverpool Classical Monthly* **16**: 64.

Vickers, M. 1993. "Alcibiades in Cloudedoverland". In Rosen and Farrell 1993, 603–18.

Vickers, M. 1994. "Alcibiades and Critias in the *Gorgias*: Plato's 'Fine Satire'". *Dialogues d'histoire ancienne* **20**: 85–112.

Vickers, M. 1995. "Heracles Lacedaemonius: the Political Dimensions of Sophocles *Trachiniae* and Euripides *Heracles*". *Dialogues d'histoire ancienne* **21**: 41–69.

Vickers, M. 1997. *Pericles on Stage: Political Comedy in Aristophanes' Early Plays*. Austin, Tx.: University of Texas Press.

Vickers, M. 1999. "Alcibiades and Melos: Thucydides 5.84–116". *Historia* **48**: 265–281.

Vickers, M. 2000. "Alcibiades and Aspasia: Notes on the *Hippolytus*". *Dialogues d'histoire ancienne* **26**: 7–17.

Vickers, M. 2001. "Aristophanes *Frogs*: Nothing to do with Literature". *Athenaeum* **89**: 187–201.

Vickers, M. 2005a. "Aspasia on Stage: Aristophanes *Ecclesiazusae*". *Athenaeum* **93**: forthcoming.

Vickers, M. 2005b. *Oedipus and Alcibiades in Sophocles*. Xenia Toruniensia 9. Toruń: Wydawnictwo Uniwersytetu Mikołaja Kopernika.

Vickers, M. 2005–6. "The *Dramatis Personae* of Alma-Tadema's *Phidias* and the *Frieze of the Parthenon, Athens*". *Assaph: Studies in Art History* **10–11**: 235–9.

Vickers, M. 2007. "A Legend of Wild Beauty: Sophocles' *Antigone*". *Classics Ireland* **14**: 44–77.

Vickers, M. 2008. *Sophocles and Alcibiades: Echoes of Contemporary History in Athenian Drama*. Stocksfield and Ithaca, NY: Acumen and Cornell Univertsity Press.

Vickers, M. 2010. "Hagnon, Amphipolis and *Rhesus*". In *Ergasteria: Works Presented to John Ellis Jones on His 80th Birthday*, N. Sekunda (ed.), 76–81. Gdansk: Akanthina.

Vickers, M. 2011a. "Alcibiades, 'a classical archetype for Alexander'". In *From Pella to Gandhara: Hybridisation and Identity in the Art and Architecture of the Hellenistic East.* S. Chandrasekaran, A. Kouremenos and R. Rossi (eds), 11–16. Oxford: BAR International Series 2221.

Vickers, M. 2011b. "Antigone's Creon and the Ephebic Oath". *Scripta Classica Israelica* **30**: 1–8.

Vickers, M. 2012 "Alcibiades and the Irrational". *Scripta Classica Israelica* **31**: 151–60.

Vickers, M. 2014a. "The Caryatids on the Erechtheum at Athens: questions of chronology and symbolism". *Miscellanea Anthropologica et Sociologica* 15: 119–33.

Vickers, M. 2014b. "Politics and Challenge: The Case of Euripides' *Ion*". *CW* 107: 299–318.

Vickers, M. and Briggs, D. 2007. "Juvenile Crime, Aggression and Abuse in Fifth-century Athens: a Case Study". In *Children and Sexuality: From the Greeks to the Great War*, G. Rousseau (ed.), 41–64. Basingstoke: Palgrave Macmillan.

Vickers, M. and Gill, D. W. J. 1994. *Artful Crafts: Ancient Greek Silverware and Pottery.* Oxford: Clarendon Press.

Visser, T. 1998. *Untersuchungen zum Sophokleischen Philoktet: Das auslosende Ereignis in der Stuckgestaltung.* Stuttgart: B. G. Teubner.

Vogt, J. 1960. "Das Bild des Perikles bei Thukydides". In *Orbis: Ausgewählte Schriften zur Geschichte des Altertums*, 47–63. Freiburg: Herder.

Volkmann, R. 1885. *Die Rhetorik der Griechen und Römer in systematischer Übersicht.* 2nd edition. Leipzig: B.G. Teubner.

Wallace, R. W. 1994. "Private Lives and Public enemies: Freedom of Thought in Classical Athens". In *Athenian Identity and Civic Ideology*, A. Scafuro and A. Boegehold (eds), 127–55. Baltimore: Johns Hopkins University Press.

Warren, J. 2004. *Facing Death, Epicurus and his Critics.* Oxford: Clarendon Press.

Wassermann, F. M. 1940. "Divine Violence and Providence in Euripides' *Ion*". *Transactions and Proceedings of the American Philological Association* **71**: 587–604.

Waterfield, R. 1996. Review of Gill 1996. In *Bryn Mawr Classical Review* 96.11.10.

Watson, P. A. 1995. *Ancient Stepmothers: Myth, Misogyny and Reality.* Mnemosyne Supplement 143. Leiden: Brill.

Waugh, E. 1984 [1961]. "An Act of Homage and Reparation to P.G. Wodehouse". In *The Essays, Articles and Reviews of Evelyn Waugh*, D. Gallagher (ed.), 561–8. London: Methuen.

West, M. L. 1972. *Iambi et Elegi Graeci*, vol. 2. Oxford: Clarendon Press.

Westlake, H. D. 1968. *Individuals in Thucydides.* Cambridge: University Press.

Westlake, H. D. 1979. "Ionians in the Ionian War". *Classical Quarterly* **29**: 35–41.

Westlake, H. D. 1980. "The *Lysistrata* and the War". *Phoenix* **34**: 38–54.

Westlake, H. D. 1981. "Decline and Fall of Tissaphernes". *Historia* **30**: 257–79.

Westlake, H. D. 1985. "Tissaphernes and Thucydides". *Classical Quarterly* **35**: 43–54.

Westlake, H. D. 1989. *Studies in Thucydides and Greek History.* Bristol: Bristol Classical Press.

Whitman, C. 1964. *Aristophanes and the Comic Hero.* Cambridge, MA: Harvard University Press.

Wiedemann, T. E. J. 1983. "ἐλάχιστον ... ἐν τοῖς ἄρσεσι κλέος: Thucydides, Women, and the Limits of Rational Analysis". *Greece & Rome* **30**: 163–70.

Wiesehöfer, J. 1980. "Die 'Freunde' und 'Wohltäter' des Grosskönigs". *Studia Iranica* **9**: 7–21.

Wiesehöfer, J. 2002. "Tissaphernes". *Der Neue Pauly* 12/1, 622. Stuttgart: Verlag J.B. Metzler.

Wilamowitz-Moellendorff, U. von 1893. *Aristoteles und Athen* 1. Berlin: Weidmann.

Wilamowitz-Moellendorff, U. von 1893 "Excurse zum Oedipus des Sophokles". *Hermes* **34**: 55–80.

Wilamowitz-Moellendorff, U. von 1927. *Lysistrate: Aristophanes*. Berlin: Weidmann.

Wilamowitz-Moellendorff, U. von 1982. *History of Classical Scholarship*, H. Lloyd-Jones (ed.). London: Duckworth.

Wilkins, J. 1987. "Aspasia in Medea?" *Liverpool Classical Monthly* **12**: 8–10.

Willetts, R. F. 1958. *Ion*. In *Euripides III*, D. Grene and R. Lattimore (eds), 177–255. Chicago: University of Chicago Press.

Will. W. 2003. *Thukydides und Perikles. Der Historiker und sein Held*. Bonn.

Wilson, N.G. (ed.) 2007. *Aristophanis Fabulae*. Oxford: Clarendon Press.

Wilson, P. 2003,"The Sound of Cultural Conflict: Critias and the Culture of *Mousike* in Athens". In *The Cultures within Ancient Greek Culture: Contact, Conflict, Collaboration*, C. Dougherty & L. Kurke (eds), 181–206. Cambridge: Cambridge University Press.

Winckelmann, J. J. 1764. *Geschichte der Kunst des Altertums*. Dresden: Waltherischen Hof-buchhandlung.

Wind, E. 1966. *Pagan Mysteries in the Renaissance*, 2nd edn. New York: Barnes and Noble).

Wohl, V. 1999. "The Eros of Alcibiades". *Classical Antiquity* **18**: 349–85.

Woodhead, A. G. 1967. *The Study of Greek Inscriptions*. Cambridge: Cambridge University Press.

Wolf, P. 1954. "Libanios' Kampf um die hellenische Bildung". *Museum Helveticum* **11**: 231–42. Reprinted in Fatouros and Krischer 1983, 68–83.

Wolff, C. 1965. "Design and Myth in Euripides' Ion". *Harvard Studies in Classical Philology* **69**: 169–194.

Wright, M. 2005. *Euripides' Escape-Tragedies. A Study of* Helen, Andromeda, *and* Iphigenia among the Taurians. Oxford: Oxford University Press.

Wuerker, M. 1992. *Standing Tall in Deep Doodoo: A Cartoon Chronicle of Campaign '92 and the Bush-Quayle Years*. New York: Thunder's Mouth Press.

Wunder, E. (ed.) 1831. *Sophoclis Tragoediae*. Göttingen and Erfurt: W. Hennings.

Wycherley, R. E. 1946. "Aristophanes and Euripides". *Greece and Rome* **15**: 98–107.

Wysocki, L. 1988. "Aristophanes, Thucydides, B. viii and the Political Events of 413–411 BC". *Eos* **76**: 237–48.

Zangrando, V. 1997. "Lingua d'uso ed evoluzione linguistica: alcune considerazioni sul diminutivo". In López Eire 1997: 353–60.

Zeitlin, F. I. 1989. "Mysteries of Identity and Designs of the Self in Euripides' *Ion*". *Proceedings of the Cambridge Philological Society* **35**: 144–197.

Zeitlin, F. I. 1999, "Aristophanes: the Performance of Utopia in the *Ecclesiazousae*". In *Performance Culture and Athenian Democracy*, S. Goldhill and R. Osborne (eds), 167–97. Cambridge: University Press.

Zuntz, G. 1963. *The Political Plays of Euripides*. Manchester: Manchester University Press.

Index Locorum

General Index